THE QUAKERS AND THE
ENGLISH LEGAL SYSTEM

The QUAKERS *and the* ENGLISH LEGAL SYSTEM *1660–1688*

CRAIG W. HORLE

UNIVERSITY OF PENNSYLVANIA PRESS   *Philadelphia 1988*

upp

Copyright © 1988 by the University of Pennsylvania Press

Library of Congress Cataloging-in-Publication Data

Horle, Craig W.
  The Quakers and the English legal system, 1660–1688.

  Based on author's thesis.
  Bibliography: p.
  Includes index.
  1. Quakers—Legal status, laws, etc.—Great Britain—
History.   I. Title.
KD4102.Q3H67   1988   342.41'087   87-30140
ISBN 0-8122-8101-2   344.10287

Designed by Adrianne Onderdonk Dudden

Contents

Abbreviations and Short Titles

ARB MSS	A. R. Barclay MSS. 2 vols. Library of the Religious Society of Friends, London.
Baker, *Legal History*	J. H. Baker. *An Introduction to English Legal History*. 2d ed. London, 1979.
BL	British Library, London.
Cockburn, *Assizes*	J. S. Cockburn. *History of English Assizes, 1558–1715*. Cambridge, 1972.
CSPD	Mary Anne Everett Green et al., eds. *Calendar of State Papers, Domestic Series, 1603–1704*. 85 vols. London, 1857–1972.
CTB	William A. Shaw et al., eds. *Calendar of Treasury Books, 1660–1718*. 32 vols. London, 1904–1962.
DWL	Dr. Williams' Library, London.
Dowdell, *Hundred Years*	E. G. Dowdell. *A Hundred Years of Quarter Sessions: The Government of Middlesex from 1660 to 1760*. Cambridge, 1932.
Essex Sessions	D. H. Allen, ed. *Essex Quarter Sessions Order Book 1652–1661*. Essex Record Office Publications, vol. 65. Chelmsford, 1974.
FLL	Library of the Religious Society of Friends, London.
GBS	MS Great Book of Sufferings. 44 vols. FLL.
HMC	Historical Manuscripts Commission.
Holdsworth, *English Law*	William S. Holdsworth. *A History of English Law*. 16 vols. London, 1903–32.

HSP

Historical Society of Pennsylvania, Philadelphia.

Kesteven

S. A. Peyton, ed. *Minutes of Proceedings in Quarter Sessions for the Parts of Kesteven in the County of Lincoln, 1674–1695*. Lincolnshire Record Society Publications, vols. 25, 26. Lincoln, 1931.

London Sessions

Hugh Bowler, ed. *London Sessions Records 1605–1685*. Catholic Record Society, vol. 34. London, 1934.

Meeting for Sufferings

MS Minutes of Meeting for Sufferings, FLL.

ORS

MS Original Records of Sufferings. 8 vols. FLL.

Oxfordshire

Mary Sturge Gretton. *Oxfordshire Justices of the Peace in the Seventeenth Century*. Oxford, 1934.

PRO

Public Record Office, London.

Warwick Records

S. C. Ratcliff and H. C. Johnson, eds. *Warwick County Records 1629–1690*. 8 vols. Warwick, 1935–53.

WRO

Wiltshire Record Office, Trowbridge.

Wing

Donald Wing, ed. *Short-Title Catalogue of Books Printed in England, Scotland, Ireland, Wales, and British America and of English Books Printed in Other Countries, 1641–1700*. 3 vols. New York, 1951.

Yearly Meeting

MS Minutes of London Yearly Meeting, FLL.

Preface

The Restoration of the Stuart monarchy in 1660 ended a remarkable period in English history. The Interregnum had been characterized by many of the same problems which had plagued the monarchy, but it had also witnessed an outpouring of religious fervor rarely seen in that island. One of the most enthusiastic and radical of the many fringe groups was the Quakers. Given their peculiar social habits, their embarrassing manifestations of scriptural enthusiasm, and their broad range of "testimonies" for Truth, their survival beyond the early years of the Restoration seemed distinctly improbable. Thirty years later, as the Stuart monarchy again resided in exile, the Quakers were still highly visible. In fact, they had flourished despite seemingly brutal and continuous "persecution." Richard Baxter, the distinguished Presbyterian minister, when writing about the Quakers and the first Conventicle Act, expressed dismay, tinged with gratitude, that "the fanatics called Quakers did greatly relieve the sober people for a time, for they were so resolute, and gloried in their constancy and sufferings."[1] This "glory" in sufferings was also stressed by Isaac Penington, a Quaker who, to alleviate his brethren's concern for him, wrote to them from Aylesbury gaol: "[The Lord] made my bonds pleasant to me, and my noisome prison (enough to have destroyed my weakly and tenderly educated nature) a place of pleasure and delight, where I was comforted by my God night and day."[2] This portrait of resolute Quakers joyfully suffering hardships at the hands of hardhearted "persecutors," and their inevitable victory with the Toleration Act in 1689, was perpetuated by official biographies of early Friends,[3] by Joseph Besse's *Collection of the Sufferings of the People called Quakers for the Testimony of a Good Conscience*,[4] and by generations of Quaker historians. Modern biographers have tended to concentrate on early Quaker martyrs such as Richard Hubberthorne, Edward Burrough, and James Nayler; on the "First Publishers of Truth"; or on Quaker women, particularly Margaret Fell,[5] while neglecting the generation of Quakers who led the legal defence against sufferings.[6] Even William C. Braithwaite, the doyen of Quaker historians, helped to reinforce the image of "sweet sufferings":

> The story throughout is radiant with the thronging faces of witnesses for Truth, plain men and women, aglow with the Inward Light, who felt a spirit that outlived all wrath and contention, and wearied out all exaltation and cruelty, its crown meekness, its life everlasting love unfeigned.[7]

That the Quakers suffered heavily for their religious beliefs is quite likely, but there is another side to the story, for we are dealing with flesh and blood human beings, not mythical saints. Since 1950, but mainly within the last decade, a number of historians have examined the genesis of the Quakers, the role they played during the Interregnum and Restoration, particularly the former, and their history and development in several counties into the eighteenth century.[8] The result has been a reevaluation of the true extent of Quaker sufferings and of their alleged passivity in the face of them. The first revision came in 1950 with Arnold Lloyd's *Quaker Social History 1669–1738*, a provocative but highly flawed work, whose author implied that the Quakers may actually have suffered less in purely legal terms than other dissenting groups because of their willingness to organize against persecution.[9] Unfortunately this book itself "suffered"—from poor organization, a sloppy use of sources, and a lack of any serious analysis of the legal system that the Quakers encountered. Alfred Braithwaite, son of the eminent Quaker historian, in a series of articles, attempted on a small scale to rectify some of Lloyd's carelessness by examining several legal tactics employed by seventeenth-century Friends.[10] The county studies of the past decade by Helen Forde, Nicholas Morgan, and Wayne Spurrier[11] have generally supported Lloyd's contention that the prosecution of Quakers may not have been as severe as many Quaker historians have implied. Nor, as Arnold Lloyd and Alfred Braithwaite had indicated, were Friends as passive towards sufferings as was previously believed.

The primary reason for the relative dearth of studies about the true nature of Quaker "persecution" is the paucity of research into the English legal system as it pertained to religious dissent. Only one historian, for example, has attempted to analyze any of the mechanics of law enforcement as it applied to Quakers, although he restricted himself to the early Restoration and provided a suggestive rather than a detailed analysis.[12] Although many fine legal scholars have recently scrutinized seventeenth-century law enforcement in England, they have tended to focus on lower-class criminality, particularly crimes of violence or passion.[13] Nonconformity has generated little enthusiasm, in part because religious criminality is rather unexciting; in part because the harshest period of prosecution was restricted generally to the period 1660–1689, and in part because of the perceived shortage of dissenting records. Whatever the reasons, there is still lacking a thorough study of the English legal system and its interaction with groups like the Quakers during the late Stuart period when the machinery of enforcement had been fully restored after the chaotic years of the Interregnum, and when the prosecution of religious dissent reached its apogee. Without easily accessible accounts of the law-enforcement system, Quaker historians have failed to provide a detailed study of the assorted tactics Quakers employed in their own defense during these years. If the Quakers, as generally believed, maintained their lawbreaking principles but were not "persecuted" to the degree once maintained by their apologists, then the legal system and Quaker reactive tactics need to be scrutinized.

One purpose of this study is to provide a detailed analysis of the legal system—its officers, procedures, jurisdictions, and laws as they were applicable to religious dissent, particularly to the Quakers. The legal system, of course, was not static. Consequently, the second purpose of this study is to view law enforcement in action. Legal records, however, rarely indicated the religion of the accused, while seventeenth-century Quakerism lacked any official lists of members. County lists of those considered as Friends can be compiled from the Quaker registers of births, marriages, and deaths; from Quaker meeting minute books; from Quaker sufferings records; and from supplemental sources. Such complete lists have been compiled only by Helen Forde for Derbyshire.[14] It is to be hoped that more historians will focus on county studies of Quakers or other Dissenters, keeping in mind that any legal analysis will also depend on such extant legal sources as quarter sessions, assizes, church courts, superior common-law courts, and Chancery. To undertake county reconstructions or even a representative sampling for a nationwide study would be extremely difficult and inordinately time-consuming. Nor would they present a complete picture of the nature of the prosecution and the harassment suffered by the Quakers. Normally, therefore, a national study would need to await future detailed county studies. Fortunately, the Quakers have given us another way to examine the legal system in action. Unlike most seventeenth-century religious bodies, the Quakers kept superb records, which have survived—accounts of sufferings, minutes of the Meeting for Sufferings and the London Yearly Meeting, and the legal advice they received and recorded in the "Book of Cases." Also extant is much of their voluminous correspondence, as well as their printed tracts. From these magnificent sources there emerges an exacting, though perhaps prejudiced, portrait of the legal system in operation. It is one of a system alternately efficient and inefficient, consistent and inconsistent, petty and lenient, violent and passive, but above all, so bewilderingly convoluted that it often defied the comprehension of contemporaries, including those called upon to administer the law. In some respects, it was this complexity and obscurity that enabled the Quakers to mobilize their resources and confront the law and its agents with legal tactics, which often were equally complicated. Thus the final purpose of this study is to elucidate the Quaker legal response—their ideas for law reform, their tactics, and their ultimate success or failure. As a by-product, the study will also focus on the quality of legal counsel Friends received and the vulnerability of the English legal system to manipulation and confrontation. Inevitably insight should be gained into the interplay between seventeenth-century law enforcement and religious dissent, and the precise reasons for Quaker survival as a sect into the "Age of Toleration."

Any work of this length involves the help and support of many people. I would like to thank the staffs of Friends House Library, in particular Edward Milligan and Malcolm Thomas; Dr. Williams' Library; the Public Record Office; and the British Library for their kind assistance. The Society of Friends in London also provided valuable financial help and access to manuscripts through employment in their library. My thanks also to Dr. Richard Dunn for enabling me to return to the profession as associate editor of the *Papers of William Penn*, and for his encouragement in finishing the Ph.D. dissertation that led, in turn, to this book. Drs. Edwin Bronner, Thomas Green, and Lois Carr kindly read the manuscript and made invaluable suggestions for its improvement. My colleagues, Drs. Marianne Wokeck and Joy Wiltenburg, and my dear friend, Dr. Jerrold Casway, also provided much appreciated support and advice. My long-suffering Ph.D. supervisor, Dr. J. S. Cockburn, deserves special thanks for his patience, his friendship, his suggestions, and his willingness to confront the bureaucratic nightmare caused by a long-delayed dissertation. Finally, I owe more than I can adequately express to my "significant other" Susan, whose love and support have been incomparable. This book would never have reached fruition without her.

Notes

1. Matthew Sylvester, ed., *Reliquiae Baxterianae* (London, 1696), pt. 2, 435–37.

2. Quoted in William C. Braithwaite, *The Second Period of Quakerism*, 2d ed. (Cambridge, 1961), 11.

3. In the seventeenth and eighteenth centuries, particularly after 1689, many early Friends were immortalized by official publications of their *Works* or their *Journals*; these included Thomas Aldam (1690), John Burnyeat (1691), William Caton (1689), Joseph Coale (1706), Stephen Crisp (1694), William Ellis (1710), Thomas Ellwood (1714), Margaret Fell (1710), George Fox (1694), Roger Haydock (1700), Gilbert Latey (1707), Ambrose Rigge (1710), and Oliver Sansom (1710). A number of these were reprinted in the eighteenth-century series edited by John and A. R. Barclay, *A Select Series, Biographical, Narrative, Epistolary, and Miscellaneous . . . Intended to Illustrate the Spiritual Character of the Gospel of Christ*. 8 vols. (London, 1835–1845).

4. 2 vols. (London, 1753). Although Besse is a useful source for Quaker sufferings, relying on manuscript and printed sources, he often omits valuable details, and also editorializes in such a manner as to give the impression of unduly harsh and continuous enforcement.

5. For example, see Elisabeth Brockbank, *Edward Burrough: A Wrestler for Truth, 1634–1662* (London, 1949); Elisabeth Brockbank, *Richard Hubberthorne of Yealand, Yeoman-Soldier-Quaker, 1628–1662* (London, 1929); Emelia Fogelklou, *James Nayler, the Rebel Saint* (London, 1931); Mabel Brailsford, *A Quaker from Cromwell's Army: James Nayler* (London, 1927); Mabel Brailsford, *Quaker Women* (London, 1915); E. E. Taylor, *The Valiant Sixty* (London, 1947); Isabel Ross, *Margaret Fell: Mother of Quakerism* (London, 1949); Helen Crosfield, *Margaret Fox of Swarthmoor Hall* [London, 1913]; L. V. Hodgkin, *A Quaker Saint of Cornwall, Loveday Hambly and Her Guests* (London, 1927); L. V. Hodgkin, *Gulielma, Wife of William Penn* (London, 1947); and Emily Manners, *Elizabeth Hooton* (London, 1914).

6. The one exception is William Penn, the subject of many biographies, most of which are inadequate.

7. Braithwaite, *Second Period*, 22.

8. For example, see Christopher Hill, *The World Turned Upside Down*

(1972; paperback reprint: Harmondsworth, 1975), chap. 10; Christopher Hill, *The Experience of Defeat* (London, 1984), chap. 5; Hugh Barbour, *The Quakers in Puritan England* (New Haven, 1964); Richard Vann, *The Social Development of Early Quakerism* (Cambridge, 1969); J. F. Maclear, "Quakerism and the End of the Interregnum: A Chapter in the Domestication of Radical Puritanism," *Church History* 19 (1950):240–70; J. F. MacGregor, "Ranterism and the Development of Early Quakerism," *Journal of Religious History* 9 (1977):349–63; Alan Cole, "The Quakers and the English Revolution," *Past & Present* no. 10 (November, 1956):39–54; Alan Cole, "The Quakers and Politics 1652–1660." (Ph.D. thesis, Cambridge University, 1955); Helen Forde, "Derbyshire Quakers 1650–1761" (Ph.D. thesis, University of Leicester, 1976); Helen Forde, "Friends and Authority," *Journal of the Friends Historical Society* 54 (1976–80):115–25; Barry Reay, *The Quakers and the English Revolution* (London, 1985); Barry Reay, "Popular Hostility Towards Quakers in Mid-Seventeenth Century England," *Social History* 5:387–407; Barry Reay, "The Social Origins of Early Quakerism," *Journal of Interdisciplinary History* 11 (1980–81): 55–72; Barry Reay, "Quaker Opposition to Tithes, 1652–1660," *Past & Present* no. 86 (February, 1980):98–118; Barry Reay, "The Authorities and Early Restoration Quakerism," *Journal of Ecclesiastical History* 34 (1983):69–84; Barry Reay, "The Quakers, 1659, and the Restoration of the Monarchy," *History* 63 (1978):193–213; Nicholas Morgan, "Lancashire Quakers and the Oath, 1660–1722," *Journal of the Friends Historical Society* 54 (1976–80): 235–54; Wayne W. Spurrier, "The Persecution of Quakers in England, 1650–1714" (Ph.D. diss., University of North Carolina, 1976); see also Craig W. Horle, "Judicial Encounters with Quakers 1660–1688," *Journal of the Friends Historical Society* 54 (1976–80):85–100.

9. Lloyd, *Quaker Social History* (London, 1950), 97–105.

10. "Imprisonment Upon a Praemunire: George Fox's Last Trial," *Journal of the Friends Historical Society* 50 (1962–64):37–43; "Early Friends' Experience with Juries," *Journal of the Friends Historical Society* 50 (1962–64):217–27; "Early Friends and Informers," *Journal of the Friends Historical Society* 51 (1965): 107–14; "George Fox's Last Imprisonment," *Journal of the Friends Historical Society* 51 (1965):159–66; "Early Friends Testimony against Carnal Weapons," *Journal of the Friends Historical Society* 52 (1968–71):101–5; "Were Penn's Jury 'Starved?'" *Journal of the Friends Historical Society* 53 (1972–75):58–61.

11. See n. 8, preceding. Wayne Spurrier's dissertation, although focusing on Kent and Essex, attempted through printed sources, particularly Besse's *Sufferings*, to examine the extent of prosecution nationwide. Although his conclusions are admirable, his methodology is not. With the exception of the two counties he examined, he failed to utilize any manuscript sources or to examine the nature of the legal system or the laws under which Friends suffered. Nor did he examine harassment of Quakers or the types of crimes for which they were prosecuted. It is a useful work, but far from complete.

12. Reay, "Authorities and Early Restoration Quakerism."

13. See, for example, J. S. Cockburn, ed., *Crime in England 1550–1800* (London, 1977); J. A. Sharpe, *Crime in Seventeenth-Century England: A County Study* (Cambridge, 1983); Douglas Hay et al., eds., *Albion's Fatal Tree: Crime and Society in Eighteenth-Century England* (London, 1975); J. M. Beattie, "The Pattern of Crime in England, 1660–1800," *Past & Present* no. 72 (1974):47–94; Buchanon Sharp, *In Contempt of all Authority: Rural Artisans and Riot in the West*

of England, 1586–1660 (Berkeley and London, 1980); E. P. Thompson, *Whigs and Hunters: the Origin of the Black Act* (London, 1975); John Brewer and John Styles, eds., *An Ungovernable People: the English and their Law in the Seventeenth and Eighteenth Centuries* (London, 1980).

14. It should be noted that Richard T. Vann and David Eversley, in preparation for their forthcoming book, *Friends in Life and Death: The Demography of the British and Irish Quakers*, have prepared lists of Quakers from the "digests" of births, marriages, and deaths. But while those records are very useful for their purposes, severe gaps in them, particularly for the Restoration period, force the legal historian to augment them with monthly and quarterly meeting records and with sufferings records. The local historian would also be well advised to scrutinize records of other dissenting groups and the Catholics in the county under study, for official legal records do not provide the religion of the offender. Only a thorough knowledge of local families will enable accurate identification of Quakers. It is also important to know when the individual is first mentioned in Quaker records, for earlier offenses may have taken place prior to association with the sect. I strongly urge both religious and legal historians to focus on detailed county studies of dissent in the seventeenth century.

Introduction

MORRIS DANCERS FROM THE NORTH

A while ago there came to . . . Bristol certain Morris dancers from the north, by two and two, two and two, with an intent here to exercise some spiritual cheats, or (as may well be suspected) to carry on some levelling design, and our soldiers here, having nothing else to do . . . struck in with them in their quaking, . . . but His Highness (by breath from his mouth) hath driven away these northern locusts from us and given a command for the remove of their abettors and favourites. . . . His Highness hath gained much upon the hearts of our citizens by this act of grace and duty.

Ralph Farmer, *The Great Mysteries* (1655), prefatory epistle dedicated to
John Thurloe, Secretary of State

The Interregnum was a period of intense religious excitement and speculation that not only affected the older "Puritan" sects—the Presbyterians, Independents, and Baptists—but also resulted in the emergence of many smaller, more radical groups. Despite mutual jealousy and competition, all the sects saw this period as the Age of the Spirit, an identification that helped to create millenarian expectancy that, in turn, interacted with the political events of the time. Religiously and politically, the first decade of the Interregnum was dominated by the Puritans. But their preeminence was uncertain, for it was an era of individualism, thanks in part to the increasing number of "masterless men," including those in the New Model Army. It was this army, aided by increased social mobility during the Civil War, that linked up numerous radical groups that had hitherto existed as lonely outposts in the north and west of England. Class and generational tensions, exacerbated by a "tradition of plebian anti-clericalism and irreligion," also played a part.[1] Laymen often found themselves actively and independently searching for the "truth," if not in Scripture, then within themselves. They were also searching for answers to what they viewed as legal, social, and political oppression. It was this milieu, combined with disillusionment with those Puritans in power, that was to influence the

rapid growth of the Quakers—the strongest radical challenge to Interregnum Puritanism and the Restoration monarchy.

A spontaneous movement that "unconsciously rested on many
precedents and predecessors,"[2] the Quakers in the early 1650s were
strongly northern in their outlook and membership. Yorkshire, Lancashire, Westmorland, Cumberland, Cheshire, Durham, and Northumberland contained only one-seventh of the population of England
at that time. But 160 out of 250 of the "most active Friends" during
that period came from that region, a factor that may help to account
for much of the character of early Quakerism.[3] The northern counties, more so than the rest of England, were heavily reliant on agriculture and pasturage; and although some of these regions may have
begun to experience a degree of prosperity in the early 1650s, they
were generally among the poorest counties in the country. This fact
was particularly true of Westmorland and Cumberland. In 1649, the
year the plague spread north from Manchester, there were said to be
thirty thousand impoverished, starving families in Cumberland alone,
and that tenants there were complaining of rising rents and continual
royal levies. Similarly, Cartmel and Hawkshead, in Lancashire, were
areas of serious discontent caused by the excessive tithe demands of
two lay impropriators, the Roundhead Nathaniel Nicolson, and the
Royalist Thomas Preston, the latter recouping his fortunes after having been heavily mulcted by the parliamentary authorities. Parts of the
north had a strong tradition of Lollardry, while tenant farmers in the
northwest, as far back as the Pilgrimage of Grace, had exhibited a
marked dislike for nobles, clergy, and tithes.[4]

The Anglican Church had shown little interest in the north. Most
of the tithes had gone to nobles or to the universities who had kept the
money. The clergy of the region had been long considered the most
ignorant in England, a situation exacerbated by the pathetic stipends
that caused the bishops "to admit mean scholars rather than have
none."[5] Following the defeat of the Royalist armies and the bank-
ruptcy of the traditional clergy, there developed in the north a spiritual vacuum far more serious than in the more traditional Puritan
centers of the south and east, a void which was not filled adequately
either by the Puritan sects or by Catholic missionaries. Although by
the 1650s the north contained a fairly large number of Puritan pas-
tors, few of them were of any merit, and some had only recently been
put in by the Triers and Ejectors.[6]

Educational facilities in the north were also unsatisfactory, the region on the whole having both fewer and poorer schools than anywhere in England; and there is evidence that small private schools run by clergymen were much rarer in the north and west than in the south and east. This failure by the clergy may help to account for the disproportionately high number of schoolmasters among early Quaker leaders.[7]

Given the situation in the northern counties, it is not surprising that the majority of early Quaker leaders were involved with agriculture. Although some were "substantial freeholders or allodial tenants," well educated and locally influential, the majority were probably moderately educated tenant farmers from families with a long tradition of independence and individualism. While not desperately poor, they were forced to work hard to extract an unglamorous living. They were likely, as well, to work at several trades to supplement their income.[8] Many had served in the parliamentary armies and consequently had been exposed to the various currents of radical thought then in circulation.[9] In any event, it is probable that a tradition of independence, individualism, and disdain for formalized religion and education, combined with a slowly rising level of prosperity in the face of demands from landlords and impropriators, helped to mold early Quaker thought. While neither theoretical socialists nor egalitarians, many of those who became Quakers in the northwest bitterly opposed the claims and pretensions of the "highbred and powerful." Secular radicalism joined with spiritual Quakerism to produce an explosive reaction against perceived evils in English society.[10]

Yet more than indignation against the highbred and powerful or mere self-interest motivated many of these individuals. They were spiritually troubled, having both separated from the Established Church and experimented with the various Puritan sects in their quest for the "truth." These "Seekers" often met together to read the Bible and to discuss religious matters, and some were already engaging in the method of worship later to be used by Friends. These and other separatists, including some Ranters, were to form the nucleus of early Quakerism, which only gradually developed its own character.[11] Quaker theology would provide a focus for the "instinctive" radicalism of many of these separatists, as well as easing their spiritual malaise. It would also appeal to many radical Puritans, for although Quaker theology tended to be antithetical to the central Puritan emphasis on the

Word and the ordinances, Quakerism carried forward "a development already well advanced within radical puritanism; was an emphasis, a fusing and a systematization of beliefs which had appeared earlier but which had then been more hesitant, sporadic and unrelated."[12] Furthermore, in common with other sectaries, the Quakers were convinced that the "saints" would ultimately rule the world.[13]

Briefly,[14] the Quakers believed in the existence of an inner "Light" or "Spirit" of Christ, which was present in everyone, whether converted or not, from the Beginning. This Light was the pure and perfect love of God and the key to perfection and the everlasting kingdom. Following the transgression of Adam, however, many people were denied the ability to know this Light, perfection was lost, and the capacity to sin, along with the inevitability of death, became man's fate. Although God later made a Covenant with the Jews and gave the Law to Moses, men were still unable to partake of the Light, but were bound instead by external laws and ordinances. There were some exceptions. Moses, the prophets, and John were all chosen by God to prepare the world for the coming of Christ. They had been, as a consequence, "redeemed" out of the world's spirit and allowed to experience the love of God by means of the Inner Light. With the crucifixion of Christ for the sins of man, every individual was once again capable of discerning the Light. The Quakers claimed that Christ had brought, therefore, the "Second" Covenant, that of "Light and Peace," which would be everlasting and unchanging and which superseded the First Covenant of God with the Jews. The apostles, following in the tradition of Moses, the prophets, and John, were also redeemed out of the world's spirit in order to spread the word that the kingdom of God and everlasting life were there for all to enjoy simply by obeying the inner Christ.

Unfortunately, claimed the Quakers, a lengthy period of "apostasy" had taken place during which the message of Christ and his apostles had been distorted, and outward ordinances and practices that ignored the Light had again developed (or had continued from the First Covenant). This distortion, they argued, was originally the work of the Catholic Church and the Pope, but had been continued by post-Reformation Protestant ministers who were nothing less than false prophets leading their people to "condemnation." This apostasy was continuing in England despite the overthrow of the Catholic and the Anglican Church and of the monarchy, all of whom had contributed in their own way to the obscuring of Christ's message and to the continuance of external ordinances.[15]

Friends believed, therefore, that the work of the Lord had not been accomplished, and consequently he had again chosen "saints" to spread the message and to warn all those who refused to come to the Light that they would be destroyed, as would any who dared to "persecute" his servants. These saints were the Quakers, selected by God and enabled by him to reject the ways of the world and to experience the Light within, by which they were able to "come to the mountain of the house of God established above all mountains, and to God's teaching," and who, in turn, would "teach His ways."[16] Friends saw themselves as the new apostles, sharing the identical apostolic spirit; as a result they had entered into the same state of perfection that Adam himself had known before the Fall. They were free from sin and, in a metaphorical sense, from death. Christ was speaking in their hearts, and would speak in those of all men and women who would reject the temptations of the world and seek the "indwelling Christ." For the Quakers, personal experience of Christ without the aid of the Scriptures was certain.[17]

Quakerism did not imply simply a mystical communion between man and an inner spirit, for Friends could not and did not, like members of other sects, view themselves as an isolated minority resisting interaction with mankind except as converts joined them. Instead they believed they were the "true" church and the real ministers of God. As a result, Quakerism was an aggressive, "enthusiastic" religion that demanded total conversion of all those with whom it came into contact and whose adherents were determined to spread the message, not only within England, but throughout the world. Of itself, that need not have posed a threat to the state, but the implications of the "Second" Covenant, when combined with the radicalism of early Friends, led to unlawful modes of behavior and principles that relegated the Quakers to the rank of criminals throughout the period to be studied.

Symbolic of the criminality of the Quakers was the role played by traveling ministers, known as "First Publishers of Truth."[18] Although Friends had carried the Puritan concept of "prophesying" to its ultimate expression by eliminating a separate ministry and relying completely on extempore lay preaching in meetings according to the movings of the Lord, they had encouraged the development of itinerant preachers. Normally traveling in pairs, they helped spread the faith by appointing and holding meetings, keeping a watchful eye over newly "convinced" friends, debating with other sects, and entering into churches during divine service, either to preach or to challenge ministers to defend their sermons. These traveling ministers were to be well versed in Quaker thinking, with the strength of conviction and character necessary to undertake arduous and often hazardous missions. They were either self-supporting or assisted by voluntary contributions of the faithful, often administered from organized funds set up, in part, for that service. Rejecting the concept of autonomous congregations, Friends had linked together their scattered meetings under the guidance of itinerant ministers. By thus combining group democracy with centralized spiritual leadership, they were in a position to organize themselves against their antagonists.[19]

At first their meetings were gatherings of the "world's people," at which two or three of the First Publishers, ostensibly moved by the Lord, preached at great length but often with little erudition, in an effort to gain conversions. These "threshing" meetings often attracted hundreds, and sometimes thousands, of spectators and were held in fields, large halls, private homes, or on moors and mountains. In time, smaller "retired" or "silent" meetings were encouraged for new converts, usually in the homes of Quakers or their sympathizers. Although these were open to the public, they were not primarily directed to the need for "convincements," but were intended to strengthen the faith of those already inclined to Quakerism.[20] After the Restoration, the two types of meeting tended to coalesce; thereafter the normal Quaker meeting was composed of Friends, with the public being welcome to attend. It involved silent waiting on the Lord, and although that often resulted in preaching or praying by a recognized "public" Friend, the meeting might well be completely silent. In addition, these gatherings were increasingly held in houses either leased or built by Friends for that purpose, an important development as the laws against meetings stiffened.[21] The "silent" meeting would prove to be an ordeal for authorities charged with preventing large-scale Quaker gatherings:

> We met together often, and waiting upon the Lord in pure silence . . . and harkened to the voice of the Lord, and felt His word in our hearts, to burn up and beat down all that was contrary to God, and we obeyed the Light of Christ in us. . . . And while waiting upon the Lord in silence, as often we did for many hours together, with our minds and hearts toward Him, being stayed in the

Light of Christ within us, from all thoughts, fleshly notions, and desires, in our diligent waiting and feare of His name, and harkening to His word, we received often the pouring down of the spirit upon us and the gift of God's holy, eternal spirit as in the days of old, and our hearts were made glad, and our tongues loosed, and our mouths opened, and we spoke with new tongues as the Lord gave us utterance, and as His spirit led us . . . and to us hereby was the deep things of God revealed, and things unutterable was known and made manifest, and the glory of the Father was revealed.[22]

The development and the activities of the First Publishers illustrate a number of important aspects of Quaker belief that either broke the law or were liable to be challenged by the authorities. First, the Quakers were determined to hold their meetings, notwithstanding their potential illegality. The meeting for worship, Friends insisted, was an essential vehicle for spreading the word, while also providing the support and reinforcement that each Quaker needed. Although Friends believed that all those living in accordance with the Light were in unity and fellowship, they realized that vigilance was necessary, for the world was a temptation, with "fleshly-minded men" ready to draw them "from the spirit into the flesh and so into bondage." Similarly, Friends needed protection from the internal threat, the Devil or "Tempter," who would also try to lure them into condemnation.[23] The meeting for worship provided that protection. In addition, the Quakers were convinced that they were following the dictates of God and the pattern of behavior of Jesus and his apostles. To Friends it was a crucial matter of conscience. Edward Burrough in 1661 went so far as to warn the House of Commons, then considering a bill to prevent Quaker meetings, that if the bill became law, "he was so far from yielding conformity thereunto, that he should . . . meet among the people of God to worship Him, and not only so, but should make it his business to exhort all God's people everywhere, to meet together for the worship of God notwithstanding that law and all its penalties."[24] Meetings were held on Sunday and usually on one or two weekdays, and Friends were also determined that they should be public, both as a means of encouraging potential converts to attend, and as a witness to their own testimony of faith. Thus Bristol Men's Meeting in 1678, when granting permission to any Friends who so wished to retire from the public meeting on Sunday afternoons "to wait upon the Lord

in the pure silence of all flesh," added a caveat that "lest such meetings . . . be an occasion of hurt to our testimony as to encourage
Friends to withdraw from our public meetings or meet privately in
time of persecution, Friends doth propose that such meetings may dissolve and not be in such times, but that in times of persecution Friends
may publicly meet together as heretofore."[25] Religious meetings held
apart from an established church were generally acceptable in the
heady, millenarian days of the Interregnum. But with the restoration of the monarchy and the Anglican Church, meetings of religious
dissenters, except on a very small scale, became anathema. Given
Friends' inflexible attitude on the necessity and openness of those
meetings, conflict with the law was inevitable.

Second, many First Publishers were defiantly aggressive about the
sect's northern origins. In 1654 George Fox warned that the Quaker
"army" was "coming up out of the north against you terrible ones,"
while in that same year both Francis Howgill and John Camm, disillusioned with London and with Lord Protector Cromwell, thanked God
for separating "the people of the north . . . from the world and from
the pollutions of it."[26] Friends were well aware of the attitude of many
Englishmen towards the north. "O thou north of England, who art
counted as desolate and barren, and reckoned the least of the nations," lamented Edward Burrough, "yet out of thee did the branch
spring and the star arise which gives light unto all the regions round
about."[27] Such provincial chauvinism would scarcely pacify troubled
local authorities in other parts of England, viewing with suspicion
these northern invaders whose means of support were not always
clear. In an age characterized by intense suspicion of new arrivals,
local magistrates were susceptible to the fear that laxity towards religious radicalism could promote a new breed of wandering messiahs.
These magistrates were therefore prepared to treat all new arrivals, be
they minstrels, tinkers, or Quakers, as vagabonds.[28]

Third, those same authorities might also be concerned with what
they regarded as "profane" traveling on the Lord's Day, as First Publishers or local Friends traveled to meetings, often over some distance.
The Quakers did not alleviate such concern by their principle that
every day was the Lord's Day upon which they could serve Him. "I
have Christ about me and in me," claimed John Love, "and therefore
cannot choose but remember Him continually."[29] James Nayler chided
the Presbyterians that they had a day "to abstain from the world and

days to conform to the world."[30] As a result of this attitude, the Quakers were willing to travel to their meetings on Sundays, and to maintain their daily routine, whether on Sundays, fast days, or holy days, by opening their shops, carrying on their trades, or working their land. Once again, a Quaker testimony implied conflict with custom and law.

Fourth, ministering Friends were also viewed with suspicion for their preaching in market places and streets and for their intrusions into churches during divine service. Quakers scarcely considered the possibility that such interruptions might be both unwarranted and unlawful. Believing themselves to be the new apostles, they felt obliged to emulate Christ, who had gone into the Temple, and his apostles, who had entered the synagogues "to testify of Christ Jesus." Friends also asserted that they were simply following the pattern of early Protestant reformers, such as Martin Luther, John Calvin, and John Wycliffe, and "those persons which in Queen Mary's days went into the Popish steeplehouses, to bear witness against their superstitions."[31] The Quakers vigorously opposed specified places of worship, believing that the "true Tabernacle" was "made without hands," and that therefore the coming together of the faithful could occur anywhere, as the First Publishers had demonstrated. Friends were acting in accordance with their own bitter hatred of ministers and of formalized religion, based in part on their northern experience. The only true ministers, Friends argued, were those both living in and moved by the Spirit of Christ. Others who assumed the title of minister, but who lacked "the same spirit which was in the Apostles of Christ" were "none of His ministers."[32] Consequently, the Quakers vilified the "hired" ministers who preached formal sermons with prescribed time limits. Friends therefore assumed the right to interrupt such sermons, either to proclaim the Quaker message or to challenge the minister in debate, much to the astonishment and annoyance of his congregation. "They cry up liberty of conscience," Thomas Underhill complained, "but are not willing to give it to others."[33] The Quaker justification for this apparent infringement of the religious toleration they demanded for themselves was succinctly expressed by Thomas Morford, who had been criticized by a Baptist minister for interrupting the latter's sermon. Morford complained that

> had not that been a false prophet that was speaking he would have been subject to me, or to the spirit of the Lord in me who had His

word to declare, for so are the spirits of the true prophets and not to limit the spirit of the Lord, but if anything be revealed to another that stands by, the first is to hold his peace though he be not bid be silent, for our God is the God of order and when He moves one to speak that is silent, the other that is speaking which is guided by God's spirit, stops and is silent.[34]

But even if the Quakers had waited until the end of divine service, they would still have been in violation of the law.

Fifth, the willingness of Friends to thrust themselves on unwilling ministers and congregations was symptomatic of another Quaker testimony—their refusal to contribute, through rates, tithes, oblations, or other obligatory dues, to the Established Church. It is hardly surprising that the Quakers, with their background and attitudes, would hold such a view. They protested that Christ had, with his Second Covenant, ended the necessity for tithes by instituting the "unchangeable" ministry—that of his "saints," who would preach gratis at any time and in any place. Jesus and his apostles had done so, living off the voluntary contributions and offerings of the faithful; and therefore Quaker ministers would do the same. Such self-maintenance, Friends averred, should also apply to meeting places.[35] Although Friends were not alone in their opposition to compulsory maintenance of the established religion, there was strong support for such a system from many of the landed gentry, themselves often lay impropriators; from the universities; from many conservative Puritans who saw the need for a state-maintained church to propagate "sound" religious doctrines as opposed to the whimsies of Quakers and other radicals; and from the restored Anglican Church.[36] Once again, conflict between the Quakers and the law seemed certain.

Furthermore, their belief in the absolute necessity of holding their own meetings, combined with their denial of compulsory maintenance of an established religion, led Friends to oppose resolutely the attending of obligatory divine service. Their stance on this issue was again uncompromising, for they never subscribed to the concept of occasional conformity, often practiced by other sects. This staunch nonattendance made them liable to prosecution under the recusancy laws.

The direct activities of traveling Friends, while illustrating potential areas of conflict with the law, did not exhaust such possibilities, for the Quakers had developed other testimonies, some of which had grave secular implications. Of particular importance was their position on swearing. In accordance with their theory of the Second Covenant, and drawing on the injunction in Matthew 5 : 33 – 37 and James 5 : 12 against swearing, Friends refused to take any oath, including those enjoined by the law. They restricted themselves instead to yea and nay, thereby remaining within the doctrine of the Inner Light. In 1658 Gilbert Latey, in a letter to Henry Scobell, clerk of the Privy Council, made this point clear when he warned the authorities that all those who swore were "out of the spirit and out of the power that they were in that could not swear, to which power every soul must be subject that is a follower of Christ and the Apostles." Therefore, he added, "take heed how you cause any to swear and sin against Christ and the Apostles' doctrine." [37] Of all the Quaker testimonies, this contained the greatest potential for conflict with the law, for oath-taking was a fundamental requirement of common-law procedure. Although based ostensibly on a religious concept, this Quaker belief (despite their arguments to the contrary) could be properly viewed by the authorities as a civil matter. Refusal to take an oath left Friends liable to numerous civil disabilities; but more significantly, it exposed them to the charge that they were Catholics in disguise,[38] for the normal test in England to distinguish Catholics from Protestants was the use of specific oaths. Although Friends vehemently denied that accusation, contemporaries remained skeptical, and a recent historian of English Catholicism has lent some credence to those doubts by claiming that the Quakers were "the opposite of Protestant Christianity." Their theology, he argues, had "an archaic character more reminiscent of pre- than of post-Reformation Christianity," with its roots in "traditional northern society," while Quaker uncertainty about the need for the Scriptures reflected "a more general lack of esteem for the bible in the north." At the very least, he believes, Quakers and Catholics were complementary.[39]

Adherence to the Second Covenant also led Quakers to refuse to use "carnal" weapons. All those who lived in the Light, they argued, had been "redeemed" from strife, and therefore from the need to bear arms or to take an oath, the latter having been necessary only to adjudicate an end to strife.[40] Their development of a "pure" pacifist stance—opposition to all forms of violence—was delayed until the Restoration; but while some Friends wavered before 1660, the nature of Quaker theology consistently demanded a willingness to refrain personally from using weapons.[41] In 1660 George Fox endeavored to allay the suspicions of the new government in relation to the equivocal

attitude of some Friends in the previous year. "Taking up arms out-
wardly," he proclaimed, "we utterly deny, and it is not our principle,
nor is it in the Covenant, and life, and peace with God and the Light
with men." This doctrine was expanded in January 1661 after mass
arrests of Quakers following a rising of Fifth Monarchists. "We know
that wars and fighting proceed from the lusts of men . . . out of which
lusts the Lord hath redeemed us, and so out of the occasion of war. . . .
All bloody principles and practices, we, as to our own particulars, do
utterly deny, with all outward wars and strife and fightings with outward weapons, for any end or under any pretence whatsoever."[42] Refusal to bear arms conflicted with Restoration demands for men and
weapons for the militia.

The activities discussed thus far were obviously susceptible to legal
prosecution. Less clear were the issues of blasphemy and heresy, for
these were largely subjective matters, better suited for theological
debate than for the normal processes of the law. Nonetheless, the Quakers were vulnerable on a number of points. Guidance by an Inner Light
worried Quaker opponents, who measured their own faith in accordance with scriptural commands. The Quakers, they feared, seemed
to judge the Scriptures by their own spirit.[43] Similarly, many opponents were suspicious of the rather lax Quaker attitude toward the
Trinity and the symbolism of the Crucifixion and the Resurrection, as
well as their claim to be free from sin, a claim not always in accord with
their behavior.[44] There were also the "enthusiastic" manifestations of
Quakerism exhibited by many early Friends who "shook" and "trem-
bled" in meetings, went "naked as a sign," engaged in lengthy fasts,
viewed themselves as faith healers, and spoke often of their "miracu-
lous" escapes from death and of the "judgments" delivered by God
upon their "persecutors."[45] Their language was often passionate and
violent, as Vavasor Powell, a Baptist, discovered after he had mocked
the Quaker claim to perfection. He was more than mildly chastised by
Morgan Watkins: "O, thy sottish blindness makes thee grope at noon
day, strain at a gnat, and swallow a camel. Why dost thou pray against
sin, while thou believest thou cannot be delivered from it on earth?"[46]
Contemporaries often linked the Quakers with the Ranters and the
Anabaptists. Ephraim Pagitt, in his *Heresiography*, reflected the common view that the Quakers were a northern English "upstart branch
of the Anabaptists," composed mainly of the "dregs of the common
people," whose "pride, conceitedness and ignorance," drove them into

"esteeming no men but themselves, condemning all laws, magistrates, ancient worship, prayers, and sacraments, and confining salvation within the circle of their own giddy, unclean heads."[47]

Pagitt's diatribe illustrated another aspect of Quakerism that not only brought it into confrontation with the law, but generally affronted many who might have been sympathetic to much of Quaker thought. This was Friends' "social" testimony—their insistence on plain speech, relative simplicity of dress, and an absolute refusal to show any outward sign of respect, even to those in authority to whom it was traditionally given. In effect, the Quakers challenged all the symbols of a stratified society. While proclaiming their respect for authority, Friends promulgated ideas that implied a desire to turn the world upside down. "When the Lord sent me forth into the world," wrote George Fox, "he forbade me to put off my hat to any, high or low, and I was required to 'thee' and 'thou' all men and women, without any respect to rich or poor, great or small. And as I travelled up and down, I was not to bid people 'good morrow' or 'good evening'; neither might I bow or scrape with my leg to any one." Not surprisingly, "this made the sects and professions . . . rage."[48] It was normal seventeenth-century practice to acknowledge anyone in passing, often by doffing the hat while uttering some elaborate courtesy; and whereas the hat was generally worn in the house and in church, it was not worn in time of prayer nor particularly in the presence of superiors. The use of such terms as "thee" and "thou" was commonly restricted to those within a family, to intimate friends, and especially to social inferiors.[49] Friends also reacted against fancy dress and superfluous luxury at a time when clothing clearly differentiated one class from another. William Morris, a Quaker, complained that if Friends went into the "parish temples" they would find men "daubed with lace, their hats and their garments hung with ribbons . . . their heads powdered like millers, their breeches like coats, cuffs near the elbows, and boothose tops to the heels," and women "with naked necks and collars about them, their arms pinioned like felons condemned, with manifold like abominable attire."[50] Fancy dress implied more to Friends than simple vanity in looking smart. "God is against you," warned James Nayler, "you proud and lustful, wanton ones, who make it your greatest care to deck yourselves in your proud attire, inventing new ways and fashions to make yourselves glorious in the sight of men, that they may bow down and worship you." Any gestures that implied respect or subservience to men deeply troubled Friends, who viewed such behavior as responsible for the oppression of the poor by those in power, who were respecting men and not God. Thomas Aldam typified the attitude of Friends when he complained of "oppression in racking of rents, oppression in tithes, oppression amongst the gentry, priest[s] and judges, justices, lawyers, all receiving gifts and rewards contrary to the teachings of the Lord." As a result, he stressed, the "law and truth" were "corrupted."[51] J. F. Maclear believes that Friends saw themselves as the "champions of the socially disinherited," and thereby yearned for the establishment in England "of a new social order." This orientation was not, he adds, "humanitarian benevolence," but rather "a viewpoint which was conceived in the knowledge of divine judgment on a world of social injustice and fashioned in an atmosphere laden with intense millenarian expectations."[52]

While Quaker attacks on the ways and customs of the world elicited reactions of scorn and anger from opponents, no laws were necessarily infringed. But, as always, Friends went further. They refused, in keeping with their testimony, to doff their hats when in court or when speaking to any magistrate. As Christopher Hill notes, the authorities might not view this action as an "innocent eccentricity," for such refusal in the presence of superiors "was a long-standing gesture of popular social protest."[53] Contemporaries were naturally concerned that lack of respect could be taken further than hat-honor and simplicity of speech and dress. Thomas Fuller, writing in 1655, warned that "such as now introduce Thou and Thee will (if they can) expel Mine and Thine, dissolving all property into confusion."[54] In practical terms, refusal to doff their hats could be construed as contempt of court and of magistracy. In any case, intemperate attacks by Friends upon judges, justices, and lawyers were unlikely to evoke any sympathy from those charged with enforcing the law.

Friends, for their part, did not consider themselves as social revolutionaries. To some extent their demand for simplicity was an effort to break down the proud, rather than to exalt the humble, for only by driving out that pride could the sinner be capable of coming to the Light. This question was one of conversion, rather than social reform. The Quakers were also clearly enunciating their own uniqueness as a sect by breaking away from the fashions and customs of the world, thereby maintaining an internal feeling of discipline and detachment from their society.[55] Understandably, many contemporaries failed to see such subtle nuances in the actions of early Friends.

Quaker inward discipline and relative detachment from the world led them to develop an organization sufficient for them to both survive and expand. That expansion was quite remarkable, reaching geometrical proportions between 1652 and 1657, as Quaker numbers increased from about five hundred in 1652 to five thousand in 1654, and to at least twenty thousand three years later. By 1660 there may have been as many as forty thousand adherents, although precise figures are impossible to ascertain. It does appear that their numbers continued to increase dramatically during the Restoration, reaching a peak about 1680.[56] "These vipers," complained one M.P. in 1656, "are crept into the bowels of your Commonwealth, and the government too. They grow numerous, and swarm all the nation over; every county, every parish. I shall turn Quaker too," he added, "but not in that sense." Henry Cromwell, in Ireland, echoing that concern, warned that the Quakers were "our most considerable enemy."[57] Organizational ability played a considerable part in this expansion and in holding the movement together,[58] and was one of the features which distinguished the Quakers from many other radical sects which had emerged during the Interregnum. The Quakers became a state within a state, with a network of meetings for business as well as for worship. Registers were kept of births, marriages, and deaths; "sufferings" were recorded; and care was taken of Quaker poor, apprentices, and prisoners. Funds were established to aid the work of traveling ministers, both in England and abroad.[59] Implicit in this organization were two further challenges to the law—Quakers' insistence on conducting their own marriages and burials, in accordance with their own principles, rather than those of the state or the Established Church. Friends believed that God had joined man and woman before the Fall, and therefore, as they had come to share in the perfection that existed prior to the Fall, they too would be married by God and not by man. "The right joining in marriage is the work of the Lord only, and not the priests or magistrates, for it is God's ordinance and not man's. And therefore Friends cannot consent that they should join them together, for we marry none; it's the Lord's work, and we are but witnesses."[60] The Quakers insisted on rigorous procedures before marriage was allowed to take place and, from 1656, provided a marriage certificate that could be shown to the civil authorities, but only if the couple was so inclined.[61] As for Quaker burials, they were to be conducted in their own burial grounds because Friends could not "give their dead bodies to the world." Such burials were to be according to "the manner of the holy men of God, recorded in the Scriptures of Truth, and not after the customs of the heathen." Quakers and neighbors would gather in silence at the graveside; if any were moved to minister, they did so.[62] The resemblance between a normal meeting for worship and gatherings at burials was not lost on authorities anxious to deal firmly with the Quakers. Certainly from the point of view of the restored Anglican Church, Quaker marriages and funerals were equally unlawful and ungodly.

By the end of their first decade of existence, the Quakers had developed a collective set of principles which threatened the foundation of the English legal system. They were a large and expanding group of potential criminals, motivated by inflexible and powerful religious convictions. Although many of the outward symbols of Quakerism were not peculiar to them, "it was the characteristic mark of Friends that they invoked these symbolic actions as invariable rules of conduct demanded by their religion."[63] Even after millenarian excitement and the more "enthusiastic" aspects of Quakerism had died away during the Restoration and the focus of the movement had shifted from the north to London and its environs, Friends remained bound by lawbreaking testimonies. They also retained in the minds of many contemporaries an unfavorable reputation that they had deserved in their early years, but that became increasingly less applicable as the Restoration progressed. As late as 1672 they would still be characterized in an official report as "rude, saucy, unmannerly with all the ugly names that belong to an ill-bred person; it is no wrong to them to say they are mad and fitter for Bedlam than sober company."[64] In the circumstances, conflicts with the law were inevitable if the authority of the state was to be maintained. The Quakers, in fact, had often been prosecuted during the Interregnum,[65] but had survived and expanded. Yet with the restoration of Charles II, the return to power of many Royalists eager for revenge, the strong backing for the king from the Presbyterians and other conservative Puritans, and the apparent hostility of many of the populace towards religious radicalism, the outlook for the Quakers became deeply unsettled. By 1662, according to Quaker sources, thousands of Friends had already suffered some form of legal restraint. In that year, moreover, Parliament enacted the so-called Quaker Act[66] directed against their meetings and their refusal to swear, and prescribing punishments of fines, imprisonment, abjuration of the realm, and transportation. Since the Quakers steadfastly maintained their principles, the possibility of their surviving as a unified religious entity was doubtful. In 1689, however, the Toleration Act[67] was passed, and the Quakers, still numerous and still asserting many of their testimonies, were included. Thereafter, the state gradually accommodated Friends to its own system, tolerating and protecting their meetings, tacitly permitting their marriages and burials, accepting their affirmation in many instances rather than an oath, and relying on distraint for tithe and militia offenses instead of harsher sentences.[68] In effect, Quaker criminality had been either legitimized or rendered relatively harmless.

How were the Quakers able to survive, and why did the Anglican Church and the English government fail to eradicate them? The answers to these questions have a significance beyond the experience of a single sect. It is not the purpose of this book to denigrate or play down the persecution of the other English dissenting sects during this period. The late Stuart kings and their supporters clearly preferred an England unified, like France, around one established faith. As will be seen, this orientation left such dissenting bodies as the Presbyterians, Independents, Baptists, and Quakers outside the legal system. Arnold G. Matthews' *Calamy Revised*, the State Papers Domestic, the Roger Morrice MS Ent'ring Book, and C. E. Whiting's *Studies in English Puritanism*[69] all indicate the harassment and prosecution of the Presbyterian and Independent ministers, thousands of whom had been ejected from their livings in the first years of the Restoration. Whiting also chronicles the persecution of the Baptists. Nor were the Quaker efforts to record their sufferings unique. John Foxe's sixteenth-century *Book of Martyrs* traverses much of the same ground.[70] As stated previously, the Quakers had much in common with other dissenting sects. The Quakers, however, are worthy of special attention for several reasons. First, they went much further than the other sects in the sheer breadth of their principles, which they were firmly resolved to follow, even when the result was provocative, confrontational, and illegal. Combining these principles with organizational skill, they represented a threat to the social, legal, and political fabric of England at a particularly volatile period in its history. Second, the Quakers were despised by the other sects, who had often themselves resorted to persecution of Friends during the Interregnum. Third, the Quakers retained into the Restoration a reputation for eccentric, unrestrained, and uncivilized behavior that colored the attitudes of many people, both inside and outside the law enforcement system. Fourth, Quaker sufferings records are the only such documents extant for a religious sect in the seventeenth century. Furthermore, as we will see, the astonishing details of legal advice in those records, as well as the use to which they were put, is unique. Finally, the Quakers alone, of all the religious groups, developed a sophisticated legal defense organization, whose tactics provide rare insights into the operation of the legal system. For these reasons, the Quakers are an invaluable source for legal historians. The value of this documentation, however, does not preclude the necessity of viewing the survival of the Quakers and their testimonies within the context of Restoration politics and the common law tradition. In this way, and using the Quakers as our model, we can better understand the limitations of royal power, as well as the strengths and weaknesses of the English legal system in the late seventeenth century.

Notes

Unless otherwise indicated, all manuscript sources are located in the Library of the Religious Society of Friends, London. In the Notes and Bibliography, for seventeenth-century tracts the Wing number is given following the date of publication. At the risk of losing some of the flavor of seventeenth-century prose, but for ease of comprehension, all manuscript and primary printed quotations have been modernized in punctuation, capitalization, and spelling. The only exceptions are archaic words or awkward tenses, such as "arse," "doth," and "believeth." Archaic words whose meanings are obscure are explained in footnotes.

1. Christopher Hill, *The World Turned Upside Down* (1972; paperback reprint: Harmondsworth, 1975), 25 passim; see also J. F. Maclear, "Quakerism and the End of the Interregnum: A Chapter in the Domestication of Radical Puritanism," *Church History* 19 (1950):241. Barry Reay sees the New Model Army as a "major source of Quaker recruitment" (*The Quakers and the English Revolution* [London, 1985], 20–21).

2. Henry J. Cadbury, in William C. Braithwaite, *The Beginnings of Quakerism*, 2d ed. (Cambridge, 1955), 547.

3. Hugh Barbour, *The Quakers in Puritan England* (New Haven, 1964), 41; see also Reay, who adds that many of the northern Quakers were women (*Quakers and Revolution*, 69).

4. Richard Vann, *The Social Development of Quakerism* (Cambridge, 1969), 56; Barbour, *Quakers*, 77; Bruce Gordon Blackwood, "Agrarian Unrest and the Early Lancashire Quakers," *Journal of the Friends Historical Society* 51 (1965): 72–74; Hill, *World Upside Down*, 77, 79; C. S. L. Davies, "Popular Religion and the Pilgrimage of Grace," in *Order and Disorder in Early Modern England*, ed. Anthony Fletcher and John Stevenson (Cambridge, 1985), 58–91.

5. Barbour, *Quakers*, 79–80.

6. Hill, *World Upside Down*, 79; John Bossy, *The English Catholic Community 1570–1850* (London, 1975), 393; Barbour, *Quakers*, 81–82. In February 1682 Thomas Robertson, a Quaker minister from Westmorland, having been arrested in Bristol for preaching, became involved in a scriptural argument with William Gulston, Bishop of Bath and Wells. Robertson insinuated at one point that the Anglican Church had not really existed for thirty years. "Do you not think," queried Gulston, "that there was an Episcopalian church in Oliver's days?" Robertson retorted that "if there was such a church, they never told us of it, nor sent us neither epistle nor gospel, but left us to the devourers and Presbyters and the like" (T. Robertson to George Fox [February, 1681/2, Bristol], ARB MSS, fol. 148).

7. Barbour, *Quakers*, 83; Hill, *World Upside Down*, 76; Vann, *Social Development*, 56.

8. Vann, *Social Development*, 56, 58; Barbour, *Quakers*, 74–75. Most of these men held their lands by customary tenure (Barbour, *Quakers*, 75); see also Ernest E. Taylor, "The First Publishers of Truth: A Study," *Journal of the Friends Historical Society* 19 (1922):66–81; Reay, *Quakers and Revolution*, 5; Barry Reay, "The Social Origins of Early Quakerism," *Journal of Interdisciplinary History* 11 (1980–81):61.

9. At least ninety Quaker leaders "had been in arms for Parliament" (Alan Cole, "The Quakers and the English Revolution," *Past & Present* no. 10 [November 1956]:39). For the names of these Friends, see Margaret Hirst, *The Quakers in Peace and War* (London, 1923), 527–29.

10. Barbour, *Quakers*, 83–84.

11. Barbour, *Quakers*, 31–32; Reay, *Quakers and Revolution*, 5. The Ranters were a "movement rather than a sect" who "combined a variety of seemingly contradictory views from a mystical pantheism to a robust plebeian materialism." They were notorious among contemporaries for their conviction that moral law "was no longer binding upon true believers" (A. L. Morton, *The World of the Ranters* [London, 1970], 17). For their connection with early Quakerism (despite Friends' disavowal of any such connection), see Hill, *World Upside Down*, chap. 10; Geoffrey F. Nuttall, *Studies in Christian Enthusiasm* (Pendle Hill, Pa., 1948), chap. 6; Russell G. Schofield, "Some Ranter Leaders and their Opinions," *Bulletin of The Friends Historical Association* 39 (1950): 63–73; J. F. McGregor, "Ranterism and the Development of Early Quakerism," *Journal of Religious History* 9 (1977):349–63. For an analysis of the rank and file of the Quakers, see Vann, *Social Development*, especially chap. 2; Barbour, *Quakers*, chap. 3.

12. Geoffrey F. Nuttall, *The Holy Spirit in Puritan Faith and Reason* (Oxford, 1946), 151.

13. Maclear, "Quakerism and Interregnum," 246. For the influence of millenarian excitement on the spread of Quakerism, see Geoffrey F. Nuttall, *The Welsh Saints 1640–1660* (Cardiff, 1957), 70–72; see also T. L. Underwood, "Early Quaker Eschatology," in *Puritans, the Millennium and the Future of Israel*, ed. Peter Toon (London, 1970), 91–103; Pamela Oliver, "Quaker Testimony and the Lamb's War" (Ph.D. thesis, University of Melbourne, 1977), chap. 4.

14. The following paragraph is based on the *Journal of George Fox*, ed. John L. Nickalls (London, 1975), chaps. 1 and 2. While no longer considered the "founder" of Quakerism, Fox remained until his death in 1691 the outstanding spokesman and organizer of the sect; see Cadbury, in Braithwaite, *Beginnings*, 547; see also Reay, *Quakers and Revolution*, 4; W. S. Hudson, "A

Suppressed Chapter in Quaker History," *Journal of Religion* 24 (1944):108–18; and Henry J. Cadbury, "An Obscure Chapter of Quaker History," *Journal of Religion* 24 (1944):201–13.

15. These ideas permeated Quaker writings during this period. Typical examples include Edward Burrough, *Something in Answer to a Book* (B6036), 26ff., in Francis Howgill, *The Fiery Darts of the Divel Quenched* (London, 1654; H3159); Henry Clark, *A Rod Discover'd* (London, 1657; C4457), passim; Anthony Pearson, *The Great Case of Tythes Truly Stated* (London, 1657; P989), 4–10; George Fox the Younger, *A Noble Salutation and a Faithful Greeting* (London, 1660; F2007), passim; see also Pamela Oliver, "The Quakers and Quietism" (Master's thesis, University of Melbourne, 1972), chap. 1.

16. Fox, *Journal*, ed. Nickalls, 16.

17. Fox, *Journal*, ed. Nickalls, 27–39; L. Hugh Doncaster, "That State in Which Adam Was," *Journal of the Friends Historical Society* 41 (1949):13–24; see also Robert Wastfield, *An Equal Ballance* (London, 1659; W1033), 35.

18. The basic work on the activities of these early Quaker leaders is Norman Penney, ed., *The First Publishers of Truth* (London, 1907). As the century progressed, ministering Friends were often known as "public" Friends (Arnold Lloyd, *Quaker Social History* [London, 1950], 124–25).

19. Nuttall, *Holy Spirit*, 85–86; Cole, "Quakers and Revolution," 48. For more information on the early Quaker funds, see Braithwaite, *Beginnings*, 135–37.

20. See George Fox, *A Collection of Many Select and Christian Epistles. Second Volume* (London, 1698; F1764), 13 (Epistle 14). For examples of the different types of meetings, see Francis Howgill and Edward Burrough to Margaret Fell, 27.i [March].1655, in Caton MSS, 3:164–69; Swarthmore MSS: The Letters of John Audland, 23–35.

21. Lloyd, *Social History*, 124, 129–30.

22. Edward Burrough, in George Fox, *The Great Mistery of the Great Whore Unfolded* (London, 1659; F1832), prefatory epistle, B2.

23. Fox, *Journal*, ed. Nickalls, 16–17.

24. "A Brief Account of the Proceedings of Parliament Concerning the People of God called Quakers," in *Letters &c of Early Friends*, ed. A. R. Barclay (London, 1841), 102; see also George Whitehead, *The Christian Progress* (London, 1725), 263.

25. *Minute Book of the Men's Meeting of the Society of Friends in Bristol, 1667–1686*, ed. Russell J. Mortimer, Bristol Record Society, vol. 24 (Bristol, 1971), 130–31.

26. George Fox, *Newes Coming Up Out of the North* (London, 1654; F1867), title page; Francis Howgill and John Camm to Margaret Fell, 27.i [March].1654, London, in ARB MSS, fol. 20; see also Edward Pyott et al., *The West Answering to the North* (London, 1657; F1988 [wrongly attributed by Wing to George Fox]); Anthony Pearson, *To the Parliament of the Commonwealth of England, Christian Friends* (London, 1653; P992), 1.

27. Edward Burrough, *To the Camp of the Lord* (1655; B6037), in *The Memorable Works of a Son of Thunder and Consolation*, ed. Ellis Hookes (London, 1672 [not in Wing]), 66.

28. Hill, *World Upside Down*, 48–49; Barry Reay believes that much of the mobility was "predominantly short range"; consequently, there had been little contact between north and south, adding to suspicion and hostility towards northern "First Publishers" (*Quakers and Revolution*, 68–69).

29. Quoted from unnamed source in Braithwaite, *Beginnings*, 425.

30. James Nayler, *A Salutation to the Seede of God*, 4th ed. (London, 1656; N311A), 23; see also Daniel Baker, *A Single and General Voice* (London, 1659; B485), 16–17.

31. *A Declaration of the Present Sufferings* (London, 1659; B5993 [wrongly attributed by Wing to Edward Burrough]), 26.

32. Gervase Benson, *A True Tryal of the Ministers* (London, 1655; B1903), 3, 5.

33. T. Underhill, *Hell Broke Loose* (London, 1660; U43), 31.

34. In a letter to George Fox and Francis Howgill, 6.iii [May]. 1659, Waterford, in Swarthmore MSS, I:26.

35. Fox, *Journal*, ed. Nickalls, 184; Pearson, *Tythes*, 3; George Fox, *The Law of God the Rule of Law-makers* (London, 1658; F1856), 21. Quaker bitterness against tithing cannot be overstated: see Barry Reay, "Quaker Opposition to Tithes, 1652–1660," *Past & Present*, no. 86 (February 1980):98–118. Conversely, several Cumberland Friends, who were lay impropriators and now refused to pay tithes, "also for conscience sake could not receive tithes" (GBS, 1:236–38).

36. Hill, *World Upside Down*, 16, 51–52.

37. In *Extracts from State Papers Relating to Friends 1654–1672*, ed. Norman Penney (London, 1913), 38; see also George Fox, *A Journal*, ed. Thomas Ellwood (London, 1694; F1854), 180–81; George Fox, *A Small Treatise Concerning Swearing* (1675; F1906), in *Gospel Truth Demonstrated in a Collection of Doctrinal Books Given Forth by . . . George Fox* (London, 1706), 469–82.

38. For such charges, see Richard Baxter, *The Quakers Catechism* (London, 1655; B1362); William Prynne, *The Quakers Unmasked* (London, 1655; P4045); William Brownsword, *The Quaker-Jesuite* (Kendal, 1660; B5215); Underhill, *Hell Broke Loose*, 30.

39. Bossy, *English Catholicism*, 391–94.

40. See Fox, *Epistles*, 95–96 (Epistle 123).

41. See Nuttall, *Holy Spirit*, 110–12; he emphasizes the spirituality of Quaker millenarianism, which precluded any use of force. For other views, however, see Barry Reay, "The Quakers, 1659, and the Restoration of the Monarchy," *History* 63 (1978):193–213; and W. Alan Cole, "The Quakers and Politics 1652–1660" (Ph.D. thesis, Cambridge University, 1955), chaps. 1, 2, and 9.

42. George Fox, *Our Covenant with God* (London, 1660; F1871B), broadside; George Fox et al., *A Declaration from the Harmless and Innocent People of God Called Quakers* (London, 1660[1]; F1786).

43. Nuttall, *Holy Spirit*, 26–28.

44. Friends themselves were unclear on some of these issues; see Nuttall, *Holy Spirit*, 159, 175; T. L. Underwood, "The Controversy Between the Baptists and the Quakers in England 1650–1689: A Theological Elucidation" (Ph.D. thesis, University of London, 1965), 2; Maurice Creasey, "Early Quaker Christology" (D. Phil. thesis, University of Leeds, 1956), 71; H. H. Brinton, "The Two Sources of Quaker Mysticism," *Friends Quarterly* 8 (1954):10–13. Jeremiah Ives, a Baptist, agreed that the Quakers were perfect—"in the art of deceiving, lying and equivocation" (Jeremiah Ives, *The Quakers Quaking* [London, 1656; I1103], 33).

45. For the Quaker attitude towards these, see Edward Burrough, *Something in Answer to a Book* (B6025), in Howgill, *Fiery Darts*, 23; James Nayler,

Weaknes above Wickednes (London, 1656; n327), 3; Richard Hubberthorne, *Truth Cleared, and the Deceit* (London, 1654; h3241), 5; Kenneth L. Carroll, "Early Quakers and 'Going Naked as a Sign,'" *Quaker History* 67 (1978):69–87; Kenneth L. Carroll, "Quaker Attitudes Towards Signs and Wonders," *Journal of the Friends Historical Society* 54 (1976–80):70–84; Henry J. Cadbury, ed., *George Fox's "Book of Miracles"* (Cambridge, 1948); Edward Byllynge, *A Word of Reproof, and advice* (London, 1659; b2903), 79–94; Fox, *Journal*, ed. Nickalls, 140, 164, 195–96. For the attitudes of contemporary critics, see Richard Blome, *The Fanatick History* (London, 1660; b3212), chap. 5; Underhill, *Hell Broke Loose*, 32–39; Francis Higginson, *A Brief Relation of the Irreligion of the Northern Quakers* (London, 1653; h1953); Thomas Collier, *A Looking-glasse for the Quakers* (London, 1657; c5290), 1–3.

46. Morgan Watkins, *The Perfect Life* (London, 1659; w1068), 34.

47. Ephraim Pagitt, *Heresiography*, 5th ed. (London, 1654; p180), 136.

48. Fox, *Journal*, ed. Nickalls, 36.

49. Braithwaite, *Beginnings*, 490–93; Barbour, *Quakers*, 164; see also Lloyd, *Social History*, 67.

50. William Morris, *All You Perticuler Baptists in Ireland, These Things are to you* [not in Wing], in George Fox, *Severall Warnings to the Baptized People* (n.p., 1659; [not in Wing]), 3–4.

51. James Nayler, *A Discovery of the First Wisdom* (London, 1656; n273), 23; Thomas Aldam to Lieutenant-General John Lambert, n.d., York Castle, in ARB MSS, fol. 125; see also Edward Burrough, *A Message for Instruction . . . how far the Magistrates Power Reacheth* (London, 1658; b6013), 1–3; Anne Audland, *A True Declaration of the Suffering of the Innocent* (London, 1655; a4195), 5; Henry Clark, *Here is True Magistracy Described* (London, 1660; c4455), 5; William Tomlinson, *Seven Particulars, Containing* (London, 1657[8]; t1851), 1.

52. Maclear, "Quakerism and Interregnum," 243–44.

53. Hill, *World Upside Down*, 247.

54. Thomas Fuller, *Church History of Britain* (London, 1655; f2416), III, dedication to Book VIII, quoted in Hill, *World Upside Down*, 247.

55. Barbour, *Quakers*, 163, 167–68.

56. Barbour, *Quakers*, 181–82; Braithwaite, *Beginnings*, 512; Cole, "Quakers and Revolution," 48, 53. This was out of a population of approximately five and a half million.

57. *Diary of Thomas Burton*, ed. J. T. Rutt, 4 vols. (London, 1828), 1:96; T. C. Barnard, *Cromwellian Ireland* (Oxford, 1975), 109.

58. Although organization strengthened the Quakers, it did provoke several schisms by those who believed that such organization was incompatible with the concept of living by the leadings of the Inner Light; see L. Hugh Doncaster, "Diversity and Unity in the Society of Friends," *Friends Quarterly* 19 (1975):107–14; Pamela Oliver, "The Problems of Authority, Discipline and Tradition in the First Century of English Quakerism," *Friends Quarterly* 19 (1975):115–25; Kenneth L. Carroll, *John Perrot* (London, 1971). The worst separations, however, occurred during the Restoration as Quaker organization became more sophisticated; see William C. Braithwaite, *The Second Period of Quakerism*, 2d ed. (Cambridge, 1961), chap. 11.

59. See Fox, *Epistles*, 94 (Epistle 121); see also Braithwaite, *Beginnings*, chap. 13.

60. Fox, *Epistles*, 62–63 (Epistle 67), 281 (Epistle 264); see also Doncaster, "State in Which Adam Was," 23.

61. Fox, *Epistles*, 62–63 (Epistle 67), 280–82 (Epistle 264); Braithwaite, *Beginnings*, 145–46; Lloyd, *Social History*, 48–51.

62. Fox, *Epistles*, 148 (Epistle 190); Barclay, ed., *Letters of Early Friends*, 279.

63. Cole, "Quakers and Revolution," 44; see also Oliver, "Lamb's War," 1.

64. BL: Stowe MSS 186, fol. 16, as quoted in DWL: G. Lyon Turner MSS, Bundle 9, ln82.

65. During the Interregnum, Friends had published numerous tracts either tabulating their sufferings or discussing individual cases in detail. In 1660 they estimated that "there hath suffered imprisonments, putting in the stocks, whippings, loss of goods, and other abuses for keeping a good conscience towards God and man, before the King came into England, 3170 persons" (quoted in Braithwaite, *Beginnings*, 464). Braithwaite believes that while the number is substantial "and testifies to the intolerance of many Puritan magistrates," many of the prosecutions were "petty" and resulted in twenty-one deaths, compared with over three hundred during the Restoration (*Beginnings*, 465).

66. 13 & 14 Chas. II, c. 1.

67. 1 W. & M. st. 1, c. 18, whose proper title is "An Act for Exempting their Majesties' Protestant Subjects, Dissenting from the Church of England, from the Penalties of Certain Laws."

68. Braithwaite, *Second Period*, 599–600. Other statutes favorable to Friends were 7 & 8 W. III, c. 6, for easier recovery of small tithes, and 7 & 8 W. III, c. 34, which provided for an affirmation instead of an oath.

69. Arnold G. Matthews, *Calamy Revised* (Oxford, 1934); DWL: Roger Morrice MS Ent'ring Book, 3 vols.; C. E. Whiting, *Studies in English Puritanism from the Restoration to the Revolution, 1660–1688* (London, 1931).

70. First published as *Actes and Monuments of these latter and perilous dayes, touching matters of the Church, wherein are comprehended and described the great persecutions & horrible troubles* . . . (London, 1563).

Chapter One

THE LAW
IS A WILDERNESS

Thou may at leisure inform thyself and so me of Friends judgments in the case, but it is not at present in my mind to seek a way out of it by lawing it off. If there should a way probably seem, the law being such a wilderness, I choose rather to be here at quiet at present than encumbered in it.

Tobias Hardmeat to William Ingram, 27.xi [January].1683/4, Huntingdon prison, concerning his imprisonment as executor of a will (ORS, fol. 366)

It's the agreement and advice of this meeting that Friends take care in all counties & places where they suffer by distress of their goods, or imprisonment of their persons, whether by warrant from the justices of the peace, by indictment at the assizes or sessions, or process sent down to the sheriff's office, that they procure and send up with their sufferings exact copies of all warrants for distress, & such like, which they may generally procure from the constable, tithingmen, or headboroughs, & the copies of all mittimus's granted or made by justices of the peace, which they may have from the gaoler, & which the jailer is bound to deliver (by law) on demand to the prisoner, according to the Habeas Corpus Act. . . . And likewise to procure copies at large of all indictments at assizes or sessions, which they may have from the clerks of the peace & clerks of the assize & copies of all writs & process[es] issuing out of any of the courts at Westminster, which are directed to the sheriffs which they may have from the undersheriff's office, which may not only demonstrate the sufferings more exact, but be a better means & proof here to endeavour for their redress.

London Yearly Meeting, 5 June 1682, 1:106–7

I

The concerns expressed above reflected in part the most perplexing aspects of Quaker principles—the laws that those principles infringed, the manner in which the resultant criminality could be brought to the attention of the authorities, and the processes the legal system would employ once prosecutions and actions were begun. To average Quakers, the number of law-enforcement agencies, laws, and procedural technicalities to which they were liable must have presented a bewildering and depressing picture. In fact, the complexity, the confusion, and the uncertainties of the English legal system had led during the Interregnum to serious, though unavailing, efforts at reform.[1]

Perhaps aware of this legal quagmire, George Fox in 1657 called upon Friends to lay their "sufferings" before the judges of assize who, in turn, influenced the justices of the peace and lesser law-enforcement officers.[2] Perhaps moral persuasion could succeed where legal expertise was wanting. But that tactic depended on both the willingness of those who enforced the law to aid unpopular religious radicals and the flexibility of the legal system.

All English subjects were bound by two legal systems: *lex non scripta*, or unwritten law, and *lex scripta*, or written law. The most important part of *lex non scripta* stemmed from English custom and practice, and also from associated judicial decisions over many years. This category also included parliamentary statutes enacted before the reign of Richard I that had been neither repealed nor altered by contrary usage or subsequent acts, as well as elements of Roman civil law and the canon law of the Roman Catholic Church. An amalgam of civil and canon law was evident in the Anglican Church courts, although after 1660 the civil lawyers who dominated those courts accorded greater acceptance to common-law principles and standards.[3] Another combination of legal systems arose with the development of the equity jurisdictions of the courts of Chancery and Exchequer. Like the post-Restoration church courts, Chancery and the equity side of Exchequer were heavily influenced by common law and to a lesser degree, by canon law. Their rules of procedure were extremely complex, but the equity they dispensed was a "system of remedies," not the "do unto others" philosophy urged by the Quakers on all courts.[4]

Lex scripta, on the other hand, comprised statutes enacted since 1189 by mutual consent of the Crown and both houses of Parliament, and profoundly affected religious dissent; for the English Reformation had produced a legislative partnership in ecclesiastical matters between the king, as the new head of the church, and Parliament. Membership in the church became a prerequisite for full rights in the state; Quakers and other religious Dissenters were liable to prosecution by both ecclesiastical and secular authorities.[5] In theory, statutes could be augmented by royal proclamations. Because of a controversial history under the early Stuarts, however, proclamations by Charles II and James II proved to be little more than royal efforts to stimulate particular aspects of law enforcement, and were "weak instruments unless addressed to willing ears."[6] Yet from the Quaker perspective, proclamations urging stricter application of the penal laws against Dissenters were as potentially dangerous as was new legislation.

Despite being restricted in the use of proclamations, the monarch, as the "principal conservator of the peace within his dominions," was the most significant force in the legal system. His foremost servants in enforcing the law (as well as in helping to formulate the common law) were the twelve judges of the three superior common-law courts—King's Bench, Common Pleas, and Exchequer. All judicial appointments lay with the king, and throughout most of the Restoration the judges held office at his pleasure. Unlike most law-enforcement officers, however, they were salaried.[7]

The three Westminster courts, rivals and competitors for litigants, had expanded their jurisdictions over common pleas, a dangerous precedent for groups like the Quakers. As for the court of Chancery, by the seventeenth century, it was involved almost exclusively with matters of property, including tithes, which were a particularly controversial issue for Friends. The chancellor, acting as sole judge, also held office at the king's pleasure, but unlike the superior common-law judges, did not ride on semiannual assize circuits.[8]

Judges of the three superior common-law courts visited most English counties twice yearly as judges of assize empowered to hear and determine treasons, felonies, and misdemeanors; to deliver gaols, by either trial or proclamation; and to entertain civil actions.[9] The assize judges were assisted by legally trained staffs, often members of the country gentry, and were dependent on fees.[10] Assizes were important for effective law enforcement, not only as criminal courts, but also as conduits for conveying central government concerns to the localities. Before leaving for their circuits, the judges frequently received from the lord chancellor, the Privy Council, or the king himself instructions either to enforce or to ignore particular laws, or to scrutinize the justices of the peace and other local officials.[11] The charge given, in turn, by the judges to grand juries on their circuits therefore indicated royal policy, but often reflected their own individual priorities. Assize judges also provided valuable information to the Crown on political, social, and religious attitudes in the localities and on the inclinations of local magistrates and other law-enforcement officers. While on circuit, judges also entertained petitions, frequently from beleaguered Quakers, and received delegations of concerned citizens. Hospitality was provided by local dignitaries, who no doubt interjected their own feelings about Whitehall policy with which they disagreed.[12]

Of further significance was the potential impact of assizes and judicial power on local officials. For example, all justices of the peace were required to attend assizes, where they witnessed the trial of suspects they had bound over. As amateurs, justices were able to solicit advice on the interpretation of statutes or methods of procedure. A judge might even leave behind detailed precedents to be followed by the justices in their sessions. He might also fine magistrates for procedural errors or negligence, and he could rectify such errors.[13]

Although the assize judges exercised a powerful influence on local law enforcement, the ultimate weapon for maintaining order was the militia, which in the Restoration comprised the former "trained bands" put on a statutory basis[14] and recruited by property owners who hired and equipped the soldiers. Although inadequately trained, the militia, with ninety thousand foot and six thousand horse, was able by sheer numbers to act as an effective weapon against recalcitrant Dissenters. Officered by the gentry, many of whom harbored bitter resentment against Quakers and other sectaries, it could be a dangerously disruptive peacekeeping force. The militia in each county was under the command of the lord lieutenant, normally one of the small elite of great nobles and a member of the Privy Council. As the "immediate military representative of the Crown," he possessed extensive patronage, including virtually all deputy lieutenancies, commissions in the militia, positions on the local bench, and other privileges that the local gentry were eager to attain. In addition, he often combined his office with that of *custos rotulorum* (the ex-officio chairman of quarter sessions) and was the dominant justice of the peace in his county.[15]

While the military arm of the Crown in the county was the lord lieutenant, the civil arm was theoretically the sheriff, another officer appointed by the Crown. From a Quaker standpoint, his most significant powers were his right to chose county gaolers; his execution of the writs and commands of the Westminster courts; his custodial responsibility of criminals before and after trial; and his authority to command anyone to find sureties to keep the peace. The sheriff also visited each hundred, an administrative county subdivision, in his jurisdiction twice annually to hold his tourn, or court, which by 1660 was generally restricted to preliminary inquiries on matters to be dealt with at the court of quarter sessions. Many hundreds had fallen under the control of lords who held their own semiannual "courts leet," a right also claimed by some boroughs. The sheriff also presided over the county court, which met every lunar month to hear pleas of debt or damage up to 40s., and to pronounce outlawries. These last courts lacked any effective means to coerce reluctant defendants to appear; in the event, the justices of the peace had appellate jurisdiction over them. The sheriff's staff, appointed by him and dependent on fees, included the undersheriff, who spent much time dealing with writs and processes; and bailiffs of hundreds, who were usually called upon to execute writs, impanel juries for cases originating within their hundred, command petty constables to render returns of recusants, notify particular individuals that they were required to take the Oaths of Allegiance and Supremacy, and levy distraints—the last a particularly hazardous and unpleasant duty. These tasks often brought them into confrontation with the Quakers. Worse still, while bailiffs were usually men of "moderate standing," those underbailiffs and special bailiffs who assisted them were often shiftless ne'er-do-wells.[16]

The most significant local law-enforcement officers over whom the Crown exercised patronage were the justices of the peace, who supervised virtually every official of county, hundred, and parish.[17] Justices of the peace were created in several ways, but the most common was appointment by the king by commission under the Great Seal upon the recommendation of the lord chancellor. Although two fourteenth-century statutes[18] specified that six or eight justices, including two lawyers, should be named in each commission, by the seventeenth century neither stipulation was strictly enforced, a reflection of the enormous appetite of the country gentry to hold the office. Many justices, in fact, were in the commission for more than one county as well as serving in Parliament. Assize judges were also included in the commissions of counties within their circuits, and as a courtesy the commission might include the entire Privy Council, the attorney general, the solicitor general, and numerous officeholders and local dignitaries.[19]

Justices of the peace were judges of record who exercised their authority only within the county or counties for which they were in commission. They had therefore to reside within the county, were required to be members of the Established Church, and in effect were to be country gentlemen or members of the nobility. Justices were policemen as well as judges, for they could make inquiries, issue warrants, receive informations, record examinations, take recognizances for keeping the peace, make arrests, and imprison suspects. Each justice, in some circumstances, could act summarily on his own view, on the confession of an offender, or on the examination and proof of witnesses, a power capable of being increased by statute. The record of a justice or his testimony in some cases was "of as great force as an indictment upon the oath of twelve men, and in some other cases of greater force than an indictment."[20]

A substantial amount of work was handled by one or two justices acting out of sessions, usually as the result of constables bringing petty offenders to them at their homes. Often one justice might send for another to assist him. Ironically, there was nothing to hinder a justice from taking action, either wittingly or unwittingly, in cases already disposed of by another county magistrate; and he could even arrive at a different determination.

Of greater significance was the power accorded any two justices, one of whom was of the *quorum* (those justices with legal training), to inquire into all felonies, trespasses, and other named offenses committed within their jurisdiction, and to receive, hear, and determine indictments. By the mid-seventeenth century the principle that the quorum should consist of legally qualified justices had been undermined with the transfer of more serious crimes to assizes, the difficulty of assembling justices at sessions, and the gentry's desire for the prestige associated with membership of the quorum. Fortunately, many of the gentry had acquired legal knowledge at either the universities or the Inns of Court, and some had received a reasonably good education.[21] Significantly, however, one of the most important offices in the law-enforcement system was virtually unpaid.[22]

The main forum for the work of the justices of the peace was the court of quarter sessions.[23] The number of magistrates active in sessions work varied from county to county, but it was always far smaller than the number named in the commission.[24] The justices in quarter sessions left most serious felonies to assizes, limiting themselves largely to the trial of misdemeanors, most of them statutory and all noncapital. Nonetheless, the jurisdiction of assizes and quarter sessions overlapped considerably, and matters could be referred from one to another.[25] Both the numbers of justices generally present at sessions and the legal and professional competence of those who held the office would be matters of great importance to the Quakers. To some extent, the clerk of the peace, normally a member of an Inn of Court, helped to bring a degree of professionalism and continuity to quarter sessions. As with most other law-enforcement officials, however, the clerk and his assistants depended on high fees for procedural services, including the preparation of indictments or informations.[26] At quarter sessions one of the justices, normally the *custos rotulorum*, if present, or his deputy, would give the charge to the juries, keep order during the proceedings, ascertain the decision of the bench, and pronounce the sentence or order of the court. If a lawyer were present, he would doubtless rule on points of law; but there was no sanction for this custom, although in 1663 Chief Justice Hyde at Hertford assizes told the justices to abide by the rulings of their legally qualified brethren, and not, as had been commonly the case, to "put to the vote of many ignorant justices on the Bench according to their fancy and opinion."[27] In the event, the charge was of considerable importance, for it reminded grand jurors of their duty to make presentments; and it also directed their attention to the matters within their purview, thereby influencing both the character of those presentments and the jurors' willingness to bring in "true" bills of indictment.[28]

Since quarter sessions met only four times each year, the justices, to facilitate administrative and judicial matters in the intervals between sessions, usually divided responsibility for the several hundreds in the county and acted when out of sessions for their particular hundred, with all the justices of that hundred meeting together monthly. These monthly sessions discharged much routine judicial and administrative work, including minor offenses over which the justices had summary jurisdiction. These offenses often included Quaker criminality, as did the "special" or "privy" sessions, often divisional in character and convened by any two or more justices, one of whom was of the quorum. They had jurisdiction over the same matters as monthly sessions and were usually informal gatherings of two or three justices in an alehouse or the home of one of the magistrates. Gatherings of justices outside quarter sessions were often referred to as "petty" sessions.[29]

Justices were county officers, of course, but the basic unit of local administration was the parish, whose officers included petty constables, churchwardens, surveyors of highways, and overseers of the poor. The essential link between the parish officers and the justices was an officer of the hundred—the high constable, whose remuneration was very small. This office was of considerable importance to local law enforcement, including the restraint of Quaker criminality. High constables administered the orders of the lieutenancy to the militia, organized watch and ward, directed the hue and cry after suspects, punished rogues and vagabonds, and presented both nuisances and those who failed to attend church. They circulated warrants and orders from quarter sessions to lesser officers within their jurisdiction and oversaw their proper execution. Above all, high constables were expected to keep the justices informed of the general state of local affairs and were therefore required to attend both monthly and quarter sessions.[30]

Below the high constables in the local hierarchy were the unpaid parish petty constables, appointed by the justices. Like bailiffs of hundreds, petty constables had an unenviable job, for they were also in many respects the true "policemen" of England—keeping the peace, executing writs, making distraints and arrests, collecting rates, conveying prisoners, escorting vagabonds to their places of lawful settlement, and seeing that watch and ward were duly set. At quarter sessions, they partly represented the parish, partly served the king by sitting on constables' juries, and partly served the justices by presenting defaults in the parish, and giving in both lists of papists and eligible jurors. Few offices carried such burdensome and unpopular duties.[31]

Another parish officer with whom the Quakers came into conflict was the churchwarden, elected by the parishioners according to local custom. Churchwardens were entrusted with the maintenance of the church structure and furnishings and were responsible for collecting the parish rate for those purposes. They also oversaw the regular attendance and behavior of the congregation, and they alone levied fines for recusancy, or refusal to attend the Established Church. But they did act with other unpaid, elected parish officers, the overseers of the poor, in levying and distributing numerous statutory forfeitures. Remaining parish officers included the aletaster—no doubt a popular post—the surveyor of the highways, and the beadle, who was effectively a manorial officer apprehending and punishing rogues at the request of the justices. Quaker criminality included their own refusal to take the requisite oath of office when called on to serve in these parish offices, and even in such minor village posts as the pinder, who impounded stray livestock, and the swineherd, the hayward, and the neatherd.[32]

Quakers might also be prosecuted in manorial courts, over which the lord or his steward presided, as well as in the many borough courts which exercised civil jurisdiction usually conferred by charter. Borough courts were normally courts of record, whose geographical and financial jurisdiction was usually limited, as also was their jurisdiction over actions. These courts assumed a bewildering variety of titles, ranging from the Norwich Guildhall to the Bristol Tolzey, and were normally presided over by a recorder.[33]

Quaker criminality often led to imprisonment, which brought them into contact with several other law-enforcement agents, including the coroner, a county official elected by the freeholders and suitors in the county court. His primary task was to inquire into sudden and unexplained deaths, such as those caused either by soldiers dispersing illegal conventicles, or by brutal treatment in gaol. Coroners also attended the county court, where they pronounced outlawries.[34] Most prisoners, of course, came into close contact with two other officers—keepers of houses of correction and county gaolers. Houses of correction, often known as Bridewells after their London prototype, were established under the Elizabethan and Stuart poor-law legislation, not as prisons for the detention or punishment of criminals "but as an adjunct of the relief of destitution." At least one was built in every county, and was intended to serve as a workhouse for the idle, shiftless, and disorderly, and in many respects resembled a primitive factory. They were often used, however, as places of detention for criminals.[35] Justices of the peace in quarter sessions had exclusive control over these buildings and their keepers, who were paid a salary from the county rates and were dismissible at will. The justices also made arrangements for the diet, the employment, and the correction of the inmates.[36]

The county gaol was a different proposition. Legally it was the property of the Crown, administered by the sheriff, who appointed and dismissed the gaoler and who was ultimately accountable for gaol security. But while responsibility for the building and repair of county gaols lay with the Crown, in practice the justices regarded gaols as within their competence and part of their general obligation, a view no doubt encouraged by justices of assize. Gaols were normally used to hold suspects awaiting trial and convicted felons awaiting execution. But they were also places of punishment for some statutory offenses, as well as for those who refused to put in bail, give sureties, or pay fines, typical Quaker offenses. In fact, during the Restoration, the combination of Quaker recalcitrance and severe enforcement of the

laws against religious dissenters resulted in the prisons becoming ab-
normally crowded, a situation exacerbated by the fact that gaols were
simply not built for long-term housing of prisoners. Incarceration also
meant payment of fees upon admittance and discharge, and for even
the most rudimentary necessities. Prisoners could refuse to pay, of
course, with predictable results made worse by the fact that the gaoler's
office was a property right.[37] If the prisoners were unpopular, like the
Quakers, redress could be limited, particularly as those imprisoned
for misdemeanors, debt, failing to find sureties, or simply awaiting
trial, were generally not entitled to public support. Medical attention
was supposed to be provided at the county's expense, and after 1667
some work was to be found for prisoners,[38] but those who refused to
pay fees were forced to rely on the willingness of gaolers to permit
provisions to be brought into the gaol by relatives or friends. During
the Restoration, some attempt was made to regulate gaolers' fees and
to allow prisoners to provide their own food and bedding without
interference.[39]

Seventeenth-century prisons scarcely resembled their modern
counterparts, for prisoners wore ordinary clothes; organized work was
rare; and men, women, and children were unsegregated, although, in
theory, felons were to be kept apart from those imprisoned for less
serious offenses. There were also numerous local gaols, particularly
for debtors, such as Wood Street Compter and Poultry Compter, both
in London. The Fleet prison in London was a national prison for debtors and bankrupts, but it also held persons charged with contempt of
the courts of Chancery, Exchequer, or Common Pleas. The Marshalsea in Southwark, the prison of the court of King's Bench, was for
debtors, as well as for persons confined under the sentence, or charged
with contempt, of that court. Overcrowding in county gaols could lead
to incarceration in local gaols, including the Compters, for offenses
other than debt.[40]

As if the attentions of secular courts and officials were not sufficient, the Quakers were also liable to prosecution by the ecclesiastical
authorities. Although the criminal and corrective jurisdictions of the
church courts had been abolished during the Interregnum, they were
reinstituted shortly after the Restoration. Nonetheless, English common lawyers, distrustful of overweening clerical legal power, believed
that the common law and its courts were superior to the church courts
and their laws. In England, they argued, ecclesiastical courts derived

their authority either from the king's commission, such as the infamous court of High Commission (abolished in 1641), or from the laws of England. This fact meant, in effect, that the use of canon law was severely restricted and that ultimately the limits and the extent of ecclesiastical jurisdiction were prescribed by English law.[41]

The bishop of each diocese had a consistory court, generally in the cathedral town, administered by his chancellor or "official" who would therefore be the "ordinary" competent judge.[42] The bishop had the right to withdraw cases from the cognizance of the chancellor if he wished to hear them himself; he could also devolve some of his diocesan powers to local commissaries. Decisions could be appealed from the consistory court to the provincial court of the archbishop, either the Chancery court at York or the court of the Arches in London.[43] Below the bishop's consistory court was the archdeacon's court,[44] headed by his chancellor, whose primary concerns were ecclesiastical discipline, church attendance, and the correction of moral offenses. As in the secular sphere, there were many exceptions to the general pattern. These were the peculiars, self-contained jurisdictions, exempt from that of the ordinary diocesan courts.[45] At the pinnacle of the ecclesiastical court structure stood the provincial courts of the archbishops of Canterbury and York. Those of the former included the court of the Arches, the normal appellate court for the province, and a court of first instance in all ecclesiastical causes. There was also the Prerogative court, which supervised the rights of the archbishop in testamentary matters where the deceased had goods exceeding £5 in value in more than one ecclesiastical jurisdiction (diocesan or peculiar). In such cases the necessary probate or administration had to be obtained from that court, located at Doctors' Commons in London. Finally, there was the court of Peculiars held by the dean of the Arches at Bow Church for the thirteen London parishes which were exempt from the diocesan jurisdiction of the bishop of London. In the north the provincial courts of the archbishop of York included those of Chancery and Prerogative (equivalent to the courts of the Arches and Prerogative in the south).[46]

Ecclesiastical discipline was maintained and the general condition of the church ascertained by means of the visitation. The bishop had the right every four years and the archdeacon annually to visit their respective jurisdictions. Similarly, the archbishops had the right to visit their dioceses (effectively as bishops) every fourth year, and to visit their provinces upon their accession to the see. Local commissaries also frequently traveled on circuit. During visitations, all inferior jurisdictions were inhibited, and the causes normally heard in those courts went to the visitor and provided a valuable source of fees. It was an unwieldy system, but the prospect of fees to the visitor's officers was ample incentive to continue it. Where criminal presentments were made by churchwardens to the visitation court, those cited were required to appear at correction courts held some months later for trial and, if convicted, punishment.[47] In fact, extensive criminal responsibility was placed upon the churchwardens, answerable to the church courts as well as to the justices of the peace.

Since the abolition of the court of High Commission, the temporal jurisdiction of the ecclesiastical courts had been in rapid decay, with a consequent expansion in the jurisdiction of the common-law courts, including many matters formerly belonging to both sets of courts concurrently. The only capital offense within the purview of the ecclesiastical courts was heresy, punishable until 1677 with death by fire.[48] Statutory felonies could be tried only in the common-law courts. The usual punishments in church courts, therefore, were excommunication or penance, both of which could be commuted to fines, although normally only the more prosperous could afford the fees, in addition to the charges of absolution and other costs. Not surprisingly, the efficiency of church discipline depended to a large extent on how seriously an offender viewed excommunication. Despite this caveat, church courts could often utilize the secular authorities to assist them by imprisoning offenders; also, excommunication could have serious legal consequences. Furthermore, ecclesiastical jurisdiction over probate, marriages, burials, and tithes could create considerable difficulties for groups like the Quakers.[49]

Because of their principles, the Quakers were subject to a myriad of law-enforcement agencies, both secular and ecclesiastical, all of whom appeared to have one common denominator—the king. Head of church and state, he controlled the appointment and the dismissal of virtually all the major officers at the national and county levels, including the lord chancellor, lords lieutenant, sheriffs, and justices of the peace. Through them he could indirectly control lesser officers, as well as the militia. The Crown also enjoyed the patronage of numerous lucrative legal posts, and during much of the period held, at pleasure, the patents of the superior common-law judges. By the use of proclamations and orders in council[50] the king could influence reluctant local law-enforcement agencies to prosecute the law.

As we will see, the Crown could also issue declarations, which normally took two forms—those of intended policy which the Crown hoped Parliament would convert into statute and those attempting to suspend penal laws. Like their Tudor predecessors, all the Stuart kings claimed as their prerogative the right to dispense with laws in particular cases, or to suspend them altogether. Although a contentious position, the royal claim in the ecclesiastical sphere was strengthened by its legacy, derived from the English Reformation, of the vast papal powers of dispensing and suspending. The king could argue with some validity that he could suspend the penal laws by virtue of his role as supreme head of the Anglican Church, thereby providing him with another method of influencing law enforcement.[51]

The king could also mitigate the impact of the law by granting, as a matter of grace, charters of pardon to individuals or groups, or by ordering his attorney general to secure a writ of *supersedeas* from the Chancery to halt an action brought by or on behalf of the Crown.[52] Nor was he powerless in matters of legislation. He could actively intervene in parliamentary elections, or could attempt through a judicious combination of patronage and bribes to develop a "Royalist" faction in the House of Commons. More significantly, the Crown could tamper with the charters of corporate towns, who returned almost eighty percent of the membership of Commons. Since the granting of municipal charters was a royal prerogative, they could be declared forfeit by means of the writ *quo warranto*, which alleged some misuse or other irregularity in the rights granted to the corporation. The Crown could then issue a new charter on terms more favorable to itself, including the right to remove any member of a corporation, to extend royal power over appointment of their sheriffs, and to give royally appointed magistrates a greater voice in borough affairs. The early Stuarts, as well as Oliver Cromwell, had effectively remodeled corporations. In any event, the king could also control Parliament by his right to prorogue and dismiss that body at will, often to prevent "undesirable" legislation.[53]

For the period under study, therefore, a vast law-enforcement system was headed by two kings with substantial potential to destroy or protect religious dissenters, but whose father had been executed, who themselves had been forced into exile, and whose loyal followers had seen their lands and fortunes confiscated, all by Puritan zealots. That background did not bode well for any religious dissenters, let alone those belonging to one of the most radical religious sects of the century. Nor did the outlook brighten when Quakers examined seventeenth-century legal procedure and the laws which could be utilized against them.

II

The legal system which the Quakers and other religious dissenters faced during the Restoration was, then, immensely complex. What follows is an examination of the procedures and laws which directly affected the Quakers, and which were also generally applicable to other dissenting groups. In one sense, the Quakers were fortunate in that the crimes resulting from their principles were not felonies, but misdemeanors,[54] which normally incurred fines, distraints, and imprisonment rather than loss of life or limb. But this was of scant consolation to Quakers separated from their families, friends, and work by imprisonment, or to those whose goods, chattels, or lands were confiscated by the Crown or by their personal adversaries. Among those misdemeanors were unlawful religious gatherings, or conventicles, restricted not only by statute but also by common law as a form of criminal trespass "with force and arms"; recusancy; vagrancy; disruption of church services; and travel or work on Sundays and holy days. Common law also prohibited simple nuisances, a wide class of misdemeanors[55] encompassing such public Quaker activities as standing in a street or a walkway proclaiming their message to passers-by, or going naked "as a sign." Quaker principles also rendered them liable to imprisonment for contempt by their refusal to appear to a prosecution or action,[56] to swear on oath, to pay either fines or fees, to put in sureties for the peace or good behavior, or to put in bail or any recognizances for themselves.[57] Sureties were widely utilized, under both statutory and common law. For example, they were required, particularly for good behavior, from anyone who abused a law-enforcement officer executing his office, or from those who showed contempt to a magistrate, even when he was not performing his duty. Similarly, if a "contempt" or "disturbance" had been committed in any court of record, the presiding judge could impose a "reasonable" fine upon the offender.[58] These strictures could be applied to Quakers who protested against law-enforcement officers' executing the law against them, or who refused to remove their hats either in court or in the presence of judicial and civic dignitaries when out of court. Also, justices of the peace, in order to prevent a breach of the peace, or on complaint or information of an actual breach, could issue warrants for suspects to be brought before them to provide sureties for good behavior or the peace, or to be bound over to the next sessions or assizes. Any refusal to provide sureties resulted in imprisonment. A justice's warrant was indisputable, even if he had exceeded his authority. Therefore a constable or other officer, on receipt of a warrant, was to act quickly to locate the suspect, explain the issue, and require him in the king's name to accompany him to the justice. If the suspect refused, he was to be arrested and imprisoned immediately. It was essential, however, that the officer show the warrant or at least tell a suspect what it contained. It was unimportant in whose name, if any, the warrant was issued, as long as it was subscribed by one or more justices, and contained the day, year, and place of issue. Legal commentators, such as Dalton, emphasized that in all instances where one or more justices acted out of sessions, a written record of all the matter and proofs in the case should be made, suspects should be heard in their own defense, and credible witnesses examined. Quakers would complain that, where they themselves were involved, these constraints were too often ignored. The law also demanded that whenever suspects were imprisoned, the committing officer was to draw up a *mittimus*, or warrant of committal, which contained full information relating to the prisoner and the offense. A defective mittimus could overturn a case.[59]

These kinds of activities by law-enforcement officers were one method by which Quaker criminality became known and was proceeded against. Quakers and other Dissenters could also be "presented," or accused, before the appropriate court by a jury or by individual law-enforcement officers. Petty misdemeanors were presented by juries at the sheriff's tourn and at local courts leet, while justices at their monthly sessions could receive presentments from constables, churchwardens, and overseers of the poor.[60] The most significant presentment agency, however, and one which sat at all quarter sessions and assizes, was the grand jury, impaneled by the sheriff and representing the entire county. With its power to make preliminary inquiries and to initiate criminal process, this body was essential for effective law enforcement. After receiving the charge from the bench, the grand jury presented crimes from its own knowledge, before scrutinizing presentments made in court by high and petty constables, either on scraps of paper or formally while sitting on hundred juries. The grand jury also acted on bills of indictment engrossed on parchment by the clerk on the instructions of individual victims, the preliminary inquiries of leets and tourns, and the activities of justices of the peace, either out of sessions or on presentments made to them in their monthly sessions. After hearing some or all of the evidence in private, the grand jury returned the bill either as true, in which case a trial on the indictment followed, or as *ignoramus*, in which case the matter ended, although the bill of indictment could be laid before another grand jury. A similar procedure was followed with presentments.[61] The indictment was drawn in Latin,[62] in technical language, and it was essential that the form and wording precisely satisfied legal requirements.[63] Thus it was possible for Quakers to challenge indictments as well as mittimuses for insufficiency. Not all suspects were present in court; recusants (including Quakers), for example, were unaware that they were being presented. Proclamation would be made at the conclusion of the sessions or assizes calling on those named to appear and stand trial at the next such gathering.[64]

Misdemeanor prosecutions were also commenced by "information," a method which avoided the grand jury and the collective presentment process. Although there were several types of informations, the most significant for the Quakers was the *qui tam*,[65] which was brought by an informer upon a penal statute "as well for himself as for our lord the King." A creation of statute, the *qui tam* procedure was intended to promote active law enforcement by giving a financial incentive to informers, who not only shared in the fine, but were not liable for costs. *Qui tams* were allowable before justices of the peace, of assize, and of the superior courts, and normally required trial by petty jury.[66] The government viewed informers as a necessary evil, for they acted, in effect, as an auxiliary police force helping to uncover political, economic, and religious crimes. To Quakers and other religious dissenters, the ability of informers to prosecute recusants and conventiclers was a serious threat.

Prior to the summoning of a petty or trial jury, the indictment was read aloud in English and the defendant was asked to plead. If he pleaded guilty, he was set aside to await sentencing at the close of the sessions or assizes. Alternatively, he could plead not guilty, and agree to be tried "by God and country." Any delay at this stage was discouraged: in cases of misdemeanor any perverse plea or a refusal to plead (normal Quaker practice) was considered a confession of guilt. Other pleas, however, were available to the defendant. Suspects accused of misdemeanors could traverse, that is, deny or take issue with the chief matter of the indictment. While not constituting a formal plea of guilty or not guilty, this measure postponed a trial until the following sessions or assizes, provided that the defendant agreed to enter recognizances for his appearance. Those accused also had the right to demur to, or challenge, the jurisdiction of the court on the grounds that the crime contained in the indictment could not be tried before that court.[67] A demurrer was another potentially useful delaying tactic.

All those arraigned for misdemeanors were tried separately from those arraigned for felony. When a sufficient number of defendants had been arraigned, the petty jury was impaneled, either from members of hundred juries or, more usually, from freeholders warned by the undersheriffs and bailiffs to be present for that purpose. Since jurors were unpaid, absenteeism was common; jury slots therefore were often filled by talesmen, bystanders picked ostensibly at random. Although peremptory challenges without cause or challenges with cause were allowed to felons, there does not appear to have been any specific regulation regarding such rights in cases of misdemeanor. In the event, any attempt to challenge jurors had to be made prior to the swearing of the jury. While jurors could request informal directions on matters of law, they were judges of fact, not of law, which was determined by the judge, a point often disputed by Quakers. All verdicts of guilt or innocence had to be unanimous. The court might ask that the jury return a special verdict, that is, merely to state the facts and leave the verdict to the discretion of the court.[68]

Those found not guilty were discharged after paying their fees, but could still be bound to good behavior or even sent to the house of correction if it appeared from the evidence that they had "misbehaved." Those found guilty had until the end of the sessions or assizes to prepare a motion in arrest of judgment. Normally the sentence then followed. Refusal to pay a fine, which was normal Quaker practice, led to imprisonment unless recognizances to pay it were given. In effect, this requirement meant that many Quakers who came into conflict with the law faced perpetual imprisonment. It was possible for the accused, prior to conviction, to obtain a writ of *certiorari* from King's Bench or Chancery in an effort to avoid or at least to postpone judgment, but this method related only to technical flaws in the record and did not involve a review of the facts of the case. It was, of course, difficult and expensive to travel to Westminster and to purchase a writ that would often simply delay proceedings. After judgment, it was possible to secure a writ of error from King's Bench which, like a *certiorari*, demanded the record of the case. But it could not be used to quash summary convictions, the latter often the result of activities of justices of the peace acting out of sessions.[69]

All of these possibilities, however, were predicated on the appearance of the accused to stand trial. The methods of coercion available to the legal system were critical. The most significant process in common law actions was the writ *capias ad respondendum*, instructing the sheriff to arrest and imprison the offender for an original contempt in not appearing when first demanded. Often the sheriff, unable to claim expenses and liable to damages if he erred, might yield to the considerable temptation to do nothing, returning the *capias* endorsed *non est inventus*, meaning "he cannot be found."[70] The offender would then be threatened with process of outlawry, an extremely complicated procedure involving writs *alias capias*, *pluries capias*, and *exigent*, all of which needed to be returned *non est inventus* before the outlawry took effect. After the *exigent* was so returned, the coroner pronounced the outlawry at the county court, resulting in a *capias utlagatum* from King's Bench, again demanding the offender's arrest for the contempt of not answering. This contempt could only be purged by paying the fees and charges for the writs and then appearing to the action, steps Quakers were seemingly unwilling to take. Imprisonment for contempt did not preclude the possibility that the prisoner's goods and chattels could be forfeited to the king or to the plaintiff in satisfaction of his demands.[71]

Presentment, information, and the initiative of law-enforcement officials were three of the means by which Quaker criminality was uncovered. A further method involved individuals seeking to redress personal wrongs. Quakers were particularly liable in disputes resulting from their refusals to pay tithes or to swear on oath to the probate of a will, or from the questionable legality of their marriages and the consequent bastardy of their offspring. Legal proceedings began when the aggrieved made a complaint in due form. In local courts the complaint itself was sufficient to initiate process. Where the plaintiff wished to bring an action in the court of Common Pleas or King's Bench at

Westminster or at assizes, however, and was not himself in Westminster, he had to purchase an original writ from Chancery. This writ was a precept in the king's name containing a summary of the matter or cause of complaint. The sheriff again featured prominently, for the writ was sent to him in the county where the action was brought, and he was commanded to begin process against the defendant. The writ was returnable into one of the Westminster courts, or before the justices of assize locally. In such cases, it was essential not only to appear but also to answer the complaint. Fortunately for the Quakers, an answer to a suit in Common Pleas or King's Bench did not require an oath, although nonappearance could lead to process of outlawry.[72]

In the equity court of Chancery and on the equity side of Exchequer, however, an answer had to be made on oath. In these jurisdictions, procedure began with a bill of complaint[73] (rather than an original writ), which was a written petition to the court showing the plaintiff's complaint of wrong done to him by the defendant, the damages he had thereby sustained, and a request for process for redress to begin. Bills of complaint were engrossed on parchment and also included an interrogatory section—specific questions to be answered by the defendant. After the bill was filed, a *subpoena ad respondendum* was issued requiring the defendant to appear to answer the suit, but unlike most other writs, this one was served by the plaintiff or a messenger rather than by the ubiquitous sheriff. But the subpoena contained no information as to the cause of the complaint, and equally disturbing was the willingness of both Chancery and Exchequer to issue the subpoena before the bill was exhibited. These characteristics made it difficult for a defendant to plan a defense and also encouraged vexatious suits. Another problem could be the date to appear, which might not give the defendant sufficient time to make an appearance, even though the court might allow further time. As with common law, the defendant could delay the action by putting in a demurrer, which in equity was an assertion that the law did not compel an answer because the facts, even if true, did not entitle the plaintiff to succeed. If the defendant answered—something Quakers were unlikely to do—a complicated process of pleading commenced.[74]

Failure to appear had serious consequences. Both Chancery and Exchequer had their equivalent of outlawry. Rather than a *capias*, the important writ was an "attachment" addressed to the sheriff, whose action again was decisive. In Exchequer, continued failure to appear

led to an *alias* attachment, *pluries* attachment, an attachment with proclamation, and finally a commission of rebellion which declared the defendant to be a rebel, liable to both arrest by anyone in any county and
sequestration of goods and chattels. If the defendant did appear, but
failed to answer on oath, an attachment was issued and if he refused to
answer, having been twice brought into court on writs of *habeas corpus
ad testificandum*, then the bill was taken as *pro confesso*, and sequestration ensued. In Chancery, the procedure for nonappearance was
greatly abbreviated, with an attachment, attachment with proclamation, and commission of rebellion, although it does not appear that a
sequestration would ensue in that court for nonappearance, but only
for refusing to answer.[75]

Unfortunately for the Quakers, both King's Bench from the Interregnum and Common Pleas from the Restoration, each eager to at-
tract litigants, permitted an easier and cheaper method of procedure
in cases of debt, including tithe disputes. Procedure began with a fictitious action of trespass, which enabled the court to have the defendant
imprisoned in his own county and then transferred to Westminster by
writ of *habeas corpus ad deliberandum et recipiendum*. Once there, he was
a prisoner of the court, which then allowed the fictitious action to be
dropped and replaced by a declaration of debt which, in effect, was
the equivalent of the equity bill of complaint. Once the defendant had
pleaded, the trial took place in his county at assizes.[76] By this device
King's Bench and Common Pleas were able to avoid the costly and
time-consuming procedure based on an original writ out of Chancery.

The Quakers and other Dissenters, of course, were also at risk
from church courts and their officials. Because the canons passed by
convocation in 1603 were not binding on the laity, the significant factor in clerical legal power was the extent to which common and statute
law confirmed or superseded such canons. Despite the erosion of
much of its jurisdiction, the church still retained considerable sanc-
tions over marriages, tithes (and related church payments), the licensing of schoolmasters, and the probate of testaments involving goods
and chattels. As noted previously, the penalty of excommunication
had potentially serious ramifications, for excommunicates in England
could be imprisoned. The church also had other effective weapons. In
testamentary disputes (which in some instances were heard in temporal courts) involving the legality of marriages, the bishop would be
consulted on their validity, a devastating prospect for the Quakers. Of

equal concern was the power of church courts, when the probate oath had been refused, to transfer the normal right of executorship or administration of a will to others who were prepared to take that oath.[77]

To some degree, the methods by which Quaker criminality became known to church courts approximate those in the temporal sphere. Thus officers known as apparitors resembled informers, for they identified any offenders against church law living in the diocese to the churchwardens, who then presented them to an ecclesiastical judge. Apparitors sent to the bishop quarterly lists of recusants, heretics, and schismatics with records of their appearances before any court, and informed him simultaneously of cases where proceedings taken against offenders had been stopped for any reason, and where unlawful marriages, sequestrations, and legacies to charitable uses had taken place. They also cited any executor or administrator in order to prove a will or undertake an administration, provided that fourteen days had elapsed since the death. Apparitors were not alone in making presentments. Churchwardens presented annually to the bishop or ordinary all schismatics and disturbers of divine service, and (in conjunction with ministers) all those who did not receive Easter communion. Ministers had the power to make similar presentments, either with or without churchwardens, and presented all popish recusants annually.[78]

Procedure in the church courts, whether by presentment or by personal suit, normally began with a citation requiring the defendant to appear. In personal suits, when appearance was made, the plaintiff entered a "libel," which resembled the bill of complaint in equity and the declaration of debt at common law. This required an answer from the defendant on oath, an unacceptable requirement for Quakers. Failure to appear to a citation or to answer on oath to a libel resulted in excommunication. If the offender remained contumacious, that is, willfully stubborn and disobedient, for forty days afterwards, the plaintiff could obtain a *significavit*, or certificate of the offense, from the bishop who had granted the letters of excommunication. This certificate was sent to Chancery, where a writ *de excommunicato capiendo*[79] could then be purchased commanding the sheriff to imprison the offender until the contempt was purged. Similarly, in cases of presentment rather than personal suit, the appropriate bishop could himself employ the same remedy. In tithe cases, it was also possible for the church authorities to utilize the justices of the peace to imprison offenders. Even if offenders appeared, answered on oath, and agreed to be tried, any contempt for a court's judgment also resulted in excommunication and possible imprisonment.[80] The risk of Quakers' being imprisoned on process originating in the church courts was obviously substantial.

III

Quaker criminality was defined by numerous pre-Interregnum statutes, augmented by further legislation during the reign of Charles II. Before examining the milieu within which Restoration legislation was enacted, it is instructive to analyze briefly the end result—that is, the laws and penalties facing Friends through much of the period. Quaker meetings for worship, like those of other dissenting sects, were viewed by the church as a vehicle for the propagation of religious schism, and by the state as a venue for conspiracy. The Restoration government added the "Quaker" Act and two Conventicle Acts to the 1581 Elizabethan Conventicle Act.[81] Taken together, these statutes had one major objective—the prevention of large-scale meetings held under the "pretence" or "colour" of any religion differing from the liturgy or practice of the Church of England. With the exception of the Elizabethan Conventicle Act (which implied that any such gathering, no matter how small, was illegal), these acts permitted dissenting meetings of fewer than five persons aged sixteen or over, either at an uninhabited site or in an inhabited dwelling. Members of the household were not included in calculating the numbers present in an inhabited dwelling. Some degree of toleration, therefore, was permitted to Quakers and other Dissenters, albeit on a scale most of them regarded as insufficient. The statutory methods for convicting those attending such meetings varied, often depending on whether the offense was the first, the second, or the third. In any event, offenders were liable to jury trial on indictment at assizes or sessions and to summary conviction by justices of the peace or similar officers of other jurisdictions, either by confession, "notorious evidence of the fact," or by the oaths of witnesses. Those who allowed a meeting on their premises and those who taught or preached in the meeting, were also liable to conviction. Punishments varied, depending on the nature of the offense, but included imprisonment, fines, and distraints. In some cases, swearing an oath to abjure the realm was required, with refusal resulting in a death sentence. Either eventuality led to permanent forfeiture of goods and chattels and loss of all lands for life. Offenders were also liable to transportation to English overseas possessions for seven years. Nor was poverty an excuse where distraints were involved, since the second Conventicle Act allowed the fines of impoverished offenders to be levied on others who had been present and who were more capable of paying. That was also the case where a preacher or a teacher was unknown or had fled. The two Restoration Conventicle Acts also included penalties for the defaults of law-enforcement officials, and gave significant power to the militia and to the civil authorities to suppress or prevent such meetings and to make arrests, although a warrant from a justice or chief magistrate was necessary. The second Conventicle Act gave sweeping and controversial rights and rewards to informers, encouraging them to prosecute conventiclers. That act did provide a limited right of appeal, the only redress permitted by any of these statutes.

Unauthorized religious meetings could also be prosecuted at common law as riots. The pretext was the unlawfulness of the meeting according to the Elizabethan Conventicle Act, but rather than proceed on that statute, complicated by its recusancy provisions and severe penalties, the authorities could treat the meeting as a riot. That approach involved trial by jury, with the right, if the verdict was guilty, for the court to inflict an unlimited, albeit "reasonable" fine, with imprisonment on refusal to pay. Some authorities preferred this tactic over use of the second Conventicle Act, for the latter relied on distraint rather than imprisonment for refusal to pay fines. In addition, the common law required only three or more persons to constitute a riot. Most seventeenth-century legal commentators insisted, however, that a riot should involve violence or the intent to commit a violent act, a point often futilely emphasized by Friends.[82]

The Restoration authorities also had weapons available to harass Quaker "First Publishers of Truth" and others traveling to meetings. They could be treated, for example, as vagabonds, on the pretext that they were able-bodied persons begging for food and money. Two statutes[83] in force during the Restoration authorized the apprehension of such persons, who were then to be stripped to the waist, whipped, and sent back home, or to the town through which they had last passed without having been punished. Normally, confession or the oaths of witnesses before two or more justices were prerequisites for vagrancy convictions. But traveling Quakers could also be prosecuted for non-observance of the Lord's Day (Sunday), or any of twenty-six other holy days. Two pre-Interregnum statutes,[84] as well as 29 Chas. II, severely restricted the right to work, sell goods, or travel on those days, under penalty of two hours in the stocks or fines by distraint in the temporal courts, together with excommunication in the church courts. Even worse, after 1677 any person who traveled on the Lord's Day and was robbed could not bring an action against the thief, nor would any hundred be charged with or be answerable for that crime.

Church and state also viewed with alarm the Quaker habit of entering churches to engage ministers and congregations in debate, often disrupting the service. Such disruption was liable to imprisonment under a Marian statute[85] originally enacted to protect Catholic clergy from molestation during the sermon, or during Mass or some other divine service. Although an Act of June 1657[86] extended liability to interference with a minister while he was going to, or returning from church, the Restoration government chose to rely on the Marian statute, apparently countenancing Quakers who disrupted the routine of ministers and congregations outside the church itself. Parishioners, of course, might take matters into their own hands and forcibly discourage such activities.

Ironically, probably the only time that Quakers attended the Established Church was to disrupt it. The Restoration government, however, by means of nine Jacobean and Elizabethan statutes, demanded regular attendance at divine service.[87] The anti-Catholic origins of several of these statutes resulted in some confusion as the terms "recusant" and "popish recusant" were often intermixed, a point the Quakers and other Dissenters would seize upon. Taken together, these statutes called for all those aged sixteen or over to attend divine service regularly and to take the sacrament at least twice each year. Failure to attend was punishable by fines of 12*d*. per week, £20 per month and/or loss of all goods and chattels and two-thirds of the offender's real estate. Inability to pay the 12*d*. fine resulted in imprisonment. Refusal to take the sacrament was punishable by fines of £20 for the first year and £40 for all subsequent years. Recusants were forbidden to persuade anyone either to attend unlawful assemblies, or to forgo attending church or taking the sacrament. Nor were recusants themselves to attend unlawful assemblies. These offenses were subject to three months' imprisonment; failure to conform within that time would require taking an oath to abjure the realm, with refusal to do so resulting in death as a felon. Recusants were also barred from employment under the Crown, from holding any legal or medical post, and from working as schoolmasters or servants. They were disabled from acting as executors, administrators, or guardians. The right of recusant husbands and wives to inherit from one another was severely restricted. Nor could recusants initiate suits at law or come to any place where the king was located. With some exceptions, they were forbidden to live within ten miles of London unless they provided their names to the lord mayor or the justices of the peace. In fact, they were not permitted to stray further than five miles from their homes without a license, for which an oath was necessary. The penalties for noncompliance, graded according to the personal wealth of the offender, were imprisonment, abjuration of the realm, the permanent loss of all goods and chattels, and forfeiture of lands for life.

The Quaker testimony against swearing was countered by equally severe legislation. Normal legal practice prevented those who refused to swear from sitting on juries, recovering stolen goods, suing for debts, carrying on trades in corporate towns, probating wills involving goods and chattels, giving evidence to defend titles, entering into copyholds, answering suits either in equity or church courts, or holding any law-enforcement position which required an oath of office. By 1660 numerous enactments required other specific oaths. Two Elizabethan statutes[88] had introduced the Oath of Supremacy acknowledging the Queen and her successors as supreme over the Anglican Church. The employment disabilities for refusal were similar to those for recusancy. But refusal also resulted in an indictment and trial, with guilt punishable by *praemunire*, which placed the offender outside the king's protection and involved forfeiture of goods and chattels, loss of all income from real property, and imprisonment for life or at the king's pleasure. If the offender subsequently refused a second tender of the oath within three months, he was guilty of high treason. The numbers of those to whom the oath was to be retendered were severely restricted but, unfortunately for the Quakers, they included anyone who verbally or in writing slandered the rites or ceremonies of the Established Church. Several Jacobean recusancy statutes[89] also demanded oaths as a means of proving conformity, one of which was the Oath of Allegiance or Obedience, to be tendered to all the leading officials in church and state. Bishops and justices of the peace were given wide latitude in tendering it to anyone convicted, indicted, or merely suspected of failure to either attend church or to take the sacrament twice in the past year. Refusal to take this oath led to imprisonment; continued refusal resulted in praemunire (except for married women who were simply imprisoned until they took the oath). All popish recusants were also, ipso facto, excommunicated until they conformed and swore the oath. Furthermore, any person who refused to take the oath was disabled from holding any office, from utilizing or practicing common and civil law, and from gainfully practicing surgery, the "art" of an apothecary, or any liberal science.[90]

The Restoration government, as part of its anti-Dissenter policies, introduced further statutory offenses involving oaths. Thus the 1661 Corporation Act[91] demanded the Oaths of Allegiance and Supremacy and an oath against the Solemn League and Covenant in order to hold any office in a corporation. Although directed mainly against the Presbyterians, it would also effectively broaden the number of offices from which the Quakers were excluded by their refusal to swear. The 1662 Act of Uniformity,[92] aimed at Presbyterian ministers, could also affect any Quaker schoolmaster or private tutor and instructor, for a license had to be purchased from the ecclesiastical authorities, and a declaration subscribed disavowing both the Solemn League and Covenant and the proposition that it was lawful to take up arms against the king, and agreeing to conform to the liturgy of the Established Church, on pain of imprisonment and fines.

The 1662 "Quaker" Act[93] was ostensibly directed against "Quakers and others," who maintained that the swearing of an oath was contrary to the law of God, and who then willfully and obstinately refused, or encouraged others to refuse, to take a lawfully tendered oath. In fact, the only penalties were to be levied on Quaker offenders who assembled illegally, leaving them liable to substantial fines or imprisonment for the first two offenses, and abjuration of the realm or transportation for a third offense. Only by taking the oath that the court tendered and by posting security not to attend any further unlawful assemblies could the offender be discharged. Trial by jury was permitted *only* for the third offense.

The first Conventicle Act in 1664 reiterated that Quakers and other sectaries were obstructing justice by refusing to take oaths. Those liable to prosecution now included anyone legally served with a process or other summons to appear in a court of record (except courts leet) as either a witness or a juror, or to be examined on interrogatories. It also included anyone simply "present in court." Refusal in these circumstances to take any "judicial" oath tendered in the court of King's Bench or at assizes was sufficient for conviction. If the refusal took place in any other court, the offender was imprisoned until the following assizes or gaol delivery, where the oath was again tendered. A second refusal resulted in transportation. The same procedure also occurred when any person refused to answer on oath a bill exhibited against him in any court of equity or any suit in the ecclesiastical courts, or who refused to take an oath in those courts when called upon either as a witness or for examination on interrogatories. In effect, this act provided an alternative to the lengthy and expensive processes normally associated with contempt of those courts. The conviction could be overturned, however, if the offender came into court or before a justice of the peace and took an oath that he did not hold the taking of an oath to be unlawful and that he had not refused to swear on that account, a clever way to avoid the self-incrimination implied in the Quaker Act, but still an unacceptable proviso for the Quakers.

The 1665 Five Mile Act,[94] although ostensibly directed against those who were or had been in holy orders, also included those "pretending" to holy orders, a phrase sufficiently vague to encompass Quaker ministers.[95] All such persons were to subscribe to the declaration in the Act of Uniformity, and were also to swear to the "Oxford" Oath, which again recited the unlawfulness of taking up arms against the king and which bound the swearer to forsake any attempt to alter the government in church and state. Any person who refused to take the declaration and oath and who had been convicted of preaching in an unlawful assembly, was not to come within five miles, except in passing on the road, of any corporation or borough sending burgesses to Parliament. Nor was he to come within five miles of any locality where he had, since 1660, either held holy orders or preached in a conventicle. Those who, in addition, did not attend divine service or failed to behave in an orderly fashion while there, were forbidden by the act to teach in any public or private school or to take in boarders for instruction. The normal fine was £40, but any two justices of the peace could sentence an offender, without trial, to six months in gaol simply on oath made to them of any offense against the Act.

As for Quaker wills and burials, two Restoration statutes involving oaths put these in greater jeopardy. Whereas wills involving personal estates were to be probated on oath in the ecclesiastical courts, 29 Chas. II, c. 3 tightened procedure involving written and unwritten (nuncupative) wills bequeathing lands or tenements. A minimum of three witnesses was now required to attest and subscribe written wills. Although not specified, the witnesses were probably required to attest on oath. With unwritten wills, where the estate exceeded £30, oaths were to be required of at least three witnesses present at the time the will was made. As for burials, 20 Chas. II, c. 3 insisted that all corpses were to be buried in wool, with proof to consist of a sworn affidavit of two or more witnesses. Failure by the relatives of the deceased or by some other individual to present this affidavit to a local parson or minister within eight days of the burial resulted in a fine of £5, levied by distraint normally on the goods and chattels of the deceased or of anyone involved in dressing or placing the body into the coffin.

Quaker opposition to the use of "carnal" weapons had, prior to the Restoration, resulted only in dismissal from army and navy posts.[96] But the Militia Acts of 1662–63[97] gave lords lieutenant power to require all persons, according to the value of their estates, to provide horses, men, and arms, and to pay towards the maintenance of the men for the days they served. Rates were to be set towards furnishing ammunition and other equipment. Moreover, if their landlords defaulted, tenants were to provide horses, armed horsemen, or armed foot soldiers on pain of fines up to £20, although they could deduct the costs from their rents. No individual charged had to serve in person, but could instead provide a replacement. Quakers would therefore be liable for refusing either to serve in person, to find any replacements, or to provide in any way towards raising and supporting the militia. Perhaps most insulting, as well as alarming, for the Quakers, was the indemnification granted to those who had acted in the militia between 2 February 1659 and 20 July 1661 "as touching the assaulting, detaining or imprisoning any person suspected to be a fanatick, sectary or disturber of the peace, or seizing of arms, or searching of houses for arms or for suspected persons."[98]

The most difficult laws to interpret and to enforce against Quakers were those relating to blasphemy and heresy. Primary jurisdiction in such matters rested after 1660 with the church courts,[99] the sole exception being the obsolete writ *de heretico comburendo* which permitted the burning of heretics, but which was finally abolished by the statute 29 Chas. II, c. 9.

Finally, the Quakers were obligated, like everyone else, to pay towards the maintenance of the Established Church through tithes, church rates, and customary dues. Unfortunately, tithes and church dues became subject to extremely complex rules of procedure and severe penalties for nonpayment.[100] Much of the complexity surrounding tithe payments resulted from the English Reformation, with its immense changes in land ownership as laymen took over many of the former monastic lands and "impropriated" the tithes originally belonging to those monasteries. Tithes owned by laymen became temporal inheritances assuming the same characteristics as other land. While there remained many men in holy orders who had claim to tithes, either in their own right, or as part of agreements reached with lay impropriators, the intrusion of laymen into the tithing system had transformed the question of jurisdiction over tithe disputes.[101]

At the Restoration, three sixteenth-century statutes,[102] enacted to end the confusion over tithes caused by the Reformation, partially regulated tithe procedure and were sources of controversy, often involving Friends. The most significant and contentious statute proved to be 2 & 3 Edw. VI, c. 13, which permitted triple damages against any person who carried away his tithes before dividing and setting them forth. The statute failed, however, to specify in what court the suit was to be filed, an oversight which would be seized upon by the Quakers, who wished to restrict all tithe litigation to the church courts. Yet the Act also stipulated that it was lawful for every party to whom tithes were due to watch their tithes being justly and truly set forth and severed from the nine parts, and then to take them away without molestation. But if any tithe payer carried away the tithes before they were set forth, willingly withdrew them, or prevented the tithe owner from taking them away, then on proof given to an ecclesiastical judge, he was liable to pay twice their value as well as the costs of the suit. The church courts, however, lacked effective process to coerce payment, although the statute did provide that in cases where a defendant, having been sentenced in the church courts, refused payment of tithe or damages, he would be excommunicated and liable to imprisonment on the writ *de excommunicato capiendo.*

Although the appropriate court for suits for triple damages was left unclear, all the other statutory methods had firmly limited suits to ecclesiastical courts. But the legal issues would be further complicated during the Interregnum by the suppression of church court jurisdiction, by a further upheaval in ownership of church lands, and by the tremendous upsurge of radical opposition to the tithing system. Although the consequent right of justices of the peace to distrain for tithes, permitted during the Interregnum, ended in 1660, temporal court intervention had grown. It was asserted, for example, that the Exchequer, as a court of revenue and with equity jurisdiction, had always possessed authority over tithes, a right acknowledged for Chancery as early as 1575. Therefore, the equity side of Exchequer during the Interregnum had allowed tithe cases to be prosecuted by anyone who merely suggested that he was a debtor to the Crown, since he would be less able to pay the debt if he did not receive his tithe. This was equivalent to the *quo minus* procedure on the plea side of that court which had tended to restrict this privilege to bona fide Crown debtors. Both of these methods continued into the Restoration.[103]

Similarly, the courts of King's Bench and Common Pleas, again vying for litigants, utilized legal fictions to broaden their jurisdiction over tithes by allowing an action of debt to be brought against any of their prisoners, the latter having been arrested originally on a false pretext.[104] To some extent, the need for this fiction was irrelevant for tithes, because the clause in 2 & 3 Edw. Vl, c. 13 that awarded their triple value had been interpreted by contemporary legal authorities as allowing an action of debt in any of the king's courts of record. In practice, actions on that statute normally were brought in the courts of King's Bench and Common Pleas. If a defendant refused to appear to the suit, he would be imprisoned locally and a writ of *habeas corpus ad deliberandum et recipiendum*, procured by the plaintiff, used to bring him to the court at Westminster, where he was to appear and put himself upon the country. The case was then returned to the county of origin for trial at the next assizes. There the plaintiff had to substantiate the amount of tithe claimed, and the jury then brought in a sum which the judge, bound by the statute, tripled.[105] In effect, tithes and church dues could leave the Quakers liable to imprisonment; double value with costs; triple value; sequestration of estates, both real and personal for contempt of court; and outlawry, also for contempt. If the amount owed was under 40*s*., the tithe owner could sue in a local civil court, normally the county court, and hope to obtain an order from the justices of the peace authorizing distraint, apparently even in cases of nonappearance. Although this action may have been legal during the Interregnum, there is little doubt that after the Restoration it was not. The Quakers, like other parishioners, were also liable to pay rates to maintain the fabric of the parish church, although these were normally cognizable only in the ecclesiastical courts.[106]

Clearly, state and church after 1660 had at their command an astonishing array of laws and jurisdictions, often overlapping, to deal not only with the Quaker challenge, but also with religious dissent in general. As indicated, many of the statutes originated during the reign of Charles II, thereby implying a concerted and continuing effort either to eliminate religious dissent or to render it harmless. If so, why did the Quakers appear to flourish? For at least a partial answer to this question, we must examine Restoration politics and religion and how they affected the legal system.

Notes

1. See Edmund Heward, *Matthew Hale* (London, 1972), chap. 3; Veall, *Law Reform*; William Sheppard, *Englands Balme* (London, 1657; s3183); Nancy L. Matthews, *William Sheppard, Cromwell's Law Reformer* (Cambridge, 1984), 186–230.
2. Swarthmore MSS, 2:97.
3. Matthew Hale, *The History of the Common Law of England*, ed. Charles M. Gray (Chicago and London, 1971), 4, 17, 19, 44; Ronald A. Marchant, *The Church Under the Law* (Cambridge, 1969), 3, 240; see also Brian P. Levack, *The Civil Lawyers in England 1605–1641* (Oxford, 1973). Until the nineteenth century a single case was not considered binding, although a well-established custom was viewed as strongly persuasive (Theodore F. T. Plucknett, *Concise History of the Common Law*, 5th ed. [London, 1956], 347).
4. Baker, *Legal History*, 84–97; W. J. Jones, *The Elizabethan Court of Chancery* (Oxford, 1967), 10–11, 18, 420; see also Marchant, *Church Under Law*, 2; W. H. Bryson, *The Equity Side of the Exchequer* (Cambridge, 1975). Although the Exchequer's equity jurisdiction developed later than that of Chancery, the two courts employed virtually identical procedure.
5. Hale, *Common Law*, ed. Gray, 6; Holdsworth, *English Law*, 1:589–91; 4:81; 8:403.
6. Dowdell, *Hundred Years*, 14; J. D. Eusden, *Puritans, Lawyers and Politics in Early Seventeenth Century England* (New Haven, 1958; reprint [Hamden, Conn.], 1968), 94–96; Holdsworth, *English Law*, 6:303; Robert Steele, ed., *A Bibliography of Royal Proclamations of the Tudor and Stuart Sovereigns and Others Published Under Authority 1485–1714* (Oxford, 1910), xxxii. Numerous proclamations were issued during the Restoration, often involving the enforcement of the penal laws against Dissenters and Catholics; see Chapter 2, The Government and "Matter of Religion."
7. Michael Dalton, *The Countrey Justice*, 5th ed., rev. and enl. (London, 1635), 1; Bryson, *Exchequer*, 53–55; Holdsworth, *English Law*, 1:195; 6:155; Edward Foss, *The Judges of England*, 9 vols. (London, 1848–64), 7:4; William S. Holdsworth, "The Constitutional Position of the Judges," *Law Quarterly Review* 48 (1932):33; Holdsworth, *English Law*, 1:254–55. The judges of

the court of Exchequer were known as the chief baron and the puisne barons. After the execution of Charles I in 1649 and until the Restoration, the King's Bench was known as the Upper Bench. The judges during the Interregnum and early Restoration normally held office during good behavior, but the appointment of William Wylde to Common Pleas in 1668 heralded a return to tenure during the king's pleasure. The one exception was the chief justice of the King's Bench, who normally was appointed by royal mandate without specified tenure, but this also changed to "during pleasure" with the appointment in 1676 of Richard Rainsford (Alfred F. Havighurst, "The Judiciary and Politics in the Reign of Charles II," *Law Quarterly Review* 66 [1950]:64–65). The House of Commons in 1680, concerned about the reversion to patents held during pleasure, ordered the preparation of a bill to require the king to appoint judges "during good behaviour" (*Journals of the House of Commons* 9:683 [17 December 1680]). A dissolution ended this effort.

8. Baker, *Legal History*, 38–43, 46, 53, 86, 88, 96; J. H. Baker, "Criminal Courts and Procedure at Common Law 1550–1800," in *Crime in England 1550–1800*, ed. J. S. Cockburn (London, 1977), 26; *Guide to the Contents of the Public Record Office*, 3 vols. (London, 1963, 1968), 1:7, 47; Jones, *Chancery*, 23, 306, 317–18.

9. Cockburn, *Assizes*, 19, 23, 59–61; Baker, "Courts and Procedure," 28. There were exceptions to the normal assize pattern in Bristol, London, Middlesex, Westminster, Southwark, Colchester, Isle of Ely, County Palatine of Chester, and the city and county of Chester; see Baker, "Courts and Procedure," 26, 30; Cockburn, *Assizes*, 23, 29–30, 34, 38, 47, 164n; Baker, *Legal History*, 19–20; *Guide to Public Record Office*, 1:127.

10. J. S. Cockburn, "Seventeenth-Century Clerks of Assize—Some Anonymous Members of the Legal Profession," *American Journal of Legal History* 13 (1969):315–32.

11. For examples of such instructions after 1660, particularly in relation to the penal statutes against Catholics and Dissenters, see PRO: P.C. 2/65, 123; J. G. Muddiman, *The King's Journalist 1659–1689* (London, 1923), 235; DWL: Roger Morrice MS Ent'ring Book, 1:263, 310, 329, 424; John Gutch, ed., *Collectanea Curiosa: or Miscellaneous Tracts Relating to the History and Antiquities of England and Ireland*, 2 vols. (Oxford, 1781), 1:391–93. Cockburn, however, believes that there was a decrease in formal charges to assize judges after the Restoration (*Assizes*, 184–87).

12. Cockburn, *Assizes*, 7–9, 58, 65.

13. *Kesteven*, xxxiv; Cockburn, *Assizes*, 168, 171–72; *Essex Sessions*, xxii; Anthony Fletcher, *Reform in the Provinces* (New Haven and London, 1986), 92–94.

14. By 13 & 14 Chas. II, c. 3.

15. J. R. Western, *Monarchy and Revolution* (London, 1972), 48, 145, 160; *Warwick Records*, 8:xiv; *Kesteven*, xxxvii; Cockburn, *Assizes*, 186–87; Anthony Fletcher, *A County Community in Peace and War: Sussex 1600–1660* (London and New York, 1975), 175; Anthony Fletcher, *Reform in the Provinces*, 316–48. "One of the recurring themes in the state papers and newspapers of the early months of the Restoration is the eagerness of the gentry to join the militia" (I. M. Green, *The Re-establishment of the Church of England 1660–1663* [Oxford, 1978], 181).

16. *Kesteven*, xiv–xx, xxxvi, lviii–lix; *Warwick Records*, 1:xx, lxi; 7:liv–lv; 8:lxi; Baker, *Legal History*, 23; Baker, "Courts and Procedure," 31; Holds-

worth, *English Law*, 1:135; T. E. Hartley, "Undersheriffs and Bailiffs in some English Shrievalties, c. 1580 to c. 1625," *Bulletin of the Institute of Historical Research* 47 (1974):164–74; Dalton, *Countrey Justice*, 133–34; M. J. Ingram, "Communities and Courts: Law and Order in Early-Seventeenth-Century Wiltshire," in *Crime in England*, ed. Cockburn, 125; see also *Guide to Public Record Office*, 1:78. The Crown did not appoint where a municipal corporation had its own sheriffs. London had the additional right to appoint the sheriffs of Middlesex (Western, *Monarchy and Revolution*, 67–68). In some counties hundreds, also known as wapentakes, were part of other administrative subdivisions, for example, the ridings of Lincolnshire and Yorkshire, the rapes of Sussex, and the lathes of Kent (H. M. Jewell, *English Local Administration in the Middle Ages* [Newton Abbot, 1972], 47–50). Jurisdictionally, a hundred or group of hundreds was known as a bailiwick.

17. Unless otherwise stated, the following discussion of the justices of the peace is based on these sources: Dalton, *Countrey Justice*; L. K. J. Glassey, *Politics and the Appointment of the Justices of the Peace 1675–1720* (Oxford, 1979); Norma Landau, *The Justices of the Peace, 1679–1760* (Berkeley, 1984); Fletcher, *Reform in the Provinces*, especially chaps. 1, 3–4; Fletcher, *County Community*, 128, 177; *Essex Sessions*, ix–xii; *Kesteven*, xxvii–xxviii; *Warwick Records*, 4:ix–x; 8:xxxvii; Baker, *Legal History*, 24; Baker, "Courts and Procedure," 28–29.

18. 12 Ric. II, c. 10; 14 Ric. II, c. 11.

19. Beginning about 1670 the assize judges were regularly omitted from the commissions. This practice continued until 1685, after which they were again included (Cockburn, *Assizes*, 61).

20. The quote is by Dalton, in *Countrey Justice*, 8–9.

21. In a less favorable light, the Inns of Court were in decline by the mid-seventeenth century; see Wilfrid R. Prest, *The Inns of Court Under Elizabeth I and the Early Stuarts 1590–1640* (London, 1972).

22. For more on the "inconsiderable perquisites" justices of the peace could earn, see *Warwick Records*, 5:xix–xx; 7:xl; *Essex Sessions*, xiii; Glassey, *Justices*, 22–23.

23. Also known as the "principal" or "open" sessions (William Lambarde, *Eirenarcha, or of the Justices of Peace*, rev. and enl. ed. [London, 1614], 593). Numerous jurisdictional anomalies existed in relation to these sessions. The archbishop of York and the bishops of Durham and Ely, for example, held sessions within their liberties by statutory authority. Many cities and boroughs held sessions by charter wherein the mayor and some aldermen or jurats were permanent justices, as was a legally qualified, salaried justice called a "recorder" (Baker, "Courts and Procedure," 30; Dowdell, *Hundred Years*, 1). The most notable jurisdictional exceptions were London and Middlesex (see *London Sessions*, vii–ix, 7), while other interesting anomalies included Bristol and Chester; see Elizabeth Ralph, *Guide to the Bristol Archives Office* (Bristol, 1971), 49; Cockburn, *Assizes*, 47n; *Guide to Public Record Office*, 1:172; J. S. Morrill, *Cheshire 1630–1660* (London, 1974), 1–3, 7–8; Dowdell, *Hundred Years*, xx.

24. Thus from 1674–82 in Warwickshire only 37 out of a commission of 109 ever attended sessions, with an average attendance between 10 and 11. In early seventeenth-century Cheshire, attendance averaged 8 out of an effective bench of about 40, and there was lacking a "hard core of 'professional' justices who turned up sessions after sessions." In Kesteven in the last half of the seventeenth century "little more than one-third were active magistrates" (*Warwick Records*, 7:xxxvi–xxxvii; 8:li; Morrill, *Cheshire*, 9; *Kesteven*, xxxn).

25. Cockburn, *Assizes*, 92; *Essex Sessions*, xxii–xxiii. For a detailed list of offenses dealt with at quarter sessions, see *Warwick Records*, 3:xii.

26. *Essex Sessions*, xiii; *Warwick Records*, 5:xxxii; 7:xl; *Kesteven*, xxxvii– xxxviii; Fletcher, *County Community*, 144; Baker, "Courts and Procedure," 16. For a list of fees payable to the clerk and his assistants, see *Oxfordshire Justices*, lix–lxii.

27. *Warwick Records*, 7:li; Baker, "Courts and Procedure," 30.

28. Dowdell, *Hundred Years*, 2. For an excellent example of charges delivered to quarter sessions' grand juries, see Sir Peter Leicester, *Charges to the Grand Jury at Quarter Sessions, 1660–1677*, ed. Elizabeth M. Halcrow, Chetham Society, 3d ser., vol. 5 (Manchester, 1953).

29. Morrill, *Cheshire*, 8–9; *Kesteven*, xxxv, lxxix–lxxx; Fletcher, *Reform in the Provinces*, 122–35; Fletcher, *County Community*, 137; *Essex Sessions*, xiv; Lambarde, *Eirenarcha*, 623–24; *Oxfordshire Justices*, lxxxiv; see also Dowdell, *Hundred Years*, 8–9; Baker, "Courts and Procedure," 30.

30. *Essex Sessions*, xiii–xiv; Dalton, *Countrey Justice*, 46–47; *Oxfordshire Justices*, xxiii–xxiv, lvii–lxv; *Kesteven*, xl–xlv; Morrill, *Cheshire*, 10–11; *Warwick Records*, 7:lvi–lviii; William Lambarde, *The Duties of Constables, Borsholders, Tythingmen and such other lowe and Lay Ministers of the Peace*, enl. ed. (London, 1614), 5, 19, 34; Fletcher, *County Community*, 141–42. Watch and ward were primitive security systems involving able-bodied members of the community; see *Kesteven*, lx–lxi; Dowdell, *Hundred Years*, 21–24.

31. Dalton, *Countrey Justice*, 3–4, 46–47; Lambarde, *Duties of Constables*, 5–6, 9, 11 passim; *Warwick Records*, 7:lviii; *Kesteven*, xlvi–xlix, l–liii; Dowdell, *Hundred Years*, 18; *Essex Sessions*, xiii.

32. *Essex Sessions*, xiii–xiv, xix; *Kesteven*, lv–lviii; Marchant, *Church Under Law*, 183; Lambarde, *Duties of Constables*, 72–73; *Oxfordshire Justices*, lxvi–lxvii; Dalton, *Countrey Justice*, 93–94, 96–97; *Essex Sessions*, xiii–xiv, xix.

33. Holdsworth, *English Law*, 1:148–49, 182, 184–85; Baker, *Legal History*, 25–26. For a list of the various titles of these courts, see Holdsworth, *English Law*, 1:149n.

34. *Kesteven*, xxiv–xxv; Dalton, *Countrey Justice*, 3.

35. *Warwick Records*, cviii. Yet in Oxfordshire they were neither seen nor used as prisons in the seventeenth century (*Oxfordshire Justices*, lxxix–lxxx).

36. *Essex Sessions*, xxi; *Warwick Records*, 7:cviii–cx; Dowdell believes that the keeper's income was derived from fees (*Hundred Years*, 11).

37. *Warwick Records*, 7:civ–cv, cvii; *Kesteven*, xxi–xxiv; Cockburn, *Assizes*, 107–8; *Essex Sessions*, xxi–xxii; Veall, *Law Reform*, 15. The scale of fees varied from county to county (*Warwick Records*, 7:cviii).

38. By 19 Chas. II, c. 4.

39. By 22 & 23 Chas. II, c. 20.

40. Veall, *Law Reform*, 14–16; *Kesteven*, xxii; *Warwick Records*, 7:cvii–cviii; Gerald Cragg, *Puritanism in the Age of the Great Persecution 1660–1688* (Cambridge, 1957), 101–2; *Guide to Public Record Office*, 1:154.

41. Hale, *Common Law*, ed. Gray, 21–22, 28. The claim of common-law superiority was particularly important in tithe disputes, to which Quakers were vulnerable.

42. Holdsworth, *English Law*, 1:599. The bishop of Chester was unique in having two consistory courts (Marchant, *Church Under Law*, 14). An "ordinary" was an officer instituted by common law to exercise ordinary jurisdiction in ecclesiastical causes, while an "official" was the deputy of the bishop,

either the chancellor or often the latter's appointee. Sometimes it referred to the archdeacon's substitute "in the executing of his jurisdiction" (William Sheppard, *An Epitome of All the Common & Statute Laws of This Nation now in force* [London, 1656], 793).

43. Holdsworth, *English Law*, 1:599; Marchant, *Church Under Law*, 14; Baker, *Legal History*, 111. The court of the Arches received its name because it was built on arches.

44. Archdeaconries were composed of deaneries headed by rural deans. These boundaries were similar to those of the hundred and the wapentake, and therefore the court of the rural dean had been the "ecclesiastical parallel of the hundred court" (Dorothy M. Stenton, *English Society in the Early Middle Ages*, 4th ed. [Harmondsworth, 1971], 218). Annual visitations by the archdeacons effectively destroyed the function of the rural deans to correct offenders, leaving those deans with only testamentary duties (Marchant, *Church Under Law*, 128).

45. Marchant, *Church Under Law*, 91; Baker, *Legal History*, 111; J. A. Sharpe, "Crime and Delinquency in an Essex Parish 1600–1640," in *Crime in England*, ed. Cockburn, 91–92; Holdsworth, *English Law*, 1:600, 604; see also G. I. O. Duncan, *The High Court of Delegates* (Cambridge, 1971).

46. Holdsworth, *English Law*, 1:601–2; Marchant, *Church Under Law*, 12–14. For more on Doctors' Commons, see G. D. Squibb, *Doctors' Commons: A History of the College of Advocates and Doctors of Law* (Oxford and New York, 1977).

47. Marchant, *Church Under Law*, 19, 115–17, 122, 145, 190, 235. From a Quaker viewpoint, one of the most important crimes presented was nonattendance at church.

48. Abolished by 29 Chas. II, c. 9.

49. Holdsworth, *English Law*, 6:112–13; Veall, *Law Reform*, 11; Baker, "Courts and Procedure," 32; Marchant, *Church Under Law*, 2–3, 112–13, 212, 220, 222; Jones, *Chancery*, 390–417.

50. For a discussion of the Privy Council's role in government, see Chapter 2, The Government and "Matter of Religion."

51. Holdsworth, *English Law*, 6:217–24. For Restoration judicial actions on the right of the Crown to dispense and suspend, see A. F. Havighurst, "James II and the Twelve Men in Scarlet," *Law Quarterly Review* 69 (1953): 531–32; Western, *Monarchy and Revolution*, 15–16.

52. Baker, *Legal History*, 420.

53. For the efforts of Charles II and James II to carry out such policies, see Chapter 2, The Government and "Matter of Religion."

54. Contemporaries tended to obscure any difference between misdemeanors and what are presently known as civil wrongs, such as Quaker marriages, often viewed as clandestine; testamentary disputes arising from such marriages; and Quaker refusal to pay tithes.

55. Baker, *Legal History*, 361.

56. Actions were of many sorts, including personal, criminal, penal, and popular; see, for example, Sheppard, *Epitome of the Laws*, 5–6; Baker, *Legal History*, chap. 4.

57. A surety for good behavior necessitated keeping the peace to the safety of many, while a surety for the peace generally protected the safety of the individual who caused it to be granted, although in some cases the measure was taken for the safety of all the king's subjects. Unfortunately for the Quakers, surety for good behavior (unlike surety for the peace) did not re-

quire force or violence to take place for forfeiture. See Dalton, *Countrey Justice*, 158, 170–71, 186–87, 326; Sir Edward Coke, *The Fourth Part of the Institutes of the Laws of England* (London, 1644), 180; Sheppard, *Epitome of the Laws*, 795; *Kesteven*, lxv, lxvii).

58. Dalton, *Countrey Justice*, 3, 171, 188, 191–92. Neither the county and hundred courts nor the courts baron were courts of record (Sheppard, *Epitome of the Laws*, 365).

59. Dalton, *Countrey Justice*, 2, 8–9, 13, 18, 22, 25, 104, 140, 154–56, 328–29, 347; Cockburn, *Assizes*, 102–3; Lambarde, *Duties of Constables*, 19–20, 27, 82; Cragg, *Age of Persecution*, 45–46.

60. Sheppard, *Epitome of the Laws*, 365; Baker, *Legal History*, 414; *Kesteven*, lxxv.

61. Baker, "Courts and Procedure," 19–20; Baker, *Legal History*, 415; *Kesteven*, lxxi–lxxii; Cockburn, *Assizes*, 67–68, 111, 113; *Warwick Records*, 4:viii; 6:xxii; *Oxfordshire Justices*, xvi, lxxxvii; Holdsworth, *English Law*, 1:322. Chief constables or bailiffs for their hundreds compiled lists of those qualified to be jurors. These lists were then scrutinized by the appropriate justices and sent to the sheriff to be incorporated into the freeholders book from which jurors were chosen. Generally the grand juries, composed of no less than 13 and no more than 23 members, contained the most sufficient freeholders in the county who were not assigned to the commissions of the peace, although in some counties they consisted solely of high constables (*Kesteven*, lxxi–lxxii; *Warwick Records*, 6:xxii; Cockburn, *Assizes*, 67). All that was needed to find a true bill was a majority vote of the grand jury (Baker, *Legal History*, 415). The hundred jury in some areas had virtually disappeared, having been replaced by petty constable and headborough presentments to the high constables, who included them with their own presentments to the grand jury. In any event, the hundred jury or constables presented nuisances and defaults similar to what the grand jury did for the county, although they did not have to restrict themselves to the hundred (*Kesteven*, lxxii–lxxiii; *Warwick Records*, 7:li–lii; *Oxfordshire Justices*, lxxxvii).

62. Indictments were written in English during the Commonwealth.

63. For more details on the nature of indictments in this period, and in particular their potential for challenge, see *Warwick Records*, 6:xxv, xxvii; *Kesteven*, lxxv; Dalton, *Countrey Justice*, 401–3.

64. *Warwick Records*, 6:xxvii. It is likely that a writ of attachment ensued, causing the sheriff to require sureties for appearance, with imprisonment on refusal until the next sessions or assizes.

65. *Qui sequitur tam pro domino rege quam pro seipso.*

66. Giles Jacob, *A New-Law Dictionary* (London, 1729); Baker, "Courts and Procedure," 20–21; Coke, *Fourth Institute*, 172.

67. Lambarde, *Eirenarcha*, 541; Dalton, *Countrey Justice*, 157, 407; Sheppard, *Epitome of the Laws*, 19; *Kesteven*, lxxvi; *Essex Sessions*, xviii; Baker, "Courts and Procedure," 34; Jones, *Chancery*, 206, 208. Where a traverse was pleaded, it was possible for a writ *venire facias* to be issued immediately to return a jury to try the case at the same sessions or assizes (*Kesteven*, lxxvi).

68. Sheppard, *Epitome of the Laws*, 1050–51; Baker, "Courts and Procedure," 23, 35–36; Cockburn, *Assizes*, 120; Baker, *Legal History*, 66, 71, 73, 417; *Kesteven*, lxxii. Petty jurors, like grand jurors, were to be 40s. freeholders, or to have 40s. worth of goods if a resident of a town or city. Only men were allowed to serve, as women were excluded by custom. Jurors were not to have

been convicted of any "notorious" crime, nor were they to be related to or allied with any of the parties. There was no age limit. The use of talesmen appears to have been frequent (Baker, "Courts and Procedure," 19; Baker, *Legal History*, 416; Cockburn, *Assizes*, 118; *Oxfordshire Justices*, lxxxviii; Hale, *Common Law*, ed. Gray, 161; *Kesteven*, lxxii).

69. Baker, "Courts and Procedure," 40, 46; Baker, *Legal History*, 119, 129, 424; Lambarde, *Eirenarcha*, 574, 578; *Kesteven*, lxxvii; Cockburn, *Assizes*, 130–31; Jones, *Chancery*, 187; Baker, "Courts and Procedure," 46.

70. Baker, *Legal History*, 52–53. The normal procedure for misdemeanor indictments was the issuance of the writ *venire facias ad respondendum* from the justices to the sheriff. If the latter returned answer that the accused had sufficient goods, a writ of *distringas* was issued for distraint of goods until the accused appeared. If the sheriff, however, simply returned the writ *nihil habet*, then a writ *capias ad respondendum* ensued (*Essex Sessions*, xviii; Lambarde, *Eirenarcha*, 522–23; *Warwick Records*, 6:xxvi; Sheppard, *Epitome of the Laws*, 7).

71. Richard Burn, *The Justice of the Peace and Parish Officer*, 11th ed., 4 vols. (London, 1770), 4:42–44; Sheppard, *Epitome of the Laws*, 7, 1079–80; *Warwick Records*, 6:xxvi; Lambarde, *Eirenarcha*, 522–23; *Essex Sessions*, xviii; *The Proceedings of the Barons of the Exchequer, at Westminister, in their Court of Equity, for Tythes and Oblations* (London, 1705), 16–17; Coke, *Fourth Institute*, 172; Baker, *Legal History*, 53. An outlawry for contempt was punishable by forfeiture of goods and chattels. If the outlawry was on a popular action or suit by an individual, then it was followed by a writ of inquiry sued out by the plaintiff, which led the sheriff to impanel a neighborhood jury to value the offender's lands, goods, and chattels. It then returned the writ under its seal. Seizure followed. If an individual who had been indicted was imprisoned in another county, the justices could award a writ of *habeas corpus ad deliberandum et recipiendum* to remove him before them (Burn, *Justice of the Peace*, 4:45; *Proceedings of the Barons*, 16–17; Alfred W. Braithwaite, "Early Tithe Prosecutions: Friends as Outlaws," *Journal of the Friends Historical Society* 49 [1960]:152; Lambarde, *Eirenarcha*, 526).

72. Sheppard, *Epitome of the Laws*, 6; Baker, *Legal History*, 49–50; Bryson, *Exchequer*, 93; *Proceedings of the Barons*, 16; *Kesteven*, xv.

73. Known as an "English" bill because it was in the vernacular (*Guide to Public Record Office*, 1:8; Bryson, *Exchequer*, 93–94; Jones, *Chancery*, 193). For more on what was contained in the bill, see Bryson, *Exchequer*, 97–105.

74. Jones, *Chancery*, 177–80, 190–91, 214; Bryson, *Exchequer*, 101, 108, 110, 114, 120; Baker, *Legal History*, 69. The subpoena did not have to be served on the defendant personally. Refusal to appear carried a penalty of £100, but this amount was only to frighten the defendant, since the sum could not be levied. It was possible in cases of old age, infirmity, prohibitive distance, or severe weather to move for a commission to be appointed to take the answer in the country. If a demurrer was rejected, a fresh subpoena was issued requiring an immediate answer. A defendant could not demur after an answer was put it. By the mid-seventeenth century, it was possible to answer to one part of a bill, to demur to another, and to plead to other points (Jones, *Chancery*, 177, 209–11, 221; Bryson, *Exchequer*, 110, 118–123).

75. Bryson, *Exchequer*, 110–13; Jones, *Chancery*, 225, 229–33; Baker, *Legal History*, 88; *Proceedings of the Barons*, 20; Francis Plowden, *The Principles and Law of Tithing* (London, 1806), 320.

76. Baker, *Legal History*, 38–43; *Guide to Public Record Office*, 1:114;

Sheppard, *Epitome of the Laws*, 17. To gain jurisdiction, King's Bench pretended that the defendant had committed a trespass in Middlesex (over which the court had jurisdiction), but that he could not be found there, a contempt that permitted the court to issue a writ of *latitat* to have the offender imprisoned in his own county. He was then brought to London by writ of *habeas corpus ad deliberandum et recipiendum* and imprisoned in the Marshalsea, over which King's Bench had jurisdiction. A declaration was then put in for the debt. When challenged in 1661 over this procedure, King's Bench resorted to writs for imaginary trespass "and also [*ac etiam*] to answer in a plea of debt." Common Pleas, anxious to keep pace with King's Bench, had developed by the 1670s its own "fictitious writs of trespass to land" in conjunction with *ac etiams* (Baker, *Legal History*, 42–43).

77. *Jura Ecclesiastica: or A Treatise on the Ecclesiastical Laws and Courts . . . By a Barrister of the Middle Temple*, 2 vols. (London, 1742), 1 : 165; Plowden, *Law of Tithing*, 103; Baker, *Legal History*, 112, 394; Jones, *Chancery*, 391–92, 495; Marchant, *Church Under Law*, 63–64.

78. Marchant, *Church Under Law*, 31–32, 58; Lambarde, *Duties of Constables*, 70, 73–74, 82.

79. Unfortunately, like the bishop's certificate, this was commonly called a *significavit*, from the beginning of it: *Rex vicecomiti . . . salutem. Significavit nobis venerabilis*. If the sheriff returned *non est inventus*, a *capias* followed and imprisonment still took place (see Richard Grey, *A System of English Ecclesiastical Law*, 4th ed. [London, 1743], 404, 406; Book of Cases, 1 : 224; *Jura Ecclesiastica*, 1 : 180–81). Quaker records, therefore, while generally mentioning writs *de excommunicato capiendo*, occasionally speak of imprisonment by a *capias* following a *significavit*.

80. Plowden, *Law of Tithing*, 243–45, 247; Marchant, *Church Under Law*, 19; *Guide to Public Record Office*, 1 : 42; Hale, *Common Law*, ed. Gray, 23; Holdsworth, *English Law*, 1 : 631.

81. See 13 & 14 Chas. II, c. 1, effective from May 1662; 16 Chas. II, c. 1, effective from July 1664; 22 Chas. II, c. 1, effective from May 1670; 35 Eliz. I, c. 1. See also *The Statutes at Large*. Quaker meetings during the Interregnum had been effectively exempt from prosecution as a result of the "Instrument of Government" of 16 December 1653, provided they did not disturb the peace. The "Humble Petition and Advice" of 25 May 1657 and the Lord's Day Act of 26 June 1657 had been far more equivocal in their attitude towards religious toleration. But the vagueness of each of these measures made them relatively ineffectual in prosecuting such meetings (C. H. Firth and R. S. Rait, eds., *Acts and Ordinances of the Interregnum 1642–1660*, 3 vols. [London, 1911], 2 : 821–22, 1053, 1162–70).

82. Sir Edward Coke, *First Part of the Institutes of the Laws of England or a Commentary upon Littleton* (London, 1628), 176; Lambarde, *Eirenarcha*, 175–76; Dalton, *Countrey Justice*, 91, 120, 218–21; Sheppard, *Epitome of the Laws*, 891–92. The last two authorities were more equivocal on the subject of what constituted this offense, believing that assemblies which broke the peace or did any unlawful act might be liable, although the latter offense was closer to common trespass than riot. See also *Warwick Records*, 6:xxx.

83. See 39 Eliz. I, c. 4; 1 Jas. I, c. 7. The Interregnum, by an Act effective from 1 July 1657, had confirmed the Elizabethan statute, but broadened liability to any person who wandered or traveled about without any sufficient cause. Nor was suspicion of begging to be a prime consideration, thus provid-

ing a more effective weapon against peripatetic Quakers at whom it may have been primarily directed (*Acts and Ordinances*, 2:1098–99; John Towill Rutt, ed., *Diary of Thomas Burton*, 4 vols. [London, 1828], 1:114).

84. 1 Chas. I, c. 1; 3 Chas. I, c. 1. Any items exhibited for sale would be forfeited; travel or work without reasonable cause resulted in fines by distraint.

85. 1 Mar. st. 2, c. 3.

86. *Lord's Day Act*, 26 June 1657 (*Acts and Ordinances*, 2:1162–70).

87. 1 Eliz. I, c. 2; 23 Eliz. I, c. 1; 29 Eliz. I, c. 6; 35 Eliz. I, c. 1; 35 Eliz. I, c. 2; 1 Jas. I, c. 4; 3 Jas. I, c. 4; 3 Jas. I, c. 5; 7 Jas. I, c. 6. The Interregnum had been relatively tolerant in this matter, modifying or repealing several of the Elizabethan recusancy laws, although there still existed enough laws against popish recusants that could have been applied to Quakers. Oliver Cromwell in 1655, by proclamation, called for the imposition of the 1643 Oath of Abjuration on all those suspected of being popish recusants, and in 1657 Parliament legitimized this use of the Oath. Generally, however, Quakers were liable to fines of 2s., 6d. each Lord's Day only if their meetings, after June 1657, were considered improper religious services not conforming to the vague criteria of the "Humble Petition and Advice" (Braithwaite, *Beginnings*, 446; *Acts and Ordinances*, 2:254–56, 423–25).

88. 1 Eliz. I, c. 1; 5 Eliz. I, c. 5.

89. 1 Jas. I, c. 4; 3 Jas. I, c. 4; 3 Jas. I, c. 5; 7 Jas. I, c. 6.

90. The Interregnum on 9 February 1649 had repealed the Oaths of Allegiance and Supremacy, but had introduced the Oath of Abjuration, an equally severe weapon (*Acts and Ordinances*, 2:1, 1170–80).

91. 13 Chas. II, st. 2, c. 1. This statute, however, was essentially directed against the Presbyterians.

92. 14 Chas. II, c. 4.

93. The problem with this statute was the self-incrimination necessary to prosecute successfully those who viewed oaths as contrary to God's law. The first Conventicle Act rectified this weakness; see below.

94. 17 Chas. II, c. 2.

95. In fact, William Penn was imprisoned for six months in 1671 under this Act; see Richard S. Dunn and Mary Maples Dunn, eds., *The Papers of William Penn*, 5 vols. (Philadelphia, 1980–87), 1:191–204.

96. For example, see Braithwaite, *Beginnings*, 218–19, 229–31, 252, 519–20.

97. 13 & 14 Chas. II, c. 3; 15 Chas. II, c. 4.

98. The indemnification was granted by means of two statutes: 13 Chas. II, st. 1, c. 6; 15 Chas. II, c. 4. That the militia had often acted violently toward sectaries in that period is evident from Quaker records. See Chapter 3, The Tyranny of the Law.

99. During the Interregnum these were civil matters. Perhaps the most famous blasphemy trial of that period involved James Nayler, a prominent Quaker, who at Bristol in 1656 emulated Christ's entry into Jerusalem. He was tried and imprisoned by Parliament (see William Bittle, "James Nayler: A Study in Seventeenth-Century Quakerism" [Ph.D. diss., Kent State University, 1975]; Braithwaite, *Beginnings*, 244–73).

100. For a fuller analysis of this matter than what follows, see Craig W. Horle, "Partridges Upon the Mountains: The Quakers and the English Legal System, 1660–1688" (Ph.D. diss., University of Maryland, 1985), 104–11.

101. Christopher Hill, *Economic Problems of the Church from Archbishop*

Whitgift to the Long Parliament (Oxford, 1956), chap. 2; Plowden, *Law of Tithing*, 254–55, 264, 270; Hill, *Economic Problems*, 25, 48, 125, 138–39. By 1603 there were close to four thousand impropriated livings (Hill, *Economic Problems*, 144). As early as the Interregnum, the Quakers complained bitterly about tithes inheritable as other temporal possessions (see Anthony Pearson, *The Great Case of TYTHES, Stated* [London, 1657; P989], 28, 30; John Crook, *Tythes no Property* [London, 1659; c7225], 1).

102. 27 Hen. VIII, c. 20; 32 Hen. VIII, c. 7; 2 & 3 Edw. VI, c. 13. The first two of these, while restricting all suits to the ecclesiastical courts, did permit the ecclesiastical judge to issue a certificate to two justices of the peace to imprison anyone who, after judgment was rendered in the church court, refused to pay the tithes or duties decided upon. This stipulation presupposed, of course, that those cited actually appeared and answered. Quakers rarely did, leaving them vulnerable instead, to the writ *de excommunicato capiendo* for contempt in not appearing or in not answering.

103. *Acts and Ordinances*, 1:567–69, 996–97, 1226; 2:1467–69; William Sheppard, *The Parsons Guide: or the Law of Tithes* (London, 1654; s3204), 23; Plowden, *Law of Tithing*, 378–80; Eric J. Evans, "A History of the Tithe System in England, 1690–1850, with special reference to Staffordshire" (Ph.D. thesis, University of Warwick, 1971), 84; Baker, *Legal History*, 45; *Guide to Public Record Office*, 1:92; Bryson, *Exchequer*, 17–18, 94–95. Procedure in Exchequer involved local imprisonment on an Exchequer process for nonappearance to a suit, followed by a writ of *habeas corpus ad deliberandum et recipiendum* to transfer the offender to London to the Exchequer bar. If he did not answer the bill and pay the costs of the suit, he was imprisoned in the Fleet. Motion was then made for a serjeant of arms to institute a search in the country for the offender, who would not be found, of course, being a prisoner in London. Consequently the sheriff returned *non est inventus*. That began the process towards sequestration (*News from the Country: or the Plough Man's Lamentation* [London, 1706], 5–6). If the offender entered his appearance, however, then the bill was filed for him to answer. If he refused to answer, he was imprisoned in the county where he lived. If he did not pay off this contempt and appear, process issued forth against him as above until a sequestration occurred. He was kept in prison until the sequestration was satisfied (*News from the Country*, 6–7).

104. See n. 76, preceding.

105. William Watson, *The Clergyman's Law, Or: the Complete Incumbent*, 4th ed. (London, 1747), 607, 609; Sheppard, *The Parson's Guide*, 23; GBS, 1:60–61, 77, 199–200; 2:10; 3:594–95, 780–81, 823, 996; 4:206; 5:3–4, 500; 6:45; Meeting for Sufferings, 6:198; ORS, 1:8. The action was apparently laid only for a contempt of the statute for not setting out tithes; subtraction of tithes was limited to the ecclesiastical courts (Plowden, *Law of Tithing*, 379–80; Evans, "History of Tithe System," 84).

106. Braithwaite, "Early Tithe Prosecutions," 149–50; Burn, *Justice of the Peace*, 1:331; *Clergyman's Law*, 598. The Quakers were also liable to oblations, obventions, and offerings which were the "customary payments for communicants at Easter, for marriages, christenings, churching of women, burials and such like" (Burn, *Justice of the Peace*, 4:265). Another payment, which like church rates was restricted to church courts, was the mortuary, a fixed money payment on the death of a parishioner on the pretext that it was a recompense to the parish church "for his personal tithes and oblations not duly paid by the deceased party in his life-time" (*Clergyman's Law*, 598; see also Sheppard, *The Parson's Guide*, 30–31).

Chapter Two

THE GOVERNMENT AND "MATTER OF RELIGION"

No man shall be disquieted or called in question for differences of opinion in matter of religion, which do not disturb the peace of the kingdom and . . . we shall be ready to consent to such an Act of parliament as, upon mature deliberation shall be offered to us, for the full granting that indulgence.

From the Declaration of Breda, 4 April 1660

For providing therefore of further and more speedy remedies against the growing and dangerous practices of seditious sectaries and other disloyal persons, who, under pretence of tender consciences, do at their meetings, contrive insurrections, as late experience hath shown.

Preamble of the 1664 Conventicle Act

I
1660–1672

A significant factor in seventeenth-century English law enforcement was the power of the Crown to appoint and dismiss officials, to augment legislation as well as assist in its enacting, and to provide direction and impetus to enforcement. The Crown's influence, however, could be circumscribed by others, most notably the landed classes, particularly through their representatives in Parliament. Had the Crown and Parliament been unified in their approach to religious dissent, law enforcement might have demonstrated more consistency than is indicated by Quaker records. In fact, they were at cross-purposes over religion throughout the period.

Charles II's sympathy for Catholicism was bolstered by his hatred of the divisions within Protestantism. For him, the Catholic Church, with its rich tradition, unity, authoritarianism, and inculcation of obedience was a perfect complement to strong monarchy.[1] Yet while Charles might have wished to be a Catholic monarch, he was primarily a survivor, determined to avoid another exile; consequently he often compromised when under pressure. While not therefore well-disposed toward the Anglican Church or the Dissenters, Charles was forced to maneuver carefully between implementation of toleration for Catholics and the powerful and sustained opposition to that policy by Anglicans and many Dissenters.

The suddenness with which the Restoration occurred added a further complication. Despite the rapturous reception of the restored monarchy, there remained a strong undercurrent of militant Puritanism.[2] Charles was bound to consider the aspirations both of the Presbyterians who had engineered his return, and of his importunate Royalist supporters. The unknown factor was the reaction of the radical sectaries, including the Quakers. Charles apparently viewed toleration as the safest method of ensuring a peaceful reign, but he underestimated both the resistance to that policy and the breadth of Quaker principles, which extended well beyond toleration of their meetings. In April and October 1660, Charles issued declarations calling for liberty for "tender" consciences, although predicated on Parliamentary enactment.[3] He believed that by this means alone he could create an Established Church led by bishops supported by elected presbyters. Parliament was to disabuse him of this notion. Charles did emphasize that toleration was dependent on the peaceful deportment of those who differed from the Established Church. To demonstrate his good intentions, he helped to procure the release from a Lancashire prison of George Fox, the prominent Quaker leader.[4]

Although Charles may have been willing, albeit cautiously, to assist the Quakers, others were not so well-disposed. The Convention Parliament, dominated by Anglican and Presbyterian Royalists, looked unfavorably on toleration for Quakers or any of the radicals. The election had revealed bitter animosity toward the military and civilian leadership of 1659 and particularly towards those who had caused the ouster of Parliament in October 1659. The reasons for this were not hard to discover. Many who had supported the Commonwealth regarded the army leaders and their supporters as hypocrites, who had used the abolition of monarchy to line their own pockets. In addition, Presbyterians and Anglicans were alarmed at radical calls for religious toleration and the abolition of tithes. Above all, many Englishmen were tired of the Puritans and their legislation against vice, sport, and other forms of diversion. The masses, who had rarely been firm supporters of the army or Rump Parliament, particularly despised the Puritan strictures against amusements on the Lord's Day, their only day of leisure. Nor had those Puritans when in power done anything truly to ease their burdens. As a result, many preferred "the publican to the Pharisee."[5] Equally foreboding for the Quakers, the politically active gentry, many of whom were to sit in the Cavalier Parliament, elected in 1661, quickly indicated through the militia, Corporation Act commissions, and grand juries, their dislike of what they perceived as the indulgent policy of the court. They were therefore anxious to accelerate the reestablishment of the Anglican Church, especially as they were well aware that their own social predominance was closely connected with that church and its vast apparatus of patronage, tithes, and leases of church lands. Those ties were to become even stronger after 1660, for the realization of that connection had been brought into sharper focus by the religious anarchy of the Interregnum. The gentry would now react rapidly and sharply against those who opposed the ecclesiastical hierarchy and the social order.[6] Another difficulty for the Quakers was the Presbyterians, whose titular leader, Richard Baxter, vehemently opposed toleration, partly out of dislike for the Quakers and other radicals, but mainly out of antipathy towards the Catholics. He favored instead an Anglican church whose doctrine would comprehend Presbyterians.

During the Restoration, a number of themes came to the fore, the inherent conflict of which amply reflected the potential duality within the law-enforcement system. First, dissent generated an atmosphere of tension and fear, seen particularly in the widespread belief that Quakers and Baptists were actively engaged in plotting. Action taken against those groups by Parliament, the Privy Council, and local law-enforcement officers was often in marked contrast to the equivocal responses of Charles II. In September 1660 the House of Lords ordered that meetings of Quakers and Anabaptists in Northamptonshire be suppressed because they were involved with Major-General John Lambert, were plotting against state and church, and were dispersing scandalous papers. The Lords feared that a residue of support remained for the ex-Commonwealth soldier and politician in the county where his humiliating capture had taken place in April 1660. In mid-December 1660 the government preempted an apparent plot led by Major Thomas White, and including Major-General Robert Overton, against the king and General George Monck, a pointed reminder of the potential danger that still remained. In reaction, the privy council complained on 2 January 1661 that the liberty allowed in the October Worcester House Declaration was being abused by "factious" persons meeting in great numbers at unusual times to conspire against the government in church and state. The solicitor general was ordered to prepare a proclamation commanding Anabaptists, Quakers, and other sectaries to forbear meeting under "pretence" of worshiping God at such unusual hours and in such large numbers. They were not to leave their parish precincts to attend any worship service in accordance with their beliefs; otherwise the justices of the peace were to proceed against them under the laws against riotous and unlawful assemblies.[7]

Only four days later a rising of Fifth Monarchists, led by Thomas Venner, a nondescript wine cooper, took place in London. Initially successful, it was soon crushed, but provoked a proclamation on 10 January prohibiting meetings of Anabaptists, Quakers, Fifth Monarchists, and others except in parochial churches or private houses. Meetings elsewhere would be considered unlawful assemblies, and those attending them were to be bound over to good behavior and to appear at quarter sessions to be tendered the Oath of Allegiance.[8]

Law-enforcement authorities reacted throughout England. A typical response was that of the West Riding quarter sessions, encouraged by William Lowther, which issued an order on 11 January, ostensibly for the West Riding, but also recommended to quarter sessions in other parts of Yorkshire. Citing the "great" assemblies of Quakers and Anabaptists where, it added, magistracy was disowned and others "seduced" to their "dangerous and blasphemous opinions," it forbade all such gatherings. Justices of the peace were to cause any offenders to find sureties for good behavior and for appearance at the following assizes or sessions. Those unable to provide such sureties were to be imprisoned as "idle, wandering people." Less than a week later, the Privy Council ordered all lords lieutenant and their officers to be particularly careful in preserving the peace and to disarm, apprehend, secure, and imprison leading dissidents.[9]

On 8 May 1661, the first day of the newly elected and Royalist dominated Cavalier Parliament, Lord Chancellor Hyde, influenced no doubt by the refusal of Quakers to take any of the oaths then in force, insisted on the imposition of some sort of oath, "tender" conscience notwithstanding. With this encouragement and in the belief that the laws as they stood were inadequate in suppressing Quaker meetings, the House of Commons acted on 26 May 1661. It was moved that the Quakers, already numerous, were growing yet more so; that despite their release from prison by proclamation, and their receipt of indulgences and fair promises from the king, they remained arrogant and dangerous seducers of the king's subjects; and that they continued to meet in great numbers. The House therefore was asked to enact a measure to cope with the refusal of Quakers, Anabaptists, and others to take oaths or to stop their unlawful assemblies. A committee was appointed and may have been provoked to harsher measures when a prominent Quaker, Edward Burrough, warned them that the Quakers would ignore any such statute and that he would personally encourage them to defy it. The committee thereupon made the penalty for a third offense the same as in the Elizabethan Conventicle Act—abjuration of the realm, or if refused, death as a felon. The House, however, concerned perhaps about Quaker martyrs, moderated this penalty after prolonged debate, and by 19 July 1661 the bill was read, passed, and sent to the Lords.[10]

The attitude of the House of Lords was already evident. It had committed for study a Quaker petition of 28 May 1661 in order that recommendations could be made "to consider of a proper remedy to cure the distempers of these people." When the committee reported on 31 May it demanded a promissory oath for the Quakers, "such a one as no good subject can or ought to refuse" and also rejected their demand to continue wearing their hats when customary respect was due, and any right to refuse the payment of tithes. But it referred to the whole house the issues of Quaker meetings and their refusal to attend church or observe Lord's Days. Numerous changes, delays, and conferences of both houses took place, during which members of Commons argued that there were other sects even more dangerous than the Quakers. Rather than attempt to name them, however, Parliament ultimately directed the bill against Quakers and "others." It received the royal assent on 2 May 1662. Rumors of yet another plot by Quakers and Baptists in October 1662 led to the arrest of substantial numbers from both groups, particularly in London and Surrey.[11]

Having been assured by Charles that he adhered to Protestantism and was ready to cooperate with Parliament in "matters of religion," the Commons introduced a conventicle bill on 27 March 1663. By 30 June it had passed its third reading, but was intentionally delayed by the House of Lords to prevent it from becoming law. Perhaps hoping to forestall action on the measure, Charles announced to the Lords in July that he had charged the judges going on circuit to punish vigorously "seditious meetings of sectaries and to convict the papists."[12]

But once again the Quakers would be victims of rumor. The government learned that an armed rising in Yorkshire would include the Quakers, although they assured Sir Thomas Gower, sheriff of Yorkshire, that they had refused to take part. They would not, however, provide Gower with the names of those who had solicited them to participate. On 5 August 1663 the government, taking the rumors seriously, informed the lords lieutenant that, as disaffected elements were continuing their frequent assemblies in which they devised plots, the militia was to be placed in a state of readiness. When the rising finally took place at Farnley Wood on 20 October 1663, a fully informed government quickly rendered it harmless.[13] Two justices in the northwest, however, were anxious to assign blame, at least in part, to the Quakers, who had generally remained aloof. Philip Musgrave and Daniel Fleming incessantly warned Whitehall about the activities of the Quakers and especially of two of their leaders, George Fox and Margaret Fell.[14] The Privy Council had also received complaints about Quaker activities in Colchester. On 27 November 1663 it ordered the earl of Oxford, lord lieutenant of Essex, to raise troops to secure and preserve the peace and to prevent unlawful assemblies of Quakers and other sectaries. On 23 March 1664 the council praised the bailiffs of Ipswich who had imprisoned John Crook, former Bedfordshire justice turned Quaker, for refusing to take the Oath of Allegiance, and ordered them to proceed according to law against Crook and other Quakers taken with him.[15]

Overall, the Privy Council remained relatively tolerant toward the Quakers during the Northern Plot agitation. The Commons, however, took the initiative and reintroduced the conventicle bill on 21 March 1664. Seditious conventicles, it was asserted, had been the genesis for the plotting that had culminated in the Farnley Wood uprising. Under pressure from the Lords, the Commons broadened the bill to prohibit meetings contrary to the liturgy "or practice" of the Church of England. The statute went into effect on 1 July 1664. Apparently the pressure exerted by justices like Musgrave and Fleming had contributed to its passage, for the Speaker of the House, Sir Edward Turner, when presenting the bill to Charles, spoke of the chronic interruptions of that body by letters, petitions, and motions "representing the unsettled condition of some counties by reason of phanaticks, sectaries, and nonconformists," who while differing "in their shapes and species," were all "no friends to the established government in church and state."[16]

Despite the new law, an informant on 20 June 1664 warned Sir Joseph Williamson that the Quakers generally, with some Anabaptists and Fifth Monarchists, were determined to meet in greater numbers than formerly and were conspiring with others "of a far different persuasion from themselves in matters of religion" to join in opposition. "I fear," he added, "that if there be a severe proceeding against them upon the Act, they will appear ten thousand in a body and demand the making good His Majesty's declarations for liberty of conscience."[17] The effective date of the Act was significant, for the assizes would be held shortly afterwards, enabling the judges to stimulate and direct enforcement at the local level. Opposition to Quakers appeared to be hardening. Charles himself doubted Quaker protestations of non-involvement in the Northern Plot. When George Fox asked Gilbert Latey, a Quaker, to assist both him and Margaret Fell in obtaining release from prison, Latey lamented that Lord Albany, whose help he had sought, claimed that "nothing could be done and that neither the king nor chancellor would do anything at all for us. Neither could any man be heard to speak for us."[18]

On 10 August 1664 the Privy Council warned the lord mayor of London that substantial numbers of Quakers and other sectaries had recently arrived in London, driven there by the actions of country justices who had disturbed and frightened them out of their usual meeting places. The newcomers were greatly augmenting the numbers of London conventicles, "the redress and suppression whereof we do likewise effectually recommend unto your especial care." London was not to become, the council stressed, "the general rendezvous and receptacle of seditious persons." On 21 September 1664 the council wrote to the sheriff of Lancashire about reports of large numbers of Quakers and other "fanatics" resorting to the imprisoned George Fox, "which we have reason to believe to be in order to the carrying on some contrivances & designs for disturbance of His Majesty's peace." The gaoler was commanded to deny any access to Fox, and to prevent him from preaching or speaking to anyone coming to the doors or windows of the gaol.[19]

The Quakers ironically saw their position further weakened when numerous Anglican clergy fled from London during the plague of 1665. Many Nonconformist clergy entered into pulpits deserted by the Anglicans and preached to the dying, while the Quakers also continued to meet, proselytize, and assist in caring for the sick. Archbishop Sheldon remained firmly at his post, but the sight of Quakers and other Dissenters carrying on religious work in London caused him to press Parliament to retaliate. He vigorously encouraged passage of an act to prevent Dissenters from preaching or teaching within five miles of any corporate or parliamentary borough, or any place where they had formerly preached. The "Five Mile Act" was passed quickly, and went into effect on 24 March 1666.[20] Although primarily directed against the Presbyterians, it could be applied to Quakers.

In 1667–68 efforts were made in Parliament to introduce measures for comprehension and toleration, moves greeted in both Houses by savage opposition led by Seth Ward, bishop of Salisbury, and Archbishop Sheldon, both fearful that the Crown might support comprehension. The Commons petitioned Charles to issue proclamations "to restrain the disorderly and tumultuous meetings of Dissenters . . . and . . . to put the laws in execution against Conventicles."[21] Since the first Conventicle Act was about to expire, many members of the Commons looked for an even tougher measure to replace it. Under intense pressure and anxious to propitiate Parliament while carrying on secret negotiations with the French, Charles issued a proclamation on 10 March 1669 calling for enforcement of the laws against conventicles.[22]

On 28 April 1669 the new conventicle bill passed the third reading; but the Lords took little action, and Parliament was adjourned by a king hoping to forestall a draconian statute while he continued his tortuous negotiations with Louis XIV. But on 8 June 1669 Archbishop Sheldon, having been assured of support by an equivocating monarch, called on the archbishop of York and all the bishops to certify to the king the name of any justice who, having received a complaint, failed to act against dissent. The clergy were also to enquire within their jurisdictions into the number of conventicles, the names of those attending, who preached and by what right, and "upon what hopes they look for impunity." Sheldon also stressed the necessity of seeking help from the civil magistrates.[23] As if to affirm his support for Sheldon, Charles issued another proclamation on 16 July 1669, charging the justices to execute the laws for suppressing conventicles, which were, he added, being held in greater numbers than formerly and were endangering the public peace.[24]

When Parliament reconvened in mid-October 1669, the Lords continued to resist any action on the new conventicle bill. After another recess, they moderated some of the more severe passages in the bill before finally submitting it to the Commons, although only after

Saturday and Sunday sessions, two formal protests, and "seemingly unprecedented visits to the House . . . by the King while the debate was in progress."[25] Under pressure from the bishops and the Commons, Charles signed the bill into law on 11 April 1670, only six weeks before signing the secret Treaty of Dover with France. On 10 June, one month after the new Conventicle Act went into effect, Charles ordered Christopher Wren, his surveyor-general, to pull down the seats and pulpits of all the dissenting meeting houses in London, Bristol, and other corporations.[26] Fortunately for the Quakers and their fellow Dissenters, Charles prorogued Parliament in April 1671 just as the Commons, having already launched severe anti-French and anti-Catholic attacks, was busy with a bill to strengthen the Conventicle Act. The Commons had also passed a bill designed to prevent Catholics from holding office, but it lapsed in the Lords because of the prorogation. Fortuitously, the impecunious Charles received additional money from Louis XIV in September 1671, ironically at the same time that he was investigating the possibility of an indulgence for Dissenters.[27]

The potential indulgence illustrates a second theme relative to dissent and the Quakers in this period. Despite the rumors of plots and an occasional abortive uprising, Charles generally pursued a policy of toleration based on his perceived rights of dispensation and suspension, to be confirmed, he hoped, by Parliament. Although toleration for Catholics was probably his long-term goal, Dissenters, including Quakers, would also benefit. But this policy was unpopular both with his supporters and with the conservative Presbyterians led by Richard Baxter. In November 1660 Charles had opposed a Parliamentary attempt, supported by moderate Presbyterians, to convert the Worcester House Declaration into a statute. The move was defeated by 183 votes to 157. Charles opposed the measure because it challenged his prerogative in ecclesiastical affairs and therefore implied that his declaration alone lacked the authority to create a modified episcopacy. Passage of the bill would have set a precedent severely restricting the Crown's ability to secure future toleration for Catholics by means of a similar declaration. Charles was also extremely annoyed at the opposition to toleration by Baxter and the more rigid Presbyterians.[28]

Despite that setback for toleration, the Quakers were still assisted by Charles, much to the chagrin of local law-enforcement officials anxious to be rid of these troublemakers. Early in November 1660 Charles received a paper signed by thirty-six Friends protesting that the Northamptonshire order by the House of Lords had been used as a pretext to beat and abuse Quakers in that county. Three days later, Charles told Friends that he had ordered the judges of assize to deal "tenderly" with them. Again on 23 November the Privy Council appointed a committee to consider the various Quaker papers and addresses, and to examine the causes and lengths of Quaker imprisonments, with an eye toward finding methods for releasing such prisoners, and toward preparing a proclamation or declaration for Charles to issue on that sect's behalf. When the committee seemed to be procrastinating in its deliberations, Thomas Moore, a prominent Quaker, appeared before the king in council on 14 December 1660. Charles promised that Quaker meetings would not be disturbed nor would Quakers be indicted for recusancy. Moore, wary that what Charles said "within these walls," would be ignored by law-enforcement officials, asked the king to signify his pleasure publicly "by proclamation or declaration." Charles reassured him that Quaker meetings would not be disturbed, so long as Friends lived "peaceably." On 17 January 1661 Charles issued a proclamation, but not the one the Quakers had envisioned, although it did prohibit any person, because of some previous irregularities, from searching a house without a warrant from the Privy Council or the lord lieutenant addressed to a constable.[29]

A week later, the council ordered the lord mayor of London and the justices of Westminster and Southwark to release, with exceptions, the Quaker prisoners within their jurisdictions. The exceptions illustrated the king's lack of understanding of Quaker principles, for he refused to release those who were "ringleaders" and "preachers," while those released were to provide sureties for good behavior. But when the lord mayor asked the council for clarification, he was told to allow the law to take its course with those Quakers imprisoned for refusal to take oaths, but that those gaoled only on suspicion were to be set free, albeit upon posting bond. Given these limitations, the gaols probably remained full. On 4 March, however, prior to the judges of assize going on circuit, the council declared that the king, troubled daily with petitions from prisoners asking for freedom, was giving the lords lieutenant discretion to discharge all those, except for ringleaders, arrested merely on suspicion of plotting.[30]

On 3 May 1661 the council expanded the king's pardon, to be published on his coronation day, to include all the Quakers. Yet when it appeared on 11 May 1661, the pardon demanded payment of fees for lodging, diet, and other essentials. Again underestimating Friends, Charles added that he expected "returns of loyalty and all due obedience," for he did not intend to give them impunity "if they shall offend in the future." Yet the council, on 17 May 1661, ordered the keeper of the Gatehouse at Westminster to release immediately six Quakers without payment of fees.[31]

Hitherto Charles's actions had been based on a mistaken premise that the Quakers resembled other dissenting sects. He assumed that they had particular ringleaders and preachers and that they would readily bind themselves to keep the peace, take oaths to gain freedom, and pay the normal fees when gaoled. Now he began to understand that they were more than a religious problem, and that he would either have to make greater concessions to empty the gaols of these criminals, or forget about including them within his envisioned toleration. Nonetheless, on 22 August 1662 he celebrated the first entrance of his queen into London by ordering the release of Quakers imprisoned in London and Middlesex for unlawful assemblies. But once again, ringleaders, preachers, and those indicted for refusing the Oath of Allegiance were excepted. When the rumors of a plot in October resulted in large-scale arrests, the government again contemplated releasing the Quakers. The Privy Council, having sent for Edward Byllynge, future governor of West New Jersey, and several other Friends, offered them a paper to sign to gain the prisoners' release, which promised on behalf of all Quakers neither to take up arms nor plot against the king. Much to the king's dismay, as well as that of many of their brethren, they refused. Charles must have wondered if his efforts were worth the trouble.[32]

On 26 December 1662 Charles took the unusual step of issuing a declaration proposing that the Crown's prerogative power of granting indulgences to individual Dissenters "should be confirmed by Parliament," possibly when the new session opened in February 1663. When he attempted to persuade Baxter that the Presbyterians should send addresses of thanks to the court for the proposed toleration, he was rebuffed. They desired comprehension, not toleration, and opposed any inclusion of Catholics within either option.[33]

On 2 January 1663 Charles ordered the release from Newgate of all those who had been "brought thither from unlawfull meetings & against whom there is no other accusation," although giving Sir Richard Browne the right "to detain such as he shall think dangerously seditious, as preachers &c." Two weeks later, the king ordered that all those imprisoned in Southwark, "having unlawfully assembled themselves under pretence of preaching & praying to the disturbance of the public peace" were also to be released, excepting those suspected of being "dangerously seditious" or "seducers of others."[34]

When members of Parliament reassembled on 18 February 1663, Charles referred to his forthcoming draft bill, stressing his wish that if the Dissenters acted "peacefully and modestly under the government," he would possess "such power of indulgence to use upon occasions as might not needlessly force them out of the kingdom, or staying here, give them cause to conspire against the peace of it."[35] To forestall opposition, a compromise court measure was introduced in the House of Lords on 23 February, bestowing on the Crown parliamentary sanction for the dispensing power that Charles claimed, a right which would have enabled him to effect both comprehension and toleration, although the bill specifically excluded Catholics. In addition, the religious qualifications of the Corporation Act were to remain in force, a concession to the political aspirations of the Anglicans in Parliament. On 27 February 1663 the king told a group of Congregational ministers that he was doing all he could, but that they should attempt to meet as modestly as possible "because there are those that will make advantage against you." He added that the Commons was fiercely antagonistic to dissent, but that he hoped the Lords would pass the measure he had just introduced. He would try to move by degrees. "I am against persecution for religion and shall be as long as I live. I would have no man punished for that that he cannot help. No man can believe but as brought to it from God."[36] As anticipated, the House of Commons proved to be hostile, but a greater blow to Charles was the resistance of the House of Lords, led by the bishops, who caused the withdrawal of the indulgence early in March 1663. An adjournment followed, at the end of which Lord Chancellor Clarendon delivered a major speech in the Lords, assuring Parliament of the king's unwavering adherence to Protestantism, and his readiness to cooperate in religious and political matters. Charles, he insisted, could be trusted in his use of the indulgence. Unwisely, however, Clarendon admitted to Parliament his own personal reservations about the bill. The measure was "discreetly shelved."[37]

Modern historians have had difficulty in discerning the motives of Charles II; contemporaries were no clearer. The critical element in law enforcement, as in politics, is perception. How did law-enforcement officials perceive the attitude of Charles toward Dissenters, and in particular toward the Quakers? Sir Daniel Fleming and Sir Philip Musgrave were typical of many justices of the peace—men from substantial landed families with a tradition of county leadership and of loyalty to the Crown. They were distinctly unhappy with the direction of royal policy. Writing on 14 January 1664 to Secretary of State Williamson, Musgrave spoke of the many Quakers indicted at Appleby quarter sessions for an illegal meeting. "They are a very dangerous people and," he stressed with some bitterness, "I hope will not have encouragement as formerly." Two days later Fleming also wrote to Williamson detailing the actions of the justices against Quakers at the sessions at Lancaster, Kendal, and Appleby. "I doubt not," he asserted, "but this proceeding against them here will break their meetings & other designs in a short time." Echoing Musgrave, he added sardonically, however, "if they procure not somewhat by way of favour from you at Whitehall which will not a little encourage them & discourage others." On 28 January 1664 Fleming again wrote to Williamson, complaining about the activities of Margaret Fell, but reiterating his frustration with other royally inspired law-enforcement agencies:

> *If we receive any encouragement from you herein, we'll tender her the oath,* & so *praemunire* her according to law, which will be the only way to take effectual course with her, who is the chief maintainer of that party in this country. *I find a coolness in several honest justices to act* against them by reason they several times have committed divers Quakers heretofore & still, when the judges came their circuit, they either picked some hole in their mittimus, & so set them at liberty, or else fined them next to nothing, whereby they cast all the odium on those who committed them. But I hope we shall have no more of this, but that every one will act heartily to his power in his proper sphere.[38]

Reiterating this theme of Whitehall support, Fleming on 19 February 1664 wrote to Sir Henry Bennett, the other secretary of state, lamenting the apparent timidity of the Lancashire justices in tendering the oath to Margaret Fell, "until I communicated your letter unto them, upon sight whereof we agreed forthwith to send for her." When she refused to take the Oath of Allegiance, she was imprisoned at Lancaster until the following assizes where, Fleming added, "we hope the judges will tender her it again that so she may be praemunired, which will . . . encourage our justices to act smartly against them."[39] Fleming was obviously concerned about the manner in which the judges intended to handle this case, as well as that of George Fox, who had also been imprisoned for the same cause. Consequently, Fleming decided to attend the assizes to justify the imprisonment of the two Quakers and to acquaint the judges with the potential political and religious ramifications for the county if they were not prosecuted at assizes. En route he met several other justices, who all agreed to wait until they heard the charge to the grand jury before speaking with the assize judges, Thomas Twisden and Christopher Turner. The charge, delivered by Twisden, disappointed Fleming and his fellow justices, who believed that it lacked severity against the sectaries. They were further disturbed by rumors that the judges had no intention of proceeding against imprisoned Quakers, including Fox and Fell, but were going to remand them to sessions. That afternoon the justices waited upon Twisden and found that he was, as suspected, unwilling to proceed against the Quakers. They acquainted him with their perception of the general condition of the county and the degree to which a refusal by the king's judges to act decisively against dissent would encourage the sectaries while simultaneously discouraging the justices. To clear themselves from charges that they were acting purely from personal pique against the Quakers or solely on their own initiative, they showed Twisden the letter from Bennett which had encouraged their actions against Margaret Fell. Twisden compromised, agreeing to proceed against Fox and Fell as examples, but leaving the other Quakers to the justices at sessions who, encouraged by such action, could then act aggressively. Content with these developments at Lancaster, Fleming traveled to the Westmorland assizes, where he witnessed the conviction of several plotters and the binding over to sessions of many others for lack of evidence. "The judges," exclaimed Fleming, "have acted here very handsomely both against the traitors and Quakers."[40]

But if Musgrave, Fleming, and the other justices believed that Charles would change his policy, they were mistaken. By 1667 the events of the previous two years had raised the possibility of relief for the Quakers and other Dissenters. The plague and the Great Fire of London had shown the Nonconformist ministers in a heroic light, particularly when compared with the Anglican clergy. Furthermore, many Englishmen blamed the fire on the Catholics, who increasingly replaced Protestant Dissenters as the focus of hate and suspicion. There were also hints that trade was suffering from persecution due to the strength of the Dissenters in the trading community. In 1667 the Dutch fleet sailed up the Medway, a critical factor in Lord Chancellor Clarendon's fall from power. His replacement, Orlando Bridgeman, although not a supporter of the Quakers, was strongly sympathetic towards the Presbyterians, while the void left by Clarendon's departure as adviser to the king was filled by a "Cabal," none of whose members was strongly sympathetic towards Anglicanism, and one of whom, Buckingham, openly favored toleration. "The Nonconformists are mighty high," wrote Samuel Pepys, "and their meetings frequented and connived at, and they do expect to have their day now soon, for my Lord Buckingham is a declared friend of them, and even of the Quakers."[41] Anglicans who were favorably disposed towards the Nonconformists also appeared more willing to speak out in favor of toleration, now that Clarendon was gone.[42]

Toleration, however, still proved elusive. The Privy Council had referred the question of Quaker prisoners in Sussex to eight of its members, including Bridgeman. Their report called for the release of all the Quaker prisoners, except those detained for tithes and failure to pay for church repairs. This mild recommendation encountered opposition within the council so severe that it was agreed to send a letter in the king's name to the Sussex justices, leaving them to distinguish between those Quakers who were "fit objects of His mercy," and those who were "ringleaders of faction in contempt of the laws." Charles himself had apparently favored the release of all the Quakers, especially those who had been praemunired and were therefore at his mercy.[43] This setback, and the failure of parliamentary efforts for toleration and comprehension, led Charles, aware of the precariousness of his restoration, ostensibly to reverse direction and to indicate his active support for the strict enforcement of the second Conventicle Act. At the same time, however, he was finalizing his secret negotiations with Louis XIV, which would, he hoped, free him from financial dependence on Parliament and enable him to press forward with a possible indulgence. By 1672, with the approach of war with Holland, Charles was particularly eager to pacify the Dissenters, who might logically view such a war with reservations, if not outright alarm. Charles was also aware that those same Dissenters, and particularly the Quakers, were defying the second Conventicle Act, despite widespread use of soldiers to disperse such meetings. Aside from his personal motives, the king's stark choice was either to continue to support the violent suppression of conventicles with the risk of serious disorder or to grant religious toleration with the constitutional and political risks such a move entailed. All members of the Cabal favored an indulgence, as did the king's Catholic brother James. On 15 March 1672, the day on which the war against Holland began, Charles issued a Declaration of Indulgence suspending the penal laws against Protestant Dissenters and Catholic recusants, and permitting Dissenters to worship publicly after obtaining licenses, and Catholics to worship in private.[44]

Two other trends also appeared to favor the Quakers. First, the Restoration witnessed the institutionalization of Nonconformity as the demarcation between Puritans and Anglicans became firmly established. The primary influences behind this development were the Baxter-led Presbyterians, the Anglican clergy, and the parliamentary Royalists. In September 1660 all the clergy ejected since the beginning of the Civil War were restored. From 25 March 1661 to 25 July 1661, the Savoy conference between the Presbyterians and the Anglican bishops unsuccessfully attempted to reach some form of accommodation, as the bishops strongly resisted any scheme permitting Presbyterian comprehension within the Anglican Church. Nonetheless, when the reactionary Cavalier Parliament assembled for the first time in May 1661, the Presbyterian members opposed the efforts by Congregationalists to secure toleration, thereby enabling the Royalists in Parliament to consolidate further their political and religious dominance. That became evident with the legislation they supported. Thus the Corporation Act imposed an Anglican sacramental test upon officers and members of municipal corporations. The Act of Uniformity denied statutory dispensing and suspending privileges to the king, and deprived all clergy who failed by August 1662 to give their public assent to the revised Book of Common Prayer. By December 1661 convocation had finished the revisions, which had been unfavorably received by the Presbyterians. Consequently, about 1,800 ministers were ultimately affected.[45] These developments, combined with the first and second Conventicle Acts and the Five Mile Act, ensured that the majority of Presbyterians and Congregationalists would be classified with the Baptists, Quakers, and other radical sects as Dissenters, or Nonconformists, deprived to a large extent of religious and political rights. That did not mean, of course, that the Quakers were supported by other Dissenters: in many respects the old Puritan divisions remained as serious as they had been during the Commonwealth. But the Quakers would not be isolated in their demands for religious freedom; nor could law-enforcement agencies focus attention solely on them.

The second development of potential benefit to the Quakers was the concern of Parliament and the Crown to limit prosecution to the normal constraints of the law. At the peak of the hysteria surrounding the Venner plot in January 1661, Charles had issued a proclamation forbidding the search of any house without a warrant to a constable either from the Privy Council or from a lord lieutenant.[46] Similarly, in the Militia Act of May 1662 Parliament permitted a lord lieutenant or two deputy-lieutenants periodically to issue search warrants for weapons to such persons as they saw fit, *provided, however,* that one was a commissioned officer and the other a civilian magistrate. Searches between sunset and sunrise were restricted geographically, nor could they be made without a warrant that specifically directed such a search. Force could be used only if resistance was encountered.[47] Although troops were used to suppress conventicles, the English government generally relied on the weapons of justice and not of men. As will be seen, however, Quaker freedom from restraint and physical abuse would remain tenuous.

II
1673–1685

Although law-enforcement officers may have been confused previously by the king's wavering attitude toward Quakers, the Declaration of Indulgence seemed to make his position clear. Quakers and other Dissenters, along with the Catholics, were to be tolerated. Parliament, however, had not been consulted. In fact, the following two decades were to see an intensification of some of the trends that had already surfaced in the first decade of Charles II's reign. The most dramatic trend—and one that deeply affected English politics until the Revolution—was the influence of English Catholicism, particularly at court. Another was the relative poverty of the Crown, a perennial problem for English monarchs, but one that enabled Parliament to retain political leverage despite its increasing opposition to the pro-French and pro-Catholic tendencies of the Crown. Another continuing theme was the division among the Dissenters, most of whom strongly opposed toleration for the Quakers. Finally, the Anglican bishops in the House of Lords remained steadfastly antagonistic toward toleration or comprehension for Dissenters, unless they themselves dictated the terms. The interaction and impact of these various forces on the English body politic prevented a consistent and uniform approach to law enforcement, while assisting the Quakers in their efforts to survive as a serious religious entity.

Although a majority of Dissenters appeared to be content with the Declaration of Indulgence, many of them, along with the Anglicans, were alarmed over the liberty permitted to Catholics. Suspicion about this proviso focused on James, duke of York, and rumors abounded that the Presbyterians intended to unite with the bishops against the Catholics. Ominously, several of the assize judges expressed doubts about the legality of the Declaration, while ardent Royalists like Daniel Fleming were dismayed at what was viewed as the greatest prerogative act "as hath been done this good while."[48] With the Dutch War going badly, and the accession of William of Orange raising the embarrassing specter of Charles waging war against his own nephew, English public opinion, assisted by Dutch propaganda, came to view the war and Indulgence as part of an international Catholic conspiracy. The reemergence of virulent anti-Catholicism among his subjects prompted Charles to postpone meeting with Parliament as long as possible, but without dissolving it, for fear that a new Parliament might reflect negative public opinion. His precarious finances finally compelled him to recall Parliament in February 1673. But the Commons refused to consider any supply, preferring instead to denounce the Declaration, particularly its provision for Catholics, as an illegal and dangerous extension of royal power. The Dissenters in Parliament, a distinct minority, advocated statutory action either to establish toleration or comprehension, to give parliamentary sanction to the Indulgence, or at least to suspend some of the penal laws temporarily. Commons initially voted that "penal laws cannot be suspended but by act of parliament." But fearful of driving the Dissenters into an alliance with the Catholics, the Commons next adopted "the liberal policy which they had rejected in 1668" and passed a bill for the ease of Protestant Dissenters. Nonetheless, the Quakers were effectively excluded.[49] On 3 March 1673 Charles, under duress, issued a proclamation banishing priests and calling for the enforcement of the laws against Catholics.

Five days later he reluctantly rescinded the Declaration of Indulgence. The Commons, meanwhile, passed the Test Act, essentially excluding Catholics from holding office under the Crown.[50]

To the dismay of the Dissenters, the House of Lords, impelled by the bishops and anxious to sabotage any efforts on behalf of dissent, seriously amended the bill for ease to Protestant Dissenters. Charles also opposed the bill, because it failed to provide toleration for Catholics, while uniting the more conservative Protestant elements. Preferring that the Presbyterians and other Dissenters remain outside the Anglican Church, he adjourned parliament and the bill died. Frustrated, Charles now moved towards an alliance with the earl of Danby, whose policies were encouraging the intolerant Anglicanism that the Dissenters opposed. Charles's support for the Catholics had been further undermined by the forced resignations under the Test Act of Lord Treasurer Clifford and James, duke of York. The king, therefore, ordered the enforcement of the penal laws and the exclusion of Catholics from his presence.[51]

Constant maneuvering by the king and Parliament had accomplished little for the Quakers or for other Dissenters. But the confusion at the pinnacle of the legal system was doubtless reflected at all lower levels, with the result that active "persecution" appeared to lag during the 1670s, particularly as the shifting alliances and chronic bickering continued at Whitehall and Westminster. His pro-Catholic, pro-French policy in disarray, Charles appointed Danby as lord treasurer. The Cabal disintegrated, and the earl of Shaftesbury, now a fierce defender of the Dissenters, assumed the role of a virtual opposition leader in the House of Lords. Along with Buckingham and Halifax, he campaigned for the dissolution of Parliament, a goal not supported by the Commons, whose members could lose their seats in a new election. Parliament met again early in 1674, but when the Lords introduced another comprehension bill, it was prorogued by Charles on 24 February 1674. He was not prepared to see the Catholics further isolated. The House of Commons, however, had talked of limitations on the Crown, had debated the possibility of judges' holding tenure by good behavior, and had launched savage attacks on several of the king's ministers, all of which indicated the further deterioration of relations with the Crown.[52]

Parliament did not meet again until 13 April 1675, by which time Danby had begun to revive the policies attempted by the Crown from

1669 to 1671—encouragement of religious persecution combined with increased organization of the king's supporters in the Commons. Suddenly the Dissenters were courted by the duke of York, who hoped to enlist their help in securing the succession and in repealing the Test Act. In return, the duke agreed to encourage Charles to issue a new Declaration of Indulgence and to dissolve Parliament; a new Parliament would, he hoped, support toleration. At the very least, he was anxious to siphon off Dissenter support for any anti-Catholic policy.[53]

In any event, the only positive result was a royal pardon for Bristol Dissenters under prosecution by Bishop Guy Carleton. Rumors circulated of an intended proclamation pardoning all religious transgressions, but Danby cautioned Charles against this. At the end of October 1674, acting on Danby's initiative, Charles convened at Lambeth a conference of the bishops to give him "advice" on religion, but unlike previous conferences of this kind during his reign, he neither invited nor consulted with the Nonconformist divines. Rather than the rumored proclamation pardoning religious offenses, the conference called for the existing laws against Catholics and Dissenters to be put into execution, and demanded that Charles assert publicly that his licenses, long since recalled, lacked either his authority or encouragement. On 3 February 1675 the beleaguered king issued an order in council embodying these recommendations. Furthermore, in the spring session of Parliament Danby, with the king's support, proposed a test designed to eliminate from Parliament anyone who was not a loyal Anglican, but this effort fell when a jurisdictional dispute led to the prorogation of Parliament. Despite the increasing pressure from James for a dissolution, Charles kept Parliament prorogued until 15 February 1677.[54]

By that time, Charles was profoundly disgusted with Parliament, and in particular with the Presbyterian members who had opposed the French alliance, toleration for Catholics, and the prerogatives of the Crown. Moreover, they had supported, with one exception, a petition in the Lords on 20 November 1675 calling for the dissolution of Parliament. A positive note for the Quakers, however, was the gradual ascendancy within the Presbyterians of moderates who favored toleration. Charles, meanwhile, was also tinkering with the judiciary. His dismissal of William Ellis in June 1676 was the first of several attempts to install judges who would be more amenable to Stuart dynastic policy. This could be beneficial for the Quakers, if the king called on his judges to support a policy of nonenforcement of the penal laws or to rule on the constitutionality of Declarations of Indulgence. Alternatively, a royal policy of strict enforcement of the penal laws might devastate the Quakers. When Parliament reassembled in February 1677, it sharply denounced royal interference with the judiciary.[55]

Unfortunately for Friends, the Commons was also examining enforcement of the recusancy laws, having requested the Exchequer as early as 1671 to take action against those certified as convicted recusants. At that time it was discovered that the Exchequer had received since 1660 the grand total of £147 15*s.* 7*d.* in recusant fines. A list of convicted recusants was drawn up, from which it was calculated that the Exchequer had suffered a shortfall of £5,000,000 in recusant revenue.[56] But local law-enforcement officers were uncertain about the proper method of proceeding with recusancy prosecutions. Sir John Lowther, having examined prosecutions in York, Lancaster, and other areas, believed in April 1674 that "there will be much difference in the method of action in the various counties, and that the judges are not so clear in their directions as was expected." Sir Philip Musgrave called for a conference of Westmorland justices to agree on a common course of action. Sir Daniel Fleming, annoyed that the justices in his area had "no public directions how to act against dissenters," wrote to Lowther that they had decided to encourage the constables and churchwardens to present lists of recusants and to provide sworn testimony to the grand jury. It was hoped to prosecute such recusants for £20 per month or forfeiture of two-thirds of their estates. Lowther, in return, expressed the approval of the justices in his area to that approach, and that they were resolved to proceed against recusants by means of the statute 23 Eliz., c. 1, "which is in general terms and not confined to popish recusants." This move was a severe blow to the Quakers.[57]

Enforcement of the recusancy laws also interested the earl of Danby, desirous to use the extra revenue generated from fines to provide salaries for sheriffs, justices of the peace, and militia officers, making them offices of profit as well as trust, while strengthening the position of the king, who had them in his disposal. Had Danby succeeded in this effort, he might well have changed the entire nature of English law enforcement. In 1674 he ordered the officers of the Exchequer to prepare lists of all convicted recusants, which lists would be sent to commissioners in each county, chosen from among members of Parliament and justices of the peace, who were then to confiscate two-thirds of each recusant's lands for the king. Richard Derham was appointed receiver of recusant revenues. This move actually forced the duke of York, interested in gaining Dissenter support, to obtain pardons in December 1674 for a number of convicted Dissenters. But in February 1676 Charles ordered the assize judges to give in charge the enforcement of the laws against recusants *and* conventiclers. Only four months later, complaining that prosecution of recusants was not being adequately carried out, Danby reverted to the "older practice of sending processes to sheriffs."[58] His grand scheme for salaried law-enforcement officers was in tatters.

In February 1677 the House of Commons introduced an unsuccessful bill calling for intensification of the existing recusancy laws. The Commons had defeated a bill from the Lords that would have distinguished between Catholics who registered themselves and would be liable to a small penalty, from those who did not register and would be liable to the oaths and severe penalties. Relations between Crown and Commons remained seriously strained, exacerbated by the fears of the opposition, ironically now in the pay of Louis XIV, that the thirty thousand troops which had been raised ostensibly for the war would be used by Charles against them. Suspicion predominated on both sides. The Commons granted a small supply, and when Danby attempted to obtain further revenues in late June, he was defeated without a division, a serious personal blow.[59]

Despite these intrigues and stratagems, the status of the Quakers had not appreciably improved, for the power of the opposition was simply one of obstruction. Its leaders failed in their attempt to bring in a bill distinguishing popish recusants from Protestant Dissenters so that the latter, particularly Quakers and Baptists, would not be prosecuted under statutes directed against Catholics. The effort was led by several Presbyterians who were increasingly aware of the need to encourage other Dissenters to assist the opposition on the hustings and thereby augment their parliamentary numbers, rather than have them continue to rely on French bribery. Charles, exasperated, finally dissolved the Cavalier Parliament on 30 December 1678, only six days after the duke of Buckingham had obtained leave in the House of Lords to bring in a bill of indulgence for Protestant Dissenters.[60] Worse still for Charles, anti-Catholicism was to receive tremendous impetus in August and September 1678 with the "revelations" of Titus Oates about a "Popish Plot." The repercussions were immediate; prior to dissolution, parliament passed the second Test Act, precipitating the downfall of Danby and his repressive policies.

The next few years were to be critical for the Quakers and other Dissenters as the country focused its venom on the Catholics. From 1679 to 1681 Charles abandoned his pro-Catholic policy and reluctantly agreed with Parliament to enforce anti-Catholic legislation. Given the propensity of legal officials to mistake them for Catholics and the general confusion over statutory terminology regarding recusants, Quakers became liable to severe prosecution. Recusants were ordered to remain within five miles of their dwellings, and were to be tendered the Oaths of Allegiance and Supremacy. The machinery for the collection of recusancy fines and the takeover of recusant estates was completely overhauled, and the commissions of the peace systematically purged as more zealous anti-Catholics were appointed. In April 1679 the Commons actively encouraged its members to provide lists of suspected papists for insertion into a bill for their easier conviction.[61]

While the Crown's efforts against the Catholics represent a new theme, the resolve of Parliament to assert itself against the Crown represents an old theme with a new twist. The major preoccupations of the three "Exclusion" Parliaments were to identify and prosecute those involved in the "Plot" and to pass a bill excluding James, duke of York, from the succession. While toleration for the Dissenters was also a priority, this would only become clear in the "Short" Parliament (October 1680–January 1681). Most Dissenters and their parliamentary allies, while generally unsympathetic to the Quakers, were concerned about enforcement of the recusancy laws against Protestants. Because Charles needed Dissenter support for a toleration which would include the besieged Catholics, and because he feared a rapprochement between the Dissenters and the duke of Monmouth, he temporarily addressed their concern. On 1 July 1680 the assize judges were instructed by the lord chancellor in council to "distinguish in their circuits betwixt the Popish & Protestant Dissenters" and to "put the laws against the former in strict execution, but be more indulgent to the latter." Moreover, he added, while not interfering with due process, they were not to encourage prosecution of those Dissenters who lived in a quiet and orderly fashion, for some who opposed the common prayer had done and would continue to do the king good service. "Various are the glosses made upon this instruction," observed Roger Morrice, a prominent Presbyterian, "by persons of various interests and affections."[62] In January 1681, following this lead, the Short Parliament moved to enact a bill distinguishing Dissenters from popish recusants, and also resolved that "the prosecution of Dissenters on penal laws against papists is at this time grievous to the people, a weakening of the Protestant religion and dangerous to the peace of the kingdom." It then endeavored to pass bills of comprehension and toleration, to repeal the Elizabethan Conventicle Act, and to investigate royal packing of the judiciary. A Commons committee soon recommended that Chief Justices North and Scroggs, along with Justice Jones and Baron Weston, be impeached for illegal and arbitrary proceedings.[63]

Ironically, as Parliament finally shifted towards the Dissenters and the principle of toleration, Charles reversed direction. He was annoyed at the support given by many Dissenters to the attempt of the parliamentary Whigs to exclude his brother from the succession, and he was also smarting from the lack of Dissenter support for the Catholics. Joining with the bishops, Charles ordered the clerk of Parliament to "forget" to present for his signature the bill repealing the Elizabethan Conventicle Act, thus disposing of it without the opprobrium a veto would have caused. He again accommodated the bishops by dissolving Parliament before comprehension or toleration had been enacted. On 19 January 1681 he ordered the assize judges to enforce the recusancy laws against papists *and others*, and to direct assize grand juries accordingly.[64]

The final Exclusion Parliament met at Oxford in March 1681 for only one week, during which time it reintroduced the comprehension bill and the repeal of the Elizabethan Conventicle Act, questioning why the latter had not been signed into law. A dissolution came swiftly. Charles now took the offensive, reinstituting an authoritarian, Cavalier policy along the lines formerly advocated by Danby, but this time without involving Parliament, which was not to meet for the remainder of his reign. The Tories, having remained loyal to the king and his brother, reaped their rewards—a monopoly of places, persecution of Dissenters and Whigs, and no open favoritism of Catholics.[65] The Crown, without the countervailing influence of Parliament, would finally provide law-enforcement officers with the firm direction deemed essential to crush dissent. This period, in fact, would be the most precarious one for the Quakers and other Dissenters.

By the spring of 1681 a "purge" had begun of the commissions of the peace. Informers came forward to discredit the Whigs. In June 1681, in response to requests from grand juries, Charles ordered the suppression of conventicles and seditious meetings. The government also attempted once again to encourage enforcement of the recusancy laws, but this time primarily against Dissenters. Towards the end of 1681 the Privy Council ordered local magistrates to strictly enforce the Corporation Act; consequently, county government officials—the lords lieutenant, deputy lieutenants, and justices of the peace—were "comprehensively purged." With the seemingly total support of the bishops, the king and his Tory supporters attempted full implementation of the laws against religious dissent. The Crown also embarked on a conscious and successful effort to gain control of corporation charters, enabling it to appoint the sheriffs, who in turn nominated the juries that would try Dissenters and Whigs. The entire apparatus of recusancy enforcement and collection was again revamped. In July 1682 it was even suggested that more money would flow into the Exchequer by introducing a discretionary levy of less than the normal penalty of £20 per month, thereby allowing for a steady mulcting, rather than the immediate ruin of the offenders. The main difficulty, of course, was to ensure that the Exchequer actually obtained the money collected by receivers and sheriffs. When Bristol Dissenters attempted to sue out writs of *certiorari* to remove recusancy indictments into King's Bench, the government intervened, with Attorney-General Robert Sawyer writing to Alderman Richard Hart on 10 January 1682 that such actions "if permitted, would be a great hindrance to the justice of the nation." He therefore enclosed "procedendos" whereby Hart and his colleagues could "proceed upon the indictment to a more speedy conviction of the defendant than the proceedings of the courts at Westminster will permit." If any writs were sent from Westminster to remove such indictments, he continued, "so soon as the clerk of your court gives me notice by letter, you shall have them superseded."[66] In March 1682 the assize judges were instructed to prosecute "fanatics" as well as papists, and in November the council instructed local law-enforcement officers to return the names of all those who failed to attend church and take the sacrament. The Anglican hierarchy was also busy. In March 1683 they instructed the Middlesex churchwardens to present every person between the ages of sixteen and sixty who failed to receive the sacrament on the following Easter Sunday. Ministers were to present any churchwarden who neglected his duty.[67]

As early as March 1684, however, there were indications that Charles was beginning to relent, for it was reported that the assize judges had received instructions to prevent the prosecution of Dissenters on those recusancy statutes which imposed the £20 per month penalty. It was also rumored that all Exchequer processes against recusants, particularly those at Bristol (including many Quakers), had been suspended.[68] Certainly, by the autumn of 1684 Charles's flirtation with anti-Catholicism appeared over, for he was probably instrumental in Sir George Jeffreys' attempt actively to assist Catholic recusants, a move that would also have benefited the Quakers. While riding the Northern assize circuit, Jeffreys had ordered undersheriffs and bailiffs to compile for his use complete lists of all those committed for recusancy. Upon returning, he told Charles in council that the judges had found many Catholics in prison. Standing up with the recusant rolls before him, he introduced a motion calling on Charles to use his pardon to discharge all recusancy convictions. Although supported by James, duke of York, and by the earl of Sunderland, Jeffreys was checked by the conservative Anglican Lord Keeper Sir Francis North, who argued that many of those imprisoned were Dissenters and not Catholics. He also forced Jeffreys to admit that while some of those on the lists were imprisoned, many simply lay under sentence of commitment. Jeffreys countered that they could, in fact, be taken up by every peevish sheriff or magistrate and would only gain freedom at the cost of large fees (an argument often advanced by the Quakers). North proposed instead that Charles could pardon individuals if he felt satisfied of their loyalty, but that the fees should be paid, since recusants were effectively compensated by their exclusion from serving in chargeable offices. He could not in all conscience, he added, affix the Great Seal to a general pardon. Nothing was done.[69]

Charles was not to be denied. In January 1685, while disclaiming any intention to extend toleration to Catholics, he admitted having given orders "to pardon the forfeitures of the penal laws to some of that religion whose loyalty he was satisfied in, and that he might extend that grace to others who could get sufficient certificates to have the like pretence to it." On 15 January a pardon for all trespasses, treasons, praemunires, pains, and penalties was, in fact, issued to a lengthy list of persons, including many Catholics. But Lord Keeper North apparently continued to block any formal toleration for Catholics.[70]

III
1685–1688

The sudden death of Charles II in February 1685 and the accession of his Catholic brother as James II led to an acceleration in attempts to aid the Catholics, even at the expense of the Dissenters. A pivotal factor would be the attitude of Parliament, which was now summoned for the first time in four years. It proved to be as firmly Anglican as any since 1660, due to the political quietism of the Dissenters since 1681 and their inability to vote, many of them having been imprisoned or eliminated by strict enforcement of the Corporation and the Five Mile Acts. Moreover, the changes in electoral procedures for burgesses in almost ninety borough charters proved to be highly effective against Dissenters, while the discrediting of the Whigs, and the aggressive electioneering of James II, Sunderland, and the assize judges also contributed.[71]

The new king's initial actions seemed to benefit the Quakers, however. Anxious to assist Catholics, James on 27 February 1685 ordered that those imprisoned for refusing to take the oaths or for failing to attend church were to be released if they would enter into recognizances for good behavior, and could produce certificates that either they or their nearest relatives had suffered for their loyalty in the Civil Wars. On 19 March and 14 April 1685 Edward Ange, the manager of recusant revenues, was ordered to delay the execution of writs that had already been sent out, while on 11 May came the first of many orders to the lord treasurer to issue stays of process, thereby halting the recovery of fines due from specified "loyal" recusants. On 6 June 1685 James ordered Ange to see that fines not yet paid into the Exchequer were repaid to the recusants. But the law was to be firmly enforced against those recusants who failed to produce such certificates.[72] Despite their uncertain loyalty to the king during the Civil Wars, the Quakers attempted to secure the necessary certificates. But Monmouth's rebellion in the summer of 1685 was a sharp setback for Dissenters in general in their quest for toleration, since it intensified the king's lingering resentment over the attempts of the Whigs, with Dissenter support, to exclude him. But the unlikely prospect of a Catholic king and Anglican Parliament agreeing on religion soon became evident, and on 20 November 1685 Parliament was prorogued, ostensibly for three months. It did not meet again until James had been exiled.[73]

Once again, the Quakers and other Dissenters found themselves in the middle of the struggle over toleration for Catholics, as James maneuvered between the Anglicans and the Dissenters, angling for support from each in turn against the other, but generally meeting with suspicion or outright hostility. For once, the Quakers were well positioned, as William Penn and Robert Barclay, two of their most substantial intellectual leaders, were both welcome at court; Penn, in fact, was to play a critical role in shaping James's attitude toward toleration of dissent.

James at first had hoped to influence Parliament to repeal the laws against Catholics while retaining those against Dissenters; therefore the government in 1685 and early in 1686 "persecuted dissenters but not Catholics and distinguished between 'loyal' and 'disloyal' religious nonconformity."[74] But the king abandoned this policy as his disillusionment with the Anglicans, and particularly with their bishops, increased. The greater his awareness that toleration for Catholics was anathema to the Anglicans, the more his approach towards the Dissenters eased. Nor was it simply opportunism, for with the continued opposition of the Tory gentry to toleration and the insults by Anglican clergy towards his religion, James grew to believe that religious persecution had prompted the often disloyal behavior of Dissenters; as a corollary, he also realized that once persecution was ended, the Dissenters would become loyal subjects. Ironically, James concluded that religious toleration was not only feasible, but inherently correct. Once having arrived at this decision, he firmly supported liberty of conscience, a position he upheld "with every sign of sincerity," until the end of his reign.[75]

While James moved cautiously toward toleration, 1686 proved to be the climactic year for the Quakers and other Dissenters. In December 1685 Edward Ange had been put in charge of revenues from conventiclers and excommunicates as well as recusants, and James had again ordered that those who failed to obtain loyalty certificates were to be prosecuted. This policy, begun by Charles II, was a shrewd method of aiding Catholics without appearing to do so, since most Tory magistrates would equate dissent with disloyalty in the Civil Wars, while Catholics were more likely to have been loyal, and therefore more capable of obtaining certificates. James was not yet courting the Dissenters actively; in fact "more conventiclers were convicted in

Middlesex in six months in 1686 than there were Papists convicted of recusancy in 1679, the worst year of the Plot."[76]

Nonetheless, in February 1686 it was rumored that an attorney who had been hired earlier by Lord Treasurer Hyde to prosecute all offenders listed in the books of Doctors' Commons was refunding compositions he had received from the Catholics for the previous six months, and had also been given the power to compound with the Dissenters. This development was followed in March 1686 by a general pardon from James, which included hundreds of Quakers and which owed a great deal to William Penn, who had received a similar order in favor of his family only six days earlier. In May the king dispatched a warrant to the keeper of Wood Street Compter, a London prison, discharging twelve Dissenters imprisoned for various ecclesiastical offenses. Neither they nor their families, it instructed, were to be prosecuted further without approval from the king.[77]

In June 1686, in *Godden v Hales*, the judges upheld the dispensing power of the Crown, and by July it was being reported that the judges had directions to enter a *nolle prosequi*, or a declaration of no further prosecution, if any Quaker or papist were presented for recusancy. By the following month, most Dissenters were able to meet freely if they petitioned James for relief, and it was widely assumed that on petition any Dissenters, including Quakers, could secure dispensations from the penal laws. By November so many congregations were petitioning for dispensations that a licensing office was established where payment of 50s. would secure a dispensation for an entire family against all proceedings for recusancy and Nonconformity, as well as a license to worship freely in the future. Proceedings that were superseded against Quakers and other recusants referred not to loyalty but to "good testimony of peaceable behaviour." One apparent obstacle to thorough implementation of this policy was Lord Rochester at the Treasury, who as late as 2 December 1686 was pressing Leicestershire justices for the king's share of conventicle fines. He was dismissed at the end of that month. In January 1687 James continued to stop proceedings against conventiclers and began to refund some of the fines; by February they were meeting openly, a practice that, for the Quakers, was simply a continuation of what they had always done. On 8 March 1687 James ordered that all proceedings against Catholics were to cease, regardless of whether or not they produced loyalty certificates.

Meanwhile, throughout the summer and fall of 1686, a committee of the Privy Council had been inspecting the commissions of the peace. In February 1687 new commissions were issued: of 455 justices inserted, almost sixty-four percent were Catholics.[78]

As a counterpoint to royal toleration, the leaders of the Anglican Church were promoting the severest prosecution of Dissenters. Roger Morrice believed that many of the bishops, resigned to toleration for Catholics, were determined to isolate the Dissenters. He was thus bemused at the specter of Dissenters, having received dispensations from the Crown, being prosecuted by the Church while Catholics were not. "Cross winds sometimes raise waves that break the force of one another and the ship is thereby preserved; sometimes they presage a tempest that destroys it when those winds center in a dangerous quarter." The spiritual courts, he added, were busy receiving presentments and issuing citations and processes, while injunctions had been sent by the bishops to ministers in their dioceses calling upon them strictly to require all churchwardens to present those who failed to attend church or who had not received the sacrament the previous Easter.[79]

Oblivious to the opposition of the Anglican hierarchy, James was determined to move beyond the mere issuance of dispensations to groups of Catholics and Dissenters; he desired to suspend the penal laws and Test Acts altogether. Dispensations were, after all, a time-consuming and cumbersome procedure, involving many people, much paperwork, and stiff fees from the beneficiaries. Some magistrates might, in any case, question the validity of such dispensations. On 18 March 1687, therefore, James announced his intention of granting a general liberty of conscience. It was rumored that William Penn had a large part in drafting it; at the minimum, it "certainly . . . reflected his views."[80] On 4 April 1687 the Declaration of Indulgence was issued, which not only permitted religious toleration, but also gave the Dissenters time to recover money which had been levied against them. On 4 June 1687 the lords commissioners of the Treasury ordered the barons of the Exchequer to discharge all Catholics whose fines had been certified to the Exchequer. It was believed, wrote Roger Morrice, that the Dissenters were to receive the same favor. In the interim, James ordered that processes for recusancy already begun but not yet certified should be superseded.[81] In December 1687 commissioners were named to inquire into sums levied on recusants since 1677 and not yet accounted for. New commissions were issued several times during 1688, some of which operated with reasonable efficiency; but they gradually ceased. The Exchequer was still attempting to extract money from the various receivers of fines whose office had been abolished in 1684. The sheriffs, of course, had also collected large sums, while some recusants had compounded with the Exchequer, that is, agreed to pay a smaller sum to discharge a debt. There was no question, however, of repaying money which had already been accounted for in the Exchequer.[82] Nonetheless, the Declaration of Indulgence of 1687, reissued in 1688, and followed in 1689 by the Toleration Act, effectively ended the severer prosecutions of Quakers and other Dissenters.

In retrospect, it is apparent that the late Stuart kings failed to provide firm and consistent leadership against Quakers or religious dissent in general. Instead, they had been ambivalent and opportunistic; and their basic lack of agreement with Parliament and the church about religious policy must have conveyed a sense of despair to law-enforcement officers anxious for a clear policy. Parliament had also shifted direction on more than one occasion. It appeared that only the Anglican Church, with its sharp bias against both Dissenters and Catholics, had acted consistently. Yet what is not clear is how this ambiguity in leadership either hindered or furthered enforcement of the law against criminal Quaker activities. Quaker records indicate that the authorities often exceeded the letter of the law in prosecuting them, engaging in illegal, unethical, and sometimes brutal tactics.

Notes

1. Miller, *Popery and Politics*, 110.
2. This situation was evident in the numerous plots in the early years of the Restoration. See Richard L. Greaves, *Deliver Us from Evil: The Radical Underground in Britain, 1660–1663* (New York, 1986).
3. The Declaration of Breda, 4 April 1660, and the Worcester House Declaration, 25 October 1660.
4. Fox, *Journal*, ed. Nickalls, 388–91. Fox had been arrested as a disturber of the peace and a conspirator (*Journal*, 379).
5. Douglas Lacey, *Dissent and Parliamentary Politics in England 1661–1689* (New Brunswick, 1969), 8, 11; Godfrey Davies, *The Restoration of Charles II 1658–1660* (London, 1955), 332, 359.
6. I. M. Green, *The Re-Establishment of the Church of England 1660–1663* (Oxford, 1978), 180, 194, 199–200.
7. John Whitehead et al., *This to the King* (London, 1660; w1983); Davies, *Restoration of Charles II*, 335–36; Greaves, *Deliver Us from Evil*, 27–29, 35–40; PRO: P.C. 2/55/48. The Privy Council was the primary executive body

under the Crown. Meeting at Whitehall usually two or three times each week, it normally comprised the great officeholders, the princes of the blood, and other leading nobles, all of whom served at the pleasure of the king. The number who attended generally varied between twelve and twenty-five, tending to be larger when the king was present. Although reflecting the king's own predilections, the important status of its members could help to influence significant decisions. But increasingly after 1660 critical decisions often were arrived at prior to Council meetings by deliberations between the king and a small group of trusted advisers, and were simply rubber-stamped by the whole Council. This development increasingly alarmed Parliament, anxious to keep decision-making as public as possible in order to protect its own power, and was yet another factor in the complex and confusing realm of legislation and enforcement. See Edward Raymond Turner, *The Privy Council of England in the Seventeenth and Eighteenth Centuries 1603–1784*, 2 vols. (Baltimore, 1927–28), vol. 1, chaps. 15–16.

8. See Greaves, *Deliver Us from Evil*, 49–53; Steele, ed., *Bibliography of Royal Proclamations*, 393. Ironically, two days before Venner's rising, the Council had ordered all lords lieutenant to tender the oaths to any persons known to be disaffected to the government or who had disturbed the peace. They were also to give sureties for good behavior (PRO: P.C. 2/55/49–50).

9. PRO: S.P. 29/28/45I; P.C. 2/55/56; see also Greaves, *Deliver Us from Evil*, 54–56.

10. Frank Bate, *The Declaration of Indulgence, 1672: A Study in the Rise of Organized Dissent* (London, 1908), 21; Barclay, ed., *Letters of Early Friends*, 99–105 and n.

11. Barclay, ed., *Letters of Early Friends*, 109–11n; Besse, *Sufferings*, 1:389–90; Ellis Hookes to Margaret Fell, 28.viii [October].1662, London (Swarthmore MSS, 1:44); Greaves, *Deliver Us from Evil*, 106.

12. Green, *Church of England*, 222; Lacey, *Dissent and Parliamentary Politics*, 53; Bate, *Declaration of Indulgence*, 40; *Journal of the House of Lords*, 11:580.

13. Anonymous to Sir Henry Bennett, 24 July 1663 (PRO: S.P. 29/77/50); Gower to Bennett, 1 August 1663, York (S.P. 29/78/6); PRO: P.C. 2/56/253–54; see also Greaves, *Deliver Us from Evil*, chap. 6.

14. See, for example, PRO: S.P. 29/83/84; 29/85/85; 29/90/38; 29/90/86; 29/90/100; 29/91/68.

15. PRO: P.C. 2/56/325; 2/57/28; see also P.C. 2/56/318.

16. Bate, *Declaration of Indulgence*, 45; Edward Pearse, *The Conformists Fourth Plea* (London, 1683; P975), 68.

17. PRO: S.P. 29/99/109.

18. Mary Fell to Margaret Fell, 27.iv [June].1664, Mile-End (Gibson MSS, 5:55); Latey to Fox and Fell, 1.vii [September].1664, London (Gibson MSS, 1:201).

19. PRO: P.C. 2/57/95, 119.

20. Braithwaite, *Second Period*, 52.

21. Roger Thomas, "Comprehension and Indulgence," in *From Uniformity to Unity, 1662–1962*, ed. Owen Chadwick and Geoffrey Nuttall (London, 1962), 198–201, 204; Lacey, *Dissent and Parliamentary Politics*, 56–58, 287.

22. Miller, *Popery and Politics*, 106–7; Thomas, "Comprehension and Indulgence," 202; Braithwaite, *Second Period*, 54; *CSPD, 1667–1668*, 276. See also Thomas Salthouse to Margaret Fell, 21.i [March].1668/9, Somersetshire (Swarthmore MSS, 1:102).

23. Lacey, *Dissent and Parliamentary Politics*, 288; Thomas Salthouse to Margaret Fell, 19.iii [May].1668, London (Swarthmore MSS, 1 : 103); British Library, Add. MSS 19,399, fol. 107.

24. *CSPD,1668−1669*, 412.

25. Lacey, *Dissent and Parliamentary Politics*, 60. For the attitude of at least one prominent justice on the necessity for a new Conventicle Act, see Leicester, *Charges at Quarter Sessions*, ed. Halcrow, 69.

26. Miller, *Popery and Politics*, 114; Lacey, *Dissent and Parliamentary Politics*, 289.

27. Lacey, *Dissent and Parliamentary Politics*, 63; Miller, *Popery and Politics*, 115−16; Thomas, "Comprehension and Indulgence," 207−8.

28. Green, *Church of England*, 127; see also Lacey, *Dissent and Parliamentary Politics*, 13, 269.

29. John Whitehead et al., *To King and Council*; PRO: P.C. 2/55/28; Swarthmore MSS, 4 : 196; Steele, ed., *Bibliography of Royal Proclamations*, 394.

30. PRO: P.C. 2/55/59, 62, 81.

31. PRO: P.C. 2/55/110, 113; Steele, ed., *Bibliography of Royal Proclamations*, 397.

32. Penney, ed., *Extracts from State Papers*, 150; Ellis Hookes to Margaret Fell, 25.ix [November].1662, London (PRO: S.P. 29/63/70).

33. Green, *Church of England*, 220; Lacey, *Dissent and Parliamentary Politics*, 52.

34. PRO: S.P. 44/10, 27; S.P. 29/67/39. Forty-seven Friends remained imprisoned at the White Lion in Southwark, perhaps owing to a broad interpretation of "dangerously seditious" or "seducers of others." On 29 January they petitioned Charles, who ordered the release of all those charged simply with meeting (S.P. 29/67/133).

35. Quoted in Bate, *Declaration of Indulgence*, 38.

36. Lacey, *Dissent and Parliamentary Politics*, 52−53; BL: Add. MSS 4107, fols. 16−18b.

37. Bate, *Declaration of Indulgence*, 38−39; Green, *Church of England*, 221−24.

38. Musgrave to Williamson, 14 January 1663/4, Hartley Castle; Fleming to Williamson, 16 January 1663/4, Kendal; Fleming to Williamson, 28 January 1663/4, Rydal (PRO: S.P. 29/90/86, 100; S.P. 29/91/68).

39. Fleming to Bennett, 19 February 1663/4 (PRO: S.P. 29/93/23).

40. Fleming to Williamson, 21 March 1663/4, Appleby (PRO: S.P. 29/95/2).

41. *The Diary of Samuel Pepys*, ed. Robert Latham and William Matthews, 11 vols. (Berkeley and Los Angeles, 1970−83), 8 : 584.

42. Lacey, *Dissent and Parliamentary Politics*, 55−56; Thomas, "Comprehension and Indulgence," 196.

43. East Sussex Record Office, Lewes: Sussex QM Sufferings (SOF 1, 79). Identical letters were sent at the same time to justices in at least two other counties (see HMC, *Various Collections*, "County of Wilts," 149−50; W. J. Hardy and William Le Hardy, eds., *Hertfordshire County Records*, 7 vols. [Hertford, 1905−31], 1 : 190).

44. Miller, *Popery and Politics*, 116−17; Thomas, "Comprehension and Indulgence," 207−9; Lacey, *Dissent and Parliamentary Politics*, 64.

45. Braithwaite, *Second Period*, 5, 7; Whiting, *Studies in English Puritanism*, chap. 1.

46. See n. 29, preceding.

47. 13 Chas. II, st. 1, c. 6 [italics added].

48. Thomas, "Comprehension and Indulgence," 210; Miller, *Popery and Politics*, 117–18.

49. J. P. Kenyon, *Stuart England* (London, 1978), 207–8; Lacey, *Dissent and Parliamentary Politics*, 66–67; Western, *Monarchy and Revolution*, 180–81.

50. Miller, *Popery and Politics*, 125; Braithwaite, *Second Period*, 86; Kenyon, *Stuart England*, 208.

51. Thomas, "Comprehension and Indulgence," 212–13; Western, *Monarchy and Revolution*, 181; Miller, *Popery and Politics*, 121, 131–32.

52. Miller, *Popery and Politics*, 121; Lacey, *Dissent and Parliamentary Politics*, 74–76, 295; Kenyon, *Stuart England*, 209–10.

53. Miller, *Popery and Politics*, 122–23, 135–37; Thomas, "Comprehension and Indulgence," 217.

54. Thomas, "Comprehension and Indulgence," 217–22; Lacey, *Dissent and Parliamentary Politics*, 71–72; PRO: P.C. 2/64, 65, 367–68; John Miller, *James II: A Study in Kingship* (Hove, Sussex, 1978), 78–79; see also Quintrell, ed., *Proceedings of Lancashire Justices*, 133–34.

55. Lacey, *Dissent and Parliamentary Politics*, 80; Cockburn, *Assizes*, 249.

56. Miller, *Popery and Politics*, 106. Nothing came of this first attempt to make the laws work.

57. These letters are in HMC, *Twelfth Report*, Appendix, pt. vii, "The MSS of S. H. Le Fleming of Rydal Hall" (London, 1890), 109–10.

58. Miller, *Popery and Politics*, 136–37, 142; PRO: P.C. 2/65, 123.

59. Miller, *Popery and Politics*, 145–46; Lacey, *Dissent and Parliamentary Politics*, 85–92.

60. Lacey, *Dissent and Parliamentary Politics*, 93; Thomas, "Comprehension and Indulgence," 221–22. Buckingham had once before, on 16 November 1675, attempted to introduce in the Lords a bill for indulgence of Dissenters. That effort was bitterly denounced by Sir Peter Leicester in his charge at Northwich on 4 April 1676. He believed that "toleration of all religions will soon destroy the right religion" (Leicester, *Charges at Quarter Sessions*, ed. Halcrow, 78–79).

61. Miller, *Popery and Politics*, 162–69.

62. Thomas, "Comprehension and Indulgence," 223; Cockburn, *Assizes*, 251 (Cockburn differs from Thomas in viewing reform of the judiciary as second in priority for the Exclusion Parliaments); Lacey, *Dissent and Parliamentary Politics*, 138–40; BL: Add. MSS 29,572, fol. 247; Morrice Entr'ing Book, 1:263.

63. J. G. Muddiman, *The King's Journalist 1659–1689* (London, 1923), 231; Lacey, *Dissent and Parliamentary Politics*, 144–45; Western, *Monarchy and Revolution*, 183–84; Thomas, "Comprehension and Indulgence," 224–31.

64. Thomas, "Comprehension and Indulgence," 224; Lacey, *Dissent and Parliamentary Politics*, 144; Muddiman, *King's Journalist*, 235 [italics added].

65. Thomas, "Comprehension and Indulgence," 230–31; Miller, *Popery and Politics*, 189.

66. Miller, *Popery and Politics*, 189–92; Kenyon, *Stuart England*, 221; G. Lyon Turner MSS, 14:183a.

67. Morrice Entr'ing Book, 1:329, 347, 362; Philip Henry, *Diary and Letters*, ed. M. H. Lee (London, 1882), 319; see also William Le Hardy and George Reckitt, eds., *County of Buckingham: Calendar to the Sessions Records*, 4

vols. (Aylesbury, 1934–51), 1:95, 111; Henry, *Diary*, 320; B. W. Quintrell, ed., *Proceedings of the Lancashire Justices of the Peace at the Sheriff's Table During Assize Week, 1578–1694*, The Record Society of Lancashire and Cheshire, vol. 121 (n.p., 1981), 145–46.

68. Morrice Entr'ing Book, 1:424.

69. Miller, *Popery and Politics*, 194; Augustus Jessop, ed., *The Lives of the Norths*, 3 vols. (London, 1890), 1:309–11.

70. Charles Lyttleton to Lord Hatton, 22.xi.1684/5, in BL: Add. MSS, 29,578, fol. 42; Miller, *Popery and Politics*, 195; see also *CSPD, 1684–1685*, 287; PRO: S.P. 44/335, 329–39.

71. Lacey, *Dissent and Parliamentary Politics*, 164; Cockburn, *Assizes*, 252–54.

72. Miller, *Popery and Politics*, 204; Western, *Monarchy and Revolution*, 195.

73. Miller, *James II*, 147.

74. Miller, *Popery and Politics*, 200.

75. Miller, *James II*, 150, 155.

76. Miller, *Popery and Politics*, 205; see also John Cordy Jeaffreson, ed., *Middlesex County Records*, 4 vols. (London, 1886–92), 4:301–9.

77. Morrice Entr'ing Book, 1:526–27, 532–33; Miller, *Popery and Politics*, 210.

78. Morrice Entr'ing Book, 1:568; Miller, *Popery and Politics*, 209, 211–12.

79. Morrice Entr'ing Book, 1:562, 569, 574.

80. Miller, *James II*, 156, 164–66.

81. Morrice Entr'ing Book, 2:142; Miller, *Popery and Politics*, 215.

82. Miller, *Popery and Politics*, 216.

Chapter Three

THE TYRANNY
OF THE LAW

Is it not strange that the Steward should appear so tender-hearted towards felons as to declare openly, it is better to err in mercy than in judgment, and be so hard on us as to err in judgment, thus to the ruinating of us. I remember I have read that King Charles I, in his sufferings, expressed that he was sensible that there was nothing worse than legal tyranny, that is oppression under pretence of the execution of a law, for you know tyranny is not legal.

Samuel Duncon to the Norwich magistrates, 1671: Arthur J. Eddington, *The First Fifty Years of Quakerism in Norwich* (privately printed, 1932), 76

I

Although the Quakers perceived that any legislation which interfered with their principles was tyrannous, inequitable, and against the law of God, their records do indicate that Samuel Duncon's concern, expressed above, over "oppression under pretence of the execution of a law" was not without some foundation. The extreme radicalism and widespread unpopularity of Friends put them at the mercy of unscrupulous law-enforcement officers. Their opposition to paying fees, an essential feature of the legal system, increased their unpopularity with officers, hindered them in court, and exposed them to the worst rigors of the prison system. The militia, officered by a landed gentry alarmed by the Quaker threat to social and religious stability, was often overzealous is suppressing their meetings. As we will see, the centrifugal forces operating within the legal system hindered Quaker efforts at redress. Worse still, corruption permeated a legal system based on "gratuitous local service," despite repeated calls for reform by assize judges in their circuit charges. Bailiffs and constables, in particular, had a reputation for embracing temptation, with one historian likening early seventeenth-century bailiffs to "brigands," while petty constables in an area like Kelvedon, Essex, had regularly been in trouble with the courts.[1] Given the crucial role played by these officers in local law enforcement, the Quakers faced hard times.[2] In fact, Friends often believed themselves to be victims of illegal actions by officers and others. But it should be stressed that while their claims were frequently justified, they sometimes criticized practices that were abhorrent by later standards yet legitimate in the seventeenth century.

That the Quakers underwent numerous prosecutions is evident from their printed tabulations, normally presented throughout the Restoration to the king and Privy Council or to Parliament; from their manuscript records; and from other, independent, sources. After the Fifth Monarchy Plot in January 1661, they complained that 4,230 Quakers were imprisoned and that more than 5,000 had already suffered since the Restoration.[3] An examination of the Middlesex sessions records shows that at least 834 out of 909 convictions from July 1664 to December 1665 were Quakers prosecuted for conventicles.[4] In 1666 Friends spoke of 400 imprisoned, 100 sentenced to transportation, and 200 having died in gaols, figures supported, in part, by the release of well over 400 Quakers under the General Pardon of 1672.[5] In 1675 they claimed that more than 8,000 had been imprisoned since 1660, a figure that had increased to 10,778 by 1680, with 243 deaths and 230 sentenced to transportation. Friends' petition to James II at his accession showed 1,460 in prison with 100 dead since 1680. John Miller has calculated that at least 776 Norfolk recusancy convictions, or twenty-five percent of the total number for that county, involved Quakers.[6] Besse's *Sufferings*, covering the period 1650–1689, indicates that 20,721 Friends had been involved in brushes with the law, with about 450 deaths.[7] In addition, Quaker records for six counties selected at random—Cumberland, Durham, Northumberland, Bristol, London, and Middlesex—demonstrate numerous clashes with the law, particularly in 1661, 1664, 1670, and the early 1680s.[8]

The Quakers complained of officers who overlooked legal prerequisites or procedural technicalities when executing the law against them. Warrants would fail to appear for arrests and distraints; mittimuses would be lacking for imprisonments. While warrants were not always technically necessary, imprisonment required a mittimus. If these documents were available, they should have been produced by the officers on request. If not, the officers were obligated by law to explain the cause of the arrest, distraint, or imprisonment. The right of Quakers to defend themselves necessitated their knowing the infraction with which they were charged, as is evident in the case of Edward Vivers of Banbury, imprisoned in 1665, and remanded by Judge William Morton at the 1666 Lent assizes on the basis of the original commitment which, Friends argued, was not a mittimus, "but a post-script, for nobody's hand and seal was unto it, nor any crime . . . expressed." The Quakers often implied that warrants for distraint based on the second Conventicle Act were being intentionally withheld to prevent defendants from knowing for what meetings they were prosecuted, thereby hindering their right allowed by that Act to appeal summary convictions by justices to the full bench at quarter sessions before a jury.[9]

Even when presented, warrants often contained discrepancies, most commonly mistakes in the offender's name, such as "Margaret" for Martha Halsey, "John" for Michael Robinson, "Andrew" for Benjamin Antrobus, "Thomas," altered to "John" before being again correctly altered, to Joseph Taylor. William Smith saw both his name and parish mistaken. Nor were warrants always correctly altered, as John Ingram discovered when the name "I. Ingram" in a warrant was subsequently scratched out and replaced by "Ambrose Sachem."[10] Quakers also protested about warrants or writs in which the name of the king was changed from Charles II to James II, the former having died before the document was served. The Quakers believed, with some justification, that the death of the sovereign terminated legal proceedings.[11]

Quakers languishing in appalling prison conditions while awaiting trial were upset when they were often ignored as quarter sessions and assizes passed. Gaolers were known to omit from their prison calendars the names of some prisoners, and the Quakers' unwillingness to pay any of the customary gaol fees provided an extra incentive to do so in their case. Alternatively, justices of the peace and judges of assize, often facing crowded dockets and more serious crimes, probably preferred to avoid contentious and emotional trials of Quakers, particularly when firm direction was lacking from the Crown. Quakers, in turn, argued that the law's commitment to due process necessitated their trial or release. Failure to do either, they believed, was "coarse law," not "due course of law."[12]

When Quakers did come to trial, the proceedings often degenerated into a raucous, public brawl. At the Old Bailey trial in June 1662 of several Quakers, including John Crook, a former Bedfordshire justice, the presiding judges, Thomas Twisden and Robert Foster, were about to swear the jury, when suddenly the prisoners began screaming for justice and for the right to be heard prior to the swearing of the jury. "So there was a great noise, the court being in great confusion, some crying, 'stay, let them alone'; others cried, 'go on to swear the jury,' which the crier in this uproar did something as if he did it." The prisoners, however, continued to demand justice from the judges, as well as freedom until the quarter sessions, "but the noise was so great that neither they could hear the prisoners, nor the prisoners them." Finally, the executioner, at the judges' command, gagged one of the prisoners, and attempted to do the same with John Crook, "striving to get hold of his tongue, having a gag in his hand for that purpose." [13] At the 1663 Lent assizes in Chard, thirteen Quakers were brought into the building, but were asked before they reached the courtroom door if they had any objections against the members of the jury, "to which the prisoners could not well return any answer, the distance being so great and some of the sheriff's men with halberds keeping the door while other prisoners were tried." Nonetheless, they were asked again, having managed, "after some difficulty," to squeeze into the court-room. The prisoners, however, "knew none of the jury," and in fact were unable to discern "which were them from other people, the throng being very great." The confusion appears to have been general, for when the court called over the prisoners' names, little heed was taken as to whether or not they answered, "for 2 of them were absent," yet the court proceeded on the assumption that all were present. [14]

The theatrical atmosphere of many trials was exacerbated by those who presided, particularly the superior common-law judges. While often resented by local officers, these judges were nonetheless prominent legal figures and direct representatives of the Crown, and were thereby influential in determining procedure to be followed against Quaker offenders. Despite royal inconsistency toward dissent, they often indicated their resolution to enforce the intent, rather than the letter, of parliamentary legislation against Quakers and other Dissenters. That was particularly clear in jury trials. During the first decade of the Restoration, Parliament, like the judiciary, demonstrated a hearty distrust of jury trial for Dissenters. The first Conventicle Act permitted the use of juries only for the third offense, for which the penalty was transportation, while the second Conventicle Act dispensed entirely with them except for appeals. To counteract potential sympathy by jurors for Quakers, where such trials were permitted, the judges often adopted the role of prosecuting attorneys, bullying prisoners and juries alike. Their charge to the grand jury often became a vehicle for making known the direction in which trials of Quakers and/or other Dissenters were expected to proceed.

A series of trials in 1664–65 in which many Quakers were liable to a third conviction on the first Conventicle Act makes clear both the atmosphere and the procedural irregularities involved in emotionally charged courtroom encounters in this period. At Hertford assizes in August 1664, for example, nine Quakers were indicted.[15] When the bill was presented to the grand jury, the presiding judge, Orlando Bridgeman, chief justice of Common Pleas, quickly discovered the inherent difficulties in prosecuting Quaker silent meetings. Having heard the witnesses testify that no preaching had taken place, the grand jury refused to find the bill. Bridgeman, aware of the potential danger in permitting such a verdict, chastised the jury: "My masters, what do you mean to do? Will you make a nose of wax of the law, and suffer the law to be baffled? Those that think to deceive the law, the law will deceive them." When one of the jurors countered that the jury needed to be careful since it was dealing with men's lives, Bridgeman, ignoring the seriousness of transportation as a punishment, quickly contradicted him: "No . . . I desire not their lives, but their reformation." The grand jury then found the bill, "at which the court seemed to be well pleased."

Four of the prisoners were then called to the bar and pleaded not guilty, but in typical Quaker fashion, embellished the plea by adding that they had transgressed no "just" law. "But you have transgressed this law," interjected Bridgeman, holding the Conventicle Act in his hand, "and you have been twice convicted already." The jury, of course, was present during this revelation about previous convictions. In fact, it was common practice for the judges to emphasize to juries that these were trials for a third offense. Bridgeman did promise the prisoners that if they agreed to forgo attending such meetings in future, he would acquit them both of the present and previous offenses. They refused and the trial proceeded. In his charge to the jury, Bridgeman left nothing to chance. After reviewing the evidence and reiterating the previous convictions, he provided a fascinating interpretation of a Quaker meeting:

My masters, you are not to expect a plain punctual evidence against them for anything they said or did at their meeting, for they may speak to one another, though not with or by auricular sound, by a cast of the eye, or a motion of the head or foot, or gesture of the body, for dumb men may speak to one another so as they may understand each other by signs. And they themselves say that the worship of God is inward, in the spirit, and that they can discern spirits and know one another in spirit, so that if you find, or believe in your hearts that they were in the meeting, under colour of religion *in their way*, though they sat still only, and looked upon each other, seeing they cannot say what they did there, it was an unlawful meeting and their use and practice not according to the liturgy of the Church of England. . . . And you must find the bill, for you must have respect to the *meaning and intent* of the law, which the king and parliament have in wisdom and policy made, not only against conventicles, but the words "assembly" and "meeting" was added, for we have had late experience of the danger of such meetings under colour of religion. And it is an easy matter at such meetings to conspire and consult mischief. Therefore, the wisdom and policy of the king and parliament, lest they should be undermined, have made this law, which is not a law against conscience, for it doth not touch conscience at all.[16]

Bridgeman had clearly indicated that conformity was less of an issue than plotting by Quakers in ostensibly religious meetings. Alarmed by his summation, Friends stressed that he was "forcing the intent and meaning of the law . . . above and beyond the express reason of the law itself or evidence of the witnesses." Bridgeman replied properly that it was his role to determine the meaning and intent of the law while the jury was simply to judge fact, that is, whether or not a meeting had taken place. Once they had determined that question, he would decide if it came within the purview of the statute. In effect, any question of religious belief or motivation was not to be considered in these trials, a severe blow to Quaker pretensions. The jury retired and within one hour dutifully convicted the Quakers, who were then sentenced to transportation.

Three more Quakers were next brought to trial, one of whom had been taken outside the meeting with his back to the entrance. Bridgeman in his summing up to the jury suggested strongly that although taken outside, the prisoner was as guilty as the rest. He then ordered the bailiff to provide a room for the jury, but to prevent anyone from speaking to them or giving them bread, drink, or candles until they brought in their verdict. Although the Quakers complained about such harsh treatment of the jury, it was, in fact, accepted practice. Lengthy deliberations were frowned upon. The jury required only half an hour to find the prisoners guilty. Bridgeman's actions in these trials set a precedent cited by justices of the peace and other local authorities.

Most similar trials of Quakers in London were presided over by Chief Justice Robert Hyde and Justice John Kelyng, both of King's Bench, assisted by Sir William Wylde, recorder of London. On 5 September 1664 at the Old Bailey, Kelyng explained to the grand jury the Quaker refusal to swear on oath and then discussed the Conventicle Act, believing, like Bridgeman, that it was concerned less with conformity than with plotting. "Whereas they pretend in their scribbles," he began, that the Conventicle Act "doth not concern them," but rather those who "under pretence of worshiping God do at their meetings conspire against the government, this is a mistake." If the Quakers conspired, he continued, "they should then be guilty of treason, and we should try them by other Laws." But the purpose of the Conventicle Act was to prevent the meetings and thereby prevent conspiracy, "for they meet to consult to know their numbers & to hold correspondency, that they may in a short time be up in arms." In any event, he believed the Act was "a merciful law," for it left estates intact, simply banishing the offenders for seven years if they refused to pay the £100 penalty. "And this is not," he concluded, "for worshiping God according to their consciences, for that they may do in their families, but forsooth they cannot do that, but they must have thirty, forty, or one hundred others to contrive their designs."[17] Kelyng had presented a legitimate point, although Dissenters, including Quakers, could not possibly be satisfied worshiping only in small groups.

Despite Kelyng's reasoned approach, the judiciary encountered serious resistance from jurors in Quaker trials. In mid-October 1664 at the Old Bailey,[18] the Quaker defendants first attempted, without legal cause, to challenge the jurors, but were swiftly reminded by the judges that such challenges were allowed only to accused felons, murderers, and traitors. Ironically, when the witnesses provided contradictory evidence, some jurors questioned the judges on the value of such testimony, only to be warned by the court that jurors who undervalued Crown witnesses risked punishment themselves. But at least two jurors then focused on the apparent silence of the meeting, and whether that, in fact, was contrary to either the liturgy of the Anglican Church or the law of the land. Hyde countered that the question of silence was irrelevant, "for they will be hushed when they hear any-[one] coming." Therefore, he insisted, it was extremely difficult to prove that Quakers met to worship God in other manner than was allowed. When the jurors persisted, Hyde interjected that they were as "disorderly" a group of jurors as he ever saw, prompting Kelyng to warn them that they were simply to regard the evidence, which clearly indicated that the defendants "were met at a seditious meeting; it's no matter whether they said anything, or did anything. . . . Though they did not exercise their gifts, they were there, . . . as some of them have said." He then had the clause read describing the illegal action. When some of the jury insisted that they were unclear as to what had occurred in the meeting, Hyde countered: "suppose one hundred or two meet in a house and, being in, shut the door, as this case is, how should you have evidence of what they did there? But you might well find their meeting to be unlawful."

In his charge Hyde again warned the jury to restrict themselves to finding the fact of the meeting which, he added, had been proved by the witnesses, while Kelyng reminded them that the records had been read in court proving the first two offenses. Nonetheless, some jurors continued to argue that the evidence was not clear-cut, and that one of the witnesses had been overheard in private admitting that he had not really seen one of the defendants at the meeting, but that having signed the list of names of those arrested, including that of the prisoner, he had to swear against him. Kelyng brushed this aside, and insisted that the evidence was clear since the fact of meeting had been proved. Such meetings, he added, were known to be illegal. Hyde, fed up with the jury and with the prisoners, warned that the court was not obliged to "suffer this," since all those exceptions threw "dirt in the face of the king and parliament." The law by which the defendants were being tried, he emphasized, was in accordance with the law of the land and Magna Carta, and therefore the court was going to overrule them. "Have a care what you say," he warned. "You will bring yourselves into a worse condition then you are in." He then gave an example of what was proper law: "If the king and parliament should make a law that two justices without a jury should adjudge a man to death for the third offence as a felon without benefit of the clergy, it would be a good law and according to Magna Carta, and the law of the land, and we should be bound to execute it." Kelyng chimed in by asserting that the Quakers despised all government, and that the Conventicle Act, as a statute, was part of the law of the land. "You see what kind of people they are," Kelyng observed, "that despise all government and law," adding profoundly, "for he that doth anything prohibited by law, it is unlawful." At long last, Hyde spoke to the jury:

> You must understand that they have been convicted upon record two times already and you have heard the records read. This is the 3rd offence, & the evidence is sufficient to prove that they were there at an unlawful assembly, and some of them confess they were there to worship God. So if you believe the evidence that they were there, you must find the bills.[19]

The court adjourned until 5:00 P.M. that day; about 6:00 P.M. the jury brought in a verdict of not guilty on four of the prisoners, but could not agree on the rest, a bizarre judgment considering that all the prisoners had admitted being at the meeting, and that nothing had been said or done. The judges were furious and gave the jury further instructions before sending them out again; about an hour later they returned with a verdict of guilty of meeting, but not of fact. What kind of verdict was that, one of the judges demanded? "Here is evidence," responded the foreman, "that they met at the Bull and Mouth. Therefore we say guilty of meeting, but no evidence to prove what they did there. Therefore we say, not guilty of meeting contrary to the liturgy of the Church of England." Hyde foolishly prolonged the farce by asking the jurors if they really believed that the Quakers had not met under color and pretense of worship. The Quakers, two jurors responded, had met to worship "in deed and in truth, and according to the Scriptures," and therefore not against the liturgy of the Anglican Church. By now, the judges must have wondered where this jury had been tutored in logic, but they learned that four of the jurors inclined for the court. The judges reminded them again to find matter of fact only and to leave the law for the court, for "we are upon our oaths as well as you." Hyde continued, "the king and Parliament have made this act to prevent seditious conventicles, as is the title of the act. Therefore you are to find they met, and we all know they meet not according to the liturgy of the Church of England." Hyde now decided to take the names of those jurors who stood out; two then sided with the four who originally favored the court, but the rest remained firm. Hyde proceeded to bind them over in £100 each "to answer for their misdemeanour at the King's Bench bar the first day of the next term."

The action of this jury created a sensation among the Dissenters and, ironically, in Parliament, the institution whose intent in enacting the Conventicle Act had been constantly stressed by the judges.[20] The episode clearly illustrated those aspects of the legal system that alarmed the Quakers. First, the judiciary apparently considered it unnecessary to prove that Quaker meetings were either religious or seditious. Although judges and juries were doubtless equally aware that Quaker meetings were religious, that fact should have been proved rather than assumed. Second, juries were subjected to severe judicial pressure to find Quaker defendants guilty. In large towns such as London, Bristol, Gloucester, Chester, and Norwich, the probability of some jurors' coming from dissenting ranks was sufficient to provoke judicial bullying and threats. Although not necessarily sympathetic to Quakers, other Dissenters were also liable to penalties under such statutes as the Conventicle Act; and so they, too, were anxious to discredit the legislation. Third, trials were liable to degenerate into unseemly debates between judges, juries, and prisoners. Fourth, the Conventicle Act itself, by permitting jury trial only on the third offense, revealed to the jury that defendants had already been twice convicted. In any event, the trial judges routinely cited previous offenses. Fifth, the large numbers of imprisoned Quakers made it difficult for witnesses to identify positively those on trial as having been at the meeting in question. Therefore the court simply relied on mittimuses whose "accuracy" would be attested by the officers who signed them.

Despite the punishment of the Old Bailey jury, the judiciary continued to experience difficulties in London. At Hick's Hall on 6 December 1664, witnesses were lacking against twelve Quakers, much to the annoyance of Hyde and Kelyng, who were told by one of the magistrates that the heavy charges involved in drawing up recognizances had dissuaded potential witnesses. Hyde ordered that witnesses were to be encouraged and were to pay nothing: if the clerks, he added, dared to make witnesses pay one groat, he would make them in turn, pay ten. A Quaker prisoner caustically remarked that it scarcely mattered, considering what had happened to the previous jury. "You scandalize us," complained Kelyng. Witnesses were soon forthcoming; and the judges examined the mittimus, called on the justice or clerk to examine the names inscribed and their own signatures to prove that the prisoners were the ones arrested, and then called on the keeper of Newgate to corroborate that he had received the prisoners. The jury found eleven of the twelve guilty; the judges sent them out again, and they convicted the twelfth.[21]

At the Old Bailey on 16 January 1665, the thirty-two Quakers on trial all admitted being at a meeting to worship God, leading Judge Kelyng to state "several times . . . that that was crime enough, being against the law." Not taking any chances, however, the judges tried to persuade the jury not to withdraw, since the matter of fact appeared so clear. One juror, Thomas Leader, resisted their efforts and encouraged his fellow jurors to withdraw, a move which clearly angered the bench. As the jury was leaving the courtroom, the judges "gave them charge, encouragement, and instructions to bring in their verdict according to the mind of the court," adding that if they brought in a quick verdict, the court "would not go to dinner till they come, and then they should be discharged." The jury failed to cooperate; and the court adjourned to dinner. Late in the afternoon, the jury found the Quakers guilty, "at which the court seemed much delighted and very well pleased, and Judge Kelyng stood up & told them they had done very well, & thanked them for their very good service." The Quakers were quick to add that "something was given by the hand of the ordinary, or priest of Newgate, into the hand of the foreman; some that saw it judged it to be a reward from the court." Thomas Leader, the obstreperous juror, published a paper about his experience on the jury and implied that it had succumbed when it became apparent that the judges were about to treat them as they had the jury that had been bound over.[22]

More Quakers were tried early in April 1665 at the Old Bailey. One of the judges summed up for the jury, "incensing them against Friends, saying they are a people that will not be subject to magistracy, and that they would not swear." One defendant asked why they bothered to bring him into court since the proceedings amounted to a phony trial, conducted merely to provide a pretense of justice for public consumption. After all, he continued, if the jury proved to be troublesome, it would be threatened or fined. Kelyng, fed up with this continual opposition, stood up and characterized the prisoner as "made of nothing but railing," but added rather pointedly that "if the jury bring not in their verdict according to the *intent and meaning* of the law, that they were not to receive it." All were found guilty. But if Kelyng believed that his problems with juries had ended, he was soon disillusioned, for in May 1665 a jury at the Old Bailey acquitted three Quakers "contrary to Judge Kelyng's mind, & what he had intended." Kelyng, in no mood to dispute the verdict, simply fined ten of the jurors one hundred marks each and committed them to Newgate until the fine was paid. Nine remained in prison for several weeks, while the tenth was not released until November.[23] The jury had claimed that they lacked sufficient evidence that the Quakers had assembled to exercise any religious worship "as the Act runs." A mystified Kelyng, when called upon by the House of Commons two years later to justify his actions in this trial, explained that the jurors had agreed with him that the defendants were above the age of sixteen; that they had been convicted twice before for attending unlawful meetings; that the Bull and Mouth tavern where they were arrested was the usual Quaker meeting place; that more than the legal number of worshipers was present; and that they should have been attending the Established Church service that day. They even agreed with him that the meeting was religious "since it appeared by the Quakers' own confession that they met to seek God in the spirit." Despite all of this, the jury refused to convict, "whereupon he did fine some of them aforesaid."[24]

Kelyng was accorded no respite from Quaker prisoners or recalcitrant juries. In June, a Quaker defendant demanded to know whether he would be discharged if found innocent; Kelyng said he would. The prisoner caustically remarked that the jury would then be sent to prison in his place. "Oh, are you thereabouts," an angry Kelyng replied, "let them look to that. If they do contrary to the law they shall suffer, but you shall be cleared." When the jurors were asked for their verdict, the foreman announced that the defendant was guilty of "breaking the law." Kelyng, enraged, "rose up and said what verdict was that?" The foreman repeated it. The recorder of London wisely said "that was enough," and the prisoner was "put in the hole."[25]

Outside of London, the assize judges, as Orlando Bridgeman had demonstrated, were equally anxious to maintain their traditional domination of trial proceedings. At the March 1663 assizes in Worcester, for instance, Judge Robert Hyde presided at the trial of Daniel Baker on the Elizabethan Conventicle Act. When Baker argued that Quaker meetings followed the example of Christ and his apostles and should not be condemned, Hyde "with fury" stood up and stressed his hope that the king's laws were not "contrary to Christ and His Apostles," but that in any event, "they were not to be disputed by such mad fellows as the prisoner, and with a loud voice cried out to the gaoler, 'Take him away.'" At Abingdon assizes in July 1665, Judge Thomas Tyrrell, presiding over the trial of three Quakers for the third offense under the 1664 Conventicle Act, conveniently ignored the lack of any records of a second offense for one of the defendants. Like his London colleagues, he also brushed aside Quaker protestations that conscience was under assault. In his summation he warned the jury that the Quakers "would be interpreters of the laws and spiritual things too," and he made clear his belief that the defendants were guilty. In marked contrast to the actions of London juries, the jury found for the king without leaving the courtroom.[26]

II

Unfortunately for the Quakers, overbearing courtroom behavior was not limited to the superior common-law judiciary, nor simply to meeting offenses. For example, at Hertford quarter sessions in October 1662, four Quakers suspected of recusancy were tendered the Oath of Allegiance by the justices, after the steward of the borough of Hertford implored them to take the Quakers "into their cognizance, for they were too mighty for . . . the town magistrates." Having refused to take the oath, the Quakers were given until the next morning to reconsider, at which time the justices attempted to convince them of the lawfulness of swearing, a debate which law-enforcement officials often unwisely undertook with Friends, believing that once they realized their "mistake" on this and other testimonies, they would relent. In fact, the prisoners complained that the court was attempting to make them examples "to affrighten others." Then Sir Thomas Fanshawe, a justice, implied that Richard Thomas, one of the Quakers, and a former officer in the Civil War parliamentary armies, deserved punishment for his having been engaged "in so horrid an act as could be mentioned." Fanshawe admitted that the king had pardoned Thomas for his role in the war, and he would also, nor "did he speak it to upbraid," but Thomas cynically commented, "& yet spoke it in open court." When the prisoners asked why the court was not trying them upon the Quaker Act, Fanshawe explained that "in some things [it] would not hit them, and therefore they were fain to make use of such laws as would." The presiding justices, unlike the assize judges, refused to permit the Quakers to speak to the jury, which deliberated for only three-quarters of an hour before returning a verdict of guilty, "delivering it with a faint, low voice." When the justices discussed among themselves whether to proceed with sentencing or to defer it to the next sessions, Fanshawe tellingly queried, "what will the country say then?" The Quakers were praemunired.[27]

Fanshawe's dislike for the Quakers surfaced again at Hertford quarter sessions in the October 1664 trial of several Quakers on the Conventicle Act. When the defendants spoke of the inner Light, he made his position perfectly clear: "But your Light is darkness and a melancholy vapour of the brain and leads you to one thing today and another thing tomorrow, and I know not what the third day." Like the assize judges, Fanshawe stressed that the Conventicle Act was not intended to hinder the Quakers from their religion, but only from their meetings. As usual, their previous offenses were read to the jury, to which the prisoners were forbidden to speak. The verdict was guilty. But in an interesting sidelight, when several more Quakers were tried for the same crime, their attempt to challenge a juror was only refused by the court because they failed to provide due cause. Unlike the assize judges, these justices appeared to believe that defendants in misdemeanor trials could legally challenge jurors, an indication of the confusion that permeated the law-enforcement system.[28]

Neither that confusion nor Fanshawe's attitude were unique. One justice who personified the often amateurish, primitive, and prejudicial character of local law enforcement was William Armorer in Berkshire. At Abingdon sessions in June 1662, Thomas Holt presided over the trial of nine Quakers for attending a meeting, but when he asked the clerk to call over the jurors, only three appeared, while the rest "hid themselves, some stooping down to hide . . . and some crept out from among the people." Continued efforts by the judge and bailiffs to procure a jury proved fruitless. Finally, the bailiffs turned to high and petty constables present in court who were "very unwillingly . . . made jurymen." The court permitted the defendants to challenge any juror, but they did not exercise that option. Having finally sworn the reluctant jurors, the court called the first witness, who proved to have nothing significant to say. Holt then called for another witness, but none appeared, which he thought was rather strange, "that an indictment should be found and Sir William Armorer's own hand to it, and none to prosecute." The bench consulted together and actually presumed to ask the jury if they personally knew whether Thomas Curtis, the most prominent defendant, attended such meetings; if so, they could find him guilty. The jury replied in the negative and rendered a verdict of not guilty. The court decided to tender the Oath of Allegiance to Curtis, but was stunned when he claimed to have already taken it. When asked for his certificate, Curtis replied that he had none, "it being 24 years ago." He was returned to prison.[29]

Armorer's problems were only beginning. At the sessions held at Reading in January 1665, after witnesses contradicted one another, the grand jury refused to find a bill against four Quakers for attending a conventicle. Armorer "rose up from his seat in great rage," and insisted on being sworn a witness against one of the defendants, Christopher Cheesman, whom he had found "twenty times at the meeting," but each time "when I came, he would tell me there was not my number,[30] so I was fain[31] to wipe my nose (wiping his finger then on his nose) and return back like a coxcomb as I went, and thus I have been plagued with him." One of Armorer's men took the stand instead to testify against the conventicle. "Jack," asked Armorer, "you remember the 23rd day of the month?" Jack, unfortunately, responded that the date was unimportant, for he knew the event well enough, at which a bystander shouted: "A rogue does not know the day of the month. He deserves to be kicked out of the court." The spectators thereupon "fell out into great laughter." After the grand jury again refused to find the bill, Armorer's demand to be sworn as a witness was accepted, "so there was only the judge, Edward Dolby, and one justice (Proctor) left on the Bench," snickered Friends, "and whether they two could make a sessions, neither of them being of the quorum, no doubt but they can tell." Despite all of this, the jury again rejected the bill. While admitting that Armorer was an honorable witness, they felt, not surprisingly, that he was a man "subject to passion."[32] That "passion" was again discernible at the April 1665 sessions at Newbury when the grand jury, by a vote of fourteen to five, rejected a bill against the ubiquitous Mr. Cheesman. Armorer, incensed, and suspicious of the religious sympathies of the jurors, threatened to tender them the Oath of Allegiance, "to which the jury cried out as one man, they would take it." The idea was dropped.[33]

Armorer successfully bullied a petty jury to find a Quaker guilty at the January 1667 sessions at Reading,[34] but at the July sessions in Abingdon he had problems with his records. At that time, no witness appeared against the Quaker defendant. The presiding justice, Thomas Holt, called for the records of the previous offenses, "upon which the clerk made diligent search and sent his man out of the court to look after them." He soon returned "with great rolls of papers under his arms," but was unable to locate the records. As Holt prepared to proceed as if it was now a first rather than a third offense, Armorer retorted that he was prepared to swear the records were true, "though they were lost." He then did so. Despite Holt's charge to the jury that this effectively proved the previous offenses, they returned a verdict of not guilty. Armorer accompanied the jury out again to "redeliberate." When they returned, the foreman pronounced the defendant guilty, "but some of the jury, not being satisfied, would not come into the court, for they did not agree to the verdict, and one of them said he would never agree to it." This rather undignified scene ended when Holt threatened to fine those jurors who failed to enter the courtroom.[35]

All of the encounters discussed thus far occurred prior to the most famous Quaker trial of the century, the results of which seriously challenged judicial dominance in the courtroom. In September 1670 the local authorities in London unwisely tried William Penn and William Meade at the Old Bailey for conspiring to commit a riot.[36] They had been arrested on 14 August as Penn was declaring at Gracechurch Street. Sir John Robinson, the lieutenant of the Tower, unsuccessfully objected against one prospective juror, Edward Bushel, for not having kissed the Bible when he was sworn. The trial quickly degenerated into a ludicrous dispute between Penn, the lord mayor, and the jury, with Penn endeavoring to elevate a misdemeanor accusation into a critical dissection of the entire common-law tradition and a case on which depended the lives, liberties, estates, and families of all Englishmen. As in many Quaker trials, confusion, noise, and a carnival atmosphere prevailed. At one point, during the recorder's charge to the jury, Penn began yelling from the dock[37] that to give the charge in the absence of the prisoners was illegal. "I say it is directly opposite to, and destructive of the undoubted right of every English prisoner," he asserted.

The jury deliberated for one and a half hours. Eight of the jurors favored a guilty verdict while the remaining four, including Bushel, favored the defendants. The bench tried to force the four to relent and the recorder blamed Bushel: "Sir, you are the cause of this disturbance, and manifestly show yourself an abettor of faction. I shall set a mark upon you, Sir." Robinson reminded Bushel that he had known him for fourteen years. "You have thrust yourself upon this jury," asserted Robinson, "because you think there is some service for you. I tell you, you deserve to be indicted more than any man that hath been brought to the Bar this day." Bushel replied that he would have willingly avoided service, but had been unable to do so. "Mr. Bushel," interjected Thomas Bloodworth, a London alderman, "we know what you are." The jury was again sent out and this time found the defendants guilty of "speaking in Gracechurch Street." A furious court refused to accept this verdict and sent the jury back. When it returned it pronounced Penn guilty of speaking "or preaching to an assembly" in Gracechurch Street, but found Meade not guilty, an absurd verdict in a conspiracy trial. The court, angry with the jury and tired of Penn's constant interjections, sent the jury out for the night without even a chamber pot. The next morning, Sunday 4 September, the jurors returned the same verdict. The court roundly denounced Bushel and properly insisted that since the charge was conspiracy, Meade could not be innocent if Penn was guilty. The jury was again sent out and returned with the same verdict. If the jury persisted, warned the court, it would be carted about the city, as in the time of Edward III. Given the previous experiences of juries in London Quaker trials, the jurors may have taken this threat seriously, or so the court wished. The jury was sent out again. Soon afterwards it sent word to the court that it had, indeed, arrived at a new verdict. The jurors were now given food and drink, but the judges decided to recess until Monday. At that time a stunned court heard a unanimous verdict of acquittal for both Penn and Meade. The epilogue was predictable; the jurors were fined forty marks each and imprisoned until the fine was paid. Ultimately they obtained a writ of *habeas corpus* and in 1671, after the issue had been argued in Common Pleas, a majority of ten of the judges decided that a jury was not to be imprisoned for its verdict.[38] The fines were rescinded and the jurors released. Judges were now prevented from unduly influencing the juries trying Friends. Or were they?

Quaker records indicate that judges could still influence juries by their charge, their interpretation of law, and their hectoring. For example, in August 1680 it was reported that Chief Baron William Mountagu in his charge to the grand jury at Cambridge assizes had warned that the Quakers "walked by a light within, & if that led them into blood they would follow it," while at East Grinstead assizes in February 1683, Justice Job Charleton "gave in his charge that there were 3 sorts that might be presented, to wit, the popish recusants; vicious persons that lay . . . about streets and in alehouses, and the dissenters that pretended conscience in not going to church."[39] At Launceston assizes, where he presided over the trial of Thomas Lower, the son-in-law of George Fox, Charleton was "very rough and wicked," refusing Lower a copy of his indictment or the right to enter a traverse, and at one point calling him a Jesuit and a "saucy fellow." Lower also complained that Chief Justice George Jeffreys at the following assizes apparently gave a savage charge, taking what Lower called "one unlucky fling" aimed at "those that downright refused to swear at all, saying such also can join in association with those that seeks the subversion of the goverment." Jeffreys did not name the Quakers, but "most people apprehended he struck at us."[40]

Perhaps the most ironical case of judicial bullying in retrospect occurred during the proceedings immediately following the imprisonment of the Penn-Meade jury. With thirteen more Quakers waiting to be tried for a riot, the court selected a new jury. According to Friends, the clerk making the selections "picked here and there such persons that were judged the most likely to answer the malicious ends and horrid designs of that bench, calling not the jurymen in order and direct course as is usual." At one point during the trial, the recorder of London "with great indignation and rage," exclaimed to one of the prisoners that he "should, be gagged, and deserved to have his tongue bored through with an hot iron & his mouth nailed to the dust." In his summing up, the recorder again made his position clear. The Quakers, he asserted, "were a refractory people, such who delighted in deeds of darkness, and . . . must be crushed, or there would be no living by them." The jury, he concluded, "must find them guilty." To the relief of the court, the jury did as instructed, "which some of these jurors had, over their cups, sworn they would do if ever they came to try the Quakers."[41]

While these misdemeanor trials often portray unsophisticated courtroom procedure and magisterial aggression, they also show the willingness of many jurors to pursue verdicts against the wishes of the bench. The last trial discussed, however, also illustrates why Friends were justifiably ambivalent toward juries, despite viewing them, in theory, as a bulwark against officious law-enforcement authorities eager to apply dubious legislation. In practice, juries were more likely, Friends believed, to be either highly prejudicial or easily frightened and intimidated, as demonstrated by the trial of four Quakers at Northampton sessions in December 1665 for a third offense on the Conventicle Act. The jury, according to the defendants, "were poor, fearful men" who the court knew "would do what they were told to do." The Quakers challenged some of them, showing what they believed was good cause, "but the clerk of the sessions said they may serve." At the April 1666 quarter sessions in the same county, John Treslove was indicted for the same crime. The foreman of the jury was William Smith, who had been "one of the greatest sticklers against the book of common prayer" during the Interregnum, having acted at that time "like an old bloodhound to hunt and persecute innocent people." With the Restoration, however, "he turned, and now is the greatest persecutor of those that do not hear common prayer, and is made use of by his now masters to be the surest hunter of any they can choose." The jury, originally ten to two against conviction, was sent out again, at which time, the "bloodthirsty" Smith forced the other ten jurors to "submit unto his will, or at least to keep silence while he spoke for them." When the jury returned to the courtroom, Smith therefore announced that it had agreed to find the prisoner guilty. The Quakers also complained that Smith had already twice served as jury foreman "upon the sentencing of the innocent."[42]

A particularly unpleasant case was related by John North, a York Quaker, whose son in 1664 had been "wilfully & maliciously & presumptuously pistoled to death at his own house door," apparently without any legal grounds, by an apothecary of the corporation. The coroner and town clerk, however, "picked & packed a jury of their own choosing . . . the foreman & chief thereof being all tenants & vassals to the mayor & aldermen of the said corporation, who dare not say the crow is black if they say she's white." They brought in a verdict of self-defense that, North protested, was "false & a great untruth, as by several credible witnesses were proved."[43] Packed or intimidated juries were not the only problem faced by Friends, as evidenced by the Abingdon assizes of July 1665, where some of the jurors in the trial of a Quaker "were so drunk that they were hardly able to speak or stand, but as they were supported by others in the throng."[44]

Quaker unhappiness over juries was matched by their concern over witnesses, whom they believed to be often either stupid or dishonest.

For example, Friends were singularly unimpressed with William Armorer's former coachman, who acted as a witness at the April 1665 sessions at Newbury. When told to put his right hand on the Bible in order to be sworn, the coachman had to be prompted by Armorer, who called to him: "Lay on the other hand, Dick."[45] In November 1662, five Quakers were convicted at Southwark sessions, basically on the testimony of a fellow named Creswell who, Friends averred, had lied, "which was signified to the jury, and also that this Creswell, who lives at The Horns in Kent Street, is known to be a very wicked man and to keep a wicked house of entertainment for drunkards & all manner of wicked persons."[46]

III

Although Quakers were understandably concerned about juries, the 1664 Conventicle Act had at least permitted their use. That was not the case with the 1670 Conventicle Act, a statute whose sophistication and unlimited potential for abuse caused Andrew Marvell to characterize it as the "quintessence of arbitrary malice."[47] This Act enabled one justice, on the oaths of two witnesses, summarily to convict anyone aged sixteen or above of attending such a meeting. The conviction was then certified to the next quarter sessions. Offenders were to be fined only 5*s.* for the first offense and 10*s.* for the second. But refusal to pay the fine resulted in distraint and sale of the offender's goods and chattels, rather than imprisonment. If the offender was destitute, the fine was levied on the goods and chattels of any capable person or persons convicted for the same meeting. Fines were to be distributed at the discretion of the justice, an excellent method of crippling particularly troublesome or offensive Quakers, although no person could be fined more than £10 in this manner. Of the money raised, either by payment of the fine or by sale of the distrained goods, one-third was to be paid to the "informer and informers and to such person and persons as the said justice . . . shall appoint having regard to their diligence and industry in the discovery, dispersing, and punishing of the said conventicles." In addition, any person who taught or preached in the conventicle was to be fined £20 for the first offense and £40 for the second, to be levied in the manner described above, but if the preacher was unknown or unable to pay, then the fine was levied on those convicted of attending. This was a particularly clever tactic aimed at fomenting discord in dissenting meetings, including those of Quakers, visited by traveling ministers, who normally departed at the end of the meeting, thereby leaving local attenders to pay the fine. Another deterrent was the clause whereby anyone who allowed the meeting to take place in his house, or other building or property was to forfeit £20, levied in the same manner. The statute permitted an appeal, but only by those whose fine had exceeded 10s., thereby excluding anyone convicted simply for being present at a meeting. Appeals had to be made in writing and within one week after payment or levying of the fine, to the full bench of justices at the following quarter sessions, where the convicting justice was to turn in the money and a record of the conviction. Only on appeal was a jury trial permitted, but if the appeal was not prosecuted or was defeated, the appellant had to pay triple costs. Although no person was punishable under the statute unless prosecuted within three months, all of its clauses were to be

> construed most largely and beneficially for the suppressing of conventicles and for the justification and encouragement of all persons to be employed in the execution thereof. And that no record, warrant, or mittimus to be made by virtue of this Act, or any proceedings thereupon, shall be reversed, avoided, or any way impeached by reason of any defaults in form.

Finally—a serious blow to all Dissenters—any justice who failed for any reason to enforce the Act was liable to a penalty of £100, one-third of which was to go to the person who sued for it, a significant incentive to justices and informers alike.

The combination of the stiff penalty on sympathetic justices, the leeway allowed "defaults in form," and the substantial financial incentive for informers provided significant impetus for illegal or unethical actions against Dissenters. But while all Dissenters were liable under the Act, the regular and public nature of Quaker meetings, along with the lingering perception of Friends as eccentric and socially abrasive, made them particularly inviting targets. In fact, while Quaker complaints were sometimes specious, their records indicate justifiable concern about the manner in which this statute was enforced, particularly, albeit not exclusively, in the early 1680s when Charles II, as has been seen, turned against the Whigs and Dissenters. Predictably, the bitterest comments by Friends were directed towards the "witnesses," generally "common" informers, a group so historically unpopular that Sir Edward Coke had once described them as "viperous vermin," while a seventeenth-century tract viewed an informer as "one of the Devil's nut-hooks, a privileged trepan or a common barrator under pretence of authority, a pettifogging caterpillar . . . [who] ferrets a conventicle just as a polecat does rabbits in their burrows."[48] The Quaker attitude towards informers, who also played a substantial role in recusancy prosecutions on the *qui tam* writ, was equally hostile, as it was also towards justices or ministers who appeared to encourage them.[49]

The Quakers were alarmed by the substantial number of cases in which informers had given false information. Normally Friends met to worship on Sunday and Wednesday (or Thursday) each week; by 1670 meetings were held either in a meetinghouse or in the home of a particular Friend. It was perfectly conceivable that informers, knowing where and when meetings were to take place, would go directly to a justice, take an oath that a conventicle was in progress, and procure warrants directed to lesser officers for distraint. Acting on the assumption that the same Quakers were present at each meeting, informers probably maintained lists of their names in order to fill in the warrants. Such assumptions increased the likelihood of false information and help to explain the numerous instances in which Quakers accused by informers of attending conventicles had actually been elsewhere—in other counties, at home, at work, or even six feet under.[50] Friends were mystified, for example, at how informers could prosecute a meeting at the home of Edward Man at Ford Green, Middlesex, swearing that two Quakers had preached, despite the fact that Man's house was situated "about 18 yards from the road and walled in." Friends concluded that "if these credible informers were in the road, if preaching had been there, it is not likely that they could distinguish it from reading at such a distance." Walter Phillips of Southwark must have been equally astounded in 1685 when convicted of attending a meeting at Devonshire House, since he "had not been there in 2 or 3 years."[51]

Informers, of course, were aware that naming a preacher was to their advantage, since the fines in which they shared would be considerably greater. On numerous occasions, therefore, informers swore that preaching had occurred.[52] Some informers, however, rather than risk an appeal by those falsely accused as preachers, preferred to entice Quakers into speaking during the silent meeting. This trick was employed, for example, at a meeting in Gloucester in 1682 when the informers asked the Quakers what they were doing. One Friend un-wisely responded, "I am here to know the will of God and then to do it." He was convicted as a preacher. Perhaps the most ingenious scheme was uncovered by Nottinghamshire Quakers. Edward Butterworth en-tered a meeting, sat down, and waited quietly until three informers disrupted the meeting. He then stood. "Blessed be the peace-makers," he exclaimed, and was pulled out of the meeting by the informers, who took him before a justice and swore against him as a preacher. Finding him penurious, the justice imposed the penalty on the others. Investigation revealed, however, that Butterworth had been planted in the meeting by the informers.[53]

Informers also convicted gatherings of Quakers that were not within the purview of the statute—instances where fewer than the re-quired number were present, or where several Quakers had gathered to consult about assisting a poor Friend or had simply visited a sick Friend.[54] Lamentably typical was the case of Jane Vickers of Raby near Bristol, convicted for holding a meeting in her house, when in actu-ality she was entertaining some visiting Friends, who were "eating some honey & butter" when the informers knocked. They were in-vited in by the naive Vickers, who proceeded to give them "a drink and some honey and butter," which they happily accepted—and then pros-ecuted their hostess.[55] More difficult to assess, but equally contentious, were prosecutions of Quaker burials as conventicles. Often the grave-site testimonies by Quakers to the deceased resulted in fines as preach-ers. Although sizable gatherings, these burials were held outside, thereby ostensibly mitigating the likelihood of plotting, which was the usual rationale of law-enforcement officials for prosecuting Quaker meetings.[56]

Some of the informers' actions were blatantly illegal. Often they took advantage of the unpopularity of Quakers to abuse them physi-cally. At Chichester in September and October 1683, for example, meetings were harassed by two informers whose modus operandi was to break all the windows and doors of the meetinghouse, while also breaking the gate to the burial ground and burning the fence sur-rounding it. Each time Friends made repairs the informers destroyed them, at one point stuffing bushes into the meetinghouse doorway "having before carried away the door," and thrusting the bushes against Friends' legs. They also "tore a Friend's scarf from her neck," all the while taunting Friends to complain to the local justice "if they would."

When Friends laid in bricks with boards as seats, the informers "broke all to pieces," and then lobbed a "serpent," a type of firecracker, into the meetinghouse "which was like to have done mischief, being a thatched house." All of these actions were performed, Friends added, "with great swearing and threatenings," the informers being "commonly drunk," and sometimes accompanied "with the rabble of rude boys and others."[57]

Complaints of this nature were widespread and may well have reflected the quality of those who acted as informers. Quakers insinuated that informers were too stupid to know if a meeting was actually religious and in manner other than according to the liturgy of the Anglican Church. Yet despite this caveat, George Whitehead lamented that if the informer declared there was preaching or praying in a meeting, "yet remembers not one sentence or word expressed," nonetheless, "such silly, ignorant, and impertinent evidence has been often accepted for conviction."[58] Worse than ignorant informers were those who were thieves, felons, or generally disreputable characters. When told by legal counsel that to be lawful witnesses, informers must not be "infamous," as for instance, "not convicted of perjury or forgery,"[59] Friends procured a copy of the conviction of Gabriel Shad, a notorious London informer, for stealing goods worth £300, an offense for which he had been burnt in the hand. They also attempted to discredit the Hilton brothers, John and George, and their retinue of desperadoes. In July 1682 Friends reported that the Hiltons had been born in Westmorland, that their father was a Catholic, that they had been educated as such, "and so they are still looked upon." The gossipy report added that John Hilton "lived a lewd, dissolute life in the country and was troublesome to his neighbours in law suits & put several to great charge when they were owing him nothing, and in short, he is accounted in his own country as the worst of men." Nor, the report added, was his brother George Hilton any better, being "one of those reputed to live upon his wits."[60]

The Hiltons, however, continued their informing activities; therefore in December 1685 Friends obtained a copy of a mittimus committing John Hilton to Newgate, having been indicted in three counties for privately compounding[61] a number of warrants issued by Sir Thomas Jenner, recorder of London, for levying fines for conventicles. Hilton had refused to obey a bench warrant issued by Chief Justice Herbert. Yet the slippery Hilton posted bond; and not surprisingly,

Friends soon obtained a copy of a warrant for his arrest. He had skipped town.[62] Similarly, in March 1685 the Quakers had taken notice of a warrant issued in November 1683 by Thomas Fletcher, a Westmorland justice, against Christopher Smith, Barnard Smith, and John Cartwright, "suspected for stealing of geese in the country, some of them being now informers in London." To emphasize their recurring concern, Meeting for Sufferings in January 1686 sent a paper to the lord mayor of London entreating him "not to countenance an idle, dissolute sort of people, turned informers against the king's peaceable & industrious subjects," who were "daily exposed to spoil & ruin by the said informers who pay the king no taxes."[63]

Although the Quakers were justified in protesting against the often uncorroborated evidence of scandalous informers, they were hindered by several factors. First, the willingness of informers to provide evidence on oath, a prerequisite of the legal system, was sufficient for a justice to proceed unless that evidence was challenged by the Quakers. The burden of proof lay with the defense to discredit such testimony. Second, informers historically have often been men and women either with criminal records or of questionable integrity, whose assistance has been encouraged by law-enforcement officers. Third, the Quakers weakened their position by unwisely characterizing as informers anyone who caused them to be prosecuted on this statute, including the civil authorities and members of the clergy executing their legal responsibilities. Thus Friends denounced Roger and William Kirkby, two Lancashire justices, for sending constables and churchwardens to Quaker meetings, with encouragement to inform, while in Sussex, they criticized James Clark, register of the bishop's court; William Snatt, a minister; and two constables, all of whom had acted as informers.[64] These men and others like them were, in Quaker eyes, as despicable as "common" informers. Despite this mistaken identification, the Quaker attitude was often validated by officers and clergy who engaged in gratuitous violence while interrupting meetings or carrying out distraints.

IV

In many respects, the violence perpetrated upon Quakers was a concomitant of popular hostility towards them. Violence was not the prerogative of informers alone; it was also employed by law-enforcement officers, soldiers, clergy, children, and mobs. Although the motives for violence are rarely easy to disentangle, such behavior, in law, was unacceptable and is perhaps the severest indictment of the English legal system found in Quaker records. Barry Reay argues that violence against Quakers, "tinged with fear and hatred," had escalated in 1659, the climactic year of the Interregnum, and continued into the Restoration. He compares it to the "Great Fear" in Revolutionary France, and believes that its genesis lay in a "mixture of xenophobia, class hatred, and a superstition which merged with the world of witchcraft . . . stimulated and encouraged by indoctrinating anti-Quaker propaganda and by the behavior of the sect itself." In effect, he concludes, the Quakers were "hated as political radicals, as social and religious deviants, and in some cases as economic middlemen."[65] While much of this may be true, Reay appears to have overlooked indications in Quaker records of simpler motives on the part of those who indulged in violent acts against them.

There were, for example, those Englishmen whose sympathies, fortunes, and ambitions were intertwined with the monarchy and who had suffered almost two decades of pent-up frustration and rage against religious radicalism. They and others were also reacting against the restrictive moral atmosphere which permeated those years. In addition, many soldiers, bored by years of relative inactivity, were doubtless anxious to reinforce their masculinity at the expense of a sect whose members they perceived as cowards. This characteristic was also found in those law-enforcement officers who engaged in violence themselves or encouraged others to do so. Ironically, a sense of moral superiority often appears in those who commit violence against individuals who refuse to fight. Of course, some of the civil authorities (and soldiers) may simply have been sadists, while others were merely frustrated by the obstinate refusal of Quakers to obey the law. Rather than question the logic or legitimacy of the laws against dissent, these officers reacted against the offenders. Nonetheless, the tacit approval and occasional impetus provided by the civil authorities helped to encourage mob violence against Quakers, particularly by young boys, always eager to assert their aggressiveness against their elders or against those who constantly reproved their unlimited potential for morally lax behavior. The "gang" mentality was another factor—a feeling of group identity, combined with physical and consequently emotional superiority over their victims. No doubt the preponderance of alcohol in the daily diet of many Englishmen was another stimulus. Fortunately, much of the violence was verbal, little more than swagger and posturing. Yet the Quakers—highly visible, socially aberrant and abrasive, but personally nonviolent—were ideal targets, not only for harassment, but also for serious physical abuse. Many illustrations can be found in Quaker records, some of them extremely graphic.

Perhaps the most dangerous offenders were soldiers, who, if permitted to exercise violence without restraint merely because the victims were unpopular, could become a politically and socially disruptive force. In fact, the militia, unaccompanied by civil authorities, often broke up conventicles, simply citing their swords or muskets as their warrant.[66] Friends in Portsmouth in 1660–61 bitterly complained about the militia after Lieutenant-Colonel William Legge, a staunch Royalist, became governor. On one occasion, a sergeant, with a company of "ungodly soldiers," descended upon a Quaker meeting, "like the raging waves of the sea, kicking and hailing Friends forth," and breaking all the windows of the house, while in another incident a meeting was dispersed and the Quakers forced to march along the street, "which was done with much cruelty, beating and kicking them on their backs." Soon, some "rude and ungodly men that were bound for Tangier" combined with the militia "in kicking and beating Friends." When they finally reached the town gate, one of the soldiers yelled to the gate guards who, not to be outdone by their fellow troops, "joined . . . in beating and kicking" the Quakers.[67]

In 1663 the king's regiment abused Friends at Horslydown, then part of London, hitting them with staves and pikes, cutting them with swords, and firing muskets close to the bodies of some of the women, burning their clothes. After that regiment left London, others arrived who acted in the same fashion, to be followed by part of General George Monck's regiment "who with no less violence then the other, fell upon Friends in their meeting." George Whitehead described the events of 9 October 1670, also at Horslydown, after the meetinghouse had been pulled down on the king's orders and the Quakers met on the rubble. Mounted and foot soldiers came to their gathering, "and one of them having a shovel, threw dirt and mire upon both men and women." He was followed by the rest of the soldiers who waded in among the Quakers, "striking and knocking down without regard to age or sex . . . until they shed blood from many." Some neighbors took the injured Quakers into their houses, only to have the soldiers force open the doors and drag the Quakers into the street, where they "plucked off their hats that they might strike on their bare heads, insomuch that many had their heads broken in a grievous manner." The soldiers, Whitehead continued, then tore the clothes of both men and women, dragging the latter through the dirt, "some of the foot soldiers impudently putting their hands under the women's coats, using obscene expressions, and very indecent behaviour." One soldier "struck one woman Friend twice on the belly with his musket and once on the breast," while another threw dirt in her face. Unfortunately, she was pregnant, and since the beating, Friends added, she "hath never been well through their abuses, whereby she did lose her child, and her own life was greatly endangered." Finally, another Quaker was taken by a soldier who "demanded his money and endeavoured to rifle his pockets, cursing and threatening, 'God damn him, he would stab him, if he did not give it him,' again swearing, 'that he would pistol him.'"[68]

At Bristol on Christmas Day 1663, Captain Thomas Smart, irritated at Quakers who opened their shops, but without the knowledge of his colonel, had three of their servants "tied neck & heels together with half hundred weights & muskets hanging about their necks in the bitter extremity of the cold weather till the eyes of some of them were observed to be out & their faces were growing black & the natural spirits of one of them ready to fail." They were finally set free by some soldiers "who were not of the guard."[69] Those Quakers lived; others were not as lucky. In August 1662, at the Bull & Mouth meeting in London, soldiers dragged out Friends, including John Trowell, who was "knocked . . . down for dead in the street & then trampled upon . . . & he lay sick ten days and then died." His body was then taken to the Bull and Mouth, where the coroner and inquest jury viewed the body, as did many others, "who judged him to be murdered, his body being black with bruises & even rotten & like a jelly." The Quakers voiced their dismay over the "grievous blows" he had endured, "one of the officers having a club in one hand about a yard long, which seemed to be as much as he could well handle for bigness & weight, with which he laid on about him without mercy, as did most of his party." Another Friend had been knocked down "five times" and the blood "lay in the streets," running down "men's faces & shoulders." At least two weapons had been broken "by force of blows over men's heads."[70] Nor was Trowell the only Quaker fatality. On 1 April 1683 the meeting at Devonshire House in London was interrupted by a party of soldiers led by Lieutenant Henry Minchard, who struck several Quakers over the head "with a large, knotty stick of crabtree." One of those assaulted was John Sparfield, "who received such a blow on his head and such a bruise in his side that he went home and . . . said he thought he should never get over it." He soon fell ill, "and spitting much blood, in about 14 days, died."[71]

Law-enforcement officers were also guilty at times of straying beyond the bounds of propriety or law by behaving with extreme pettiness or brutality. John Hellier, town clerk and later undersheriff in Bristol, was a particularly obnoxious character, who in February 1682 entered the Quaker meeting at the Friars, in company with some constables and a "rude rabble of boys," and forced Robert Gerrish, "an ancient man," in among the women Friends, telling him to preach, while calling him "friar" and "Pope" and the women "whores." As Hellier drove them all out of the meetinghouse, he thrust Gerrish again among the women, asking them "whether they would let their old friar go to prison," while pressing him to "kiss the women before he went." He finally took Gerrish to Bridewell. On another occasion he locked eighty-seven women and fourteen men in their meetinghouse for six hours, without letting them go to the toilet, telling the women "that the next time they should bring chamber pots with them." At one meeting, Hellier grabbed Rebecca Ithield's four-year-old son, lifted him up three times, each time "letting him down again in a pounding manner," while saying to him, "you rogue, will you come no more to meeting?" When the mother complained, Hellier turned on her: "You whore, I could thrust my cane down your throat." Nor was he reluctant to employ more violent methods against Bristol Quaker children, as witnessed by his behavior in July 1682 when he invaded a meeting in which children were predominant, their parents having been imprisoned. Using a twisted whalebone stick, he struck several boys on their heads and backs, almost cutting through the new hat of one of them, hit one girl "so furiously on the neck that it made a great scar as long as a man's finger," and hit another girl on her eyelid, "which hath made a scar there, and might have struck out her eye." The Quakers pointedly added that no other officer "but he" did the striking.[72]

As we have already seen, William Armorer in Berkshire was another overzealous magistrate. In January 1666, having used a sledgehammer to smash to pieces a series of interior doors in a Quaker's house, even where a key was available, he then proceeded to the meetinghouse and arrested three young men. When brought to his house, they refused to remove their hats, so he had them taken off and filled with water, and goaded the Quakers to put them back on. A constable standing by threw out the water, though, and gave them their hats, "it being very cold weather." Another time, having seen his nemesis Christopher Cheesman on the street, Armorer grabbed him, and "plucked him by the nose," warning that if he caught him at a meeting, "he would cut off his nose." It appears that Quaker noses were a favorite target, for in 1662 John Brain, a London Friend, was taken in the street by soldiers and brought to Alderman Richard Browne, who, after having the soldiers push Brain to the ground several times, ordered them "to pull off his nose also, which they spared not to assay to do, pulling him violently by the nose." For good measure, they also "played with their fingers upon his mouth," much to Browne's delight, "who laughed at the cruel & inhumane actions."[73]

At least one disruption of a meeting by civil authorities resulted in death. In Cirencester in July 1670, Thomas Masters, a justice, accompanied by other officers, broke up Friends' meeting. Robert Jenkins, a hangman, who "escaped the gallows to hang the rest," threw Quakers down a flight of stairs, one of whom, Elizabeth Hewlings, "was lamentably bruised and her shoulder separated, so she could not be recovered, but died in a short time."[74]

On numerous occasions, Friends complained about the activities of mobs of "rude boys," often tacitly encouraged by ministers or the civil authorities. But some mob action was spontaneous, and while often violent, it could also be rather silly, as in Norwich on Christmas Day 1676 when Friends insisted, as was their custom, on opening their shops. They were rewarded by snowballs, ice, and bones thrown through the doors and windows.[75]

A substantial amount of violence against Quakers also took place when goods were distrained, a highly contentious process encouraged by the second Conventicle Act and developed by the authorities into a potent weapon against dissent. However, because most legal commentators tended to focus on distraint for rent or damage-fesant,[76] there was some uncertaintly over various aspects of this punishment when utilized for nonpayment of fines. Ideally, the appropriate procedure, one often employed, called for lesser law-enforcement officers (empowered by statute) to select the goods to be taken. They were then valued by the town's official appraiser(s) and marked as distrained, but were often kept in the owner's house until such time as the officers carried them away. Public sale then followed. Although the appraised value should have given an indication of the price expected, the officers were not obliged to sell at the valuation, but only at the highest price offered.[77] As mentioned previously, the second Conventicle Act did permit an appeal after the fine was paid or levied, the latter often taken by officers to mean the time of distraint rather than of sale, another reason why goods were sometimes left in the offender's home. If the offender wished, he could then pay an amount equivalent to the fine as security to prosecute an appeal.

The imprecision surrounding distraining procedure allowed broad discretionary power to local officers, who were often confused, poorly educated, corrupt, and liable to penalties themselves should they fail to enforce the distraint adequately. Nor were they necessarily well-disposed towards Friends. In fact, the Quakers were unhappy with virtually every facet of distraining as it was practiced. First, informers were participating in distraints, either alone, with other informers, or with officers. That involvement was clearly illegal, since the statute empowered only lesser law-enforcement officers to distrain. Some cases bordered on the ridiculous, as in London in 1684 when Christopher Smith, an informer, accompanied by constables and watchmen, came to the home of Martha Halsey. After presenting a warrant for distraint, they took everything they found "from top to bottom of the house, spoiled most of her shop goods, . . . drank some, gave away some, sold some." Smith "kept the money." He and six others, who confessed they were "glad of the work," kept possession of the house for two days, pulling down her grates and copper and breaking her cistern. Their rapaciousness led them to take away "even . . . the empty bottles and old shoes." Halsey complained that they admitted "they cared not if they pulled down her house."[78] Another notorious London informer was Gabriel Shad, who came at night with a headborough, two soldiers, and others to levy a distraint on John Elson, a Quaker carpenter. After breaking open the doors, they impounded the goods and stayed in the house all night, eating and drinking everything they could get their hands on, including wine, brandy, ale, bread, and cheese, all in the name of the king. They refused to allow any of Elson's concerned neighbors to come in. One of the soldiers, with much bravado, swore he would "run his sword into some of their guts," and to prove he was serious, "drew it and run it through a hole of the door they had broke," almost wounding one of the female neighbors. Elson's wife Mary, who was home alone, was forced to stay up all night, and the following morning she witnessed four loads of household goods being hauled away, along with eight loads of timber and boards, "being trade goods," from her husband's timber yard.[79]

Elson did not accuse Shad of being intoxicated when arriving to make the distraint, but not all informers could be credited with sobriety. In 1685 two informers, Thomas Radcliff and Edward Boys, "being drunk," came with two constables to the Darlington home of Robert Truman in the evening, only an hour after they and other officers had levied a distraint there. On that occasion, they had found little, since Truman's household goods had been previously distrained. Undeterred, Radcliff "with a smith's great hammer" broke down the door, and found Truman's wife, servant, and a small child in the house. The servant was injured "with a splinter" when Radcliff smashed the door. Much to the informer's annoyance, he found little left in the house. Furious, the drunken Radcliff "fell on hacking up the bricks of the floor to take up a table that lay upon the posts fastened to the ground," screaming "whore" at Truman's wife, warning her frightened child "to get out of his presence," and grabbing the servant by the neck, "swearing he cared not what he did." He finally boasted that he was "as bad as he could be."[80]

As severe as these cases appear, they pale in comparison with that of William Bingley, a prominent London Friend, who had been fined for a meeting held on 25 October 1685. The warrant for distraint was issued to Duncomb Norris, a constable from Ludgate, who on 9 November came to Bingley's house with the beadle of the ward and five or six others, forced his way in and, according to the victim, seized his goods, "so much as my coals and candles and mine & my wife's wearing clothes." That should not have surprised Bingley, for Norris had warned him that he intended to take "fifty pounds worth of goods" for the £20 fine, and that "he would not leave . . . three pence in the house." After locking up the goods, Norris left the house in the overnight care of two watchmen, one of whom bore the majestic name of "Walkup Thorn." The next day Norris brought a city appraiser, who apparently undervalued the goods, although Bingley never received a copy of the inventory or the appraisal. The constable kept possession of the house, and gave the street door key to the watchmen who let whomever they pleased into the house "night & day," mostly "rude fellows," who sat "smoking and drinking" by Bingley's fire most of the night. Much to Bingley's concern, one of the watchmen, "a shabby fellow, who formerly was a fishmonger . . . and is now a hanger on to Newgate and Ludgate," carried the key outside with him, which he could have duplicated without Bingley's knowledge or consent. The constable then brought others into the house in order to purchase the goods, and on 12 November, still in possession of the premises, he commanded a company of porters to take away the goods. According to Bingley, Norris was not content with what he had already distrained, but tore down his bedsteads and curtains, and took away his bed and bedding. As a parting gesture, as the Bingleys were preparing a shoulder of mutton over a fire in the kitchen, Norris and his retinue entered the room and before the roast was finished, whisked away the spit, the dripping pan under it, all the dishes, chairs, stools, and kitchen table. They also interrupted the servants' dinner, taking their knives, tearing out the range while "throwing the fire about," and taking away other goods valued by Bingley at "eight or nine pounds," which were never inventoried or appraised. The constable and watchmen did not leave the house until the evening of 13 November, ending four days of turmoil for the Bingleys.[81]

While this episode was harsh, the critical issue in this, as in other distraints, was whether the goods taken covered the amount of the fine after sale. In Bingley's case, informers were apparently not involved; and the constable and the beadle were within their rights to gather the goods and to have them locked up, guarded, and appraised. A copy of the inventory and appraisal should have been provided when requested, however. Moreover, the overbearing manner in which the distrainers acted, their removing the house key from the premises, and their selling of the goods privately were by any standards unethical, if not illegal. More importantly, the opportunities for corruption which distraining afforded, combined with the often harsh treatment of the Quakers during such distraints, could undermine general respect for the rule of law. It could also contribute to the increasing alienation of those who normally opposed the Quakers, from a regime which brutalized its subjects into conforming.

Aside from violence, the most common Quaker complaints relating to distraints were underappraisal, overdistraint, and underselling. These issues, however, were extremely complex. It was natural for

Quakers to overvalue their own goods, and any claims of overdistraint need therefore to be examined with care. Yet discrepancies were often sizable, ranging as high as seven times the amount of the fine.[82] The Quakers believed that goods were deliberately undervalued, either by appraisers, if summoned, or by the informers and officers, less to promote potential sale than to quicken the ruin of those distrained upon. At the same time, Friends believed that underselling was also encouraged so that informers and officers themselves could purchase the goods cheaply. The Quakers cited many examples, including justices of the peace and even clergy. In one blatant episode, Isaac Smith, undersheriff in Cambridgeshire, when told by Quakers that it would be less detrimental to them for cattle rather than household goods to be distrained, apparently replied that he had "more need of household stuff."[83] Particularly difficult for Friends were those cases in which the original distraint, when sold, proved to be insufficient to pay the fine, leading the officers to levy yet more goods. Friends discovered from their counsel that, although irritating, this was legal.[84] The seeming lack of limitation to what authorities could distrain led Quakers to complain that distraints were often carefully calculated to destroy their ability to earn a living—a loom distrained from a weaver; bellows, anvil, vises, and other working tools from a blacksmith; a hatchet and shovel used in his work by a Cornish Friend. The Quakers emphasized that in each case other goods were available.[85] The Quakers believed that the government's misguided policy of religious "persecution" was provoking actions which, ultimately, would bring about national economic distress.[86] The suppression of the Huguenots in France would soon confirm their warning over the economic risks of destroying a productive segment of the population.

The Quakers were on less solid ground, however, when they protested about distraints made at night, or of cases where their locks and doors were broken open.[87] Although they might believe their homes were sanctuaries, if distraining was to be an effective punishment, it was imperative that officers have access to the homes of offenders at night and the right to break open locks and doors. Otherwise, Quakers and others could circumvent the law by remaining away from their homes during the day and locking up their valuables. The Conventicle Act, perhaps with this possibility in mind, had emphasized that all its clauses were to be construed most beneficially for the suppression of conventicles, and by implication this would include distraining. Doors could be broken open to suppress conventicles; it followed logically that doors could also be broken for punishment. That fact was apparently confirmed by the Crown's legal counsel, at least where the king's share was concerned.[88]

Nonetheless, the potential for abuse in the distraining process was substantial, particularly as officers and offenders were both aware that the appeal process was limited, often expensive, and given the vagaries of jury trials, not a guaranteed success. Friends often complained about goods which did not belong to them having been distrained,[89] although they were incorrect when they protested that sheep were illegally distrained from William Reynolds as payment for a fine incurred by his partner Thomas Reynolds, for as Friends' legal counsel reminded them, partners were liable for each others' debts.[90] Not legal, however, were instances in which goods previously seized and sold, but allowed by the purchaser to remain in the offender's home, were again seized for another meeting.[91] Distrainers may have been attempting to discourage sympathetic neighbors from assisting Quakers, for illegally distrained goods could be retrieved only by a replevin, a time-consuming and expensive process. Furthermore, some distraints were made on warrants as old as two years, and there is also evidence that informers were allowing fines to accumulate, particularly for recusancy, where £20 per month could quickly become hundreds of pounds. Since Quakers were often unaware they were being prosecuted either for recusancy or conventicles, they were unpleasantly surprised when officers turned up with warrants for vast sums.[92] In effect, these were other forms of harassment, particularly as the length of time between the crime and punishment made it difficult for Quakers to appeal.

The second Conventicle Act, Quakers complained, also promoted extortion, and they cited a number of cases in county Durham where informers thratened Quakers unless they privately compounded fines, or where they accepted large bribes from non-Quakers not to prosecute their Quaker relatives.[93] Any Friends involved in these transactions, of course, were not strictly adhering to Quaker practice. Nor were Friends happy that justices were often too ready to assume that Quaker offenders, particularly if prosecuted for preaching, were incapable of paying their fines. This assumption permitted such fines to be levied on the attenders and thereby helped to sow dissension among local Friends. Quakers like Richard Watson of county Durham, who insisted to the justices that he had "goods and chattels within the township of Norton . . . to the value of an hundred pounds upwards," endeavored to rectify the situation, but such efforts were sometimes to no avail.[94] Similarly, there were instances where the preacher was known, but warrants would state otherwise, thereby spreading the fines. Again the Friends involved would often approach the justices to remedy their "mistake."[95]

In Sussex in 1676 the Quakers implied that informers took advantage of the restrictions on appealing to swear against many Quakers who had not been at meetings, "knowing that this late Act yields us no relief in such a case, so that they take goods what they please and keep what they please for themselves, and say they can take more when they please, making no appraisement, nor giving any account to justices, court, or country."[96] Some informers also attempted to maximize their profits by convicting the same meeting before more than one justice. A classic case occurred in Sussex in December 1682 when two informers went to three justices, giving each of them information of a meeting at Lewes, who in turn issued three warrants to distrain "for one and the same meeting."[97]

What irritated Quakers more than any other aspect of the enforcement of this statute was the surreptitious nature of prosecution and conviction. Except on appeal, the Quakers did not have the opportunity of defending themselves, nor were the informers forced to confront them in a court of law. Conviction in the absence of the accused seemed to run counter to common-law tradition and to equity. Worse still, justices often appeared to encourage informers, disregarding as incidental their frequently false testimony. A particularly harsh offender in Quaker eyes was Sir Thomas Jenner, recorder of London, condemned by George Whitehead as an "eminent friend to, and encourager of the informers."[98]

Appeals did not go smoothly either. Friends claimed that many were deliberately obstructed or had encountered prejudice, particularly as the convicting justice often sat on the bench at appeals. Thus in Norwich, Samuel Duncon and Anthony Alexander blamed the failure of their appeal on the machinations of the mayor, the steward, and the court of aldermen. Writing to these officers, they asserted that the mayor had promised that if they appealed he would not take offense, despite having been the convicting officer. But at the trial, he had done all in his power to defeat the appeal, as had the steward, they claimed. Despite there having been only one witness, the court had told the jury that if the Quakers were at the meeting "that was enough," and thus ignored the fact that the statute demanded two witnesses and that it had not completely prohibited religious meetings. The court had also assumed that the intent of the meeting was religious and in manner other than the liturgy or practice of the Church of England, leading the Friends to complain that they had lost the appeal "upon supposition of their intentions." The court, they concluded, had acted with such arrogance that "those we employed to plead in the case, we perceive, were afraid of your displeasure, and so were subordinate to your wills, and thereby would not plead it fully according to their judgments."[99]

At the January 1677 quarter sessions in Nottingham, the Quakers complained that after they had won two appeals, the bench, at the instigation of two justices of the peace, Robert Thoroton and Pennistone Whalley, dismissed the jury, "being all substantial men, without exception when they were sworn." A new jury was impaneled "to answer their ends," the foreman being Whalley's bailiff, while another juror was his clerk. Notwithstanding, that jury deadlocked in the first appeal they tried, leading Whalley, according to Friends, to threaten the jurors that if they could not agree, *there they were likely to stay until they died, and as one died, they would chose another, until they were all dead.*" The jury then found against the appellants. The next day, another jury was selected, despite the opposition of the Quakers. Prior to the trials of the remaining appeals, Whalley uttered a memorable charge to that jury: "If they did believe that the Quakers did meet to MAKE MARRIAGES or TURN PAN-CAKES, they might find it for the Appellant, but if to WORSHIP GOD, they might find it for the king."[100]

Similarly, when Abraham Morrice, a Lincoln Quaker, had his appeal tried at Sleaford sessions in April 1676, he protested that the jury included tenants and constables from two towns where Sir Christopher Neville, who had issued the original warrant, resided. John Coddington, Neville's former servant and now his tenant, was put in as foreman. When only one informer appeared, Neville came off the bench and took an oath that "the information which he there showed upon the bench was true"; the jury found against the appellant.[101]

Even successful appeals had drawbacks, as John Lockwood learned in August 1683. He received £2 less than had been raised from the sale of his goods, for that was all the money which had been given to the clerk of the peace by the distraining constable, who still retained about 50*s*., apparently for the cost of his coach hire "when he came to make distress." The same constable also detained 31*s*. 6*d*. levied by distraint and sale on Ann Webster. In this instance, the Quakers petitioned the court to order the constable and headborough to restore the money, "your petitioners having been already at great charges about the trial . . . for the recovery of their goods & chattels distrained & taken from them." The sessions at Hicks Hall in February 1684 did order the money to be returned.[102] Such restitution, however, was not always possible, as John Elson discovered in 1683. Having been fined for being at a meeting he did not attend, Elson appealed, and paid £30 to the justice, Peter Sabb, but prior to the trial, Sabb absconded, "being an indigent person," and in order to prevent his being arrested and forced to pay his debts, went into the sanctuary of White Friars, and "in a little time after, died." Consequently, for want of the money or the record having been turned over to the sessions, the appeal was never tried. Anthony Ellwood, another Friend, had deposited £5 with the same justice for an appeal. That, too, disappeared.[103]

Another disheartening feature of appeals was the fact that after the fine or money levied was returned to the successful appellant, the costs of the trial and legal counsel had still to be paid. Successful appeals were little more than Pyrrhic victories, particularly when justices refused to discourage the testimony of perjured informers. Where, on the other hand, Quakers lost appeals, as they did at Newbury sessions, the result "proved injurious to Friends there & to the animating of informers."[104] The experience of Francis Plumstead, a London Friend, was particularly galling. After having been fined for attending two meetings and supposedly preaching in one, he appealed, claiming that he had not been present at one of the meetings nor preached in the other. The appeal was postponed from session to session until in August 1684 he secured an affidavit from the informers admitting that they had sworn falsely against him. At the trial, he produced two witnesses who testified that he had not preached. Sir Thomas Jenner, however, rather than grant both appeals, persuaded the jury to find Plumstead guilty of attending one meeting. The legal costs for the two appeals totalled £40. The same informers also retracted their testimony against two other Quakers who were still forced to prosecute appeals at great charge from session to session only to see them lost due to Jenner's dominance in the courtroom. At no time did he criticize the informers. Henry Kindon, another London Friend, prosecuted five appeals, lost three, and paid £72 in charges and fines. The primary informer against him was a woman who, Friends complained, used an alias and was later proved to have given perjured testimony. Kindon had also produced three witnesses to testify against her and pointed out, in addition, that his name had been incorrectly entered in the warrants.[105] Although Jenner may have been within his rights when handling these appeals, he would have been well advised to encourage the informers to be more accurate in their prosecutions. The frustration felt by many Quakers towards Jenner was summed up by George Whitehead when he told the Meeting for Sufferings in February 1685 that "many Friends in and about London have been frustrated in their appeals by alteration of records and by concealing of the witnesses aforehand and after . . . there having been alterations of records & warrants, both as to persons, days, & places."[106]

V

The primary goal of the second Conventicle Act was, of course, prosecution of large-scale meetings of Dissenters. Another tactic which could be used by the authorities was the demolition of meetinghouses. The Conventicle Act, if liberally interpreted, might have justified this approach, since it empowered the militia, together with law-enforcement officers, to take whatever steps were necessary to prevent or dissolve unlawful assemblies. Of greater significance was the encouragement given in June 1670 by Charles II, when he ordered his surveyor-general, Christopher Wren, to pull down the seats and pulpits in all dissenting meetinghouses in London, Bristol, and other corporate towns.[107] He followed this on 29 July with a specific order to Wren to have the Quaker meetinghouse at Horslydown "pulled down and demolished in case from henceforth any persons whatsoever shall presume to meet or hold any conventicle or unlawful assembly therein, under colour of religious worship." The order was posted on the meetinghouse door, and eventually a party of soldiers arrived with carpenters and others, who "pulled down the meeting house and carried away the boards, windows, benches, and forms and sold them." On 12 August 1670 officers and soldiers came to the Ratcliff meetinghouse in Schoolhouse Lane and took away sixty-one forms and two tables, while on 2 September a company of soldiers from the King's Own regiment, on orders from Sir John Robinson, completed the job by pulling down the meetinghouse, taking away "twelve cart loads of doors, windows, & floors, with other materials, as glass windows, casements, & lead, all the tiles being broken to pieces."[108]

These extreme measures proved to be exceptional[109] and were interrupted by the Declaration of Indulgence of 1672. But a more prolonged assault against meetinghouses began after the Declaration was rescinded and the war with Holland ended. The strategy assumed three forms: first, destruction of the interior of meetinghouses; second, the posting of guards to prevent Quakers from entering; and third, confiscation of the meetinghouse in the king's name, either by force or through the courts. Outright destruction was probably less preferable on two grounds. First, the Quakers would continue to meet on the site itself rather than in the streets, where it might be easier to prosecute them for riotous and tumultuous assembly. Second, many of the meetinghouses were either owned outright by the Quakers or leased from respectable establishment groups or individuals, including the king.[110] Destruction of such premises could cause an outcry as an attack on private property. In any event, no other Quaker meetinghouses appear to have been totally destroyed.

A typical instance of the new measures occurred in 1676 at Plymouth when the Quakers were kept out of their house and forced to assemble in the street three times a week in extreme cold and inclement weather, "abused by the rabble and scum of the people, and sometimes by the officers and soldiers of the garrison, who threw squibs of fire, and hot burning coals upon them, pushing them up and down the street, and bedaubing them with filthy excrements." At Minver, Cornwall, in October 1680 officers came to the meetinghouse and seized it in the king's name, padlocking the door and preventing the Quakers from entering.[111]

Concerted attacks on the houses began in the early 1680s when prosecution in general increased. Bristol Quakers were a constant target. On 14 December 1681 officers accompanied by "rude boys and some young men," came to the meetinghouse at the Friars, "seized the forms and benches," and proceeded to "break down the posts, rails, benches, wainscot, casements, windows, and things fixed and fastened to the freehold, contrary to law." They carried away "what they thought fit and burnt some in the place." On 20 December they continued the destruction, this time going upstairs to the dwelling of the tenant, Elizabeth Batho, throwing her chairs out the window, while the town marshal carried everything away, even sending the doors to Newgate prison. As quickly as Friends instituted repairs and added new furniture, the officers and mob destroyed them, the most serious attack coming on 27 December. Finally, three days later, after further havoc, the widow Batho, "having taken cold therein," and unable to move about with her crutch because of the ruins, sublet the house to John Woodward and moved out. She had been entitled to the house by a lease granted to John Batho, her late husband.[112] Similarly the meeting house in Temple Street was severely damaged in January 1682. Then in April, Meeting for Sufferings heard that officers and informers, bringing punch and "other strong liquors," and accompanied by fiddlers, had entered the meetinghouse, and as soon as Friends had gathered before the door, the "rude multitude" poured out of the house, struck up their music and tried to drag "several young women Friends in to them, but being prevented, after other abuses . . . sent several of the young women to Bridewell."[113]

Burning the forms, breaking the windows and doors, and general harassment became the modus operandi in many areas. Sitting tenants were also abused. Quakers retaliated by meeting in the streets. Although seemingly easier for the authorities to proceed against, these meetings, often silent, proved difficult to prosecute successfully. The authorities tended to regard such gatherings as riotous assemblies rather than conventicles, for appeal juries were unlikely to agree with the government contention that plots were being planned in public. But Friends were concerned about the possible loss of their meetinghouses. They attempted to counter government moves by leasing out a room in the premises to a Quaker, often an elderly female who, when the officers came, would contend that it was an inhabited dwelling.[114]

As has been seen, some officials resolved the matter by throwing the tenant out of the meetinghouse, the corollary of which would be the placing of their own people in possession. Thus at Bristol, when the authorities expelled Elizabeth Batho from Friars meetinghouse, they fastened up the doors with boards and sticks, claimed they were "seizing the house for the king," and put in "three or four persons," who went "in and out by a ladder through a window." It was officially seized "for want of an owner." In December 1685 at Worcester the meeting was kept outside, while the parish in which the house stood put a "poor woman" in possession, and threatened to install others. Meeting for Sufferings pointedly added, "they often formerly endeavoured to get the house from them & would know the owner."[115]

Sometimes the authorities appeared to back off. On 26 March

1686 Friends reported that the meetinghouse at Farringdon was to be seized on 30 March by the sheriff on pretext of a warrant from the attorney general, the town intending to put in its own tenant. Yet on 2 April the house was still to be seized, "no body owning it, as they say," with the intent now of converting it "to a workhouse for the poor." Troubles continued, for on 16 April the hundred constable, accompanied by a jury, came to the house just as the meeting was about to break up and inquired about its owner and use. The jury concluded that it was "a conventicle house," and valued it at 30s. a year, "though Friends manifested the owner & proffered to send for him, but was not accepted." The authorities intended to return their findings to the Exchequer and to continue legal proceedings. By order of Justice Fettiplace, the windows and doors were fastened and the woman Friend who lived there forced out. Early in May, William Parsons, the Quaker "tenant" of the meeting house[116] went to the authorities "to settle his under-tenant (one Edith Dietch, spinster) in the said house again, desiring the key to have the doors opened." Unfortunately, the officers, fearing Fettiplace's reaction, refused to hand over the key. Not one person, Friends added, was willing to appear as witnesses for them, for if anyone went to Fettiplace, claiming to be either a landlord or tenant, "he would take occasion against him & put ensnaring questions." A week later, Friends obtained a certificate from the officers explaining that the house had been locked up by order of three justices, including Fettiplace, but late in June 1686 the Quakers opened the meetinghouse doors and held a quiet meeting. Finally, on 16 July Meeting for Sufferings remarked cryptically: "about the meeting house matter, Friends think it best to let it rest."[117] Perhaps the most unorthodox legal tactic was adopted by the Woodbridge authorities who, in August 1683, prosecuted the meetinghouse "for being in the front of the town."[118]

VI

Conventicles, of course, were not the only criminal activity in which Friends engaged. But with the exception of violence, the scope for abuse in the suppression and prosecution of other crimes appeared to be less. This fact did not stop Friends, however, from objecting to prosecutions for vagrancy, recusancy, and tithes, nor as we will see, from combating them.

Although prosecutions of Quakers as vagabonds were sporadic and generally limited to the late 1650s and early 1660s, Friends pro-

tested that such accusations were both petty and illegal, since those accused were often sufficiently wealthy not to become dependent on local
rates for support, George Fox complaining that men worth as much as
£60 per year had been whipped "as sturdy beggars," and that "honest
men could hardly pass up and down to see their friends, and do their
outward occasions." Women were also vulnerable, he added, many
having been whipped on the same account. Furthermore, Edward Byllynge lamented, many of those so prosecuted had not been more than
twenty miles from home, nor out of their native county. In any event,
the Quaker system of local support led Byllynge to challenge any
"heathen" prosecutor of Friends to prove that any Quaker "hath asked
a morsel of his bread or a draught of his drink . . . for a begger we
deny, as a thief, for that which begs covets and desireth that which is
none of his own, and that which covets will steal." [119] Local officials, of
course, with neither the time nor inclination to examine the economic
status of wanderers professing to be Quakers, were probably operating within the law when they enforced the vagrancy statutes against
such persons. Strangers with eccentric religious views could only mean
trouble.

In recusancy prosecutions, the major problems for the Quakers
were procedural. At the conclusion of quarter sessions or assizes, indicted recusants were proclaimed and enjoined to appear at the next
sessions or assizes. Often Friends were unaware that they had been
proclaimed; nor was it clear whether they were to surrender themselves to the sheriff to be taken into custody, or simply to appear at the
next sessions or assizes. Neither were they clear on the precise manner
in which substantial parts of their estates would be confiscated, or as to
whether their estreats, or the record of their fines, had actually been
returned into the Exchequer and process issued. Some clerks and
local officers took advantage of these uncertainties, Somerset Friends
complaining of a racket whereby those who had been bound to attend
assizes for recusancy but who paid their fees were not questioned at
all, "as if men were called there on purpose to satisfy their greedy desires after money." [120] Quaker records also indicate that some Friends
were being illegally proceeded against for £20 per month after two-
thirds of their estate had been sequestered. Statute law permitted seizure as an alternative, rather than a complement, to the fine, nor
could the remaining one-third of the estate be liable for £20 per month,
although Friends could be proceeded against for 12*d*. per Sunday. But
Quaker complaints over being prosecuted in the ecclesiastical and secu-

lar courts at one and the same time or for one and the same offense
were groundless. This dual action was legal. More contentious were
the numerous occasions where Quakers were proceeded against for
recusancy while in prison. In fact, this was also legal, despite Thomas
Lower's belief that it was "a maxim in their own law that *lex cogit nemi-
nem ad impossibilia*, that is, the law doth not require impossibilities of
any; this for which we are now presented for (viz.) not coming to
church for 3 or 6 months past, it is impossible we could perform,
being all under a restraint."[121] Yet Friends were justifiably angry at
sheriffs who, having received writs from the courts at Westminster
calling for searches to be made for suspects in their locale, simply returned them *non est inventus*, thus preparing the way for outlawry
prosecutions. Friends would need to develop a system for learning of
potential prosecutions in advance in order to surrender to the sheriff
rather than assume any action on his part. Also illegal and unethical
were those instances in which Friends, convicted for 12*d*. for each
Sunday's absence from church, were imprisoned on a false return by
the churchwardens to the justices "that the persons . . . have no goods
or chattels sufficient for the levying of the fines imposed upon them."
That return, Friends insisted, was "notoriously known to be untrue,
the prisoners being known to be responsible, & several of them having . . . estates apparent."[122]

Procedurally, the most complex crime committed by Quakers was
nonpayment of tithes, an emotional issue for all Dissenters. As with
recusancy, a common complaint was the false return, with its serious
implications. In 1685, for example, five Lancashire Quakers were
prosecuted in the Exchequer for tithes, but refused to travel "nearly
200 miles" to London, for default of which Thomas Benson, an Ul-
verston attorney "got attachments, and so got the sheriff to return *non
est inventus* upon the several other writs issued out against them." That
was done despite the fact that the two Friends "proffered themselves
both to the bailiffs and commissioners in the writ of rebellion, and to
the sheriff upon the proclamation before they were returnable, who
refused to keep them, but returned as aforesaid, that they could not
be found, until they got sequestrations against them."[123] The most serious result of a false return was outlawry, as John Clark, of Somerset,
discovered in 1664 when he was proceeded against "so secret[ly], and
contrary to law that he never heard thereof until the execution came
upon him." He was outlawed "as a man not to be found, whereas he

constantly followed his public employments at markets and fairs & other places as his occasions required." In fact, he had appeared almost daily, "in view of the priest, his . . . neighbor, who waited for his prey, and through the help of lies obtained his end, as his father, the Devil." [124] Technically, however, the sheriff was not liable for his return, since he could claim to have tried in vain to find the offender. Again it would be important for the Quakers to be vigilant in learning of potential prosecutions.

The tortuous prosecution of a Cornwall Friend for refusal to pay tithes most clearly illustrates the many legal subterfuges Quakers and other Dissenters encountered in tithe prosecutions. In October 1660 Richard Tregennow was imprisoned at Bodmin by means of an attachment from the Exchequer for nonappearance to a tithe suit brought by James Forbes, a minister. While in prison, he was twice subpoenaed to appear at the Exchequer, and since he did not appear there, a writ of rebellion was issued. But Tregennow had been allowed to go home at harvest time by the gaoler; he was now retaken and sent to the Fleet prison in London. The warden of the Fleet, however, allowed him to return to Cornwall "for a season" to visit his wife and children. At that time, Forbes had him rearrested on a false action of debt. When Tregennow refused to post bail, he was again imprisoned at Bodmin on 27 May 1664. This phony action was an attempt to force the Quaker to break his word to the warden of the Fleet, since he would be unable to return there by Trinity Term as promised. Wisely, Tregennow quickly contacted the warden's deputy who, at his own request, allowed him to remain in prison at Bodmin. While Tregannow languished in prison, the undersheriff, "combining with the . . . priest's attorney, Thomas Dandy," sued him "to the exigent (as was alleged)." This action was the result of the undersheriff's permitting the several preliminary writs to be returned with the false response that Tregennow "was not to be found in his bailiwick," when in fact he was "in his custody." Tregennow was outlawed and a writ of enquiry executed, and his estate, which supported his wife and ten children, was undervalued, thereby prolonging the sequestration. Forbes immediately sent his bailiffs, who took away two kine, more than thirty sheep, five or six horses, two bullocks, and two oxen. Some of the horses, bullocks, and oxen belonged to Tregennow's neighbors, who were forced to buy them back for about £15. At Michaelmas, Forbes's "emissaries" returned and took eight pigs. Tregennow remained in prison, while his wife was forced to pay all the rent and taxes for the tenement, "because she lives in the house." In 1668, fearful that the prisoner might take legal action against him, his attorney, and the undersheriff for collusion in filing a false return, Forbes agreed to drop all charges provided Tregennow released him "and his agents." Tregennow replied in the affirmative and was set free. Nonetheless, in 1677 Forbes again sued the Friend to an outlawry, but Tregennow, having purchased about £500 worth of timber, decided to defend himself "to prolong time, to have a little liberty to make sale, and convert . . . [the] timber into money." In any event, he was ultimately outlawed and imprisoned in January 1682.[125] The Quakers fruitlessly complained against such legal tactics and fictions that had developed to counter nonpayment of tithes. But what alternative did the tithe owner have? Should he allow the Quakers to refuse payment? Until such time as tithes were ended, what was needed was a simpler legal method, without resorting to legal fictions, to recover them. This development awaited the reign of William III.

Other complaints made by Friends in relation to tithes were similar to those involving recusancy and illegal meetings and covered a wide spectrum, ranging from overdistraints and inflated or false claims to packed juries. In many instances the prosecutor, having had a Friend imprisoned, simply took away the wheat or corn, under the guise of court costs.[126]

VII

One punishment often awaiting Friends was imprisonment, which entailed social dislocation, but also threatened health and even life itself. Houses of correction and gaols have already been discussed. Unhappily for Friends, despite their complaints about hard conditions in gaol, contemporaries cared little about those imprisoned for the usual Quaker crimes—failure to provide sureties, to put in bail, or to pay fines. After all, the purpose of county rates was to provide county services, and not to make gaol a comfortable alternative to life outside its walls. Consequently, living conditions for prisoners were generally appalling, although often more dependent on a prisoner's ability to pay fees than on his or her offense or conduct. Fees were vital to prevent the cost of prisons from falling on public funds. Extra payments could procure such amenities as the right to have visitors; to receive provisions from friends and relatives, and to be allowed the use of pen, ink,

and paper. Privileges might also include the right to walk in the prison
yard, to go out into the town or surrounding countryside, even to go
home or to work during the day and simply spend nights in prison.[127]
The Quakers, by refusing to pay extra fees, made their time in gaol
that much more difficult.

Throughout the period extremely poor gaol conditions were often
exacerbated by sadistic gaolers. When George Fox and two other
Friends were imprisoned in Cornwall Castle, they came up against a
keeper who, by force of his appointment by the Crown lessee, Colonel
Robert Bennet, was ex-officio county gaoler with a substantial degree
of independence from the sheriff. When the keeper decided to alter
his fee agreement with the three Friends,[128] they simply made other
arrangements for their food and drink. In retaliation, he moved all
felons out of "Doomsdale" for thirteen days, replacing them with the
Quakers, who quickly realized that Doomsdale was aptly named, being
a "foul, nasty hole," without a chimney or toilet. The straw crawled
with vermin while the floor was ankle-deep with "puddles of piss"
and the excrement of former tenants. The keeper himself added to
the prisoners' woes. Having abused anyone who attempted to visit the
Quakers, he came in the evening to the felons' new quarters in the
room above Doomsdale, and proceeded, according to the imprisoned
Friends, to throw down "a pot with piss [and] excrements upon our
heads," and for good measure, "pissed down upon our heads . . . revil-
ing and raging, calling us . . . hatchet-faced dogs, devils, dumb dogs of
Egypt," while bragging that he would "nail our ears to the post." When
the Quakers implied that the sheriff or local major-general had authority over him, the keeper, somewhat perturbed, "bid a pox of God
take us, [and] that he would gag our tongues and . . . put irons upon
us, and would chain us to a post and use us like rogues." As a final
touch, he invited them to "kiss his arse and lick his arse and our noses in
his arse." What particularly galled George Fox was that the keeper, his
wife, the underkeeper and his wife, had all been branded as thieves.[129]

Unfortunately, the treatment of imprisoned Quakers often mir-
rored the violence and petty harassment they experienced outside of
prison, but also reflected the contemporary state of many gaols. The
latter often contained particularly nasty holes with appropriate nick-
names, like "little ease" in Northgate prison, which measured seventeen inches in width, nine inches in depth and fifty-four inches in
length, and into which, on several occasions, a rather large Friend,

Richard Sale, had been thrust, apparently causing his untimely death soon after his last such imprisonment. Portsmouth Quakers in 1660–61 were often thrown into a "damp, filthy hole," known as "Felton's Hole." One Friend was unfortunate enough to be imprisoned there on 24 December 1661 during a fierce storm which partly filled it with salt water, forcing him to "stand in the wet and cold and ladle out the water." He was denied a fire to dry his clothes and bedding, which were soaked; and he remained a prisoner there for almost eleven weeks.[130]

The mass arrests of Quakers during the early 1660s and 1680s often meant that gaols became seriously overcrowded, an especially dangerous situation if disease flared. Over an eight-month period in 1662 twenty-eight Quakers died in Newgate, while at least seventy-six more died there during the plague in 1664–65.[131] In February 1682, so many Quakers were imprisoned in Bristol Newgate that it resembled "the Exchange at full time." Their protests led to the formation of a committee of nine Bristol inhabitants who, accompanied by the sheriff, inspected conditions there and certified that the gaol was "very noisome in general and void of outlet for air, and therefore unfit to contain so great a number of prisoners as we find therein, being 125 close prisoners, besides the keeper and his family, 85 whereof are . . . Quakers." The latter, they added were "unreasonably thronged together, filling all the rooms in the gaol fit for lodging, except where the felons are." Some rooms had as many as nine beds, "besides several very little corners filled with 3 in a bed." Even worse, the report continued, many of the Quakers were forced to lie on the ground "in the open rooms where no bedsteads are to be placed, and spreading their mats on the ground they lie at that miserable rate that it was a grief to us to behold," that is, "some athwart the room, some under the table, being a kennel where the dogs were wont to lie, some upon the table, and some in hammocks over the table." The committee concluded that such conditions were particularly dangerous as the weather turned hotter, because of the increased likelihood of "infectious distempers to the endangering of health, not only of the said prisoners, but also of the inhabitants of this great city." This was supported by another certificate signed by four Bristol physicians.[132] Similar certificates were secured by the seventy Quaker prisoners jammed into the Norwich Guildhall in the autumn of that same year.[133]

The brutality of gaolers and the overcrowding of gaols were not the only dangers facing imprisoned Quakers. In what was a fairly common occurrence with predictable results, Stephen Harris and Joseph

Hall, the gaoler and undergaoler of the White Lion prison in Horsly-down, decided to teach the Quakers a lesson for refusing to pay the fees demanded, by putting them into the common ward with the felons. The latter immediately demanded half a crown apiece from the luckless Friends, who refused; the felons simply helped themselves, and when Harris came to the window, they told him what they had taken, and expressed their hope that "he would stand by them in what they did." Although he ordered them to return a cloak to one Friend, he allowed them to retain the stolen money and, together with his assistant, threatened the Quakers in colorful language. Given this lead, the felons warned the Friends that they would soon "be upon them again." The Quakers also protested about conditions in the ward—"a nasty, stinking hole," so crowded with the felons and several women, "which some of them called their wives," that there was no place for Friends to lay down their heads nor any stools to sit upon. Weary Friends were therefore forced to sit on the floor "among the vermin in a stinking place by the prisoners' urine."[134]

This lengthy catalogue of grievances culled from Quaker records clearly indicates that they were victims of illegal, unethical, and often violent behavior by law-enforcement officers and those under their control. Such conduct suggests a willingness by officers to ignore or distort legal restraints in response to parliamentary and royal pressure, and a concomitant failure by the legal system to protect adequately the rights of suspects viewed as political and social rebels. But rather than suffer passively, the Quakers took the offensive, gradually shaping and refining their attitude toward the law and those who enforced it, at the same time developing sophisticated, systematic, and relentless tactics in order to discourage and defeat their adversaries.

Notes

1. Cockburn, *Assizes*, 106–7; Ingram, "Communities and Courts," 123–25; J. A. Sharpe, "Crime and Delinquency in an Essex Parish 1600–1640," in *Crime in England*, ed. Cockburn, 95; see also Marchant, *Church Under Law*, 186; *Oxfordshire Justices*, lxv.

2. In fact, in June 1684 the justices in Southwark suspected that constables were being less than honest with money from the sale of distraints. Although the Quakers complained about irregularities in the distraining process, Meeting for Sufferings warned that it was not advantageous for Friends "to enquire into the concealments of monies by the officers because it may put the execution of laws the more forward, though some Friends think it might be of service to make manifest some officers defrauding the k[ing] of part of the

distresses" (Meeting for Sufferings, 3:186, 189). On the other hand, J. A. Sharpe believes that constables were more likely guilty of crimes of "omission" not "commission," and often in favor "of the offender rather than the system of law enforcement" (*Crime in Seventeenth-century England: A county study* [Cambridge, 1983], 175).

3. Robert Wastfield et al., *For the King and his Councill at White hall. Being A Brief Relation.* (London [1661]; F1436A). See also Robert Grassingham et al., *For the King and Both Houses of Parliament. The True State and Condition of the . . . Quakers* (London, 1661 [not in Wing]); *For the King and both Houses of Parliament. For You (who have Known . . .)* (London, 1660; F1436); Samuel Fisher et al., *This is to thee, O King, and thy Council* (London, 1660/1 [not in Wing]); George Fox, John Stubbs, and Henry Fell, *For the King and his Council, these* (London, 1660/1; F1822); Thomas Coveney et al., *For the King and both Houses of Parliament. Being a Short Relation* (London, 1661; F1435); *A Brief Relation of the Persecutions and Cruelties . . . Quakers* (London, 1662; B4629), 19.

4. Jeaffreson, ed., *Middlesex County Records*, 3:340–45. Of the 834 Quaker convictions, 347 were for meetings at the home of William Beane in Mile-End, 294 for meetings at the home of John Elson in Clerkenwell, 193 at the meeting house on Wheeler Street, Spitalfields. Jeaffreson does not comment on the religion of those convicted. Although Braithwaite believes that 859 of the 909 convictions were Quakers, only the foregoing meetings can be definitely identified as Quaker (*Second*, 41–42).

5. *To the King, and both Houses of Parliament, now Sitting in Westminster. Being, 1, a Representation* (London, 1666; T1490); Braithwaite, *Second*, 83–84; PRO: S.P. 29/307/166; see also Barry Reay, who emphasizes both the large number of Quakers praemunired and imprisoned as excommunicates in the early years of the Restoration ("Authorities and Early Restoration Quakerism," 76, 78).

6. Ellis Hookes, *For the King, and both Houses of Parliament* (London, 1675; H2661); *The Case of . . . Quakers . . . Especially upon old Statutes made Against Popish Recusants*, in John Whiting, *Persecution Exposed* (London, 1715), 33–34; Besse, *Sufferings*, xxxix; ORS, fols. 891–93; Miller, *Popery and Politics*, 267; see also ORS, fols. 880–90.

7. Braithwaite, *Second*, 115 and n. The number of sufferers during the Restoration period has been estimated as fifteen thousand (115n).

8. See Appendix 1. Quaker records clearly indicate that they were prosecuted under virtually every statute and law applicable to their testimonies, including their refusal to swear the oath of office as constables, churchwardens, beadles, surveyors of highways, aletasters, and tithingmen, or the oath as witnesses and jurors (see GBS, 1:135; 6:21–24, 31; Meeting for Sufferings, 1:75, 97; 5:307; 6:218; Besse, *Sufferings*, 1:7, 116, 238–39, 267, 316, 441, 449, 573, 611, 616–18, 648, 700–701, 703, 717, 760; 2:28, 163).

9. GBS, vol. 2, Oxford, 13; see also 1:389, 396; vol. 2, London and Middlesex, 10–12, 24–25, 103; 3:423; 6:396–97; Daniel Baker, *A Single and General Voice* (London, 1659; B485), 17; George Fox the Younger, *A True Relation of the Unlawful and Unreasonable Proceedings* (London, 1661; F2014)); WRO: A Collection of the Sufferings of . . . Quakers in Wilt-Shire, 1653–1702; Penney, ed., *Extracts of State Papers*, 17; Besse, *Sufferings*, 1:107, 179, 223, 348–49, 368–69; Meeting for Sufferings, 3:150, 263; HMC, *Report on Manuscripts in Various Collections*, vol. 1 (London, 1901), "The Records of Quarter Sessions in the County of Wilts," 143.

10. GBS, 5:313, 386, 397; ORS, fols. 551, 830; Meeting for Sufferings, 3:78, 351; 4:115, 250; see also ORS, fols. 6, 21; Besse, *Sufferings*, 1:472; GBS, vol. 2, London and Middlesex, 10–12; 5:314, 386.

11. Meeting for Sufferings, 3:351; 4:26; GBS, 5:387; ORS, fols. 562, 824; see also Dalton, *Countrey Justice*, 12; Baker, *Legal History*, 146.

12. Cockburn, *Assizes*, 107–8; GBS, 6:129–30, 138–39. Ironically, the Quakers would also complain that the authorities, soon after passage of the first Conventicle Act, were giving sentences of "3 or 4 days at a time that so they might proceed to banishment the sooner" (John Laurence to Albertus Otto Faber, 25.v [July].1664, Wramplingham, S.P. 29/100/110); see also John Rous to Margaret Fell, 6.vi [August].1664, Thirnbeck MSS, fol. 3; Whitehead, *Christian Progress*; GBS, vol. 2, London and Middlesex, 41–53, 58–60, 63–65, 74–76, 87–89; W. J. Hardy and W. L. Hardy, eds., *Hertfordshire County Records*, 1:169; 6:120–21, 125–26; S.P. 29/100/36; and the petition of Adam Gouldney, in HMC, *Various Collections*, "County of Wilts," 145.

13. GBS, vol. 2, London and Middlesex, 19. Crook, John Bolton, and Isaac Grey were found guilty and were committed to Newgate (*London Sessions*, 154).

14. GBS, vol. 2, Somerset, 30.

15. The following account is derived from GBS, 1:465–67; William Smith, *A True, Short, Impartial Relation* (London, 1664; s4341); Besse, *Sufferings*, 1:244–45. For the impact of Bridgeman's actions on local justices, see GBS, 1:470–77; Smith, *True, Short, Impartial Relation*. For further discussion on whether juries could judge law as well as fact, see Thomas A. Green, *Verdict According to Conscience: Perspectives on the English Criminal Trial Jury, 1200–1800* (Chicago, 1985), 200–49.

16. GBS, 1:466.

17. GBS, vol. 2, London and Middlesex, 57; see also William Smith, *The Innocency and Conscientiousness of the Quakers* (London, 1664; s4308); Besse, *Sufferings*, 1:396–97.

18. The following account is derived from GBS, vol. 2, London and Middlesex, 68–73; *The Cry of the Innocent & Oppressed for Justice* (London, 1664; c7450), 27; William C. Braithwaite, "London Friends Sentenced to Transportation, 1664–1665," 10, in FLL; Besse, *Sufferings*, 1:400–402.

19. GBS, vol. 2, London and Middlesex, 73.

20. For the reaction, see Esther Biddle to Francis Howgill, 17.viii [October].1664, London (PRO: S.P. 29/103/75); Ellis Hookes to Margaret Fell, 18.viii [October].1664, London (Swarthmore MSS, 1:47); George Whitehead to George Fox, 17.viii [October].1664, London (Swarthmore MSS, 4:61); H.P. to John Knowles, 22.viii [October].1664, London (S.P. 29/103/105); H.P. to John Knowles, 19.ix [November].1664, London (S.P. 29/105/20). The jury was not prosecuted (Braithwaite, *Second*, 45n). In December 1667 the House of Commons voted that fining juries was an innovation of dangerous consequences to the lives and liberties of the people (Braithwaite, *Second*, 45n).

21. GBS, vol. 2, London and Middlesex, 77–80; Besse, *Sufferings*, 1:403. Jeaffreson lists only eleven Quakers as convicted. They were sentenced to be transported to Jamaica (Jeaffreson, ed., *Middlesex County Records*, 3:361).

22. GBS, vol. 2, London and Middlesex, 83–86; see also Besse, *Sufferings*, 1:403.

23. GBS, vol. 2, London and Middlesex, 96–98; see also Besse, *Sufferings*, 1:405.

24. John Milward, *The Diary . . . September 1666 to May 1668*, ed. Caroline Robbins (Cambridge, 1938), 166–67. Kelyng's explanation to Commons inexplicably failed to include some of his instructions to the jury that would have put his behavior in a more favorable light; see Green, *Verdict According to Conscience*, 215.

25. GBS, vol. 2, London and Middlesex, 98; see also Besse, *Sufferings*, 1:406.

26. GBS, vol. 2, Worcester, 23; also 1:47–49.

27. GBS, 1:463–64. Besides Richard Thomas, the Quakers tried were Abraham Rutt, John King, and Henry Sweeting (W. J. Hardy and W. L. Hardy, eds., *Hertfordshire County Records*, 6:63, 72). Thomas's military background would again haunt him at Hertford midsummer sessions at the time of Monmouth's Rebellion. Described as "a person formerly in arms against King Charles I," Thomas was "therefore committed according to the late order" (*Hertfordshire County Records*, 1:352).

28. GBS, 1:471–72; see also W. J. Hardy and W. L. Hardy, eds., *Hertfordshire County Records*, 6:120–21.

29. GBS, 1:27.

30. That is, over the legal limit for attending a conventicle.

31. Compelled.

32. GBS, 1:42. In the event, Armorer recommitted the Quakers as "factious persons."

33. GBS, 1:44–45.

34. GBS, 1:52–53. The jury had originally deadlocked at six votes apiece, and were left overnight without fire or candle. In the morning, two jurors joined the six for conviction. The foreman gave that as the verdict, and before the four who believed otherwise could protest, the court passed sentence.

35. GBS, 1:56–57.

36. The following account is derived from GBS, vol. 2, London and Middlesex, 110–16; Barclay, ed., *Letters of Early Friends*, 177; Alfred Braithwaite, "Were Penn's Jury Starved," *Journal of the Friends Historical Society*, 53 (1972):58–61; William Penn, *The People's Ancient and Just Liberties Asserted in the Tryal of William Penn* (London, 1670; P1335); [Samuel Starling], *An Answer to the Seditious and Scandalous Pamphlet* (London, 1670; S5295)); William Penn, *Truth Rescued from Imposture* (London, 1670; P1362A); Besse, *Sufferings*, 1:416–18. For more on the role Penn envisioned for juries, and Starling's misinterpretation of that stance, see Green, *Verdict According to Conscience*, 228–29.

37. According to Starling, Penn was put in the dock because he "made such an uncivil noise that the court could not give the *jury* the charge" (*Answer to the Seditious*, 21). In the event, Starling insisted, Penn and Meade could still hear the charge quite clearly.

38. See *Reports and Arguments of . . . Sir John Vaughan Kt, late Lord Chief Justice . . . of Common Pleas*, 2d ed. (London, 1706), 135–58. Green believes that Vaughan took a rather narrow view of the proper role of the jury and failed to address any of the contentious judge vs. jury arguments then in vogue. For Vaughan, juries were still to judge fact, not law, but should be fined only for palpable misdemeanors, such as perjury or corruption (*Verdict According to Conscience*, 236–49).

39. Meeting for Sufferings, 2:2; GBS, 6:267; see also Thomas Amy to Thomas Rudyard, v [July].1680, Cambridge Castle (ORS, fol. 462).

40. Thomas Lower to Sarah Meade, 6.vi [August].1683, Launceston

(ORS, fol. 236); Thomas Lower to George Fox, 15.i [March].1683/4, Launceston (ORS, fol. 370). See also GBS, 3:257; 6:557–58; Norman Penney, ed., *Record of the Sufferings of Friends in Cornwall, 1655–1686* (London, 1928), 141–42; Besse, *Sufferings*, 2:165.

41. GBS, 4:4–7; see also Besse, *Sufferings*, 1:426–28. For other trials where juries proved to be difficult for the courts, see GBS, 1:84–85; vol. 2, Surrey, 5–7; 6:110–11. Perhaps Edward Sheldon, clerk of the peace, inadvertently summed up the dilemma facing many juries in Quaker trials. At Hicks Hall sessions in October 1664, the grand jury having refused to find a bill against some Quakers, Sheldon warned the jurors to "find or be fined" (GBS, vol. 2, London and Middlesex, 65).

42. GBS, 4:163; see also 1:464, 493–95; Besse, *Sufferings*, 1:534. In June 1666 Smith was again foreman, leading the Quaker defendants to object against him. Richard Rainsford, presiding justice, warmly praised his honesty and service to the king. "Thy honesty and his is much alike," sardonically commented one of the prisoners. Yet Smith was set aside, a small victory for Friends (GBS, 4:171–72).

43. J. North to Charles II, 18 February 1664 (PRO: S.P. 29/112/132); see also GBS, 1:471–74. The Quakers had scant success with inquest juries; see nn. 71, 74, below. Unfortunately for Friends, jury packing "was common and practiced on all sides" (Green, *Verdict According to Conscience*, 251).

44. GBS, 1:47.

45. GBS, 1:49. This coachman also served on the jury at the January 1667 sessions at Reading, Armorer believing "he would be a man fit for his purpose, for he hardly ever failed in any jury to bring in a Quaker guilty" (GBS, 1:52; see also 1:49).

46. GBS, vol. 2, Surrey, 6; see also John Chandler, *A True Relation of the Unjust Proceedings . . . Against . . . Quakers* ([London], 1662; c1929), 16; Whitehead, *Christian Progress*, 328–40. The witness was Humphrey Creswell; the Quakers who were tried were Daniel Rant, Robert Hasell, Henry Garrett, Richard Carter, and Isaac Jordan. See Hilary Jenkinson and Dorothy Powell, eds. *Surrey Quarter Sessions Records, 1661–1663*, Surrey Record Society, vol. 14 (Kingston, 1935), 249, 253.

47. Braithwaite, *Second Period*, 67.

48. Coke, *Third Institute*, 194; Braithwaite, *Second*, 78. A "nut-hook" was slang for a constable.

49. For example, Friends complained of ministers who encouraged informers to seek out Quaker meetings. "The men thou encouraged and employed being some idle, dissolute, and extravagant persons, not willing to take pains in the creation for a livelihood as other men do, . . . wandering from place to place to find out such peaceable meetings wherein if there be either preaching, praying, or waiting on God in silence, they trouble the magistrates, instigating *such as are willing to gratify them* (Penn, *Second Part of Continued Cry*, 5–6 [italics added]).

50. See, for example, Meeting for Sufferings, 2:210; 3:351; 4:250; ORS, fols. 246, 255, 336, 390, 395, 508–9, 534, 582, 589–90, 598; GBS, 1:384; Penn, *Second Part of Continued Cry*, 13–14; Besse, *Sufferings*, 1:322, 472, 607.

51. GBS, 5:479; ORS, fol. 148.

52. See, for example, GBS, 1:9; ORS, fols. 524, 558.

53. Meeting for Sufferings, 2:164; Penn, *Second Part of Continued Cry*,

64–65; see also *An Easie Way to Get Money* (London, 1671; E109B), 4; Besse, *Sufferings*, 1:555; Meeting for Sufferings, 2:108.

54. For example, see GBS, 1:35; Besse, *Sufferings*, 1:335, 516; 2:142.

55. GBS, 3:421. The informers admitted to four justices that they had lied about the meeting. Restitution was promised to Vickers, "yet none is yet made to her" (GBS, 3:421–22). There were also instances where Quaker business meetings were disturbed; see GBS, 3:421; Besse, *Sufferings*, 1:154, 252, 356; W. J. Hardy and W. L. Hardy, eds., *Hertfordshire County Records*, 1:326; Meeting for Sufferings, 3:329; Dix MSS, A14s. Yet Friends seemed less concerned about the disruption of business meetings; see, for example, Meeting for Sufferings, 3:325, 329.

56. See GBS, 3:946; 5:569; 6:146; Meeting for Sufferings, 3:263, 321; 4:264; ORS, fols. 129, 218, 605; Besse, *Sufferings*, 1:575; 2:76.

57. GBS, 6:271; see also Besse, *Sufferings*, 1:340–41; Meeting for Sufferings, 2:144; 3:75.

58. Whitehead, *Christian Progress*, 289–90.

59. The opinion of Thomas Corbett (Book of Cases, 1:116).

60. Meeting for Sufferings, 2:179, 187; Book of Cases, 1:114–15; see also Meeting for Sufferings, 2:138–39 where John Hilton is erroneously called "Richard."

61. To forbear prosecution in return for an agreed-upon sum of money. In effect, this practice defrauded the king.

62. Book of Cases, 1:166. Roger Morrice, a Presbyterian, also took an active interest in the Hiltons and Gabriel Shad, noting in December 1682 that they were "commonly said to be very obnoxious to the law in matters of perjury, forgery, or felony" (Morrice Ent'ring Book, 1:350; see also 1:353, 416, 623, 638). Captain George Hilton, in a lengthy rebuttal to criticism of his actions, claimed that Charles II had willingly accepted his offer to suppress conventicles, that he hired a retinue of forty others to assist him, and that he had received little reward and a good deal of aggravation because of negligent justices and constables, and fob actions by Dissenters against him and his servants (BL: Stowe MSS, 305, fols. 7–8).

63. Meeting for Sufferings, 4:1, 8, 236, 239; see also ORS, fol. 30. The Quakers campaigned strongly against informers; see Chapter 5, Quaker Legal Defense.

64. Margaret Fox to Charles II, 1684? (Thirnbeck MSS, fol. 20); East Sussex Record Office, Lewes: SOF 5/1/118–20; see also Robert Barrow to George Fox, 6.viii [October].1682, Kendal gaol (ARB MSS, fol. 138); *Cry of Oppression and Cruelty* (London, 1677; C7449A), 3; Meeting for Sufferings, 2:71, 121; 5:121, 287; Besse, *Sufferings*, 1:105; 2:159.

65. Reay, *Quakers and Authority*, 79, 95, 105. To his credit, Reay is the only historian thus far to have examined the nature of violence against the Quakers.

66. See GBS, 1:19, 81; vol. 2, London and Middlesex, 12–13; see also GBS, 1:21, 97, 440–41; vol. 2, London and Middlesex, 16–18.

67. GBS, 1:441, 446–47.

68. GBS, vol. 2, Surrey, 8; Whitehead, *Christian Progress*, 344–45; see also Besse, *Sufferings*, 1:95–96, 216, 259, 340–41, 725–26; Meeting for Sufferings, 3:75; Robert Allen, *Cry of Innocent Blood* (n.p., 1670; A1045B), 3–5.

69. GBS, 1:85.

70. GBS, vol. 2, London and Middlesex, 31; see also ORS, fol. 446; *Brief Relation of Persecutions and Cruelties*, 1–2. The Quakers often brought their dead

to a meeting house for viewing by Friends, who would meet there the next day "to go with them to the ground" (GBS, vol. 2, London and Middlesex, 59).

71. ORS, fol. 762; GBS, 5:337. An inquest was held and after two weeks the foreman of the jury and several others "were for bringing it an occasional [that is, incidental] death." The coroner advised them "they could make it no other than a natural death, so bid them hold up their hands, and 13 held up, but the foreman and 4 more dissented," to no avail (ORS, fol. 762; see also GBS, 5:337–39). London & Middlesex QM Digest of Burials records Sparfield's death "of a fever caused by blows," as on 13 April 1683, aged thirty.

72. GBS, 3:25, 47, 51, 61; see also ibid., 3:27–34, 62ff.

73. GBS, 1:45, 50; vol. 2, London and Middlesex, 22. One violent London official, Mayor John Robinson, was victimized by his own stupidity. While breaking up a meeting at the Bull and Mouth Tavern, he encouraged his officers to beat the Quakers, and then "spurred his horse to ride over Friends." Like most horses, however, the animal was "not willing to tread upon the people," and consequently "rose upon his hind legs so straight upright that John Robinson fell off backwards & pitched upon his back in the kennel & there lay till he was helped up" (GBS, vol. 2, London and Middlesex, 38).

74. GBS, 1:430. At the coroner's inquest, Thomas Masters packed the jury with "many of his tenants," while his clerk threatened Friends in front of the coroner that they would have been wiser to have kept silent, "for it should make the worst for them, for they did not deserve the benefit of the law." He added that he would excuse the hangman "for two pence." Although several eyewitnesses swore to the events, "yet the tenants, for fear of displeasing their landlord, and the coroner willing to take part with the persecutors, . . . said she died of 'God's visitation,' though several of them saw the corpse and the bruises, and said it was a sad sight to behold, and did believe she was greatly wronged" (GBS, 1:430).

75. Eddington, *First Fifty Years of Quakerism*, 94 from the Norwich QM Sufferings Book, 73); but also see the case of Elizabeth Peacock, spotted shopping at the Shambles, a London meat market, and severely beaten by a mob of butchers and others (GBS, vol. 2, London and Middlesex, 9). See also GBS, 1:23; 3:925–26, 927; 4:13–14.

76. For example, see Sheppard, *Epitome of the Laws*, 453–63. Damagefesant involved cases where goods or cattle of one man were upon the ground of another without lawful authority or license. The owner of the ground could distrain them (Sheppard, *Epitome*, 455).

77. See Dalton, *Countrey Justice*, 104. At least one legal commentator, however, believed that in cases where goods were appraised at values which effectively prohibited sale, the appraisers were to be forced to purchase the goods themselves at the appraised value, a serious disincentive to high appraisals. Edmund Wingate, *The Body of the Common Law* (London, 1655; w3006), 69; see also Chapter 5, Quaker Legal Defense.

78. GBS, 5:386–87. The warrant for distraint incorrectly gave her name as "Margaret" Halsey. See also *Second Part of Continued Cry*, 86–87; Eddington, *First Fifty Years of Quakerism*, 86–88.

79. GBS, 5:357–58; see also ORS, fol. 360.

80. GBS, 3:448. Radcliff and other Durham informers were rather active, viewing informing as an easier life than working. Radcliff, for example, had been a Darlington weaver, but took down his looms, sold his goods, and joined with Edward Boys to become informers, while turning his shop into "a

warehouse for Friends' goods, as he declared." He was encouraged in this by George Bell, a Darlington minister, who commended him "for his wit," and that he was "a fine, apt lad." Bell's wife praised the two informers for doing God "a great deal of good service, for their church was never so filled as it is now." At one point, Durham Friends complained, "there were so many informers, and they got so many warrants, and strove so hard who should be served first, that Friends knew not by which warrants their goods were taken, for many times they refused to show them, and sometimes took away Friends' goods out of their grounds, and they never knew of it till they missed them, or some neighbour came and told them" (GBS, 3:428–30).

81. GBS, 5:436–37. Bingley unsuccessfully appealed his conviction (ORS, fol. 152).

82. See GBS, 1:11–12; 4:450–51; 5:389; WRO: The Booke of Regester . . . of Sufferings of . . . Quakers in . . . Wilts, 7; Meeting for Sufferings, 2:108, 203, 205, 226; 4:37; 5:199; *An Easie Way to Get Money*, 6–7; Besse, *Sufferings*, 1:4–11, 295, 720. The Quakers complained that St. John Chernock, a justice in Bedfordshire, encouraged overdistraint "because but few would buy the goods." Consequently, Friends lamented, they were obliged to pay "for the people's disaffection to the work" (GBS, 1:11).

83. Besse, *Sufferings*, 1:97; see also 1:107, 120, 264, 338, 344, 504, 601; and 2:129; further, see GBS, 1:12; 3:422–23.

84. The opinion of Henry Pollexfen (Meeting for Sufferings, 2:204) and of John Darnell (Book of Cases, 1:158–59).

85. See GBS, 1:13; Besse, *Sufferings*, 1:10, 94, 96, 120, 172, 217, 345, 469; Meeting for Sufferings, 2:199; 3:16, 26. Sheppard believed that distraints were not permitted of "such necessary tools and instruments as are necessary to keep men in their callings and for their livelihood, as a carpenter's ax, as a smith's anvil" (*Epitome of the Laws*, 457).

86. William Penn in 1679, using the pseudonym Philanglus, epitomized the feeling of many Friends: "But since the *industry*, *rents* and *taxes* of the *Dissenters* are as currant as their neighbours, who loses by such narrowness more than *England*, than the government and the magistracy? For till it be the *interest of the farmer* to *destroy his flock, to starve the horse he rides, and the cow that gives him milk*, it cannot be the *interest* of *England* to let a great part of her sober and useful inhabitants be destroy'd about things that concern another world" (*One Project for the Good of England: That is, Our Civil Union is our Civil Safety* [London, 1680; P1334], in *A Collection of the Works of William Penn*, 2 vols. [London, 1726], 2:686). In their 1685 petition to James II, Friends noted that those in prison included several manufacturers who had employed hundreds of workers and had paid considerable taxes to the king (Besse, *Sufferings*, xli–xlii).

87. See Meeting for Sufferings, 2:141, 143, 199; 3:150; 4:37, 283; Besse, *Sufferings*, 1:172, 295.

88. PRO: S.P. 104/176/241; see also Meeting for Sufferings, 3:84. Quaker legal counsel was less certain; see Chapter 5, Quaker Legal Defense.

89. See GBS, 5:357, 386–87; ORS, fol. 360; Meeting for Sufferings, 1:34; 3:307, 312, 348; 4:132, 168; Book of Cases, 1:160; Besse, *Sufferings*, 1:679.

90. The opinion of Thomas Corbett (Book of Cases, 1:49), although later disputed by another counselor (Book of Cases, 1:117).

91. See Besse, *Sufferings*, 1:298–99, 469; Meeting for Sufferings, 3:307, 348; 4:230; see also Chapter 5, Quaker Legal Defense.

92. For old warrants, see Meeting for Sufferings, 2:218; 3:14; for accumulated fines, see GBS, 6:466–67; Besse, *Sufferings*, 1:82–83, 673; Isabel Ross, *Margaret Fell: Mother of Quakerism* (London, 1949), 320.

93. GBS, 3:452–53; see also J. C. Atkinson, ed., *North Riding Quarter Sessions Records*, The North Riding Record Society, 9 vols. (London, 1884–92), 7:27, where James Phillips at Thirsk sessions, 7 October 1679, was disabled from acting in future as an informer, having previously "under the color of an informer . . . committed several misdemeanors and received sums of money of several persons unlawfully."

94. GBS, 1:387; see also GBS, 1:393; Besse, *Sufferings*, 1:133, 179, 295; ORS, fol. 805.

95. See ARB MSS, fol. 138; GBS, 1:10; 5:377, 476; ORS, fols. 27, 360, 530, 557, 573. The Quakers would also insist that if a preacher was a stranger, or had fled, "he ought to be sought after and found (if it may be) before any fine on him, or on others for him, be set" (Thomas Ellwood, *A Caution to Constables* [London, 1683; E616], 11).

96. Quoted in Besse, *Sufferings*, 1:720. The Quakers were here referring to the limiting of appeals to fines over 10*s.*; see also Ellwood, *Caution to Constables*, 12.

97. GBS, 4:451; see also WRO: The Collection of the Sufferings of . . . Quakers in Wilt-Shire, 1653–1773, unpaginated; HMC, *Various Collections*, "County of Wilts," 150.

98. Whitehead, *Christian Progress*, 550. "These informers being accepted for credible witnesses, yet parties, swearing for their own profit and gain in the absence of the persons prosecuted . . . we think is very hard, . . . and not consistent with common law or justice. As also convicting and fining us upon their depositions, unsummon'd and unheard in our own defence. . . . This procedure appears contrary to the Law . . . of God, common justice and equity, and to the law and justice of the ancient Romans . . . and of nations" (*To the King and Both Houses . . . the Suffering Condition of the . . . Quakers* [London, 1685?; T1491], 3); see also Ellwood, *Caution to Constables*, 10–12; *A Request to the Justices not to make Convictions* ([London, 1684]; R1120); *To the King and Both Houses of Parliament. Here are some of our Sufferings* ([London, 1680]; T1489A); *An Easie Way to Get Money*, 5–6; Penn, *Second Part of Continued Cry*, 13; Meeting for Sufferings, 3:60; ORS, fol. 826.

99. S. Duncon and A. Alexander to the Mayor, steward, and court of aldermen of Norwich [January 1670] (Eddington, *First Fifty Years of Quakerism*, 71–74).

100. Penn, *Second Part of Continued Cry*, 65–73 [capitals and italics in original].

101. Penn, *Second Part of Continued Cry*, 100–101.

102. Meeting for Sufferings, 3:14, 110; Book of Cases, 1:151–52. Alternatively, the justices at Richmond quarter sessions on 17 January 1671, having been told that North Riding petty constables were "put unto great charge in and about the levying of such sums of money as are forfeited by the Quakers for their being at unlawful conventicles," ordered the reimbursement of such expenses "out of such penalties as shall be by them respectively levied, according to the discretion of the justices before whom such Quakers are . . . convicted" (Atkinson, ed., *North Riding Quarter Sessions Records*, 6:153).

103. GBS, 5:358; see also ORS, fol. 533; Meeting for Sufferings, 5:235.

104. Meeting for Sufferings, 3:149; see also *To the King and Both Houses* (1685?), 3; *A Request to Justices.*

105. GBS, 5:391–92, 397, 474; ORS, fols. 154, 519, 601, 827; Besse, *Sufferings*, 1:467–68, 474. The informer against Kindon was Anne Smith alias Bowles, while his name in the warrants was Henry Candel alias Kendal. See also ORS, fols. 397, 474.

106. Meeting for Sufferings, 3:347; see also GBS, 5:393, 453; ORS, fol. 558. Whitehead was referring specifically to Sir Thomas Jenner.

107. Braithwaite, *Second*, 68.

108. Whitehead, *Christian Progress*, 341–43; Besse, *Sufferings*, 1:696–97; Braithwaite, *Second*, 76; GBS, vol. 2, London and Middlesex, 105–6.

109. The authorities in London in 1670–71 generally preferred to use soldiers to prevent Friends from meeting in their normal places, forcing them to meet in the street. Anyone who preached was taken away and imprisoned, sometimes on the Five Mile Act, while large groups of other Friends were imprisoned for brief periods and fined. At one point, soldiers broke the doors and windows at Whitehart Court meetinghouse to gain entrance before the Quakers met, and allowed an Anglican minister to preach from the Book of Common Prayer (see GBS, vol. 2, London and Middlesex, 100–9; 4:8–11). In Chippenham, Wiltshire, late in 1670, authorities nailed shut the door to the meetinghouse which had been built on the land of Thomas Neate (HMC, *Various Collections*, "County of Wilts," 150).

110. In London and environs, all of the early meetinghouses were leasehold with terms predicated on the lives of named Friends. Among the landlords were: Christ's Hospital; the dean and chapter of Westminster Abbey; the bishop of Winchester; Charles II (either as king of England or duke of Lancaster); and the vestry of Saint Olaves. Deptford was the first freehold meetinghouse site to be purchased (George W. Edwards, "The London Six Weeks Meeting," *Journal of the Friends Historical Society* 50 [1962]:231).

111. Besse, *Sufferings*, 1:161; GBS, 3:249.

112. GBS, 3:21–23. For more on Elizabeth and John Batho, and John Woodward, see Mortimer, ed., *Bristol Men's Minutes 1667–1686*, 194, 222. On 3 January 1682, John Woodward was also forced out (GBS, 1:23).

113. Meeting for Sufferings, 2:80, 113; see also Besse, *Sufferings*, 1:54, 59–60; GBS, 3:23. The Bristol authorities attacked the two meetinghouses for failure to pay assessments towards the militia, despite Friends' contention that neither house was legally liable "to find a man in arms, not being in value £20 per annum, nor ever by them pretended to be assessed." In any event, Friends added, the penalty was fine by distraint, "not riots on houses" (GBS, 3:23).

114. For riot prosecutions, see Meeting for Sufferings, 2:89, 138–39, 155; 3:14, 88, 145, 206, 244, 265, 337, 349; 4:264, 281; ORS, fols. 199, 726, 912, 917–21, 962, 969–70, 979; GBS, 5:362, 410–12, 419–20, 459; 6:557–58; London & Middlesex QM Sufferings, 558, 630; Whitehead, *Christian Progress*, 559–64; Hardy and Reckitt, eds., *Buckingham Sessions Records*, 1:124; Quintrell, ed., *Proceedings of the Lancashire Justices*, 147. For Quaker strategies regarding their meetinghouses, see Chapter 5, Quaker Legal Defense.

115. Meeting for Sufferings, 2:83, 145; 4:228; Besse, *Sufferings*, 1:54.

116. Probably the "owner" mentioned previously by Friends.

117. Meeting for Sufferings, 5:37, 44, 77, 91, 96–97, 109, 118, 122, 160, 162, 181; see also Whitehead, *Christian Progress*, 614–15; GBS, 5:503, where Southwark meetinghouse was converted into a guard house. When the soldiers left for camp, Friends discovered £40 in damage.

118. Meeting for Sufferings, 3 : 15. In the late 1670s and early 1680s, Quaker meetinghouses were partially destroyed, locked up, confiscated or under threat throughout the country (see Meeting for Sufferings, 2 : 148, 163, 180; 3 : 14, 16–17, 60, 180, 183, 189, 263, 294, 297–98; 4 : 9, 82, 154, 182, 190, 222, 228, 271a, 283; 5 : 60, 101, 151, 198, 248, 274; Besse, *Sufferings*, 1 : 161, 171–72, 197, 223, 261, 626, 628, 676, 680, 698; Morrice Entr'ing Book, 1 : 438).

119. Fox, *Several Papers Given Forth* (London, 1660; F1901), 4; Byllynge, *A Word of Reproof*, 58–59.

120. GBS, 2 : 40.

121. Meeting for Sufferings, 2 : 160; 3 : 20, 110, 172, 281, 330; 4 : 162; GBS, 1 : 569; vol. 2, Sussex, 13; 4 : 313; 6 : 300; Lower to Fox, 23.1 [March]. 1683/4 (ORS, fol. 398). See also Chapter 5, Quaker Legal Defense.

122. Meeting for Sufferings, 3 : 38; see also Meeting for Sufferings, 4 : 26.

123. GBS, 3 : 884; see also Meeting for Sufferings, 3 : 150.

124. GBS, vol. 2, Somerset, 50; see also Besse, *Sufferings*, 1 : 317; Meeting for Sufferings, 6 : 186.

125. GBS, 1 : 164; ORS, fol. 436.

126. See Besse, *Sufferings*, 1 : 7, 119, 202, 235, 295–96, 320, 322, 677, 712, 719, 721; GBS, 1 : 199–200; vol. 2, Sussex, 9–10; 4 : 206; 6 : 45; Penney, ed., *Sufferings in Cornwall*, 39; Meeting for Sufferings, 5 : 278; 6 : 178, 205.

127. *Kesteven*, xxii–xxiii; Veale, *Law Reform*, 15; *Warwick Records*, 7:cvii; Gerald Cragg, *Puritanism in the Age of the Great Persecution 1660–1688* (Cambridge, 1957), 113–15. Despite the importance of fees for keeping up prisons, justices in at least two counties employed fines levied against Quakers for repairing or stocking houses of correction (see Atkinson, ed., *North Riding Quarter Sessions Records*, 6 : 67–68; Quintrell, ed., *Proceedings of the Lancashire Justices*, 109, 114).

128. The Friends had agreed to pay 33s. per week for the chamber, meat, drink, and "all things" for their "accommodation," but the keeper soon tired of this arrangement and demanded at least 40s. per week, while at the same time trying to prevent any alternative arrangement by the prisoners (see ORS, fol. 623).

129. ORS, fols. 304, 623; see also Fox, *Journal*, ed. Nickalls, 40, 159–62, 252–54; Fox, *Journal*, ed. Penney, 1 : 227; Edward Pyott et al., *The West Answering to the North* (London, 1657), 34–39.

130. Braithwaite, *Beginnings*, 126–27; GBS, 1:441, 447–48; see also Besse, *Sufferings*, 1 : 100–1; GBS, 1 : 22.

131. GBS, vol. 2, London and Middlesex, 29–31, 74, 100. "H.P.," writing to John Knowles on 30 September 1664 commented that Newgate was "so full of persons of all constitutions that they infect one another & have an infectious malignant fever raging among them, which sends many of them," he lamented, "to the long home" (PRO: S.P. 29/102/137).

132. GBS, 3 : 30, 38–39.

133. See Penney, ed., *First Publishers of Truth*, 180–81.

134. GBS, vol. 2, Surrey, 10–11; see also ARB MSS, fol. 89; Meeting for Sufferings, 3 : 91.

Chapter Four

THE LAMB'S WAR

Yet we do declare, as it is testified in all counties, cities, gaols, and prisons, to judges, justices, and others, that as we preach Christ Jesus alone in the things of God to be our law-giver, so do we own Him to be our king (and own magistrates in things civil) not resisting the evil, but following His example who was made perfect through suffering, and for His salvation we wait, till He alone shall plead our cause, and therefore for conscience sake we have joyfully born, and do bear so many and great sufferings, since the day we were convinced of the everlasting truth.

A Declaration of the Present Sufferings of Above 140 Persons . . . called Quakers (London, 1659), 30

That it is convenient the Friends that suffer beyond the limits and severity of the law have an understanding thereof for divers causes, and especially to be capable of laying it on the heads of their persecutors for exceeding the bounds of their own law in severity, and that they may know in what cases relief may be had, they having their liberty in the Truth to accept thereof or to suffer. . . . That in all such cases wherein Friends want information in point of law they may send up their questions to Thomas Rudyard or Ellis Hookes to procure and send them a resolve, both as to such cases wherein they may have relief and wherein they may not, that they may not remain in any groundless or uncertain expectation.

Minutes of London Yearly Meeting, 1 : 27

I

The previous chapter suggested that the Quakers were brutalized by law-enforcement officers, informers, and the militia, and that they were victimized by unethical and illegal tactics, by primitive courtroom procedure, by hectoring judges, and by intimidated juries. Their meetinghouses were often battered or confiscated; they were themselves imprisoned in primitive gaols in the care of abusive gaolers, their goods and estates often confiscated, and their livelihoods destroyed. It is a bleak and despairing picture, yet one which reflected the Quakers' own view of themselves as a people at war—the "Lamb's war" against the "Beast." This struggle was fought with spiritual, rather than "carnal" weapons; for the Quakers, in the tradition of Christ and the apostles, were determined to convert their enemies. Well aware that they often faced severe opposition, Friends knew they would suffer, but they also presupposed victory. Their strategy was one of confrontation—to bring their sufferings to bear on the consciences of those who opposed and "persecuted" them, thereby forcing the persecutor to see the Light within. To gain success, the Quakers simply could not suffer passively. As Hugh Barbour so aptly comments, this differentiated them from many other sects who viewed suffering as a "negative part of their apocalyptic outlook, a sign of the increasing power of Antichrist and the nearness of deliverance," while Friends viewed it as a "positive setting for the Lamb's victories."[1]

Sufferings, however, would also reinforce the Quakers' own collective consciousness as a "martyred" body of saints in the tradition of the apostles. To sustain that belief and to show persecutors the extent to which they suffered, Friends developed a system of collecting, recording, and printing their sufferings. Ironically, this served yet another purpose—one that did not concern early Quakers, but that became increasingly important with the passage of time. Records of suffering could be used as precedents that, when supported by legal advice and a centralized organization, could preserve Friends from imprisonment or economic ruin. In many respects, therefore, the establishment of the Meeting for Sufferings in 1676 was pivotal for the Quakers, as it clearly demonstrated their corporate resolve to combat their enemies with the latter's own weapon—the law.

Although many of the arguments and tactics employed by the Meeting for Sufferings had their genesis in earlier Quaker behavior, the willingness to utilize legal counsel on a broad scale was a decisive step for a sect which had generally condemned the legal profession. In effect, the Quakers metamorphosed from a radical sect ostensibly contemptuous of legal procedure into one which embraced those procedures to thwart their opponents and to procure their own freedom, without sacrificing their basic principles. The reasons for this change were probably twofold. First, since there is little evidence that early Friends had been involved in efforts to reform the law, they were probably ill-informed about the legal system and therefore ill-prepared to confront the bewildering complexity of seventeenth-century legal procedure. Quaker testimonies had not considered such concerns as pleas, sureties, bail, fees, and traverses. Only after extended exposure to such concepts would Friends begin to devise strategies in accord with their principles. Initially, their defense against prosecution relied heavily on their concept of equity ("Do unto others"), their belief that religious testimonies should not be prosecuted if legitimately held, and that the "Law of God" took precedence over that of man.[2] Although interesting points for debate, such arguments were scarcely calculated to sway either judges or juries. These early efforts were normally in reaction to specific circumstances and were not systematically developed. Only gradually did the Quakers realize that their survival as a sect might depend as much on the acquisition and utilization of legal knowledge as on their religious message.

Second, by 1676 Quaker leadership had shifted away from the rather isolated North to the area around London, in close proximity to Westminster and Whitehall. Many of these leaders represented a newer generation of Quakers whose interests were more commercial and professional and less agricultural—men such as James Claypoole, Thomas Rudyard, William Penn, Thomas Barker, William Bingley, John Elson, Philip Ford, William Meade, John Field, William Crouch, John Vaughton, Francis Camfield, and George Whitehead.[3] London Friends would dominate the vital executive committees of Quakerism—the Second-Day's Morning Meeting, the Meeting for Sufferings, and Yearly Meeting. Less millenarian and "enthusiastic" than earlier Friends, these men were pragmatists who understood that organization, lobbying, and legal tactics were imperatives to any strategy of survival in a hostile political and religious environment. Nor would influence at court be frowned upon; William Penn, George Whitehead, and Robert Barclay became influential courtiers during the reign of James II.

These developments should not, however, conceal the fact that prior to the 1670s Friends had haphazardly employed pressure-group tactics, and had provided positive suggestions about ending the injustices of the legal system. Almost from the beginning, the Quakers' confrontational style extended to their sufferings. They were inveterate writers of letters and petitions to those in authority, whether officers connected with their particular case, or superiors such as assize judges, justices of the peace, members of Parliament, and above all, the king.[4] As early as 1650 George Fox had written seventeen letters about his case to justices and others in authority, while in 1656 he and his fellow prisoners at Launceston, wrote to the judge, the juries, and to Major-General Desborough. In fact, it appears to have been rare for imprisoned Quakers not to write to those in power. In addition, Friends often relied on personal contact with the authorities, including the head of state. During the Commonwealth, Lord Protector Cromwell had been visited on numerous occasions by Friends demanding religious toleration, while in 1660 alone, Charles II received personal appeals from Richard Hubberthorne, Margaret Fell, Ann Curtis, and Thomas Moore.[5]

In 1657 George Fox had encouraged the Quakers to present countywide sufferings to the judges of assize, and in 1658 he began to organize a system of local recording of sufferings to be sent to London for incorporation by Ellis Hookes, Friends' salaried "recording clerk," into the "Great Book of Sufferings," and for use in petitions and printed tracts.[6] Wherever possible the Quakers published their sufferings: it has been estimated that 88 Quaker works before 1660 dealt with sufferings, either described or tabulated, while between 1660 and 1688 another 145 were published.[7] As Quaker organization expanded, the system for recording sufferings became increasingly elaborate. The notable year in that expansion was 1667 with the establishment of monthly meetings—regular gatherings of Quakers from local meetings within a definite area which would help provide direction and leadership; regulate conduct; oversee marriages; and act as a conduit for recording sufferings. Monthly meetings were in turn grouped into quarterly meetings, performing many of the same tasks. Of the utmost importance, however, was a December 1668 meeting in London of ministering Friends who decided on annual meetings, with the first to be held at Easter 1670, the beginning of London Yearly Meeting. The 1668 meeting called for the reporting of sufferings from the monthly meetings to the quarterly meetings and so to London "that nothing of the memorial of the blood and cruel sufferings of the brethren be lost."[8] By this time, London Friends were already acting formally on behalf of suffering Friends throughout England.[9] The Yearly Meeting of 1672 called for a general countrywide collection from Friends, intended in part for books to be given to "the chief rulers & others," and partly to help pay for the substantial cost of transporting packets of sufferings to London and for recording them after they arrived. For several years London Friends had expended nearly £100 annually on those services, "which do equally concern Friends in the country as the city to bear." Friends were also instructed to be "exact and brief in drawing up the sufferings in each county," paying particular attention to "times, names, . . . causes, and places of both Friends and their persecutors." These instructions and pleas for money would become common refrains. That same Yearly Meeting also appointed ten Friends to oversee the distribution and printing of books, an arrangment formalized by George Fox into the Second-Day's Morning Meeting of male ministers, which first met in London on 15 September 1673.[10] By the end of 1673, all the major committees involved with sufferings were in place except the Meeting for Sufferings. Before turning to this body, it is instructive to examine the suggestions and arguments of early Friends relative to the legal system as they experienced it prior to the mid-1670s.[11]

Quaker sufferings records, combined with their tracts, letters, and petitions, indicate that they initially had a low regard for the operation of the legal system towards them. Ironically, given their later dependence on legal advice, Friends were not well disposed towards lawyers. George Fox spoke cryptically of "the lawyers black, their black robe as a puddle, and like unto a black pit, almost covered over with blackness," while Edward Byllynge condemned the "terrible and lawless lawyer, under whose oppression the whole nation smarts."[12] But lawyers were only one part of the problem. There were also the often substantial fees charged by lawyers and other legal officials. Quaker bitterness on this issue was reflected in a tract by Paul Moon,[13] who likewise ridiculed the Byzantine complexity of Exchequer procedure, in which each step required countless officers, eagerly awaiting their fees. Moon contended that he was perfectly capable of appearing himself without counsel and of pleading and organizing his own defense. He could see no need for arcane legal jargon or for paying to obtain a copy of the bill of complaint. But the court had insisted that he appear with an attorney, that he needed a counselor to write his legal answer, that he owed 8*d.* a sheet for the bill of complaint, and that his answer was to be engrossed on parchment, again for a fee. Worse still, he lamented, even if he lost the case he was obliged to pay for services rendered, although they had done him more harm than good. In effect, he concluded, "between the counsel and the judges, they can make the poor man's cause look with what face they please & the poor man shall have no more law, but just so much as they please to measure him out, and then if the counselor that pleaded for him be but an ordinary counselor, he will have 20*s.*, if not 30, & if he be a serjeant at law, . . . then

40*s*. a fee." In any event, he added, the answer, replication, and rejoinder were full of "false" information, despite the court's protest that these were merely matters of form.[14]

The Quakers did not suggest a system of salaried officers. Nor were they unified in their opposition. Thus while some Quakers resolutely refused to pay fees, others were willing to pay "reasonable" sums in certain instances, as for example, the two Friends imprisoned at Harwich in 1660 who offered to pay the gaoler full value for everything they had used in the chamber. They did add, however, that they had "so little" of the gaoler's things in that room "that if two reasonable men would price the things, we would pay him for them, and give him the things also, or if he would not stand to that, then we would give him two shillings and six pence a week for the time we had been there."[15] But in that same year, George Fox, stressing his innocence, had refused to pay a gaoler, insisting that he would bear his own charge. It was Fox, in fact, who called for the abolition of all fees to gaolers, believing they had been the cause of too many lengthy imprisonments.[16] More than a decade later Thomas Rudyard, relying on Sir Edward Coke, Andrew Horn, and an impressive array of statutes, argued that gaolers were limited by statute to a fee of 4*d*. unless extra services were rendered. If he demanded more, refused to release prisoners after they paid the requisite fee, or stole anything from them, he should be indicted for extortion, and removed from office upon conviction. Similarly, if he used "constraint, menace, or duress" to coerce any prisoner into giving him money, that prisoner could "recover that money against the gaoler again, in an action of the case at common law."[17]

The "matter of form" which Paul Moon had complained about really irritated the Quakers. As active missionaries and "saints," they were always concerned with their public image. Edward Pyott claimed that it was contrary to law to charge a man with many apparent offenses in one indictment, as if they were "set in purposely to reproach, and wound his good name." He was concerned that if only one small part of the indictment was found, it was considered a true bill, despite all the "many falsehoods and lies therein." But, Pyott queried, how else could clerks of assize and other court clerks "fill up their bags (out of which perhaps their master must have a secret consideration)?" Despite the fact that "a few lines might serve instead of an hundred," the lawyers and court officials had to be fed "with the bread of men's children, and the ruin of their families, to maintain their long suits and malicious contentions." William Penn echoed these sentiments when writing of his 1670 conspiracy trial. "How little a grain of fact was proved," he mused, "yet how spacious an indictment was made." That indictment, he observed, was "swelled with malicious scaring phrases to suggest to the people that they were the merest villains, the most dangerous persons."[18] The Quakers often complained of their meetings being prosecuted as riots on indictments whose form included lists of nonexistent weapons, or of indictments for trespass that claimed that a man crossed over another's ground "with carts and horses, and sheep and oxen," when, in fact, he merely crossed over a hedge "on foot himself."[19] Not surprisingly, George Fox demanded that nothing be included in bills, writs, or indictments "more then the thing is."[20] Friends in a 1670 trial for riot implied that witnesses should confirm all the information in the indictment before a guilty verdict could be returned, particularly as their indictment "consisted of such matter, as meeting with force and arms to disturb the peace and continuing there riotously and tumultuously in contempt of the king and his laws, and against the king's crown and dignity," none of which, they added, had been stated by the witnesses.[21]

There was also another way to eliminate the complications of indictments and bills, and to reduce the numbers of clerks and fees. All laws and customs, Friends asserted, following the practice of the Interregnum, should be "pleaded, showed, and defended, answered, debated, and judged in the English tongue in all courts," although "entered and enrolled in Latin."[22] The Quakers also demanded that all laws be printed, so that "no man may be condemned by a law he neither knows, nor ever heard of, nor understands," a swipe at the common law, or *lex non scripta*. This would further enable Friends to defend themselves in court, without the need for legal counsel. At one point an exasperated George Fox proposed the ultimate solution—the abolition of all lawyers, counselors, serjeants, and attorneys.[23]

Another by-product of fee-paying, according to the Quakers, was the corruption of the entire legal system. By accepting gifts and rewards, judges and other legal officials were successfully tempted to favor the rich while oppressing the poor. Thus, while Friends were prosecuted for contempt in refusing to remove their hats in court, aristocrats would never be fined for such an offense, "but it is the poor that suffers, and the rich bears with the rich, and the poor have been trodden under foot." It is unlikely, of course, that a member of the nobility would ever refuse to take off his hat in court, thereby putting this statement to the test. But, as Edward Burrough succinctly commented, the hat was simply "a cover for the head, to keep from cold or heat for health's sake," and not a symbol to show respect to others.[24]

Since respect for the rich and mighty had led to the emergence of venal, corrupt magistrates, Friends provided a blueprint of the ideal magistrate. True law enforcement officers, they insisted, should be godfearing, compassionate, upright men who were to visit prisoners, take in strangers, "relieve the fatherless," and visit widows "in their afflictions." They should not swear, oppress the poor, nor act out of pride, vengeance, and wantonness. Above all, they were not to accept rewards and gifts or give anyone undue respect.[25] In effect, the only appropriate magistrates would be Quakers or those sympathetic to their ideals: in 1659 Friends had devised lists for Parliament of those they favored for office, and a list of Friends "fit to serve the Commonwealth as justices." In August 1659 when commissioners for the militia were appointed, seven Friends were chosen in Bristol, while Anthony Pearson served in the North.[26] Their tenure, however, was short-lived, and the Quakers did not actively participate in politics again until the Exclusion crisis of 1679–81.

Honest, godfearing magistrates would serve another purpose when confronted with Quaker criminality. They would be wise enough, Friends asserted, to "try into the ground and nature of such matters," in order to learn "whether it be a wilful and purposed wrong or injury done between man and man, or . . . of ignorance or want of better knowledge; or whether it be a matter of conscience or about religion."[27] In other words, such officers would see that the Quakers were not involved in any "intentional" wrongdoing. Similarly, juries were also to weigh carefully the motives of those accused. In any event, the Quakers argued, if any Friend suffered by man's law, both the law and the magistrate were unjust, since servants of God did not transgress His law.[28]

Friends realized, however, that they were likely to be prosecuted. They therefore demanded that judges, instead of badgering defendants, should act as their legal counsel, explaining proper procedure and the nature of the law under which they were charged, particularly where common law was the basis of the prosecution. "Is it not for this cause," asked Edward Pyott, "that the prisoner in many cases is not allowed counsel by the law?" As for witnesses, they must be known to be lawful, reputable, and without prejudice against the accused. It was imperative, Friends added, that the accused be confronted by witnesses, although they were not to be forced to swear to their testimony. "A man that truly and uprightly fears God," averred Edward Burrough, "will be as much afraid and make as much conscience of speaking falsely, as of swearing falsely, and out of a good conscience will testify as truly, as if he swore." As for anyone who feared to swear falsely but was not afraid to speak falsely without an oath, "this is because there is a greater punishment to such, and it is accounted a greater offence among men, to swear falsely than to speak falsely." Therefore perjury without an oath should be punished. Edward Byllynge recommended that the punishment be equivalent to that which the witness "thought to have punished the other by his false testimony." [29] The Quakers also wished to expand the role of juries into trying law as well as fact. It was not sufficient, for example, for them to find that a meeting had taken place; they were also to determine whether that meeting was actually illegal. No doubt the Quakers, aware of packed, intimidated, and frightened juries, but also aware of the awesome dominance of the judiciary within the courtroom, were looking toward juries to act as counterweights to judicial prejudice. But Samuel Starling, former lord mayor of London, and one of those who presided at the 1670 trial of William Penn, mocked the possibility of twelve jurors, "eleven of which it's possible can neither write nor read," actually presuming to judge law. Yet Friends also preferred that no one be tried except by a jury of twelve from the neighborhood "or others who shall well know each other." [30] Such jurors, vowed Thomas Rudyard, would know that the witnesses were persons "of no credit," and that the Quaker defendants were far too principled to commit the crime for which they were charged. Such juries would also know something about the matter in dispute, enabling them to "better pronounce . . . a just verdict of the fact." Of course, that might prove risky for Quakers in locations where they were unpopular. But Friends also countered that possibility by insisting that the accused, "with proper cause," could challenge any judge, juror, or witness. [31]

Predictably, the Quakers stressed that the secular courts should not interfere in matters of conscience, but should focus their attention on the "true" criminals. Who were those "true" criminals? Henry Clark enumerated them:

murderers, man-slayers, fighters, quarrellers, whores and whore-mongers, adulterers, fornicators, buggerers, thieves, robbers, swearers, cursers, drunkards, liars, cheaters, false-witnesses and perjured persons; idolaters, and image-makers, witches and the sons of Belial, amongst whom is hatred, wrath, s[t]rife, variance, emulations, seditions, heresies &c . . . and whatsoever else that is contrary to the Law that is holy, just, pure, and good.[32]

Repeatedly, the Quakers emphasized that the legitimate role of law enforcement officers was to punish "him that doth evil," to encourage "him that doth well," and to "rule the kingdoms of the earth in righteousness," in order that "justice and equity may be exalted." Drawing on their experience of gaols and gaolers, the Quakers protested against anyone keeping a gaol who was a drunkard, a swearer, or violent. Cruel and oppressive gaolers were to be removed, although Edward Byllynge offered to give them adequate compensation. Prisoners for petty crimes, like those charged against Friends, were not to be put in dungeons and nasty holes "amongst thieves and murderers."[33] George Fox, in fact, sounded a modern concern when he called for an end to long periods of imprisonment, "for that is the way to spoil people, and to make more thieves, for there they learn wickedness together." Gaols were to be repaired and kept warm and clean, while "all dungeons, vaults, . . . or other nasty holes within the same prisons" were to be "filled up, or at least never more . . . used." Wholesome prisons would also mean toilets, thereby ending instances where those confined had been forced to "lie in their own dung, and piss, and straw like chaff."[34]

Although these were valid criticisms of seventeenth-century legal procedure and enforcement, and reasonable suggestions for improvement, the Quakers' own studied refusal to cooperate with the authorities added to their burdens while ironically reinforcing their belief that the system was unjust. Often they refused either to plead properly or even to plead at all. A refusal to plead or the embellishment of pleas was frowned upon by the judiciary, and could result in automatic conviction. One can sympathize with judges like Robert Nicholas, called upon to preside at the trial of Priscilla Cotton at Exeter assizes. According to Cotton, when asked to plead guilty or not guilty,

I waited what I should say to him and I said, 'it's false what is on the paper [i.e., the indictment].' Then he said often over to me, 'guilty or not guilty?' I was to say still, 'tis false.' Then the judge said to me, 'say not guilty then.' I was not to say that word, but I said, 'tis false, what is laid to my charge.' Then the judge was mad and said, 'say not guilty.' I said to him: 'Art thou a man to judge for God and canst not rule thy self, but art angry. Be sober, man, and fear the Lord and do justice, and let not passion rule thee.' Then he raged more, and said: 'Jailer, have her away, have her away. I can not endure her. I can not abide this people.'[35]

Some Quakers also gave intentionally provocative answers. When asked his name, William Dewsbury replied that it was "unknown to the world," but that his "natural" birth was in Yorkshire. Similarly, John Otter, a London Quaker shoemaker arrested at a meeting on Christmas Day 1664, refused to give his name, and said that he had "a dwelling place where neither thief, murderer, nor persecutor could come." Unwisely, the interrogating justice, William Rider, asked where that was. "In God," replied Otter. He was committed to Bridewell as a vagabond, and ultimately sent to Virginia as a slave.[36] Friends often refused to post bail, give sureties for good behavior, pay fines or fees, or traverse the indictment. When asked to put in sureties, they frequently refused, citing their innocence and their good behavior as servants of the Lord.[37]

As for the law and its interpretation, the Quakers followed the lead of other English radicals in relying on Sir Edward Coke, Michael Dalton, William Lambarde, Andrew Horn, and William Sheppard; such timeworn clichés as "fundamental law," the "law of God," and the "rights of free-born Englishmen"; and documents such as Magna Carta, the Petition of Right, or other presumed safeguards against legal abuse.[38] Often taking these out of context or giving them undeserved status, the Quakers rarely received any sympathy either from common-law judges or justices of the peace, who paid little more than lip service to such concepts, believing instead that they were duty-bound to enforce the law as Parliament and/or the king had intended. Abstract concepts, baronial documents, the unorthodox views of some legal commentators, and the eccentric arguments of religious radicals played little part in the thinking of those who enforced the law.

A more promising approach, however, was the Quaker "strict constructionist" interpretation of statute and common law, which, like their approach to indictments, stipulated that the precise wording was critical. When the Conventicle Acts penalized those who met under "pretence" or "colour" of religion, the Quakers countered that they met in "reality" to worship God. These were not, they argued, phony religious meetings intended to foment plots.[39] Friends would often cite a statute's title or its preamble, believing that the former "should signify its nature and intent," and the latter, "the reason, or cause of it." Preambles, they asserted, were "the keys of laws." Thus the Conventicle Act was directed against "seditious" conventicles and not against the "peaceful" meetings of Friends; the Five Mile Act was against those in holy orders or "pretended" holy orders; while the recusancy laws were generally against "Popish" recusants rather than Protestants.[40]

Law-enforcement officials often ignored the original cause of commitment when dealing with the Quakers, either because of problems with the indictment, insufficient evidence, or uncooperative juries. Instead, the Oaths of Allegiance and Supremacy would be tendered, the officer knowing that Friends would not swear. As a result, the Quakers insisted that the original cause be tried alone, and that they should not be "ensnared" by an irrelevant oath, which subjected them to perpetual harassment.[41]

Although many of these suggestions and arguments were forcefully pursued and reflected weaknesses in seventeenth-century law enforcement, they were only rarely successful in persuading judges or other legal officials to forgo prosecutions. They may have had a greater impact on juries, thus prompting judicial bullying in the courtroom. Consequently, Friends were increasingly forced to engage in alternative strategies—lobbying and using legal tactics. Ironically, in light of his blistering early attacks on the legal system, the pivotal event was the lengthy imprisonment of George Fox, beginning in 1673, for refusing to take the Oath of Allegiance. The protracted and complex efforts to liberate this prominent Quaker leader, while utilizing traditional Quaker arguments and strategies, also revealed an increasing willingness by Friends, Fox included, to employ legal counsel, to pay the fees necessary for copies of indictments, mittimuses, and writs, and to combat the law with legal weapons. Yet at the same time, Friends had often operated at cross-purposes, and had demonstrated serious tactical confusion, the result of which may have been to lengthen, rather than shorten, Fox's incarceration. More than any other incident, this case focused Quaker attention dramatically on the need to provide appropriate legal counsel and strategy for those Friends who wished to utilize it, and to create a centralized committee to coordinate legal and lobbying efforts.[42] It is to the credit of the Quakers that they recognized the need for such a legal defense committee, rapidly put it together, and made substantial use of it. That committee would be the Meeting for Sufferings, the prototype of a modern legal defense organization.

II

A legal defense committee had been seriously considered as early as the December 1668 meeting of ministers in London, which announced that a meeting had been established "to look after the sufferings of the nation and beyond the seas."[43] A combination of factors prevented the emergence of a formalized Meeting for Sufferings at that time: the strict application of the second Conventicle Act which prevented London Friends from perfecting the Meeting; the issuance of the Declaration of Indulgence in 1672 which temporarily eliminated the necessity for such a body; and the aforementioned imprisonment of George Fox, a leader whose consent and tactical skills were necessary in order to implement such a policy. In April 1675, however, having gained his release, Fox stressed the need for Friends throughout the country to record their sufferings, including the names and addresses both of prosecutors and prosecuted, copies of all legal records involved, the amount of fines and distraints, the value of goods taken and the price for which they sold, and the names and residences of informers, justices, constables, and any other officers concerned. Those details were to be sent to London, to be recorded by Ellis Hookes, and prepared for presentation to Parliament at the beginning of its next session. Yearly Meeting on 4 June 1675 then instructed every quarterly meeting to send a representative to London on 18 October to discuss the best method for easing the sufferings of Friends "by such lawful and just means as may be found out and made use of." It was hoped that this proposed meeting for sufferings would enable provincial Quakers to "obtain such a general understanding of proceedings both in city and country about sufferings" that they would be capable of assisting one another. The representatives were to bring ongoing cases, including all legal documents, as well as a list of those who had died in prison. Effectively reaffirming Fox's instructions, Yearly Meeting insisted that the cases were to be "exactly and briefly stated," and were to include signatures of witnesses to the "sufferings, cruelties and . . . illegal proceedings of the adversaries." The witnesses were essential; otherwise the sufferings "would seem incredible to those in power when they are laid before them." But London Quakers were aware that many Friends were hesitant about adopting legal tactics; consequently they insisted that if any Friend wished to seek lawful remedy, he should not be "discouraged or reflected upon." Rather, such Friends should be assisted and encouraged, although the meeting cautiously added that its intention was not to encourage any Friend "either to contention, nor to take any indirect course at law either to the prejudice of Truth . . . or giving advantage to the adversary." Nor, the meeting added, was it demanding that Friends take a legal approach.[44]

At the October meeting, twelve London Friends were appointed to meet about sufferings four times a year on the Thursday of the week preceding each law term. The meeting was also to include any Friend of the Second-Day's Morning Meeting who could attend. Furthermore, one Friend from each county was to be appointed by the quarterly meeting to come to London when invited, particularly near the beginning of any parliamentary session or when the king and Privy Council were to be lobbied. Sufferings were to be presented to those in power whenever possible. But the meeting cautioned that Friends should not expect too much "in point of law." When Friends desired answers on legal matters, they were to send the questions to Thomas Rudyard or Ellis Hookes, who would respond even where relief was unlikely, so that Friends would "not remain in any groundless or uncertain expectation." Ten Quakers were nominated to draw up some examples of the most egregious sufferings for presentation to Parliament, and to prepare a book of general sufferings which had not yet been recorded in print. Quarterly meetings were also to support Friends ruined by persecution, but where serious sufferings had occurred, monthly and quarterly meetings could send up three Friends with the cases "fit to be presented to those in power."[45] The Quakers clearly intended to utilize personal pressure to a large extent.

In May 1676 Yearly Meeting continued in this vein by advising provincial Friends to press some of the "most moderate, swaying and considerate men in authority," within their counties to stop or hinder inferior officers who were "persecuting" Quakers. At the same time, where any of those local men "of interest or power" also resided at court or in London, then their names and addresses were to be sent to London Friends who would also ask their help in ending such local oppression. Friends should not, Yearly Meeting warned, use "indirect ways to free themselves, as by *habeas corpus* upon a pretended debt, or the like," although they could remove themselves to London by *habeas corpus* "to reverse an unjust judgment past either at assize[s] or sessions," provided that they maintained their religious testimony and acted in accordance with the Lord's will. Above all, no Friend was to "wrong Truth's testimony through seeking of ease to the flesh." Yearly Meeting, justifiably fearful that Friends might go to extremes in using the law, warned them against "entangling themselves in the law because of some *small irregularities in proceeding,*" although they could take action if the law was "materially transgressed and the severity of it exceeded by our persecutors."[46] A cautious use of the law, combined with a good deal of local initiative, was the recommended approach.

The Quakers soon decided that the Meeting For Sufferings needed to meet more than four times each year. On 12 June 1676, over one hundred Friends met in London, and determined that one quarter of those Friends appointed to meet prior to each law term should also gather at the home of Job Boulton in Lombard Street every Thursday, augmented by any other "faithful" Friends. Different groups of Friends would be appointed each law term, with fourteen Friends comprising the first committee. Quakers in each county were to nominate correspondents. While sufferings were still to be sent to Ellis Hookes for recording, only those where country Friends reasonably anticipated some relief or redress were to be sent to the Meeting for Sufferings. London Friends promised speedy answers about potential for relief, but insisted that before Friends sent their cases to London they should first take the advice of their monthly or quarterly meetings, or of those "faithful" Friends of the county appointed to act during the interval between such meetings. Furthermore, the cases had to be "full and short" in accordance with former instructions, for London Friends also intended to publish a monthly sheet of the most "remarkable and grievous sufferings," in order that "cruelty may not be acted in a corner, and not be known."[47]

The first official Meeting for Sufferings took place on 22 June 1676, and initially had few cases. That situation would soon change. In November 1676 monthly and quarterly meetings were instructed to appoint Friends in any town where Quakers were in prison to take care of their needs, and to keep a detailed record of the imprisonments. Those accounts were to be sent to the Meeting, as were new cases of suffering under the Conventicle Act, for presentation to Charles II. In a pivotal discussion, the Meeting also took into consideration whether or not to appoint a "standing counsel" to assist it "in mere matters of law about all such cases as God's Truth shall give a freedom to use the law in."[48] Although no results of this discussion are recorded, it appears that Thomas Rudyard and Roland Vaughan became standing counsel with the power to recommend others in difficult cases.

Yearly Meeting, strongly influenced by the same London Friends who dominated Meeting for Sufferings, often addressed many of the same general issues. Consequently, in May 1678 it recommended that Friends first present their sufferings "fairly and plainly written" to the justices of the peace at their petty and quarter sessions, or to any other important local officers. If redress was not obtained from those sources, Friends were then to turn to the judges of assize. If satisfaction remained elusive, then the details were to be presented to the king and Privy Council or to Parliament "as the case shall require." The Quakers were well aware of the importance of exhausting local avenues before lobbying the central authorities, in part because of the potential sympathy of neighbors toward Friends, and in part because of the potential antipathy of local law-enforcement officers towards those who complained to Whitehall or Westminster. Yearly Meeting also called on Thomas Rudyard and William Penn to obtain opinions from legal counsel to several questions asked previously; the responses were to be sent to the quarterly meetings to be entered into books of precedents. With a cynical eye, Yearly Meeting requested that each county keep a particular account of sufferings under the Conventicle Act partly for the purpose of laying them before the king and Parliament, but also "to compare the same with the value returned into the Exchequer." The Quakers suspected that informers, justices, or others were defrauding the king while enriching themselves at Quaker expense. Accounts of prisoners were again called for, as well as new sufferings, keeping in mind that they should always include the names of two or more witnesses to each particular case. For the present, all expenses in attending Parliament and assisting suffering Friends would come from the Quaker public stock until the quarterly meetings decided how those expenses should be met. Finally, Yearly Meeting agreed that Meeting for Sufferings, before each summer and winter assizes, was to appoint some "knowing or capable" Friends to attend the judges prior to their going on circuit, in order to give them "such cases of Friends in the respective counties as are fit for them to remedy & redress at the succeeding assizes." [49]

The pattern continued in 1679 with London Friends and the Yearly Meeting stressing the need for provincial Friends to lobby their respective members of the new Parliament; to pay their fair share of expenses incurred by London Friends, who had lobbied the king, the Privy Council, and Parliament, and who had searched through various offices, obtaining copies of records; and to support the printing by Meeting for Sufferings of all "severe and extraordinary suffering of Friends." But Meeting for Sufferings stressed that all such cases were to be "so stated as no reproach may come to the Truth by saying more than can be justified." They were therefore to be "truly dated and attested by Friends and as often as can be by those that are not Friends." [50]

One exception to the tactical approach of the Quakers occurred during the period of the Exclusion Parliaments, as Friends opted for a more active role in the political process. In 1679 William Penn campaigned vainly on behalf of Algernon Sidney. [51] Yet given the sympathetic attitude by these Parliaments to Dissenters, particularly on the issue of recusancy, Friends dramatically increased their political activity. In January 1681 prior to the elections for the Oxford Parliament, Meeting for Sufferings wrote to Friends in Northallerton about their letter of thanks to their "worthy" members Sir Gilbert Gerrard and Sir Henry Calverly. The Meeting believed that more needed to be done, for during the previous "Short" Parliament the two members had "manifested their integrity . . . and moreover in our behalf and for our redress they have concerned themselves not a little." Therefore the Meeting desired that *all Friends who are capable (and as they have freedom) may give their voices & make what interest they can in the behalf of your worthy members.*" A general letter was also sent to those Quakers in every county who were eligible and willing, to "appear and make what good interest they can in this election . . . for sober, discreet, & moderate men, such as live in love with their neighbours, that are against persecution and popery, and that deport themselves tenderly towards our Friends." In a separate letter the Meeting indirectly censured Friends in Haverford West for refusing to concern themselves in the choice of their late member, Thomas Owen. It was important, the Meeting asserted, for them to know, albeit "not by any persuasion of his or seeking to by him," about his record in that Parliament. There was not, they insisted, any member of the House of Commons who had "expressed more zeal for our relief, taken more pains in our behalf, laboured early & late in our concern before the House then . . . that worthy member." Friends were asked, if willing, to vote for him.[52]

All these efforts proved irrelevant, given the remarkably brief duration of the Oxford Parliament; the Quaker flirtation with politics ended until 1688. Apart from this short political diversion, the strategy to be employed by Meeting for Sufferings in conjunction with Yearly Meeting was clearly evident by 1680, and would continue, with slight variations, throughout the period under study. They believed strongly in sustaining, albeit with greater consistency, the tradition of confronting those in positions of authority with Quaker sufferings, both corporate and individual. The two meetings consistently encouraged Friends to send their accounts of sufferings and to make certain that they were accurate, impartial, complete, witnessed, and "without any reflections upon the magistrates & persons by whom Friends have suffered or against whom any complaint is made."[53] How unlike the stridency of earlier Quakers! Friends were to include exact copies of all warrants for distress from constables; mittimuses from gaolers; indictments from clerks of the peace and assize; and writs and processes directed to sheriffs and obtainable from undersheriffs, all of which would "not only demonstrate the sufferings more exactly, but be a better means & proof here to endeavour for their redress." Proof and accuracy were vital. Both meetings also stressed that accounts of prisoners should be regularly sent to London so that they could be assisted, and that the names of those who died in prison should be included. Wherever possible, efforts were to be made to alleviate the often appalling gaol conditions. In 1682 Yearly Meeting advised Friends to make certain that the sheriffs and gaolers permitted prisoners "to send out for beer, victuals, & other necessaries where they please," as required by 22 & 23 Chas. II, c. 20. Both meetings insisted that funds be raised and allocated throughout the nation specifically for easing the burden of sufferings. They also intended to establish a regular system for printing sufferings, to be given generally to the king, Privy Council, and Parliament in the hope that the cumulative effect of such documents would create an atmosphere conducive to toleration. Although they recognized the significant role of the king and Parliament in law enforcement, the Quakers were also acutely aware of the need to retain the initiative at the local level. In part, London Friends were wary of being inundated with requests for legal assistance beyond their capacity to give, but they were also aware of the jealousy and animosity felt by many local law-enforcement officials towards their superiors. Therefore, Yearly Meeting in 1682 recommended to provincial Friends that their quarterly meetings, for "better & more easy understanding when they are prosecuted & suffer in person & estate, contrary to law," were to buy or provide copies of the *Statutes at Large*, "to which on all occasions they may have recourse," in order to "know when & how they are injured & to whom to apply for redress."[54] The Quakers were often unrelenting in their visits, petitions, and letters, persisting until they were successful. Anyone who was deemed useful, from the king to the least important official in church or state, might find himself the object of an intense Quaker campaign.[55] Not surprisingly, such efforts were not always appreciated. In May 1680, for example, some Friends seeking to assist those imprisoned in Gloucester on a variety of charges, mainly excommunication and nonpayment of tithes, sent a letter to Meeting for Sufferings directed for John Pritchett, bishop of Gloucester. The Meeting, in turn, gathered the cases together, rewrote the letter, and agreed to deliver both the letter and the cases to the bishop. After several attempts at delivery proved unsuccessful, the Meeting learned that Pritchett was out of town at his country house near Rickmansworth. Job Boulton and Benjamin Clark were now dispatched to visit him there. The welcome they received was less than cordial, for when the bishop saw that they had kept on their hats, he ripped Boulton's off his head, "flinging it" to the other side of the room, announced that he was bishop of the diocese, and commanded Clark "to pull off his hat." This was merely the preamble, for when Pritchett began to read the letter, he spotted the words "thee" and "thou," causing him to fall "into a greater rage." He threw the letter on the ground, "and notwithstanding all moderate discourse used to him, in rage he left the room, & left them." In true Quakerly fashion, they waited until the bishop finally returned, at which point Boulton, using the words "thee" and "thou," began discussing the reason for their visit, but Pritchett "again fell in to rage & left the room, clapping the door after him." This time he did not return, so the two Friends "after considerable attendance & waiting in vain," gave the letter to one of the bishop's servants, who promised to deliver it to his angry master "as he had a convenient opportunity."[56]

The coordination between local Friends and the Meeting for Sufferings, and the hostility it often provoked, was evident also in the case of the brothers William and John Roe, of Longham Hall, Norfolk, who had been heavily distrained for recusancy, apparently on the instructions of two justices, one of whom was a minister. When William Roe came to the Meeting in London for advice, it agreed that John Edge, a prominent London Friend, should assist them, with the Meeting covering any further expenses incurred, "the steward of William's landlady (Lady Ann Cook) having taken some care in the matter already." One Friend suggested printing the case; instead it was decided early in May 1684 to lay their case initially before the lords of the Treasury, since that institution "grants commissions to persons for gathering the estreats, having purchased them." The Meeting ruled out a writ of error as impracticable, "there being a great number of Friends & others concerned in the same writ." The lords of the Treasury proved unreceptive. The brothers then had the Meeting deliver a petition to Charles II, while George Whitehead spoke with Lord Keeper Guilford, who responded that nothing could be done. As usual, Friends persevered, sending William Roe with three other Quakers to see Guilford again, hoping that he would respond differently "in the presence of the sufferer." At the interview with Guilford, the brothers also mentioned their anger with the actions of the sheriff, probably when making the distraint. Once again they failed, but Guilford, after warning them to conform, did advise them to seek legal redress against the sheriff, if he had acted illegally. Again, the Meeting petitioned the king, but to no effect. At the end of May, Roland Vaughan was sent with William Roe to the earl of Yarmouth to seek relief. Finally, on 4 July 1684 the Meeting was advised by Norfolk Quarterly Meeting "that the late sufferings of John & William Roe" should not be printed, "but respited for a while." The brothers had apparently succeeded in gaining at least a temporary respite. Yet late in the following year they again suffered a heavy distraint, and when William Roe spoke with the sheriff, that officer expressed his anger at Roe "for petitioning the king last year against him" and swore that he would ruin Roe "if he appeared against him any more." [57]

Nor was Meeting for Sufferings always welcome at court, for the 1684 Yearly Meeting epistle mentioned that Friends in London had met with "some stop in making application for suffering Friends throughout the nation . . . being advised by authority that it would be more proper for the sufferers themselves to make their own complaints." [58] But it would be wrong to assume that lobbying did not have a beneficial effect. As we shall see, many officials reacted with moderation and kindness, assisting Quakers where they could. London Friends, aware of this, called upon those elsewhere to send up "true accounts of the release or relief of Friends by name, by justices, magistrates, or other & by what means & by whom, & the time when also released or relieved."[59]

The death of Charles II did not alter Quaker tactics. On 13 February, less than two weeks after his demise, they signed a petition to James II for relief; it was delivered, along with numerous individual cases, on 3 March.[60] Throughout the spring of 1685 Friends inundated the newly elected members of Parliament with petitions recounting their sufferings, their peaceable nature, their disinclination to swear, the necessity of their meetings, and their desire for relief, particularly from prosecutions by laws originally directed against others.[61] In June 1685 they presented a brief of their sufferings to James II with a lengthier petition to Parliament.[62] James's reign would witness perhaps the most sustained effort by the Quakers to end "persecution" against them. In this effort they were assisted by the king's changing attitude toward toleration, and by the apparent power at court of William Penn and Robert Barclay.[63] Lobbying, however, was not the only strategy which London Friends had come to employ. The other main thrust of the two London meetings was the utilization of legal tactics often predicated on the advice of counsel. It is necessary, therefore, to examine those tactics that, in conjunction with lobbying, helped deter and frustrate those who prosecuted the Quakers.

Notes

1. Barbour, *Quakers*, 208–9.
2. See Audland, *A True Declaration*, 4; John Camm, *Some Particulars Concerning the Law, Sent to Oliver Cromwell* (London, 1654; c391), 4–5; Pearson, *Tythes*, 23; Besse, *Sufferings*, 1:46–47.
3. These observations are not intended to overlook the continuing contribution of older Friends, particularly George Fox, whose organizational skills and symbolic role as "founder" of the Children of Light, were still essential. Yet many early Quaker leaders were dead or were spending most of their time traveling in the ministry. See, for example, ARB MSS, fol. 139; Reay, *Quakers and Revolution*, 127, although some of those he cites as influential Quakers are highly questionable.
4. The output was tremendous. For Charles II, for example, Joseph Smith, in *A Descriptive Catalogue of Friends Books*, 2 vols. (London, 1867), 2: 62–66, lists forty-one tracts, one of which includes eleven letters, directed, at

least in part, to Charles II prior to 1675; see also Margaret Fell, *A Declaration and an Information from us* (London, 1660; F628); Fox the Younger, *A Noble Salutation*, 13–14; Fox the Younger, *A True Relation*; Daniel Baker, *The Guiltless Cries and Warnings of the Innocent* (London, 1660; B482B); Fox, *Journal*, ed. Nickalls, 379–82; PRO: S.P. 29/21/98, 29/68/74, 74I, 74II; S.P. 29/68/75, 75I.

5. Fox, *Journal*, ed. Nickalls, 59–70; Braithwaite, *Beginnings*, 458, 475–77; Swarthmore MSS, 4:196.

6. Swarthmore MSS, 2:97; 7:39.

7. Hugh Barbour and Arthur Roberts, eds., *Early Quaker Writings* (Grand Rapids, MI, 1973), 569–72. Barbour and Roberts see 340 tracts between 1660 and 1689 relating to sufferings and appeals to those in authority.

8. George W. Edwards, "The London Six Weeks Meeting," *Journal of the Friends Historical Society*, 50 (1962–64):228; Braithwaite, *Second Period*, 156–57, 255; see also Barclay, ed., *Letters of Early Friends*, 285, 309. An annual meeting had taken place from 1658 to 1661, and again in 1666 and April 1668 (Braithwaite, *Second Period*, 275–76).

9. The 1668 meeting called upon local Friends to indemnify those in London "from any damage or expence that they may be at by bail or otherwise concerning such services." Also George Fox requested that anyone who came to London because of a writ or summons should have a letter from the monthly or quarterly meeting testifying to their faithfulness, since London Friends "are fain to be bound for them here" (Book of Cases, 1:2–3).

10. London Yearly Meeting, 1:8; Braithwaite, *Second Period*, 280.

11. Some of these themes continued beyond the establishment of Meeting for Sufferings and are included here.

12. Fox, *Law of God the Rule*, 4; Byllynge, *Word of Reproof*, 20; see also Fox, *Law of God the Rule*, 25–26, where he denounces those lawyers who supported false declarations by ministers in tithe cases. Not surprisingly, early Friends rarely made use of lawyers. Alfred Braithwaite (*Thomas Rudyard*, Friends Historical Society, supplement no. 27 [London, 1956]), has found only two examples before the Restoration, although this is probably a slight underestimate. Yet the numbers do not appear to have increased substantially until the 1670s. See Chapter 5, Quaker Legal Defense.

13. Moon, *Some Passages and Proceedings in Courts*, in George Fox, *An Instruction to Judges and Lawyers* (London, [1658]; F1848), 31–40.

14. Moon, *Some Passages*, 38–39; see also Fox, *Law of God the Rule*, 24. The court of Chancery was even worse; it was notorious for its expense and delay. Cases were known to take as long as thirty years before determination. The fees of clerks were extortionate; those who drew up formal documents charged by the sheet, consequently developing large handwriting to go with wide margins (Baker, *Legal History*, 96). Fees, of course, permeated the entire legal system, and were demanded for virtually every facet of procedure; see, for example, Mary Sturge Gretton, *Oxfordshire Justices of the Peace in the Seventeenth Century* (Oxford, 1934), lix–lxii.

15. Fox the Younger, *A True Relation*, 7.

16. Fox, *Journal*, ed. Nickalls, 13; Fox, *To the Parliament of England*, 13. In 1656 Fox was one of the Quaker prisoners at Launceston who agreed to pay the gaoler 33*s.* per week for food, drink, and accommodation (see Chapter 3, n. 128, preceding). Nonetheless, the dichotomy between those Quakers willing to pay fees and those who would not became more marked as the century progressed.

17. Thomas Rudyard, *The Second Part of the People's Antient and Just Liberties Asserted* (London, 1670 [not in Wing]), 34. The fourteenth-century work *La somme appelle Mirroir des justices, vel speculum justiciariorum factum* by Andrew Horn (or Horne) (H2790 French) was translated into English in the mid-seventeenth century as *The Booke called, The Mirrour of Justices* (London, 1646; H2789), and was often cited by the Quakers.

18. Fox, *Journal*, ed. Ellwood, 197–98; William Penn, *The Peoples Antient and Just Liberties Asserted in the Tryal of William Penn* (London, 1670; P1336A), 29–30. Thomas Rudyard (*Second Part of People's Antient and Just*, 57–58) condemned indictments that were "subtle to place a small matter of fact, as they call it, in the midst of a whole sea of their decriminating and obnoxious terms, which they call law." It was, he surmised, to keep the people from "pittying them, that they may rather condemn them in their very thoughts as miscreants, not worthy to live." For more on the Quaker concern over their public persona, see Craig W. Horle, "Quakers and Baptists 1650–1660," *Baptist Quarterly* 26 (1976):218–38.

19. Fox, *Law of God the Rule*, 28. The Quakers in their bitter protests against meetings charged as riots, relied on numerous legal commentators—Coke, Lambarde, Keble, Dalton et al.—to substantiate their defense, usually to no avail. See Rudyard, *Second Part of People's Antient and Just*, 25–26; *A Legal Examination of Abuses of Law* (London, 1682; L943); Thomas Ellwood, *A Discourse Concerning Riots* (London, 1683; E618); GBS, 5:361; Besse, *Sufferings*, 1:458–60, 465–67, 469–70; Bate, *Declaration of Indulgence*, 5:412; Meeting for Sufferings, 3:243.

20. Fox, *To the Parliament of England*, 3. This demand was repeated in May 1661 by Fox and others in *For the King, and both Houses* (London, 1661; F1821), 7. Dalton believed that the formalized list of weapons was not necessary unless "the circumstances of the fact do require them, for these circumstances do either aggravate or diminish the offence" (*Countrey Justice*, 401).

21. Besse, *Sufferings*, 1:427; see also Rudyard, *Second Part of People's Antient and Just*, 57–58.

22. Richard Farnworth, *The Liberty of the Subject by Magna Charta* (London, 1664; F489), 12. "Let no man speak in an unknown tongue," asserted George Fox (*To the Parliament of England*, 3–4). Latin indictments, according to Thomas Rudyard, were only "to keep the people ignorant," especially the grand jury, "being only informed or made to understand . . . as a mercenary clark will read to them, or let them know, which besure shall be no more then whats for the interest of the prosecutors and the prisoners disadvantage" (*Second Part of People's Antient and Just*, 60). These were common complaints by radicals of the period.

23. Edward Byllynge, *A Mite of Affection* (London, 1659; B2902 [the author's name misspelled in Wing as Billing]), 3; Fox, *To the Parliament of England*, 5; see also Fox et al., *For the King and Both Houses*, 7). William Penn, when told in his 1670 trial for conspiracy, that he was being prosecuted by common law, retorted: "It is too general and imperfect an answer, to say it is the common law, unless we knew both where, and what it is. . . . Certainly, if the common law be so hard to be understood, its far from being very common" (*Peoples Antient and Just*, 11).

24. Fox, *An Instruction*, 27–28; Burrough, *Message for Instruction*, 15; see also Clark, *Here is True Magistracy*, 5; John Crook, *An Epistle of Love* (London, 1660; C7204), 11–12.

25. See Fox, *Journal*, ed. Nickalls, 54; Fox, *Journal*, ed. Ellwood, 36, 44, 55; Audland, *True Declaration*, 5; Byllynge, *Word of Reproof*, 61; Burrough, *Message for Instruction*, 1–3; Farnworth, *Liberty of the Subject*, title page; Crook, *Epistle of Love*, 11–12; George Fox et al., *The Copies of Several Letters* (London, 1660; f1778), 29.

26. Braithwaite, *Beginnings*, 460–61.

27. Burrough, *Message for Instruction*, 4–5, 19–21, 24–25; see also John Crook, *Sixteen Reasons Drawn from the Law of God* (London, [1661]; c7213), 5.

28. See Burrough, *Message for Instruction*, 3–4, 18; Anthony Pearson, *A Few Words to all Judges* (London, 1654; p988), 6–7; Rudyard, *Second Part of People's Antient and Just*, 56; Thomas Gibson, *Something Offered to the Consideration* ([London, 1665]; g678), 7–8; Farnworth, *Liberty of the Subject*, 12–13.

29. Fox, *Journal*, ed. Ellwood, 195; Burrough, *Message for Instruction*, 18; Byllynge, *Mite of Affection*, 2; see also Veall, *Law Reform*, 20; Whitehead, *Christian Progress*, 328–29; *A Request to the Justices not to Make Convictions* ([London, 1684]; r1120).

30. Samuel Starling, *An Answer to the Seditious and Scandalous Pamphlet* (London, 1671; s5296), 2; Byllynge, *Mite of Affection*, 2; see also Burrough, *To Charles Fleetwood*, 8, 10; Gibson, *Something Offered*, 7–8; Penn, *Peoples Antient and Just*, 3. The Quaker emphasis on neighborhood juries and their right to judge law were reiterations of Leveller arguments, not surprising since John Lilburne had joined their cause. As early as 1649 Lilburne had "challenged the view that the government, rather than the community at large, was ultimately responsible for determining the law." Unfortunately for Lilburne and the Quakers, there was "no basis at English common law for the proposition that jurors were the only judges of law" (Green, *Verdict According to Conscience*, 170, 175; see also chap. 5).

31. Rudyard, *Second Part of People's Antient and Just*, 50; Byllynge, *Mite of Affection*, 2; see also Farnworth, *Liberty of the Subject*, 11.

32. Clark, *Here is True Magistracy*, 4; see also ORS, fol. 435.

33. *Declaration of Present Sufferings*, 30; Fox, *Law of God the Rule*, 12; Byllynge, *Word of Reproof*, 4.

34. Fox, *To the Parliament of England*, 7, 13; Byllynge, *Mite of Affection*, 8.

35. ORS, fol. 310; see also ORS, fols. 297, 311; GBS, vol. 2, London and Middlesex, 66ff.; 6:256, 261; *Something in Answer to a Petition to Oliver Cromwell* (London, 1654; s4659), 9–10; [Samuel Curtis], *The Lamentable Sufferings of the Church of God in Dorsetshire* (London, 1659; c7691), 6, 12; GBS, vol. 2, London and Middlesex, 66; W. J. Hardy and W. L. Hardy, eds., *Hertfordshire County Records*, 1:166.

36. Edward Smith, *The Life of William Dewsbury* (London, 1836), 94–95, 117; GBS, vol. 2, London and Middlesex, 84; see also GBS, vol. 2, London and Middlesex, 21; Besse, *Sufferings*, 1:379–80; Penney, ed., *Extracts from State Papers*, 19.

37. For example, see Fox, *Journal*, ed. Ellwood, 41–42; Anthony Pearson, *To the Parliament*, 3, 7; *A Brief Relation of the Persecutions and Cruelties . . . Quakers* (London, 1662; b4629), 7–8; Penney, ed., *First Publishers of Truth*, 93–94; Penney, ed., *Extracts from State Papers*, 18–19, 29, 52; Besse, *Sufferings*, 1:63–64, 109–10, 135, 379–80, 481–82, 621, 630–31; 2:106, 165; GBS, vol. 2, London and Middlesex, 21; 3:483; 6:557–58; Meeting for Sufferings, 2:89, 122, 186, 225; 3:75, 206; 4:190, 263.

38. For example, see n. 17, preceding, and Crook, *Sixteen Reasons*, 5–6;

Whitehead, *Christian Progress*, 253, 328–29; Fox, *Journal*, ed. Ellwood, 190–91; GBS, vol. 2, London and Middlesex, 14–20; vol. 2, Salop, 7; 5:412; Penn, *Peoples Antient and Just*, passim; Besse, *Sufferings*, 1:369, 374, 409, 420–21, 426, 527; Pearson, *Tythes*, 15; John Crook, *Tythes No Property* (London, 1659; c7225), 1.

39. See Whitehead, *Christian Progress*, 266–67, 275–80; Fell, *Declaration and Information*, 4.

40. See Besse, *Sufferings*, 1:371, 445–48; Crook, *Tythes No Property*, 3; Thomas Rudyard, *The Case of Protestant Dissenters* (London, 1680; r2178), 3–4; GBS, 1:29, 509; vol. 2, London and Middlesex, 16. Sheppard, in fact, defined the preamble as "the first part of an act or statute, which is as a key to open the mind of the makers, and to show what mischiefs they intend to remedy that make the statute, and some statutes have these, and some are without them" (*Epitome of the Laws*, 917).

41. See, for example, GBS, 1:170–71, 400; vol. 2, Northamptonshire, 26; vol. 2, Oxfordshire, 9; vol. 2, Somerset, 141, 214, 226; 6:57; Penn, *Peoples Antient and Just*, 40; Fox, *Journal*, ed. Nickalls, 670–705; Besse, *Sufferings*, 1:129, 182, 204, 611, 751. This argument appeared to have the support of Thomas Smith, a lawyer with whom Friends consulted in 1680 about a case in Norwich where Quakers were arrested for meeting, but tendered the Oath of Allegiance. "It's an irregular proceeding throughout," advised Smith, "for first they were apprehended upon the account of meeting, but not duly proceeded against according to the law in that case" (Book of Cases, 1:77).

42. For this important case, see Craig W. Horle, "Changing Quaker Attitudes Toward Legal Defense: The George Fox Case, 1673–75, and the Establishment of Meeting for Sufferings," in *Seeking the Light: Essays in Quaker History*, ed. J. William Frost and John M. Moore (Wallingford, Pa., 1986), 17–39.

43. Book of Cases, 1:3.

44. Leek MSS, 61–62; London Yearly Meeting, 1:22–24. See also Leek MSS, 59–60, a general letter from Ellis Hookes to Friends in May 1675 relative to accounts of sufferings.

45. London Yearly Meeting, 1:25–29; see also Meeting for Sufferings, unpaginated section at the beginning of vol. 1.

46. London Yearly Meeting, 1:29–31.

47. Barclay, ed., *Letters of Early Friends*, 350–53; Leek MSS, 91–94; Book of Cases, 1:1–2. The exact number who attended this meeting is uncertain; Barclay, ed., *Letters of Early Friends* (347–50); Leek MSS (91–94); and the Book of Cases (unpaginated list before p. 1) give 110, 112, and 122 attendees respectively. In any event, this meeting firmly established the Meeting for Sufferings.

48. Meeting for Sufferings, 1:12–13. No doubt London Quakers, busy with their own lives as well as serving Friends, did not wish to become involved with long-winded Friends who personally attended the Meeting for advice. They insisted that those who attended for advice, assistance, or information were to present their cases in writing to "avoid long and tedious discourse" (Meeting for Sufferings, 1:13).

49. London Yearly Meeting, 1:60–62; see also Meeting for Sufferings, 1:58–60; Leek MSS, 99–104. Meeting for Sufferings also kept a "book of precedents," which became the four-volume series now known as the "Book of Cases," in FLL.

50. Book of Cases, 1:58; Meeting for Sufferings, 1:91–96, 98, 103; London Yearly Meeting, 1:69–70.

51. See R. Dunn and M. Dunn, eds., *Papers of William Penn*, 1:546, indicating that Penn actively supported Sidney's two losing efforts in 1679, but did not support his equally unsuccessful efforts in 1680–81.

52. Book of Cases, 1:81–84.

53. London Yearly Meeting, 1:83–84; see also 1:108–10, 122–23, 147, 169; and Meeting for Sufferings, 3:341.

54. London Yearly Meeting, 1:106–7, 112; see also 1:108–10, 115–18, 122–23, 139–40, 142, 144, 147, 151–52; Meeting for Sufferings, 2:207, 209; 3:42, 58, 341.

55. For letters, petitions, and papers see, for example, Meeting for Sufferings, 1:170; 2:34, 37, 46, 95–96, 102, 108, 168, 173, 175, 179–80; 3:1, 47–48, 60, 101, 123, 129, 138, 145, 149, 154, 161, 206, 214–15, 221, 224, 227, 236, 239–40, 251, 267, 305, 322; 4:86, 267. A small sampling of those visited by Friends include the marquis of Worcester; Sir John Churchill; the earl of Middleton; the duke of Albemarle; Lord Craven; the bishops of Oxon, Peterborough, Lincoln, Durham, and London; members of Parliament; sheriffs; justices of the peace; and the two late Stuart Kings (see Meeting for Sufferings, 1:75, 97, 99, 104, 167; 2:8–9, 13, 77, 79–81, 85–86, 90, 99, 101, 103, 113, 115, 121–22, 128–30, 133, 135, 143–44, 146, 158–60, 163, 169, 182, 196, 199, 226; 3:298, 301, 339, 345–46; 4:126–27, 131–33; 5:177, 301; 6:221, 239; and Book of Cases, 1:115).

56. Meeting for Sufferings, 1:125, 155, 158–59, 161–62, 173–74.

57. Meeting for Sufferings, 3:154, 159, 163, 167, 171, 174, 176, 180, 183, 201; 4:169, 175, 183. Despite the threat, the sheriff proved to be moderate; see 4:224.

58. London Yearly Meeting, 1:161.

59. London Yearly Meeting, 1:109.

60. Meeting for Sufferings, 3:352, 361; 4:4.

61. See Meeting for Sufferings, 4:51–52, 55, 57–60, 62; Besse, *Sufferings*, 1:515–16, 550–51, 644–45, 656–57, 706–7; 2:88–89, 166–67.

62. Meeting for Sufferings, 4:65; Besse, *Sufferings*, 1:xl–xliii.

63. "Mr William Penn & Robert Barclay that wrote the large Latin tract of Quakerism are very often at court & *have much acquaintance there*" (Morrice Entr'ing Book, 2:86, entry of 26 March 1687 [italics added]).

Chapter Five

QUAKER LEGAL DEFENSE

The parties arrested are not bound to give any other bail, but for their appearance to the action, & it ought not to be extravagant, let the writ say what it will, for although it be an action of debt, yet it's not a certain debt, until the jury have found it, for it may be less than in the writ or declaration; therefore, I conceive, the best way is to give bail.

Opinion of Thomas Smith in the case of Henry Jackson prosecuted for recusancy: Book of Cases, 1:78

Many Quakers proved to be receptive to the offer made by Meeting for Sufferings to provide legal advice and support, doubtless a reaction to the renewed intensity of persecution in the 1680s, and to what they perceived as harsh and illegal proceedings against them. The questions posed, although indicating a lack of legal sophistication, are valuable to an understanding of the seventeenth-century English legal system because they reflect the often unorthodox methods of law-enforcement officers, the vagueness and complexity of legal procedure, and the types of arguments that Friends wished to pursue. The answers provided by Meeting for Sufferings and Yearly Meeting, together with the opinions of legal counsel in the Book of Cases, while also confirming the complexity of the legal system, specify the strategies Friends were willing to employ. They also provide a measure of the accuracy and utility of the legal advice being dispensed, often from some of the finest legal minds in England. The legal backgrounds of Roland Vaughan and Thomas Rudyard, the original standing counsel for the Meeting for Sufferings, have not been ascertained. The extant matriculation records for Oxford, Cambridge, and the Inns of Court fail to list their names. But it is clear from some of Vaughan's opinions to Meeting for Sufferings, and from Rudyard's career in West New Jersey and Pennsylvania that each had been exposed to some degree of legal training. In any event, as we will see, and as Appendix 2 illustrates, Meeting for Sufferings often relied on other legal advisers, en-

compassing the four Inns of Court, and including eleven men who at
various times held superior common-law judgeships. Perhaps the lawyer most sympathetic to Quaker pretensions was Thomas Corbett, a
Welshman. Although not a Quaker, this member of Gray's Inn had
often acted on behalf of Welsh Friends, particularly their most prominent figure, Richard Davies, and had played a crucial role in the legal
proceedings that freed George Fox in 1675.[1] Quaker records are silent, however, on why particular lawyers were consulted, although it is
likely that Friends leaned toward those known to be sympathetic toward dissent. What follows focuses on seven categories of Quaker
crime, about which they exhibited particular anxiety, and the often dis-
parate legal tactics Friends pursued to ensure the victory of the "Lamb"
over the "Beast."

I

A significant number of the queries from Friends related to the prosecution of their meetings. An especial concern was the second Conventicle Act, and in particular the penalty of distraint and the inordinate
privileges extended to informers. As a concurrent theme, however,
Friends were anxious to devise strategies to protect their meetinghouses from confiscation by the Crown or local authorities. One tactic
the Meeting advised was to "settle" a tenant in the meetinghouse, with
a lease from the trustees, but who could claim to be the owner, thereby
preventing prosecution of the house as an uninhabited dwelling used
for the sole purpose of illegal meetings. But not just any Friend should
be a tenant, as Watford Friends learned in December 1685 after their
meetinghouse had been presented by the grand jury. Reiterating advice it had given Berkshire Friends two years earlier, the Meeting
called for "some *poor* Friend" to be installed as the tenant.[2] That message was not merely the product of humanitarian benevolence. If the
tenant were poor, he could personally avoid the steep fines laid upon
"owners" of houses where meetings had taken place. Instead, the fines
would be spread among members of the meeting. It would be a rare
Friend who would be willing to lose all as owner of a meetinghouse.[3]
Perhaps emulating the courts at Westminster, Friends on one occasion
developed a neat subterfuge of their own when Richard Heritage, a
trustee in Warwickshire, was indicted for building a meetinghouse at
Brailes. Yearly Meeting advised the trustees to place a tenant "with all

speed" in the house, to then "lay 4 acres of land to it," and to let the house and land to the tenant "upon a valuable consideration" receiving the rent "fairly for it before sufficient witnesses" and giving "receipts for the rent." Heritage was also to traverse the indictment, and to send a copy to London Friends so they could know if it was laid "on the Statute of Mortmain or the Statute of Cottages."[4] Yearly Meeting's object was to circumvent both statutes at one time. A rent-paying tenant passing as owner avoided any suggestion that the land was held in mortmain, that is, as an inalienable possession of a religious corporation. At the same time, it was legalizing the property as a cottage in accordance with 31 Eliz., c. 7, by designating at least four acres of land around the building, and maintaining continual occupation. Even more outrageous was the same Meeting's advice to Northampton Friends whose meetinghouse was involved in an action of ejectment. The owners were immediately to let the house "to the party that lives in it, from Michaelmas last to Michaelmas next, by a short lease in writing for a valuable consideration." The tenant was then to pay the half year's rent "due at Lady Day last, before sufficient witnesses" and to take a receipt "for the same." Legal counsel was then to appear to the ejectment and maintain the title.[5]

The primary motive behind many of these efforts was to avoid any involvement of meetinghouse trustees, who, after all, were the owners in trust for the Quakers as a corporate body. That concern, for example, prompted Bristol Men's Monthly Meeting in October 1682 to write to London Friends asking how best to secure their meetinghouse deeds "for their *intended uses* out of the reach of all Truth's adversaries."[6] While protecting trustees from heavy fines, the Quakers were also concerned to obscure the ultimate use of the trust. Although it was preferable, as we have seen, to put in a poor tenant, the Quakers realized that trustees might ultimately become involved. In 1682 Yearly Meeting therefore insisted that those who had agreed to trusteeship were to stand by that commitment "in time of trial & persecution," rather than provide an "opportunity & occasion" for the authorities to seize Quaker meetinghouses, as had already occurred in some instances "for want of one to own the houses." Any trustee, however, who wished to surrender that obligation could do so, the meeting hoping that their replacements would show the necessary resolve "in times of trial or necessity or persecution."[7] At least one trustee, however, William Potter of Banbury, proved incapable "in times of trial" in

1684, forcing Meeting for Sufferings to take the deeds. Unfortunately, by that time an inquisition jury had viewed Banbury meetinghouse and found in favor of the king. The house was to be officially seized in the following law term unless someone came forward to claim ownership. Finally, legal counsel advised Friends to try the case in Potter's name, "they having the writings," while assuring the fearful man that he would *"come to no damage."* [8]

Obviously, the Quakers preferred that the trustees not be involved in any way with prosecutions. That was evident in the case of the meetinghouse at Worcester. The town had taken the ostensibly empty house and put a poor woman in as tenant, expecting to add more people, since they had no knowledge of an owner. Worcester Friends asked Meeting for Sufferings if "some of the trustees may own it?" The Meeting wasted little time in responding that the feoffees in trust should not appear "as concerned in the meeting house," for that would give advantage to the prosecutors *"to enquire into the trust & for what uses,"* which could then "make it forfeited by law." Rather, the Meeting urged that the tenant whom Friends had formerly put in should go to the mayor and acquaint him "that he owns the house & is poor." Anxious to put the parish officers on the defensive, the Meeting further judged that their takeover of the house was a "violent entry," and that they should be warned by the tenant not to repeat the offense. The Quakers were audacious, to say the least. Worcester Friends, however, failing to appreciate the point, unwisely persisted. In January 1686, having reinstalled the tenant, they again wished to know whether the tenant posing as owner was "sufficient in law, or whether the trustees?" The latter were prepared, the Friends emphasized, to meet with the authorities. Meeting for Sufferings replied by sending a paper to the mayor and justices reporting that the town clerk, when he had put in the poor woman as tenant, had claimed that "it was enough if one did own it." Therefore, it was now strongly advised "that the tenant's owning it is enough." [9] But not all Friends appreciated this approach, for Sedbergh Quakers, willing to meet in private homes, had openly speculated whether or not it was worth attempting legally to reenter their seized house. Meeting for Sufferings, unwilling to risk the loss of a meetinghouse and opposed to seemingly private meetings, approached the justice involved, John Otway, in an effort to regain it. [10]

The Quakers also rented houses or rooms for their meetings, and in 1675 they asked Thomas Corbett, one of their legal counsel, whether any single individual was liable for the £20 fine when a house was rented by many Friends solely for the purpose of meetings. All were liable, responded Corbett, but he indicated a way to avoid the problem. If all the tenants or occupiers were "poor and unable to pay" or if it was not known who were the tenants or occupiers, then the penalty could not be levied, for there was no "particular provision or clause" in the second Conventicle Act "in relation to the house" as there was "in relation to the preacher or teacher."[11] Although in theory it seemed more sensible for Friends to have rented, not owned, meetinghouses, in practice there was one problem, illustrated by a case in Rutland in January 1683. The non-Quaker owner of a room rented by Friends had been obliged to pay a fine of £20. Meeting for Sufferings warned the Friends "for the future" not to take any house "entire to themselves"; in the meantime, they were "to clear themselves . . . as they see meet."[12] In other words, they were to reimburse the owner. In any event, law-enforcement agents might simply confiscate the furniture in the meetinghouse on the presumption that the tenant, although claiming poverty, really owned the premises, and was therefore capable of suffering distraint.[13] But it is likely, as with other Quaker crimes, that their staunch legal resistance helped to prevent the takeover of many of their meetinghouses by the authorities.

The meetinghouse at Sunderland, however, late in December 1688 suffered a fate worse than confiscation when a mob took advantage of the political confusion towards the end of James II's reign, and destroyed it. But the Quakers reacted quickly. John Stone, the primary trustee, successfully pursued a civil action of trespass against two men involved, and then executed a writ of inquiry attempting to prove damages of £50, which the witnesses for the defendants acknowledged. The undersheriff summed up for the jury, effectively agreeing with this assessment, but the jury, obviously not enchanted with the Quakers, brought in damages of 20s. The outraged Quakers asked their legal counsel if another writ of inquiry could be sued out and executed by another jury. Samuel Blackerby, the counsel, believed that it could. Ironically, Friends then asked if the jurors could be prosecuted, a move which would have brought sardonic smiles from the late Stuart judiciary. Blackerby wisely advised against it, since the jury had found for the plaintiff and awarded some damages. Stone appears to have taken no action.[14]

Meetinghouses, however, were only one aspect of the difficulties confronting Quaker meetings, particularly in relation to the second Conventicle Act. What made that Act so dangerous to Friends was the sweeping powers it gave, both explicitly and implicitly, to justices of the peace and informers, and its avoidance of jury trial except on appeal. Friends needed therefore to develop legal arguments which, although useful in appeal trials, could also be utilized when lobbying law-enforcement officers, Parliament, and the king. The Quakers had to either render the statute's provisions harmless or convince Parliament that it should be repealed. Friends looked to legal counsel for support, and found it initially in Thomas Corbett, whose advice was sought at length in 1675 and 1678.[15] Unfortunately, while his responses often confirmed Quaker presuppositions, they may have simply reflected a tendency of some lawyers to tell their clients what they wished to hear, rather than what was practical in a court of law. Whatever Corbett's motives—and one should not rule out an unsound grasp of the statute and proceedings involved—his advice was often unconventional at best. Predictably, many of the questions Friends posed centered on the extent to which justices could enforce the statute without infringing on the rights of both the accused and lesser officers, in particular constables.

Corbett's advice, if upheld by the authorities, would have undermined enforcement of the statute. For example, in addressing himself to the Quaker concern over convictions by justices in the absence of the accused, Corbett stressed that justices were obligated to summon the accused prior to conviction, because common law, civil law, and "the law of nature" demanded it. The rule of law, he added, was *qui statuit aliquid parte in audita altera licet quum statuerit haud aquus est*.[16] He also believed that by providing for conviction by confession or proof, the statute assumed a summons, as proof could not be given until a denial had taken place, a rather arcane view, but one suited to Friends. As for witnesses, Corbett argued that justices could not force either suspects or law-enforcement officers to testify under oath about alleged breaches of the peace. Nor could justices grant warrants to break open doors or locks for distraint. In fact, he argued, they were not obliged by the Act to issue warrants for distraint, but were merely to have suspects brought before them and to record convictions, involving themselves further only if they received a complaint and their assistance was needed. Consequently, they were not liable to the penalty of £100 for neglect if a distraint was not levied, although they should, he felt, publicly express their doubt about the necessity of issuing such a warrant, thereby avoiding an accusation of "wilful refusal" to enforce the law. Technically Corbett was correct: the statute did not specifically require the justice to issue the warrants for distraint. But there was an implicit assumption that this action was expected. Corbett was right, however, when he supported Friends' contention that justices, as *custodes pacis*, could not beat Quakers. Furthermore, the office was judicial, not ministerial; and therefore, he added, such actions were unwarranted.

What about the rights and duties of lesser officers? Once again, Corbett proved most cooperative. Any constable who failed to execute a warrant of distraint was not, he insisted, liable to the fine of £5 for neglect of duty, for he was bound *only* to inform a justice of a meeting and to endeavor to have it convicted. Ironically, Corbett contradicted this strange opinion elsewhere in his response when he admitted that a constable could be summarily fined by a justice if he failed to execute a warrant. Only in 1686 did Meeting for Sufferings appear to clarify this issue when it advised that a constable need not execute a *defective* warrant for distraint, although he would be wise to speak to the convicting justice "for his better information upon the warrant."[17] In any event, the intrepid Corbett provided another way to protect a constable who failed to levy the distraint. While admitting that distraints on this statute, since they were in the nature of an execution, and not for rent, could be made at night, he denied that constables had the right to break open doors to get at distrainable goods, even if "the justice should express it particularly in his warrant." After all, Corbett observed, "a man's house is to him as a castle of defence and so is every part or room therein." Thus Corbett again stressed that the constable was not liable for neglect if he failed to levy a distraint, either because goods were not found or were locked away. But what if the distraint took place? Was the constable, Friends queried, legally obliged to either drive or carry away the goods out of the parish where the distraint occurred in order to make a sale? Friends were not trying to conserve the constable's energy. Rather, they wished to limit the sale to the immediate vicinity, in hopes that sympathetic neighbors or relatives would refuse to buy distrained property or would return items sold to the offender. Corbett correctly responded that constables were limited to their jurisdiction, but he unwisely added that they were not liable to charges of neglect if they exposed the goods to sale, but were unable to obtain "reasonable" value for them. Yet when Friends asked if distraints had to be sold even if the offer was "much under the real value of the good[s]," Corbett hedged. The constable was not obliged to sell at "under rates," but that was only true "till after he hath kept the same a reasonable time and tried the market, fairs, and chapmen within his liberty, after which he may sell *at the best rates that are offered*, though much under the value." Corbett did not say, however, that they *must* be sold. Considering that constables, in his opinion, would not be fined, failure to sell would be an obvious way of avoiding enforcement. If all else failed, Corbett also remarked that warrants for distraint were not good if they failed to express what the offense was, and when and where it had occurred. Unfortunately, as we have seen, the Quakers were often either refused a copy of the warrant for distraint or not even told what it contained.

If Corbett's advice on distraint was not sufficient to nullify the statute, his claims as to invalid testimony certainly were, for he ruled out all those who had any vested interest in testifying. Although a generally accepted ground for exclusion in the twentieth century, this concept had not yet fully evolved in the seventeenth century, particularly for misdemeanors. Either Corbett was far in advance of his time, or simply dispensing unsound advice. Among those he viewed as ineligible were informers, who gained by the conviction, "for the law to prevent perjury admits not any interested witness"; constables and other officers, since they could receive a reward in the justice's discretion and therefore resembled the informers; anyone who contributed to the poor rate, since they were in "equal condition with such who swear to enlarge their own parish bound who never have been allowed as good witnesses in that case"; and the poor of the parish, since they received one-third of the fine and would therefore swear "for their own immediate advantage." Corbett also found a way to protect those who "owned" Quaker meetinghouses, for he advised that liability ceased after one conviction, the statute not saying "for every offence." In some respects this was all irrelevant, for according to Corbett, meetings which lacked preaching, teaching, or any other exercise of religion were legal. Unfortunately for Friends, the authorities rarely agreed with that premise. Finally, even Corbett had to admit that while the statute established a "way of trial and conviction . . . different from the common law trial by juries," it was not, as Friends contended, contrary to the "ancient, fundamental laws of England."

Friends did not rely solely on Corbett for advice relative to the Conventicle Act. In 1682 they turned to another, unnamed, counselor. Significantly, his responses were also improbable.[18] For example, he believed that justices and lesser officers should act only on information of a conventicle already assembled, and were therefore not liable to penalty for neglect if they failed to act on information about a conventicle "to be held." This opinion appears to be a misreading of the statute that insisted on *prevention* as well as *suppression* of conventicles. But he did admit that if a justice made out a warrant prior to the assembling of the conventicle, the constable *must* execute it, the warrant also enabling him to enter the meeting. Although the constable could go alone with a warrant, this counselor stressed that if the justice had been informed on oath, "he ought to go *or forfeit if he does not*." This supported the Quaker belief that justices should view the so-called crime being committed, rather than relying on the uncorroborated "evidence" of informers. Like Corbett, this counselor believed that while a constable was expected to give unsworn information, a justice could not force him to answer questions under oath. Nor could he be obliged to incriminate himself or to inform against any particular person at the conventicle. In a surprising opinion, the counselor added that the silent meetings of Quakers "*have been taken to be within the law*." While that may have been true on some occasions, it does not accord with Quaker records showing that silent meetings were often prosecuted successfully. What about informers? An informer, he observed, "ought to be a man that is not infamous, but a lawful witness," that is, neither a convicted perjurer nor forger, "whose testimony in law is not to be admitted." Friends would have preferred that informers convicted of *any* crime should be disqualified. What about constables who failed to levy distraints? This counselor, more cautious than Corbett, skirted the issue, merely stating that their authority was limited to their parishes. As for churchwardens, who Friends believed should accompany constables making distraints, they were obligated to go only if the warrant was "made to them."

Not all those questioned by Friends about conventicles were as supportive as Corbett and his unnamed colleague. In 1682 Edmund Saunders, later chief justice of King's Bench, responded obliquely when asked whether a meeting where no open or public preaching or praying had taken place was a conventicle. It was not a conventicle, he commented, where a meeting was dispersed before anything was done "of the nature of religious exercise." Nor was he noticeably sympathetic toward the Quaker children who had been holding meetings in Bristol, while their parents were imprisoned. He asserted that boys and girls under the age of fourteen who met peacefully could be asked to disperse on the assumption that they might cause a riot, and if they refused, they could be "moderately corrected by a public officer" and even imprisoned for a "convenient time." Despite Friends' implication that justices and other officers were whipping and beating these children, Saunders stoutly insisted that no magistrate would "abuse children without any cause at all." But when asked what remedy the children or their parents had against such an officer, Saunders advised that an action could be brought in the name of the wronged child and damages recovered, "to be assessed by a jury in proportion for the wrong done."[19] Unfortunately, Friends were often ineligible to carry on prosecutions, unless they could obtain non-Quaker witnesses.

In 1683 Thomas Ellwood, a prominent Quaker, selectively using the legal advice Friends had received, published *A Caution to Constables*, in an effort to discourage these officers, whose role in local law enforcement was critical, from assisting in the prosecution of Quaker meetings. Neither constables nor other officers, he advised, were obliged to be "attendant upon an informer, to be at his beck, and run like a lackey after him whensoever, or whethersoever he shall think fit to call." Nor were they bound to take notice of information given them unless they believed it was "credible"; if it was, they were only to give that information to a justice, and not to follow the informer to the meeting. Foolishly, however, many of these officers had been "tricked" by "cunning and swaggering informers" to trail along to the meetings, to observe who was there, and even to provide the informers with names and addresses of those present. This activity went beyond their duty, Ellwood stressed, adding that such overzealousness resulted from anxiety over the £5 penalty for neglect, although lawyers were uncertain how it was to be levied, "for it is not to be supposed that the officers of a town or parish, should levy the fine upon themselves." Ellwood conveniently ignored the fact that nonculpable lesser officers could levy the distraint on their colleague(s). Although addressing himself primarily to constables, Ellwood also warned justices of the peace that they must demand that informers be economically sufficient to defend themselves legally if challenged, and also be able to prove *every part* of the statutory offense. The burden of proof rested on them, he averred—an assertion that actually contradicted legal advice given to Friends. Ellwood also expanded on legal advice when he insisted that a constable, rather than sell below normal rates, could wait for a better market, and if the goods remained unsold until he was out of office, could "return them again to him from whom he took them." This opinion coincided with advice given by Meeting for Sufferings that warrants for distraint were directed to the officers "for the time being," and that distraints by their replacements were "judged illegal." In any event, Ellwood concluded, Quaker silent meetings "hath been adjudged not to come within this act." [20]

Assuming, as was usually the case, that Quaker meetings of any kind were generally prosecuted, and that justices and lesser officers enforced the statute as Parliament had intended, Friends needed to focus on alternative tactics, while continuing to encourage justices to ignore informers, and constables to forgo distraining. One obvious tactic was to appeal, a right permitted by the statute, but one predicated on obtaining a copy of the warrant of distraint, and on clearly understanding the appeal process. That officers were not always cooperative in the first instance is evident by a quarter sessions order at Hicks Hall, London, in October 1683, which condemned those constables and other parish officers who had been refusing to grant copies of warrants for distraint to offenders, thereby depriving them of "necessary instructions how to draw their appeals . . . in due time according to the said statute." The court ordered that true copies of all such warrants were to be provided to any offender. [21] The warrant of distraint was of vital importance to Quakers and other Dissenters, often surreptitiously convicted, because it was the *only* way, short of going to the justice and demanding to see the record of conviction, that they could learn for what meeting(s) they were being prosecuted. This order, however, only applied to Middlesex.

Many of the queries to Meeting for Sufferings concerned appeal procedure. It appears that the goods distrained were to be left on the premises until the time for appeal had passed. Friends wishing to appeal, according to the Meeting, should pay the amount of the fine as bond to prosecute with effect, but if the goods had been sold within the appeal period, the amount they sold for, even if less than the fine, was a sufficient bond. [22] But Henry Pollexfen, later chief justice of Common Pleas, advised Friends that if an appeal was successful, restitution should be made "according to [the] value of the goods as val-

ued by the appellant & not as valued or sold by the officers." This
statement seemed to imply that the bond should match that presumed
value.[23] Although it would be in the appellant's interest, if successful,
to value his goods arbitrarily high, this procedure would help to protect those Quakers who complained bitterly of distraints without any
appraisal or inventory, which then left open the prospect of embezzle-
ment and fraud by distrainers.

Quaker records clearly indicate their willingness to appeal for a
wide variety of reasons, albeit with inconsistent results. As early as
1676 Friends claimed to have twenty appeals pending at Nottingham
sessions, while in the summer of 1677 in London, seven appeals from
Ratcliff Meeting alone were to be heard at the following sessions. In
November 1683 Meeting for Sufferings called on Friends to bring in
accounts of appeals tried and the names of informers defeated, and in
July 1685 the Meeting heard that recently in London, sixteen Quaker
appeals had been won, seven lost, and one postponed.[24] Despite
Thomas Corbett's often eccentric opinions, the Quakers commonly
appealed on more sensible grounds, such as not having been present
at the meeting, or the meeting having not taken place at the time
claimed. In appeals of this nature, Friends apparently enjoyed reasonable success, although often depending on non-Quaker witnesses who
could swear on oath. The grounds for other successful appeals included meetings held in the street "& not in the house, as the warrants
do express"; a distraint by warrant of a justice who had subsequently
been put out of office; and a marriage supper prosecuted as a conventicle. Success was also likely for those Friends who appealed against
fines levied for preachers erroneously believed to be unknown or impoverished, or for preachers "when no words" were spoken. More
debatable, but also more likely to be successful, was the contention of
the Meeting for Sufferings that women could not be prosecuted for
preaching, the statute specifically mentioning "he" when discussing
preachers.[25]

Not all appeals prevailed. Richard Needham's claim that his goods
had been sold within the time allotted for appeal, was defeated, as also
was the effort of William Collard, who argued that the warrant had
contained the wrong name. Similarly, appeals predicated on silent
meetings were unsuccessful, while those based on literal statutory
interpretation were unlikely to succeed. As John Darnell advised, the
Quakers "would be put to prove that there were nothing taught or

spoke[n] contrary to the liturgy, instead of Friends putting the informers to prove their speaking contrary to the said liturgy."[26] This concept would also include arguments that the fines were for praying,
"whereas the act lays the fine upon preaching only," or where burials
had been prosecuted as conventicles. Justices tended to ignore such
scrupulousness.[27]

Meeting for Sufferings could not always encourage appeals. When
John Jones complained that the officers had levied a second distraint
on his goods for the same offense, Henry Pollexfen advised the Meeting to discourage an appeal, as he conceived "it lawful they might
come again, if at the first time they had not enough." Nor, as John
Darnell advised the Meeting in Richard Needham's case, did an appeal
prevent the officers from distraining for "the residue of the fine . . .
after the appeal is brought."[28] In June 1683 Richard Richardson was
advised that an appeal on the wrong occupational addition in the warrant, "schoolmaster," would be "overruled." Friends also suffered a re-
versal when they asked Francis Pemberton's opinion about convictions
in the reign of the late king Charles and new warrants issued for distraint. The opinion? The Meeting noted cryptically, "not thought necessary to record the same."[29] There was, of course, another deterrent
to appealing, as exemplified by Durham Friends who complained
"several times" to the local justices "of the wrongs done and false informations, when it was in their power easily to have addressed us." However, "they put us off, saying we might then appeal, which," the Friends
lamented, "puts us to so much charge (and costs not allowed) that
sometimes the charge . . . is as much or more than the fines." Rather
than appeal, they were "many times content to sit down with the wrong,
though it be very great and unjust."[30] Such sentiments notwithstanding, appeals were a necessary weapon in the Quaker armory against
informers, a point confirmed by Worcestershire Quakers in August
1683 when they told Meeting for Sufferings that a combination of
Quaker appeals and lying informers had resulted in the meetings'
being left alone.[31]

As Worcestershire Friends indicated, informers were a significant
factor in prosecuting conventicles. Appeals therefore, even when unsuccessful, harassed informers by prolonging the prosecution, thus
preventing them from obtaining their share of the spoils until the appeal was adjudicated. But appeals were only one tactic employed by
the Quakers to defeat the pretensions of informers. For example, in

April 1678 six Quakers, surreptitiously convicted under the Conventicle Act, complained to Westminster sessions that they had not been allowed to defend themselves in court. Surprisingly, the court ordered the two informers to appear and defend their prosecution. Meeting for Sufferings immediately sent a copy of the order to all the quarterly and monthly meetings to be used as a precedent.[32] Friends were alert to any challenges from the authorities to informers. Their interest was therefore piqued in 1685 when George Whitehead reported that the justices at the quarter sessions in London had refused the entreaties of informers to disturb a Quaker meeting being held in Peel Street. The presiding justice, Whitehead noted, told his colleagues they could neither disturb the meeting as a riot, "because no overt act [was] done there," or as a conventicle "because [there was] no . . . act of worship or preaching." In reaction, several informers petitioned against that justice "as a favourer of sectaries," but the charge was thrown out at the sessions. Realizing that Whitehead's unsubstantiated oral report would be insufficient to influence other justices, Meeting for Sufferings dispatched two Friends to inquire of the clerk of the peace "if he took any minutes of the sense of the court about the meeting . . . & what judgment the court did make thereupon."[33] Friends also gathered evidence of the unsavory behavior of informers, such as those in the North Riding who in May 1683 pretended to have a warrant that actually did not exist; the accused Quaker, Benjamin Lindley, appealed. The informers fled, and warrants were issued "to take them in any part of the county." Again, in August 1685 another informer, having already caused the imprisonment of several Friends, swore, "he being drunk," that he would bring more to prison the next day, "but going away & abusing the mayor & others, was imprisoned."[34]

Some Friends apparently were not content with simply attacking the informers' reputations. In a strange incident, Christopher Smith, a London informer, helped break up a meeting at Devonshire House in April 1686. But during a skirmish outside, Smith's periwig and hat fell off, prompting someone to grab a stick and give him "a blow upon his head," causing it to bleed. At their subsequent trial for riot and assault, Friends claimed that Smith had been accidentally struck by the staff of a constable who was guarding the door, for they were certain that none of the Friends present "did so much as lift up a hand" or offer "the least violence." In any case, they had been kept inside the house and the riot was outside, the "evil designs of mischievous persons," who had "contrived to do us hurt by making such tumults and uproars at our meeting door." Smith, himself, apparently blamed Presbyterians in the crowd for his wound. The highlight of the trial came when Sir John Holt, the recorder, in response to Quaker protestations of innocence, claimed in his summing up "that if 6 men came into a house and made a riot, all in the house were guilty of the riot." Thomas Robinson, one of the defendants, then asked: "If 6 men came to my house and go to the door and beat one another and commit a riot, how am I guilty of that riot?" At this retort, "a counselor began to laugh, and the court round about began a laughter, and looked upon the recorder." Friends were still found guilty.[35] Far more serious was an incident at Newcastle in 1684 during a distraint on John Airey, a Quaker soapmaker. After the officers broke open Airey's soaphouse doors, an informer who was with them took "some tapes out of oil casks on purpose to waste it," at which point Airey's son "threw a dishful of the soap lees in his face." As a result, the informer was likely to become "wholly blind," for one of his eyes was "clearly gone," while the other was "in great danger." The twenty-year-old son was imprisoned, and the local justice took advantage of the incident "to fall upon that meeting very severely, and," Friends added, "we are afraid they will be very hard upon the young man, there being an act that makes it felon[y], the loss of [a] member."[36]

Aside from isolated acts of violence, most of the Quakers' efforts against informers may have been beneficial in the short term. But the confrontations of informers and Quakers continued until the Act of Toleration. At one point, in September 1681, Meeting for Sufferings gave advice on prosecuting informers which rivaled for deception the actions of the informers themselves. The meeting advised a Darlington Friend whose wife had been beaten by informers, that if substantial evidence existed to prove his wife was beaten, he should not prosecute the informer in the Crown Office, the criminal side of King's Bench, for that would cost about £10. Rather he should remain "still and silent" until the next assizes or quarter sessions, and then have the clerk "draw out a bill against the persons that did so beat her." The names of witnesses would be included, one of which should be the prosecutor, but "NOT SHE, because she cannot swear." It was then to be taken, along with the witnesses, to the grand jury, who would doubtless find the bill, "*because the adverse party can have no notice that way, whereby to oppose it.*" The overall cost would be minor. Once the bill was found, the accused would be either imprisoned or forced to put in bail "to try the cause at their own charge." Meeting for Sufferings admitted that most country attorneys would recommend proceeding in the Crown Office, but the method suggested by the Meeting would "cast all the charge" on the informers, "who must traverse and try the cause at their own costs," and even if the Friend lost the case, the informers could not recover costs, "as otherwise they may in the Crown Office."[37]

The Quakers refused to concede any ground to the informers. As we have seen, Friends were particularly annoyed that justices, like Thomas Jenner in London, were either aiding and abetting informers in appeal trials, or refusing to censor their lying. As a result, Friends employed another legal weapon. As early as 1670 Buckinghamshire Quakers prosecuted for perjury two informers—Richard Aris, a "broken ironmonger," and Ralph Lacey, a "cow-stealer," who had informed against Thomas Zachary and his wife, for attending a meeting at Jordans, when in fact they were in London at the time. As a result of the efforts of Thomas Ellwood, who organized the defense and retained a Windsor lawyer named Starkey, the Zacharys had won an appeal against the conviction, but rather than rest with that, Ellwood had the informers indicted for perjury, once again employing Starkey and another Windsor lawyer named Forster. The informers were forced to traverse and were ultimately tried, convicted, and imprisoned. But the cost for legal counsel and for witnesses brought from London was over £27, which was raised by Upperside Monthly Meeting.[38] The expense of such prosecutions often necessitated a corporate effort, as Meeting for Sufferings implied when it advised a Friend that if he had sufficient evidence to exonerate himself, he should appeal, and then Friends would be *"willing to be at the charge thereof to prove the persons perjured."* On another occasion, the Meeting heard that a false oath had been taken against some Sussex Friends. It advised with counsel as to whether the evidence they had against the informers was sufficient to prove them perjured; if so, they were to proceed to indict them in the Crown Office. A month later, however, Thomas Corbett undertook to prosecute them by an information, which was a cheaper method, but also an ironical one.[39] The Meeting tended to encourage prosecutions for perjury, despite the expense, but their success was not always guaranteed, as John Newcombe of Worcester learned in October 1683 when the grand jury, despite his successful appeal, brought in a perjury bill *ignoramus*. Similarly, Christopher Moore in Somerset, having won his appeal, indicted the informer for perjury, "but by the false laying of the indictment by Philip Bennett, clerk of the peace, who hath manifested himself full of envy against the Truth and them that profess it," the grand jury "brought it in an *ignoramus*."[40]

One of the most important and detailed opinions concerning prosecution of informers came from Roland Vaughan in 1683 in response to allegations from Durham Friends that informers were engaging in widespread illegal activities, including bribery and collusion with law-enforcement officers.[41] Vaughan began by encouraging every Friend molested by informers to appeal in writing and in Latin to the convicting justice, agreeing in the presence of local witnesses "to enter into recognizance" to prosecute the appeal at the next quarter sessions. At that sessions, the justice was to give the written appeal, the bond, and his record of the conviction to the clerk of the peace, all of which would remain there until after the trial of the appeal "the 2nd sessions following." In the interim, the goods distrained would be returned to the appellant. At that same sessions, the appellant was to tender his plea, already drawn and engrossed, to that clerk in open court and to enter into a new recognizance to try the appeal at the following sessions. The court should accept this without bail. Nonetheless, he stressed that Friends must "*let such security be given to the court for the trying of the appeal, as shall be required.*" The effect of much of this strategy, as Vaughan asserted, was to irritate and discourage the informers from bothering Quakers. His only regret was that Friends had not taken "this course of proceeding" from the very first moment "when the informers began their prosecution upon the Conventicle Act," for constant appeals would have thoroughly disheartened the informers, particularly as the trial would not take place sooner than the second sessions after conviction, "for there must be 15 days between the date of the venire to summon the jury & the return thereof, which cannot possibly be in the compass of one sessions." Furthermore, this method guaranteed that Friends could publicly confront the informers. Finally, Vaughan believed that even if the informers appeared to have proved their charge, the Quakers could produce their own witnesses to invalidate the informers' evidence if it was really false,

> for though no proof will be allowed in the negative of the informers' testimony in the affirmative, yet if the appellant's evidence be able to prove that the party convicted was not at the time of the

supposed conventicle at the place mentioned in the conviction, but at another place far distant from it, such proofs are such negative evidence as in themselves do carry an affirmative. And in case such witnesses should exceed in number the informers' witnesses, all courts of justice ought to allow of such witnesses on the appellant's behalf, as affirmative evidence to destroy the first conviction of the informers before a justice out of sessions.

Nothing more clearly demonstrates the often primitive nature of English law, for this resembled the medieval and canon law institution of compurgators, or oath-helpers, who swore that the accused was honest, and therefore must be telling the truth when he denied the charge. The more serious the crime, the more compurgators needed to be produced for acquittal. In effect, as Vaughan implied, the justices' record of conviction was not to be disputed directly, nor was the informers' evidence to be crossexamined or refuted except by negative evidence on the part of the appellant's witnesses. Where defendants were concerned, the English legal system was still far from enlightened.

Finally, Vaughan included an example of the appeal in Latin "to guide such practitioners at law, as shall undertake to draw up appeals on the behalf of Friends, with the assistance of their counsel in the country." He also included a form for pleading, "drawn by very able counsel," and advised that the lawyers hired by Friends put in an exception against the willingness of courts to permit surreptitious prosecutions by ne'er-do-well informers, since it tended to encourage perjury. It was, he concluded, "against natural justice to condemn any without hearing them."

Whether Friends in county Durham followed this advice is not known. What is certain, however, is their continuing trouble with informers, and in particular John Buzier, described by Friends as a former employee of the archdeacon, "and now supposed to be very low in the world." Anxious to improve his worldly standing, Buzier, in conjunction with the mayor of Stockton, physically abused Friends at Stockton meeting in March 1684. On complaint from Friends, the bishop of Durham questioned the sheriff, who confirmed that Buzier had drawn his sword in the meeting and that he and the mayor had carried out several Quakers by the head and heels. When questioned, the mayor blamed Buzier, and his own fear of the £100 penalty. The bishop's secretary assured Friends that "for time to come," Buzier and the mayor would be "stopped from doing violence or abuse to . . . Friends."[42]

Although Friends could use the legal system to frustrate informers, they could not completely block their long-term ability to prosecute meetings. Friends therefore turned to the Crown for assistance. Shortly after James II's royal pardon of 15 March 1686, six Friends presented him with a petition against informers and the actions of Sir Thomas Jenner, and soon followed this with a "short request" from George Whitehead asking for a conference of Quakers, informers, and royal commissioners.[43] James agreed, appointing as commissioners Richard Graham and Philip Burton, the solicitors to the Treasury, who held the first meeting at Burton's chambers in Cliffords Inn on 4 June 1686. Using their recorded sufferings, Friends prepared fifty-two cases for presentation, with another forty-five in reserve, and were allowed to summon forty-four informers, including fifteen women. Two London justices were also present, the result of complaints from the informers that they had refused to issue warrants against some Quakers, "or to convict them in their absence." The Quaker arguments were organized by Whitehead, who began with cases involving false oaths, confronting the informers concerned, with the exception of John Hilton who, "in drink, and not in a fit condition," was prevented from entering by his companions, but not before commenting loudly that "he cared not a fart for the king's commissioners." He was passed over.

Whitehead next turned to the breaking of doors. He had compiled so many cases that the commissioners, he admitted, "seem'd almost weary with hearing them that day," nor were matters eased by the hot weather and the immense throng in the chambers. The commissioners, having listened to numerous cases, adjourned until 14 June, at which time the informers brought a lawyer, although Friends claimed that he was soon overwhelmed by the evidence against his clients. Whitehead waded through half the cases before the commissioners threw in the towel, insisting that they had enough information to make a report. Whitehead, in summation, called for the informers to be thoroughly "discourag'd and stopped" from any further prosecutions against Quakers, and that afternoon he pressed his case again, showing the luckless commissioners all the cases which had not been covered. But on a subsequent visit, he asked to see their preliminary report and was astonished to find that it was "very deficient and improperly drawn up: for instead of stating plainly matter of fact," they had proposed that an easier way of dealing with the Quakers was to prosecute them for recusancy rather than for meeting. When asked, the commissioners admitted that prior to drawing up their report, "some great person, or persons of the church" had pressed them to "report nothing that might disable the informers," who had given "so great service . . . to the church." Under pressure from an angry White- head, they now amended their report. But the Quakers persevered, complaining in a letter to James II on 10 July 1686 that the informers had gained revenge since the recent investigation by having several Quakers arrested and bound over to sessions, and more imprisoned, despite the fact that other Dissenters had since successfully prosecuted several informers for perjury at the London and Middlesex quarter sessions. On 11 July the king in council referred both the Quaker complaint and the commissioners' report to the lord chancellor "in order to correct the irregular proceedings of some justices and the in- formers." Friends again presented their proposals, demanding that a summons always be issued before conviction; that Quaker public meetings no longer be prosecuted; that informers be "credible per- sons, and responsible in estate," who would be able to make restitution for false prosecutions; and that a list of named informers be "utterly disabled from any further prosecuting." They also insisted that con- victing justices be barred from sitting as judges or chairmen in the trial of appeals; that no local law-enforcement officers should be forced to inform; and that no justice should be prosecuted for "not gratifying the informers." Finally, they maintained that a system which permit- ted officers "to divide, embezzle, or detain to themselves the monies levied, or any part thereof, *as some have done*," should be abolished and all the money brought into sessions, and that the right to prosecute on a penal statute for reward should also be abolished, as encouraging perjury.

Although Friends intimated that the commissioners' report "car- ried pretty much reflection on the informers" and that James II had apparently indicated his displeasure with such prosecutors, some in- formers, particularly in Nottinghamshire, Leicestershire, Wiltshire, Westmorland, Lancashire, and Lincolnshire, continued to prosecute and abuse the Quakers, forcing them to prolong their campaign. They continued to appeal prosecutions, and were also able to gain further support from James II, the earl of Huntingdon, the duke of New- castle, and many local authorities. Nonetheless, the informers demon- strated a remarkable ability to survive, aided by the £100 penalty looming over the heads of negligent justices; the Quakers were not truly rid of them until the suspension of the penal laws.[44]

Some Quakers, however, utilized still another tactic to frustrate their adversaries, including informers. Prior to a distraint, they conveyed their goods to others, ostensibly their creditors. Yearly Meeting had been particularly concerned about Quaker traders and shopkeepers whose goods were sold on credit to country Friends, believing that where distraints were likely, the goods should be returned.[45] Although the intention was laudable, these and other conveyances could be construed by the authorities as efforts to defraud the king, particularly if the conveyance took place *after* prosecution but prior to distraint. Some officers took this view, even where unjustified, as in the case of William Day of Gloucester who, before the Conventicle Act "came in force," conveyed his goods to two creditors as security for money he owed them. He was ultimately convicted under the Act, and despite the conveyance, officers tried to take away "some green hides," but Day's creditors paid 30*s.* to prevent this. Day soon moved elsewhere, after physically turning over all the goods to the creditors, who then hired a man to "tan the leather and live in the house." But the officers returned and had the goods distrained, ultimately forcing Day's creditors to redeem them for £8 10*s.*[46] The prevalence of conveyances made after conviction, however, may account for the cryptic message recorded by Meeting for Sufferings from Jeremy Owen in Cheshire that informers were "seizing goods that are made over to other men *& cannot be recovered by law.*"[47] These conveyances may also help to account for the many instances in which Friends claimed that goods distrained did not belong to them. Despite the potential for officers to ignore legal conveyances, the tactic was a legitimate tool, and did not preclude the right of creditors to whom goods had been conveyed to replevin those goods, that is, to recover them until a court adjudicated the legality of the distraint. But Quakers were also aided by kindly neighbors and relatives who bought distrained goods, but returned them to the Friends, although retaining the bills of sale, thereby preventing further distraints. Although illegal distraints in these cases were also liable to be replevined, Meeting for Sufferings on at least one occasion advised the rightful owner to bring an action of trespass against the distrainers.[48]

While the second Conventicle Act occupied much of the spotlight in terms of Quaker meetings, Friends were forced to adopt legal strategies when their gatherings were prosecuted under the Quaker Act or the common-law injunction against riots. These prosecutions generally involved trials. Therefore, one strategy was indicated by Meeting for Sufferings in the case of Friends prosecuted in Yorkshire in July 1684 for the third offense under the Quaker Act. After perusing the indictment, the Meeting advised them to "draw up their case very plainly & briefly," and to present it to the judges of assize "at their first coming in the city at their chambers." If that failed to elicit judicial favor, however, the Meeting counseled them to challenge the indictment, which omitted their convictions for the first two offenses, a necessary prerequisite before an indictment could be laid for a third offense. Unfortunately for the Quakers, clerks were not always so careless when drawing up indictments, although the authorities in Cheshire had apparently forgotten about the penalty for a third conviction on the Quaker Act. Thus the Meeting, when asked by Cheshire Friends, warned them not "to move their case at assize, lest it should put them in mind to procure an order from the k[ing] to transport them." It was better they should "let it rest."[49]

Another tactic was delay. As appeals postponed potential rewards for informers on the Conventicle Act, traversing the indictment would do so in these cases, since it postponed a trial until the following sessions. Meeting for Sufferings therefore advised Friends at Lancaster, charged with a riot in December 1683, to remove the indictment from quarter sessions to assizes, and then to traverse in order to gain time. But the Meeting did not always favor a change of venue. When William Bingley and eight others prosecuted for a riot suggested that they remove the case by *certiorari* to the King's Bench, the Meeting protested: "It's not judged safe to remove it from the mayor's court to the K[ing]'s Bench, lest it be evilly resented by one and the cause not ameliorated by the other and be an ill precedent to the country, it being a case & judgment directed from above."[50] That was a sensible piece of advice, for local magistrates were often very sensitive about efforts to supersede their authority. Although the Meeting generally advised traversing, if not change of venue, this presented two major obstacles—the bond for good behavior and the fees demanded by the clerk of the sessions. The Meeting normally advised Friends that a "moderate consideration of clerk's fees" was permissible, while recognizances that omitted good behavior were viewed as "a favour as not being designed to make a prey upon them." It was urged, however, that Friends were to traverse only if good behavior was not inserted. But not all Friends were in a position to follow the Meeting's advice even if they so desired. Many Bristol Friends, "being very poor men," refused to traverse since the security to be posted would have been greater than they were "able to undergo."[51] Yet the increasing willingness of Friends to traverse indictments reflected a growing acceptance of the need to put in bail and pay reasonable fees rather than permit their adversaries to have them immediately and perpetually imprisoned.[52] But once again, Friends appear to have been confused over the proper course of action. Thus in August 1684 at York assizes, 232 imprisoned Quakers refused to enter bail offered by Judge Richard Holloway. Taken aback, Holloway then "instanced Friends at Norwich," who had concurred with what the court desired. The following month Meeting for Sufferings heard again from the prisoners at York concerning their entering bond "as was proffered them last assize[s] by Judge Holloway." Unfortunately, they lamented, "that opportunity is passed." Imprisoned Southwark Friends, also uncertain, had queried the Meeting in July 1684 "about giving sureties," while several months earlier a Friend in Essex had questioned whether he could give surety to keep the peace, several others having entered recognizances. The meeting insisted that this was a "snare" because the authorities would always make their meetings a breach of the peace and of good behavior.[53]

Friends sometimes opted for prevention rather than delay. In May 1682 officers in Bristol, having broken up a Quaker meeting, went to their local church for services. Unhappy at lack of further prosecution, constable Ralph Olliffe pursued some of the dispersing Friends, hoping to have them imprisoned. But, "as he was driving them over the bridge, some rested." When they refused to move again, Olliffe ran to the church to get the sheriff and some more constables. Unfortunately for the embarrassed Olliffe, when they arrived at the bridge, the Quakers "were gone." In Berkshire, one of William Armorer's men, having come into the meetinghouse, saw Friends gathered inside. He left to get help, pulling the door after him, but "it being a spring lock," caught hold, "so locked himself out." He went for Armorer who demanded that the Quakers open the door, "but the Friends in the meeting sat still, for as they had no hand in shutting . . . him out, so they were not willing to let him in." Armorer broke the door down with a sledgehammer.[54]

Finally, despite the sanction Meeting for Sufferings gave to legal assistance, it was not for everyone. On 17 July 1685 it heard that Hertfordshire Friends imprisoned for meeting were "not willing to put their hands to their sufferings in order to make application to men." They chose, instead, to "trust the Lord."[55]

II

The Quakers also used legal tactics against prosecutions for refusal to swear. As we have seen, Meeting for Sufferings had counseled Friends not to rely on "small irregularities in proceeding." But in fact, legal flexibility in the matter of oath-taking was severely restricted, forcing Friends to rely on technical arguments that only a lawyer could love. A case in point was that of John Alway and Abraham Dickson, who in 1670, having been praemunired at Wells assizes, removed themselves by *habeas corpus* to King's Bench, where Chief Justice Matthew Hale, despite the misgivings of his colleagues, gave judgment for the prisoners and discharged them from their sentence. Why? The record of the original proceedings had read *preceptum fuit* rather than *preceptum est.*[56] In 1672, operating on the premise that what had worked once should be tried again, the Quakers challenged both the record and the indictment. The case involved ten Friends who had been praemunired for refusing the Oath of Allegiance. Obtaining a writ of error, they argued the case in King's Bench during Michaelmas term, presenting a litany of apparent errors, including the judgment reading *committuntur* rather than *committantur*, and the indictment mentioning the "sea," instead of "see" of Rome. The only feasible ground for dismissal was the mistake in Latin but the judges in this case, unlike that of Matthew Hale, refused to overturn a conviction because of a mistake in one letter. The writ was dismissed and the conviction upheld.[57]

These cases pale in comparison with several others that occurred in the year 1682, when Meeting for Sufferings could call on its battery of lawyers. There was, for example, the case of Erasmus Dole, a Bristol pewterer prosecuted for recusancy and also indicted for refusing the Oath of Allegiance as contained in 3 Jas. 1, c. 4. The indictment was taken to William Thompson and Edward Ward for review and legal advice. By the time these lawyers finished, the indictment was in serious jeopardy, for Thompson concluded that it stated incorrectly that the tender and refusal of the oath was at the "general sessions," rather than at the "general quarter sessions," and that it did not aver, as demanded by statute, that the oath was tendered by the "major number of the justices there present." Ward agreed with Thompson on the latter point, but disagreed on the former, believing that the type of sessions mentioned was irrelevant, for the first tender of the oath, he insisted, was to be *out of sessions*, which the indictment failed to mention. Therefore, if "it was not so tendered & refused first out of sessions, the refusal at the sessions doth not incur a praemunire. And no such proceeding appears in the record against Erasmus Dole." Ward did agree that the next tender of the oath should occur "at the general quarter sessions." Therefore, even if the oath had been first tendered out of sessions, the indictment's use of the term "the general sessions," was "not sufficient to warrant the proceedings." For good measure, he also argued that the indictment declared that the conviction for recusancy was by indictment, when it should be by presentment; therefore this was a "variance & not good." As if the lawyers were not enough, Dole himself added further exceptions, including the failure of the indictment to mention that he was a subject of the realm, or to include a recital of the Oath of Allegiance. In any event, he was permitted in April 1682 to make a declaration of allegiance, leaving out the word "swear."[58]

Emphasis on technical error, rather than scriptural exegesis, was also evident in the case of Joshua Green and three others who on 4 October 1682 had been indicted for refusing that same oath and had been praemunired at Barnsley general sessions in Yorkshire. Meeting for Sufferings, upon examining the mittimus, again debated where and how many times the oath was tendered, and whether, in fact, the second tender had been made by the majority of justices then present. They turned to Henry Pollexfen for advice, who startled them by asserting that the statute 3 Jas. 1, c. 4 permitted justices to tender the oath to "any other person whatsoever" then in court; therefore "the refusal in the court of assizes or sessions, being there tendered, though never tendered or refused before, incurs the penalty of praemunire, for which they may in the same assizes or quarter sessions indict & convict." Actually, Pollexfen had misread the statute, for there was no clause permitting justices to tender the oath to anyone simply present in court. That had been allowed by the first Conventicle Act, which was no longer in force. So much for legal expertise. Yet Pollexfen was no worse than justice Edward Dolby, who at Reading in 1666 had deflected Quaker protests by arguing that if two justices could tender the oath to anyone out of sessions, they surely had equivalent power within sessions. On the assumption that Pollexfen and Dolby were right, Friends next asked the former's advice on the kind of process which issued forth for seizure of estates from those praemunired. The next step, Pollexfen commented, was "an office or inquisition" to determine what lands and goods they had, and after that was returned, process would ensue to seize them "into the king's hands." Why were Friends examining the mittimus, rather than the indictment? Their next question clarified this. Was it legal for clerks of assize or peace, or judges of assize to deny a copy of the indictment to those prosecuted for this offense, thereby preventing the accused from "bringing his writ of error . . . if the proceedings against him appear to be erroneous?" Pollexfen concluded that such denial, "especially after conviction," was "against law." Although his opinion was correct, the authorities, wary of guilty Quakers obtaining freedom by challenging indictments, often hindered their access to such documents. What was needed, perhaps, was a radical revision in the requisite form for indictments and mittimuses, and a concurrent tightening of the rules which permitted cases to be overturned on minor technicalities. The Quakers continued to grill Pollexfen, asking if an offender could, before seizure of his estate, "make a good & lawful sale, *both of his personal & real estate*, or either, for the satisfaction of his just debts . . . or in consideration of ready money." Pollexfen repudiated this policy: "He cannot, for by the offence & conviction all his goods are forfeit, and by the offence his lands, *from the time of the offence*, so that he cannot make a good sale of lands or goods, though not yet seized."[59] Friends, of course, were concerned about the prospect of being tendered the oath and praemunired all in one sessions or assizes before they could secure their debts. No doubt Pollexfen's claim that conveyances became illegal from the time of the offense, rather than conviction, was a shock. It was, alas, also wrong. Perhaps sensing that Pollexfen was having a bad day, Friends also approached Robert Dodsworth with the same questions. In general he agreed with Pollexfen, except on the issue of conveyance. Unlike his colleague, Dodsworth believed that the offender could sell lands or goods until judgment was rendered. Citing several legal sources, he explained that a writ was directed to the sheriff to inquire into and then seize the lands, tenements, goods, and chattels held by the defendant "the day that he was put out of the king's protection," and not before. But Dodsworth added a significant caveat: "if the tender & refusal, conviction & judgment may be at one assizes or sessions, 'tis not much material whether the lands are forfeited from the time of the offence committed or the judgment given."[60] The Quakers wished to avoid this development at all costs.

In Gloucester, also in 1682, seventeen Friends had been tendered the oath. The Quakers consulted Joseph Tilly of Lincoln's Inn, much as they had questioned Pollexfen and Dodsworth. Surprisingly, he agreed that the oath could be tendered to anyone over eighteen at assizes or sessions and could result in an immediate penalty of praemunire, even though the oath had not been previously tendered. He thought, however, that the statute 7 Jas. 1, c. 6 had limited this possibility to those who had already been tendered the oath out of sessions.[61] In fact, although that statute was restrictive, both Tilly and Pollexfen had erred, for it did not imply that the earlier statute had permitted justices in sessions to tender the oath arbitrarily. Both lawyers were reading into the earlier statute something that was not there. Judicial practice, of course, might have assumed the right. Tilly's opinion, however, did give the Quakers some hope of countering efforts to praemunire them at one sessions or assizes. In addition, his response as to process once an initial refusal had taken place was far more thorough. The justices, he said, were first to commit the parties to gaol without bail until they took the oath. Then men and single women were to be praemunired, and were also "disabled to bring any action real or personal." But he added some positive, albeit highly technical, observations: the Act did not extend to annuities; rents-charge; rents-seck; and the rights to hold fairs, markets, and warrens. Nor did the penalty include "other hereditaments that cannot legally pass in grants by the word ['lands']." Most importantly, a praemunire did not result in "any corruption of blood," which meant that the offender could inherit lands and hereditaments and transmit them by descent to heirs. Returning to procedure, he added that if the parties were not in custody at the time of the conviction a *capias* would ensue "in nature of an execution," which resulted in seizure of the offender's lands into the king's hands, "as is usual in cases of treason & felony after conviction & judgment." Sometimes a commission to discover the lands might be directed to particular persons appointed by the attorney general. "But," Tilly concluded, "I take it the most usual method is by inquest of office," an inquiry initiated by writ out of the petty-bag office in Chancery, directed to the sheriff or county escheator (who certified to the Exchequer county reversions of property to the king). As for the question of conveyancing, Tilly put Pollexfen's opinion in a better light, while reassuring Friends. That question, he responded, "hath been very much controverted & seems undetermined to this day." But he personally considered that the inquest was "only from the day" the offender was put out of protection, "which is *from the time of judgment given against him*." But when asked by Friends if the sale of goods and chattels, "upon a valuable consideration," to strangers in open market by those praemunired, was "sufficient & warrantable to save harmless the purchasers from the forfeiture," he answered succinctly: "I do conceive *not!*"

After all of this exposition, Tilly suddenly offered the seventeen Quakers some hope. The indictment, he observed, was "vicious." In English law this rendered it void because of some inherent fault or defect which did not satisfy legal requirements or conditions. In this case he recommended a *certiorari* or writ of error, for the indictment failed to state which statute enacted in the reign of James I was being utilized. That was critical, he argued, because they were dealing with two distinct laws "that require & ordain the taking of this oath & different penalties inflicted for the refusal, and it . . . not appearing upon which of these 2 statutes the indictment is founded, I conceive it to be uncertain & void." Not satisfied with this, Tilly offered another reason, far more arcane: since the justices could only tender the oath to those men and women who were not members of the nobility, the indictment must mention this. It did not, and if the court objected that several of those Quakers were indicted "by the name of 'labourers' which sufficiently supplies that omission," yet the indictment could not be good "as to the women, who are indicted as the wives of such men, and their husbands' names only mentioned without any addition."[62]

Finally, the year 1682 also saw the case of Griffith Jones, a prosperous Bermondsey glover, imprisoned at Bristol in January on a mittimus characterizing him as a stranger unacquainted with anyone in Bristol, who "pretended" that he was going into Pembrokeshire and then overseas. In fact, he had purchased five thousand acres in Pennsylvania, would soon become a charter member of the Free Society of Traders, and was about to embark for Penn's colony. Yet he had been detained by the authorities and examined as a suspected recusant. Not only did he admit to being a recusant, but added that he had only received the sacrament of the Lord's Supper once in his life. He was tendered the Oath of Allegiance and imprisoned upon refusal. On 10 February 1682 he was brought by *habeas corpus* to the court of King's Bench where his counsel insisted that his mittimus failed to mention that the oath was tendered by two justices, one of whom was of the quorum, as called for by the statute. The court "admitted the exception and thereupon immediately discharged him."[63]

What is so striking about these cases is the degree to which numerous Quakers had embraced the use of legal counsel and grasped the complexities of the law. Where estates and goods were liable to forfeiture, they clearly indicated their determination to defeat the intent of the law by "securing debts" which, in effect, prevented such forfeitures. Delays and legal technicalities were seized upon. In fact, Friends often appeared to be adopting any strategy to gain their freedom and defeat their adversaries. As if to confirm this, Thomas Salthouse, one of nine Quaker prisoners at Launceston in 1683, asked Meeting for Sufferings to consult Edward Ward about their sentence of praemunire. One of the arguments Salthouse stressed centered on their having been indicted as "yeomen," which, he added, "is altogether untrue and erroneous . . . for Thomas Lower is reputed a gentleman," while the others included a fisherman, weaver, pewterer, two shopkeepers, and three laboring tinners. Salthouse concluded, however, if Meeting for Sufferings, with Ward's advice, did not believe that this or the other exceptions they offered, would "prevail for our enlargement, nor a writ of error and an arrest of judgment, then upon intimation from you with your advice and experimental precedents, we may think of *some other expedient* in order to our desired enlargement and liberty from under this . . . sentence of praemunire and perpetual imprisonment." As with other forms of prosecution, Meeting for Sufferings did not always advise taking action. Thus in June 1683 it cautioned Joseph Cobham of Essex, indicted for refusing to swear, "not to insist against them with their laws." Rather, he should "rely upon their kindness & seek to prolong the time of their proceeding to judgment thereupon."[64] Perhaps his mittimus and indictment were both in good order.

Wisely, the Quakers were not content simply to rely on the courts. They queried former Attorney General William Jones on the possibility that the king, after the oath had been initially refused by a person at quarter sessions, could have the prisoner freed "before any further proceedings." Jones responded that the king could "order his discharge" prior to conviction only if the party was imprisoned at the king's suit. Alternatively, at the time the party was indicted at sessions, the king could order his attorney general to enter a *nolle prosequi* "upon such indictment." It was also possible, he added, for the king to issue a pardon after a praemunire.[65]

While the Oath of Allegiance was obviously a primary worry for Friends, they were also concerned about oaths of office. The ubiquitous Thomas Corbett was asked in 1677 whether or not Richard Basnett, a

Friend in Norton Folgate, could lawfully and safely execute the office of headborough without taking an oath. Corbett believed he could, on the premise that the election, not the oath, "made him an officer," the oath being simply a stricter obligation on him "for the due execution of his office." There was no law or statute, he observed, which made Basnett's acting in that office either "void or penal" for failure to take the oath. In any case, the steward of the leet, as the "proper person to swear him" had dispensed with it. "I conceive," he added, that "it is not the concern of any justice of peace to enquire whether he was sworn or not." Corbett, never one to avoid controversy, then denied that any law or statute existed empowering a justice to swear constables, but only to swear sheriffs and their bailiffs, "who have return of writs from courts of record."[66] While that might be true, normal procedure was otherwise, as indicated by the fact that in November 1687 James II, anxious for allies, would specifically order that Quakers could become constables *without needing to take the oath of office*. It is more likely that many localities, "rather glad of Friends they can have," were willing to waive the required oath.[67] It was not, after all, a popular office.

Even Quaker ship captains needed to worry about oaths, for they were bound to swear to their entry and contents upon clearing their ships outward bound. Meeting for Sufferings cautiously advised that "the statute allows the content[s] to be passed on oath *or otherwise*," but went on to add that the situation was "hazardous," for one Friend had been successfully prosecuted. The meeting admitted, however, "smuggling was proved against him." Some Friends, it noted, had been subpoenaed, "but suits generally fall." Captains, therefore, could either "appear or stand it out till arrest, & then appear or go to prison, as they have freedom, which is," the Meeting concluded, "the safest advice." Similarly, there were reports of Quakers having served apprenticeships, but when their time was up, being refused the freedom of the city in order to carry on their trade. For once, the Quakers had little redress, other than requesting by petition that such Friends be admitted without an oath, and that "their promise . . . may be taken of what they are able to perform, there being several articles in the oath which the takers thereof do not perform themselves nor hardly are capable to do it."[68]

Finally, from 1676 to 1678 Friends also clashed with the court of Arches in London, which had imprisoned some Southwark Friends for refusing to pay towards repairs of the parish church and not taking

an oath when questioned. The Quakers did obtain a prohibition removing the case from the inferior church court jurisdiction into King's
Bench.[69] Their challenge was probably successful, for in Easter Term
1677 the judges of Common Pleas had granted a prohibition to
Thomas Watersfield, who had been excommunicated by the bishop of
Chichester for refusing to take an oath when presenting evidence as a
churchwarden. The prohibition claimed that "no person ought to be
cited to appear in any court Christian before any judge spiritual to
take any oath unless it be only in cases matrimonial or testamentary."
Several years later, Meeting for Sufferings ordered Roland Vaughan,
in response to a complaint from Chester similar to that from Southwark, to "draw up the state of the case by way of complaint against the
ecclesiastical court for committing the said Friends for want of an answer upon oath, *it being a case neither testamentary nor matrimonial.*"[70]

III

The Quaker defense against prosecution for recusancy centered, not
on the issue of forced conformity, but on their belief, as well as that of
other Protestant Dissenters, that the severer statutes were directed exclusively against Catholics. It was imperative, Friends believed, that
judges and others in power be convinced that Quakers, as Protestants,
were not liable to prosecution. In practice, the success or failure of their
campaign often depended on politics. In February 1675 Charles II had
ordered that process be issued against the estates of those convicted of
recusancy. But in August 1676, possibly with the vacillating king's ac-
quiescence, the Quakers actively campaigned for law-enforcement
officers and church leaders to signify to the king's remembrancer in
the Exchequer that convicted Friends were Protestant Dissenters, not
popish recusants. That officer would then draw up a plea to the attorney general for his signature, which Friends could send to the appropriate sheriff in order to suspend further prosecution.[71] Edward
Ward, of the Inner Temple, confirmed in 1679 that this was the only
way the Quakers could get relief from recusancy convictions, and that it
required the king's cooperation, for his warrant to the remembrancer
and clerk of the pipe was a prerequisite. Normally, however, such convictions could not be discharged, except "by the party's conformities
duly pleaded," although the seizures could be prevented "by a prior
title pleaded." But if any were convicted, he added, by informers, the

latter could "proceed for their parts." Therefore, the Quakers, who refused to conform, could not procure an absolute discharge, "but there may be a *perpetual stay of process* which in effect will amount to that."[72] Friends were learning that the rights of informers far surpassed their own rights.

Friends pursued a similar strategy with juries. After conviction it was usual for an inquisition jury to visit the offender's estate to assess its value; the jury's return would be sent to the Exchequer, out of which process would issue twice yearly for bailiffs to collect two-thirds of the rents and profits. Legal counsel advised Friends on methods to limit the amount seized. Where the jury of inquisition had not yet visited the estate, those Quaker recusants who had any mortgages or real encumbrances on their estates should produce them to the jury, utilizing legal assistance to convince that body that the person convicted was not possessed of any lands. But if such mortgage or encumbrance was lacking, then the attorney should still be present to observe what evidence was given to the jury to find the party possessed of land, because the jurors, "who are upon oath," must not find a person possessed of land "upon common fame or the report of the country." In any event, Quakers should satisfy the jury that they were not popish recusants, and if possible, "get the jury to put that into their return." Unfortunately, if the inquisition had already taken place, there was no remedy except either to plead some encumbrance if any existed, in the Exchequer, or to petition the king that they were not popish recusants, "and praying thereupon his majesty's directions in the law and a pardon under the [Great] Seal." In 1680 Meeting for Sufferings even advised Friends to make certain that they received sufficient notice when first returned as convicted, and then personally to encourage the jury of inquisition not to proceed.[73]

Thomas Corbett once again supported the Quaker view, believing, when asked his opinion, that it was "very hard" that Quakers were returned as popish recusants. While admitting that the statute 1 Eliz. I, c. 2 which imposed a weekly fine of 12*d.* included Protestants as well as Catholics, he conceived that the £20 per month penalty imposed by the statute 23 Eliz. I, c. 1 "was never intended" to include Protestants, "as appears by the preamble . . . and by a proviso therein, and also by the statute 3 Jac. [1], c. 4." Therefore, if Quakers were returned among papists, they should "take copies of the returns and . . . move the court thereupon." In this instance, Corbett's opinion was reasonable and contained some potential for success. But as always, he soon passed the boundaries of legal sensibility, for in February 1679 he examined all of the relevant statutes and responded to a number of important queries, including the *qui tam* action utilized by informers. While conceding that this action was allowable in the courts at Westminster, he clearly, but erroneously, thought that it did not lie before the justices in quarter sessions, nor before the judges of assize, not even by the statute 21 Jas. I, c. 4, which permitted informers to bring actions for recusancy in any county. He wisely advised, however, that in whatever court the information or action was brought, the defendant could plead "the general issue,"[74] but should not give "any special matter in evidence, but such as doth directly maintain the issue, and not any collateral matter." In other words, Friends were not to obscure matters with specious arguments, one of which would likely be the question of Protestant liability to such prosecutions. In response to Quaker fears of outlawry on such popular actions, Corbett insisted, incorrectly, that outlawries were on indictment only. In another significant, but debatable, response, he believed that Quakers incurred the penalty of £20 per month only for those months mentioned in the information "and not for any month after such conviction, for the subsequent monthly forfeitures are only upon indictments."[75]

Interestingly, Corbett's opinion on *qui tams* was confirmed by Roland Vaughan in 1683, who advised that "upon the reading of good authorities" the justices at quarter sessions had "no jurisdiction to hear & determine the matter in charge upon issue joined, unless it be upon indictment & not upon a *qui tam* . . . and therefore cannot issue process for the levying of the goods of the parties convicted of recusancy." Vaughan even expanded Corbett's opinion by arguing that *qui tams* were not permissible at all for recusancy, an interesting but uninformed premise, since he had overlooked 21 Jas. I, c. 4.[76] The views of Corbett and Vaughan, however, suited the Quaker strategy of frustrating informers, for restriction of *qui tam* actions to the central courts and assizes would force informers to travel substantial distances at great expense. As for Friends' premise that popish recusants were the appropriate target of the statutes in question, Corbett's opinion was ostensibly confirmed by Thomas Smith who, advising them in the case of Henry Jackson, stressed that the titles, preambles, and tests of the statutes in question, clearly indicated they were "only & singly intended against popish recusants."[77]

Supported by such legal advice, the Quakers in 1680 presented a lengthy petition to the king and Parliament, which argued that the preambles to the recusancy statutes applied only to popish recusants, and therefore "the prosecution of Protestant dissenters (as they have been of late) is . . . extending the sense of those statutes beyond right reason, and the intent of the law-makers." The petitioners even offered their own "Test" for distinguishing between a popish recusant and a Quaker. That petition was part of a sustained campaign by the Quakers to influence the Cavalier and Exclusion Parliaments to enact a statute limiting enforcement of the severer recusancy laws to Catholics. Early in 1678, according to Friends, Charles II had agreed that it was "very unreasonable" that Quakers should be prosecuted on statutes never made or intended against them, but at the same time he had also declined the responsibility for relieving them. Instead, he deflected them towards the Cavalier Parliament, in the direction of which they then turned, and seemed to be nearing success when it was dissolved, although Algernon Sidney warned that he had found "many parliament men very bitter upon them in private conversation," but "without knowing why." Friends continued to lobby the new Parliaments, only to be frustrated by the king's tactics of prorogation and dissolution as he fought to protect his brother's right of succession.[78]

Yet for a brief period early in the Popish Plot and Exclusion crises, Charles II had appeared willing to assist the Quakers; for Lancashire Friends in December 1678 and January 1679 obtained at least thirteen certificates from neighbors, constables, churchwardens, and overseers that they were not popish recusants. These were probably related to a warrant issued in February 1679 from Lord Treasurer Danby to the king's remembrancer and to the clerk of the pipe superseding and staying convictions and processes against a substantial number of Quaker recusants, with order to "let no process be from henceforth issued out against them without especial order & directions in that behalf."[79] Quaker hopes were further raised by directions issued in March 1679 by the Privy Council to the bishops to permit Quakers to subscribe to the declaration in the 1678 Test Act to distinguish them from Catholics. Those same bishops were also to make "strict enquiry" into the Quakers' "opinions & deportment towards the government in church & state and to certify the same to His Majesty in council." Although Friends believed that law-enforcement officers could now be persuaded that the king opposed the prosecution of Protestant Dissenters as recusants, they were soon rudely awakened. On 4 May 1679, probably after severe recriminations from the bishops, Charles revoked the March Privy Council order, and prosecutions of Quakers as recusants continued with varying degrees of ferocity.[80]

Nonetheless, the chronic confusion over Protestant and Catholic recusancy and the temporary desire of Charles II to propitiate Parliament and the Dissenters during the Exclusion crisis enabled Friends early in 1681 to again subscribe to the declaration in the Test Act of 1678 that, with royal approval, would result in the discharge of prosecutions. Thus, in February 1681 the Privy Council examined the cause of eleven Suffolk Quakers whose estates had been seized, but who had obtained a certificate from Sir Charles Crofts Read and Thomas Holland, two justices of the peace, that they had publicly subscribed to the declaration. The Quakers were ordered to be discharged and their estates returned, while the declaration was to be filed and remain on record in the court of Exchequer. In the following month William Penn, although not subscribing to the Test, saw his prosecution for recusancy superseded, the government "very well satisfied he is not or ever was a popish recusant."[81] In March 1681 at Cambridge assizes Judge William Montagu told thirteen Quakers convicted for recusancy that if they subscribed, he had orders from the king to acquit them. They did so. Montagu, lobbied by Friends when he returned to London, acquainted Charles with what had occurred, and the king, in turn, ordered their discharge. London Friends hurriedly dispatched copies of this case to Friends in other counties as a precedent.[82] Although the relationship between Crown and dissent soured markedly as the year progressed, the Quakers continued to pursue the same tactic. In September 1681 ninety-four Quakers subscribed to the declaration in Rydal, Westmorland, before Sir Daniel Fleming and his brother, while in the following month the Privy Council was petitioned by Quakers in Hereford to supersede their convictions for recusancy, as they were willing to take the same step. The petition was referred to the attorney general, Sir Robert Sawyer, for consideration. In December prominent London Friends also petitioned the council for relief. But Charles was no longer so accommodating; acting in council, he cleverly rebuffed them. After stressing that it was "not his pleasure to stop execution of the laws against dissenters," he agreed to supersede recusancy prosecutions only if Dissenters produced certificates from local "gentlemen," who were "known to be well affected to the government," that the said Dissenters were "of peaceable and quiet behaviour" and did not "give disturbance to the government." Charles would then "extend his favourable indulgence towards them."[83] The king had managed to appear tolerant while leaving the true initiative to others far less so. If the gentry gave such certificates to Quakers, an unlikely eventuality, he could simply say he was following their lead. As Friends would soon discover, the attitude of the Crown towards dissent had hardened.

Undaunted, as always, the Quakers attempted to procure the necessary certificates. In January 1682 George Whitehead and other London Friends attended the council with certificates of the quiet and peaceable behavior of Quakers in Westmorland and Cumberland, together with certificates from justices of those who had subscribed to the declaration, and certificates for Norfolk Friends from ministers and churchwardens. But the council "seemed not satisfied with such certificates, but directed new ones *particular to every one's respective case.*" Meeting for Sufferings thereupon drew up a standard short form for certificates which they sent into several counties.[84] Some justices, in fact, were surprised that the king would even consider such certificates. Sir Daniel Fleming, a bitter adversary of the Quakers, having rebuffed the efforts of some Westmorland Friends for a certificate, wrote in January 1682 to Sir Lionel Jenkins, expressing his confusion over favoritism to staunch opponents of the Church of England. "I wish to know," he added, "what would be pleasing to the king herein."[85] Nonetheless, some Friends in Herefordshire, Norfolk, and Wiltshire were able to procure certificates, with those in Norfolk also subscribing to the Test. But in the spring of 1682 it appeared that the success of these tactics could no longer be guaranteed, although Roland Vaughan in 1683 advised that where constables made presentments for recusancy, Friends should obtain certificates citing their loyalty and that they were not popish recusants. He would then try to discharge them from forfeitures entered in the Exchequer. The Quakers continued throughout 1683 to attempt to procure such certificates, but with indifferent success, and by 1685 the Crown was asking for certificates of *loyalty and sufferings for the king* or his family.[86] To the Crown, complaints by Protestants about prosecution as popish recusants were no longer relevant.

Nor were the Quakers likely to receive support from the judiciary. The Presbyterian Roger Morrice, an interested observer, did report that early in 1682 at Hertford assizes some Dissenters, indicted on the statute 23 Eliz. I, c. 1, alleged that it did not include them, and moved successfully for a special verdict. Yet Judge Thomas Jones in his charge to the three Middlesex grand juries on 31 January 1683 indicated otherwise. That statute, he commented, was against *all* recusants. A further blow followed in February 1683 when the case of a Kent Dissenter was heard by writ of error in King's Bench; the judges unanimously decided that 23 Eliz. I, c. 1 did, in fact, apply to persons of all persuasions. Morrice commented that while many lawyers had favored this view, it was only the second time that the court had judged it so, the first being in the reign of Charles I. When motion was made again on 18 May 1683 that King's Bench should hear arguments on why Protestants should not be prosecuted under that Act, the judges demurred on the ground that they had already given their opinion. A week later, counsel again moved "very fervently" to be able to present their argument, and again were forcefully denied.[87]

With the judiciary apparently unsympathetic, the Quakers turned to grand juries, relying on an approach recommended by Rowland Vaughan in September 1680, but which today would be characterized as "tampering." The undersheriff, his clerk, or the bailiffs of each hundred could inform Friends in advance of the names and addresses of all those who would serve on the grand jury at every assizes or quarter sessions. The Quakers could then visit the jurors and inform them that Quakers were being prosecuted on statutes directed against popish recusants, while those same papists "go free." Grand juries, Vaughan insisted, had not taken the time to "search into the matter, so as to make a distinction between Friends of Truth & popish recusants." The Quakers should therefore explain to the jurors that indictments were really their own presentments.[88] Vaughan feared that most grand juries saw the bill of indictment as "a kind of record," because it was sent to them "ready drawn by the clerks of the court." Yet those clerks were chosen by the court "because skilful in drawing of indictments." It was not a record, he stressed, until brought in *"billa vera."* Too often, he believed, grand juries returned an indictment true, although often only "partly true." Grand juries were also frightened of "displeasing the judges of assize," who in their charge to that body warned them "to find every indictment that comes before them" for otherwise the matter could "never be known & examined by the court." Vaughan believed that if grand jurors were made aware of their own power and responsibility, they would act accordingly and save themselves trouble by giving in presentments of their own "knowledge or understanding," rather than out of "envy, hatred or malice." Moreoover, he learned that when constables made presentments under the heading of popish recusants, the clerks would then ground the indictment in general terms of absence from church, "which the presentments cannot warrant under such . . . terms, nor ought the jury . . . find such indictments if they regarded their oaths & the truth of their knowledge." If the Quakers, he concluded, were unable to lobby the jurors prior to their assembling in court, then they should speak with them either after the charge was given and before the afternoon session or on the first night after they were sworn, "for then they will be most at leisure for the purpose."[89]

In 1682 Yearly Meeting confirmed this approach, but added that justices should also be lobbied "to prevent the grand jury's presentment." If the seizure could not be avoided, however, then Friends were "to use their interest" with the jury of inquisition "not to overrate their lands." As part of the overall strategy of Friends, all those under such prosecution were to attempt prior to conviction and distraint "to clear their accounts, & secure (or satisfy for) their debts which they owe to all persons, and suffer for their testimony with no other estate but their own." But Yearly Meeting also suggested that goods which had been distrained, yet were left in the sufferer's home "without a bailiff or keeper to keep possession," were still the property of the Friend, "though under lock or wall," who could "do with them what he pleaseth, for they are not the king's till he takes them." This suggestion conveniently ignored the question of conveyance after conviction.[90]

Although Quaker records are silent on the matter, it seems likely that grand jurors relied on their own sympathies, although generally following the direction of the court once indictments were drawn up. Thus the Quakers in 1685 followed the lead of the Crown and began to rely on certificates of their peaceable behavior and loyalty, a form of which was sent by Meeting for Sufferings to local Friends. Although it was often difficult to secure the appropriate signatories, some Quakers were successful, like those at Bury St. Edmunds and Clare, in Suffolk, who received certificates signed by four justices and two justices, respectively. Where justices were unwilling, Friends looked to others, procuring certificates in Essex, for example, from neighbors, local officers, and (in one case) a vicar. Similarly, six certificates were gathered for Quaker prisoners in Northampton, signed in three cases by two or more justices; in one case by eight neighbors, including a rector; in another by twenty-two neighbors, including two churchwardens, two overseers of the poor, and one constable; and in the last by eleven, including two churchwardens and one constable. Although not all the certificates were for recusancy, they all stressed the loyalty of the prisoners and their peaceable behavior.[91] By 1686 the Quaker attempt to relieve sufferings for recusancy would become part of their general effort, with increasing assistance from James II, to end all their sufferings.

While the Quakers struggled to obtain certificates and fought against prosecution as popish recusants, they also needed to focus on other questions of enforcement, such as instances where imprisoned or excommunicated Quakers complained of simultaneous prosecutions for recusancy. Unfortunately, Thomas Rudyard advised that it was a "maxim in law" that no person could "take advantage of his own wrong," and therefore it was not legally acceptable to plead an excommunication as a bar to prosecution for recusancy.[92] The extraordinary complexity of recusancy prosecutions often led Friends to ask Meeting for Sufferings to search in the Crown Office for prosecutions by informers, or in the Exchequer to see if convictions had been returned there, or if process was about to ensue, and for how many months. Or they might ask what the procedure entailed. These numerous requests, combined with the surprise of many Quakers that they had been indicted without their knowledge, led the Meeting to appoint Friends to attend London, Middlesex, Westminster, and Surrey sessions and assizes to learn whether Quakers were being presented for recusancy. The same procedure was also encouraged in the country at large.[93] Yet the problem continued, prompting the Meeting's request in November 1685 "that consideration be had how way may be found to give Friends timely notice before seizure on the statute of recusancy," a query repeated again on 11 December.[94]

Of course, the question then arose of what tactics Quakers should employ after their names were proclaimed in court. The Meeting generally advised Friends to "offer their bodies to the sheriffs," but to attempt to delay proceedings, particularly when dealing with *qui tam* actions. Yearly Meeting in 1682 was clear in its approach to these actions and the informers who initiated them. When asked about the advisability of appearing, that Meeting responded that on "consideration of some knowing in this case," any Friend who appeared could be prosecuted to "judgment & execution" at "small cost" to the informer. Nonappearance, however, would prevent further prosecution until the suspect was brought to one of the courts at Westminster "at the informer's cost," which could be as much as £10. That kind of money "an informer seldom can or will lay out." Consequently, "it is plain (in the sense of diverse) that not appearing is the greatest disappointment to the informer," although the Meeting left the ultimate decision to the freedom of Friends, and to the "guidance of the power of God in themselves."[95]

As with other forms of prosecution, Friends also conveyed away their goods, although once again, this strategy was not always successful, as Meeting for Sufferings learned from Richard Sherring, who had "delivered full possession of all to his creditors by bill" and had left his home, "but that day the bailiffs coming, the creditors left possession to them."[96] Ironically, the Quakers had few problems with the recusancy statute that contained the most severe penalties—the Elizabethan Conventicle Act (35 Eliz. I, c. 1), which numbered among its punishments abjuration of the realm and death as a felon without benefit of clergy for those who refused. With several exceptions, most notably the case of Richard Vickris in the early 1680s, the Act was rarely employed by the authorities. When it was used, Friends countered with their usual phalanx of prominent lawyers, who employed virtually every legal weapon imaginable, successfully preventing either abjuration or death as a felon.[97]

Yet it appeared that death was the only true release from recusancy prosecutions. When asked about the rights of heirs to discharge confiscated estates, Yearly Meeting cited the case of Nathaniel Owen's wife Anne, who had died nine months after forfeiture of two-thirds of her estate. After her death, an affidavit was made before a baron of the Exchequer that Nathaniel's "said wife was educated in the Protestant religion, generally known & reputed a Protestant, was married to him, the said Nathaniel, [and] had one child now living." The child's right as an infant was pleaded before the barons of the Exchequer, who thereupon discharged the land from the seizure and sequestration, "except only for the 9 months the said Anne was living after the seizure."[98]

IV

When the Quakers resisted prosecutions for tithes and rates, they encountered stiff opposition, in part because these had been initiated by
private, rather than royal suits, thus minimizing (as with informers)
the king's usefulness to imprisoned Friends. When legal tactics were
employed, such as the right to appeal decisions from inferior church
courts to those of the archbishops, they met with minimal success, as
seen in the case of three Kendal Friends who appealed their imprisonment for small tithes to the archbishop's court at York. When the
prosecuting minister, William Browsword, swore to the legality of his
prosecution, the court demanded that the appellants testify on oath or
be cited for contempt.[99] Thus Friends' refusal to swear effectively nul-
lified the ecclesiastical appeal process. Yet Friends did have one potentially useful weapon. As early as 1661 Bray D'Oyley, prosecuted for
tithes by Richard Bloxham in a hundred court, demurred to that
court's pretense to jurisdiction over tithes, and produced the statutes
32 Hen. VIII, c. 7 and 2 & 3 Edw. VI, c. 13 to prove it. But when the
jury asked to see the statutes, the presiding steward refused, charging
them "to find for Bloxham," which they did. Ironically, the amount in
the declaration was then tripled by the court, as required by the
Edwardian statute cited by D'Oyley.[100] The Quakers, as always, were
undeterred. In 1668 they solicited the advice of John Merefield and
John Haggatt about the ability of the county court to meddle in tithe
cases; both men agreed that such courts had no power to hold pleas
for any cause arising on an act of parliament unless specifically empowered by the act: the statute in question, 2 Edw. 6, c. 13, did not
convey such power. The best strategy, they advised, was for the defendant to demur to the court's jurisdiction. But, Friends queried, what
happened if they failed to put in a demurrer, or their having done so,
the court rejected it? Could the defendant bring an action against the
freeholders who judged against him, or against the sheriff or county
clerk? "If the court proceed," responded Merefield, "where it hath not
cognizance of the cause, all the proceedings are before no lawful judge
coram non judice," leaving the sheriff, the county clerk, the bailiff, and
the freeholders liable to "an action at the suit of the party injured."
Similarly, when William Bishop sued John and Edward Corbet in an
action of debt for tithes on the same statute in the county court, the
Quakers turned for advice to Thomas Hunt, who also recommended

demurring to that court's jurisdiction, which lacked cognizance "in any action upon breach of any statute, because in all such actions a fine is to be made to the king, and no court can impose a fine but a court of record," which the county court was not. As Bray D'Oyley had discovered, however, legal advice did not always translate into success in court, for the county court proceeded to give judgment for the plaintiff. Since 1661, however, the legal sophistication of the Quakers had greatly increased, and they were able to have the case successfully argued by Hunt the following term in King's Bench, which thereupon issued a prohibition, stating that all pleas of debt for not paying tithes based on 2 Edw. 6 or any other penal statutes were cognizable only in the central courts at Westminster, "and not in any county court."[101] This was an important victory for the Quakers. Although some successful prosecutions against them still occurred in local courts, they were rare, no doubt reflecting the increasingly successful use of this legal tactic.[102] As Thomas Titley found out in 1679, however, it was imperative that Friends demur to the jurisdiction prior to conviction; otherwise, the proceedings were legal.[103]

In tithe prosecutions, as with those for recusancy, Meeting for Sufferings believed that Quakers should not assist their adversaries in any way, nor give any appearance of sanctioning such prosecutions. When Nathaniel Owen, sued in 1678 in Chancery, asked if he should surrender to the Fleet on an order of the master of the rolls, the Meeting counseled that it was preferable *"to be taken by his adversary than voluntarily to surrender his body."* Similarly, it advised Yorkshire Friends in 1687 to ignore a subpoena. In January 1688 instructions were sent by Roland Vaughan to Friends in nine counties to prevent excommunications for failure to pay tithes. Sometimes Meeting for Sufferings was simply unable to assist Friends in any way, as in the case of William Somkey, whose name in the warrant was spelled Zomkey: "the mistake in the letter 'Z' for 'S' is not material."[104]

One person the Meeting would doubtless have wished to assist was Richard Tregennow, whose lengthy struggle with James Forbes has already been described. In July 1682 he was able to write to James Brain in London that Forbes "hath yielded his breath and is gone to his last home to receive the reward of his actions." It appears that Forbes, an illegitimate Scot, had failed to leave a will, and that two men were quarreling over the estate. Tregennow hoped to take advantage of the death and the quarrel to secure his release, believing that neither man, once he was freed, would have him reimprisoned, "so as the proverb is, 'between the lip and the cup'." He added that he lacked the skill to know quickly what steps to take, "but if any Friend or counsel be treated with, and they consult the business, what charges or fees it come at shall be readily paid on demand, and if anything may be done," he stressed anxiously, "pray brother be quick in it." Sadly, Thomas Rudyard responded that as Tregennow had been outlawed and imprisoned, "the death of his adversary will not discharge him, nor can he be acquitted till the executor or administrator acknowledge satisfaction on record." The Meeting reluctantly endorsed the letter as having been read on 14 July 1682 and that there was "nothing needful to transcribe nor enter."[105]

While Tregennow's case might elicit the Meeting's compassion, that of William Wilkins, a Nailsworth Friend, aroused its anger. Imprisoned in Gloucester castle on a King's Bench process at the suit of an impropriator for tithes, Wilkins wished to remove himself by writ of *habeas corpus* to King's Bench, but queried if the marshal there would give him liberty, how much the move would cost, and whether the impropriator could proceed against his goods if he remained where he was. "Friends can not direct any one," the Meeting retorted, "to remove himself from the gaol where his adversary had committed him, in order only to go into another gaol," for he would then become a prisoner in a place of his own, not the impropriator's, choosing. Nor could he then complain about any abuse or hard use by the gaoler "when on his own election he enters the gaoler's house." Moreover, the potential for liberty from the marshal was uncertain and would be extremely expensive. In any case, by removing himself to the King's Bench, he enabled his adversary to proceed against him to judgment, whereas if he remained where he was, his adversary had to remove him to King's Bench by *habeas corpus*, and could not proceed further against him "unless he voluntarily appears to the suit by an attorney." Also, if Wilkins removed himself, he aided his adversary at his own charge, but if he stayed in the country the charge would fall on his adversary to remove him. In effect, "if his adversary remove him hither, he then will have all the advantages as if he had removed himself."[106]

The statute which most annoyed the Quakers was 2 Edw. VI, c. 13, upon which triple damages for not setting out tithes could be levied, and under which many Quakers had suffered,[107] but there appeared to be little that Friends could do to mitigate its impact. At the same time, they vehemently opposed the jurisdiction which the court of Exchequer had presumed over tithes; for nonappearance would lead to writs of rebellion, then sequestration. Even worse, nonappearance was likely for Friends, given that court's insistence on an oath. Thus Yearly Meeting, condemning the "arbitrary jurisdiction of the Exchequer," left it to Friends' "liberty & freedom in the Truth" whether or not to appear. But it also implied that Friends might do well to appear and answer without an oath, as a public demonstration of both the Quaker testimony against swearing and the severity of the court in prosecuting Quakers "to contempts, rebellion, and sequestration" simply for not swearing to their answers.[108]

The advice given to provincial Friends from London was not without error. Thus Meeting for Sufferings in March 1687 heard from Lancashire of a tax instituted for repair of the church at Prescot, with a double penalty, levied by distraint on those who refused to pay. Some Quakers, having already suffered such distraints, asked the Meeting whether churchwardens could either distrain or bring an action of debt, since the assessment was made by a majority of the vestry. This tax with distraint was, they added, "a new thing," whereas Friends formerly "only suffered by excommunication." Roland Vaughan responded that they should quietly suffer distress, "it being the easiest way for them." But Lancashire Friends were like any other Quakers. They persisted with their questions until Vaughan turned to Edward Ward, of the Inner Temple, for further opinion. He advised that the repair of churches was an ecclesiastical function, and therefore the tax, "if not paid," was to be recovered in the church courts, "by the censures and proceedings thereof." There was no right of distraint in this case, he conceived, either by common law or statute law; those who undertook the distraint would be "trespassers" and therefore "liable to damage for so doing." When the Lancashire Friends also questioned the legality of the penalty, Ward agreed that it was not legal. "The tax itself & costs in the ecclesiastical court for not paying it" were all that could be legally recovered.[109] Local parishes now discovered what many others already knew. It was not a simple matter to challenge the Quakers.

V

It would appear that the threat of excommunication, the primary weapon of the church courts, had failed to frighten the Lancashire

Friends mentioned above. Nor did it seem to scare many other Dissenters, for the number of excommunicates was immense. For example, in the early seventeenth century, about fifty thousand, or five percent of the population of the dioceses of York, Norwich, and Chester were habitual excommunicates.[110] Even after the Restoration, it remained a common penalty, particularly against recusants, who often remained excommunicate for years. All Quakers, of course, should have suffered this sanction; for that reason, no doubt, Derbyshire Friends stopped recording excommunicates after 1663, and the same is probably true for other counties.[111] Yet as mentioned previously, church authorities could secure secular assistance by means of the writ *de excommunicato capiendo* to imprison excommunicates,[112] and could also threaten marriages and wills. Friends were certainly worried about potential imprisonment, often requesting Meeting for Sufferings to search the Crown Office to see if that writ had been filed, in order to surrender themselves to the sheriff rather than risk the expensive fines which would follow a return of *non est inventus*.[113] Imprisonment, of course, also involved the activities of sheriffs and gaolers. Meeting for Sufferings asked Thomas Corbett if a sheriff was liable to an action for allowing some liberty to excommunicates? While admitting that the King's Bench could fine that officer for his neglect, Corbett believed that in this instance there was no action at common law against him, because the judgment upon which the imprisonment was grounded came from the spiritual court, and therefore it was not a writ of execution "to retain the party till he satisfy any sum of money or costs of suit," but was only "in nature of an attachment." As to whether gaolers could put excommunicates, or those committed for misdemeanors or contempts, among felons, Corbett thought not, relying upon the statute 22 & 23 Chas. II, c. 20 which forbade prisoners for debt being placed in the same room with felons. Corbett envisioned the above-mentioned crimes as "clearly within the equity and meaning of that statute, as prisoners for debt are within the letter of it," for executions for debts were "of greater concern" than either misdemeanors or contempts for not paying debts or duties. Corbett had further good news for Friends, when they asked if the right of justices to imprison excommunicates simply on certificate from a bishop was still in effect. Although he replied in the affirmative, he added that "it hath been sometimes, *though but rarely*, put in execution since the king's restoration."[114]

The Quakers, of course, could combat individual abuses. Among the cases disputed were those where the bishop swore a *significavit* which failed to list one of the causes or offenses contained in 5 Eliz. I, c. 23, the relevant statute; [115] the issuance by a cursitor in Chancery of a *capias* writ without a certificate from the prerogative court, and his failure to enroll it in the Crown Office; [116] a mittimus which failed to make it clear upon what statute contumacious Friends were imprisoned; [117] and a Friend imprisoned and then freed by a gaoler who again called for him, but without a writ having been issued. [118] As for those Friends prosecuted in both the ecclesiastical and secular courts for the same offense, Yearly Meeting, having consulted with "some knowing in those matters," advised that in cases where statutes specifically prohibited double punishment for the same crime, the accused Friend could plead the first prosecution as a bar to any further prosecution. However, if the ecclesiastical court refused to accept that plea and did not grant a stay, the Friend could "suggest the whole matter" in any of the superior courts at Westminster, with the likelihood of obtaining a prohibition "to stay the procedure in the ecclesiastical court." [119]

As we have seen with nonpayment of tithes, the Quakers were distinctly unhappy over the presumed power of the church courts to demand an oath in such cases when Friends did appear and were ready to answer. That requirement would lead to excommunication and imprisonment, when some Friends apparently preferred to argue their case. Roland Vaughan, therefore, formulated a set of instructions to avoid the oath. When Friends were cited they should appear in person or by a proctor retained for that purpose, and should demand copies of the libels exhibited against them "in the presence of some persons who can make affidavit of such demand if occasion require." Upon obtaining the copies, they were to retain able counsel to draw up their answers, and then go with that counsel and present their formal signed answers. If the court demanded an oath attesting the truth of the answers, counsel was to insist that they ought to be accepted without an oath, on the grounds that no ecclesiastical court had the power to administer an oath "in any case other than in causes matrimonial or testamentary." If that failed, however, and any Friends were prosecuted for contempt for not answering, and were subsequently imprisoned, they should "by their counsel" inform the court of King's Bench that they had "tendered their answers as aforesaid, before the sentence of excommunication was pronounced against them, which according to law ought to have been accepted, though not sworn unto," and then should "pray the court to grant a *supersedeas* for their enlargement, being proceeded against . . . contrary to law." [120] Nothing more dramatically illustrates the change in Quakerism by 1688 than this advice, when contrasted with Paul Moon's tract in 1658. [121]

Ironically, the Quakers could not always rely on the attorneys they hired. Windsor Friends late in 1678 retained John Vining, who for £3 per person claimed he could secure their freedom, but refused to explain how. Meeting for Sufferings decided to investigate and found that Vining had "no way consistent with Truth to discharge them." They dismissed him. Yet two years later three Friends imprisoned at Salisbury on writs *de excommunicato capiendo* told Meeting for Sufferings that on the recommendation of Ellis Hookes, the recording clerk of that Meeting, they had hired an attorney named Vining and paid him £30. Vining had not changed, for the Friends complained that he had failed to assist them in any way. The Meeting dispatched two Friends to speak with him. Presumably, he was not recommended again. There was also the immortal Peter Peele, "an apostate Quaker, formerly a tailor and now pretending to be a solicitor" who, according to Thomas Tyler and Thomas Bennett, imprisoned at Chelmsford in 1678, was about to have them discharged. It was soon discovered, however, that he was simply following the prescribed course of having the Quakers post bond to conform. William Meade, a member of Meeting for Sufferings, was not impressed: that procedure, he noted, "may be done without more wit or learning then usually attend a porter." Peele's offer was turned down. [122]

Nor were these isolated instances, as evidenced by Yearly Meeting's lengthy warning in 1680:

> Friends having notice and information of the treacherous & clandestine courses, now & some time past, taken & used by one or more solicitors and attorneys inhabiting in and about London in discharging or pretending to discharge our Friends in Truth from their imprisonments upon writs of *excommunicato capiendo* and such like process by such ways & courses as consist not with their testimony to the Truth, and for large and extravagant fees & sums of money, & taking monies of others not doing any thing for their relief. It is therefore the advice and counsel of this Meeting that all Friends have a due care & regard how they employ & entertain the said persons or any such without the counsel & advice of some knowing Friends to intermeddle or manage such cases for them,

. . . we being certainly informed that although they pretend to
procure Friends discharge in such a course, that their testimonies
for the Truth shall not be wronged, yet we know that their course
of proceeding has been generally a betraying thereof, of which we
have had *many instances* to the grief of the faithful.[123]

Early Friends, of course, could have told their later brethren what they
themselves always knew—lawyers were not to be trusted.

VI

Potentially the Quaker crime with the most serious ramifications was
their marriage within their own meeting. Canon law stressed that marriages were legal only if they took place in the parish church or chapel
before a minister and after banns and granting of a license by the
proper authority.[124] If Quaker marriages were illegal, the children of
such unions were illegitimate, and technically could be challenged
over inheritances. That, in turn, could have destroyed the Quakers by
undermining their ability to bequeath lands and goods to their heirs.

Of paramount importance was the attitude of the secular courts,[125]
for at worst Friends prosecuted in ecclesiastical courts would be excommunicated and possibly imprisoned. One of the earliest recorded
cases involving Quaker marriages was that of Cuthbert Hunter, who
in August 1654 was brought before Judge Hugh Wyndham at Newcastle assizes, accused by information of fornication and adultery.
Hunter admitted that he had not been married either by a justice or
minister, leading Wyndham to judge that he had broken both the law
of God and of man, and must therefore put in sureties for good behavior or be imprisoned. He chose the latter.[126]

Hunter's imprisonment, while unfortunate for him, did not signal
the loss of freedom for all Quaker husbands and wives, and the bastard-
ization of Quaker children. This fact soon became evident.[127] In October 1658 William Ashwell and Anne Ridge had married at a meeting
in Lincoln, but two years later Ashwell became mortally ill. Before
dying, he made a will leaving his personal goods, house, and land to
his wife and, after her death, to their unborn child. Since it was copyhold land, he sent for some copyholders to surrender it accordingly,
but died before they arrived. Legally speaking, therefore, he had died
intestate because the copyhold estate of inheritance was not settled
nor disposed of in his lifetime. His wife gave birth to the child, Mary,

who was presented to the manor court and accepted by the tenants as next heir in law to her father, and thus admitted by the lord of the manor as tenant, with her mother Anne as guardian. Anne Ridge Ashwell then married John Theaker, who shared the estate until John Ashwell, brother of the deceased, brought a writ of ejectment against Anne and Mary, on the premise that Anne's first marriage had not been legal, and that Mary was therefore illegitimate, leaving him, John Ashwell, as the legal heir. Martin Mason, a Friend, alarmed by the implications of this case, wrote to the two judges of assize, John Archer and Edward Atkyns, who were to try the case. If the marriage was not upheld, he warned, it would strike at the root of religion, make the Quakers fornicators and whores, and bastardize their children. "Shall the want of a mere punctilio in the formality of the law deprive so many thousand innocent people of protection by the law when the body or substance of the law is so clearly answered?" The trial took place at the 1661 Nottingham summer assizes. Recognizing, even at this early date, the importance of legal counsel in a case of this dimension, the Quaker defendants were represented by the former judge, Richard Newdigate, and by Charles Dallison of Lincoln's Inn. They introduced three non-Quaker witnesses who testified that William and Anne had been solemnly married in open meeting. They also produced the marriage certificate signed by those present, both Quakers and others, and proved that the child had been conceived within the time of wedlock. Finally, they cited Sir Edward Coke's opinion that in cases where one of the parties to a marriage had died, the marriage might not then be called into question since it would bastardize and disinherit the issues, who were less able to defend the marriage than the parties themselves, if both were alive. Judge Archer, in a major pronouncement for the Quakers, told the jury that "as for the Quakers, he knew not their opinions, but did believe that they did not go together like brute beasts (as had been said), but as Christians." He therefore believed that the marriage of William Ashwell and Anne Ridge had been lawful, and their daughter Mary legal heir to the lands in question. He then provided a precedent for the jury, the case of a man "that was weak of body and kept his bed in that condition," but who desired "to take a woman present to be his wife." They each declared that they took one another as man and wife, "and all the bishops at that time did conclude it to be a lawful marriage." Furthermore, Archer added: "There was a marriage in paradise, Adam took Eve, and Eve took Adam and none other present." It was, therefore, "consent of the parties that made a marriage." Not surprisingly, the jury found for the defendant.

But a single judgment might not constitute a sufficient precedent to protect Friends. Soon there were others. In June 1667 William Smith and Alice Cliffe married in Lincolnshire, but he died in February 1669, leaving her as executrix. Despite this designation, his eldest brother received the administration from the bishop's court on the grounds that the marriage had been unlawful. The Quakers hired William Ellis, a serjeant-at-law, who advised them to bring an action of trover and conversion to recover damages against the brother on the premise that he had converted to his own use goods or chattels in which the plaintiffs had a legitimate claim, but which the defendant had refused to recognize. The case came to trial at the winter assizes of 1670 before Judge Hugh Wyndham, but "the matter proving difficult," and the bishop of Lincoln with some of his court's proctors sitting on the Bench, Ellis moved for a special verdict. It was finally argued before the judges about three years later, but Ellis "proving faulty," Friends turned to John Coates, a long-time associate clerk of the Midland assize circuit, whom Ellis had employed. By that time, however, the marriage was apparently not the central issue, but rather whether the will, although unproved, or the administration, was good. The judges ruled "clearly for her with costs & damages." The victory, by implication, validated her marriage.[128]

Despite these successes, Meeting for Sufferings in December 1679, as a precautionary measure, asked Thomas Corbett whether a man and woman who agreed to take each other to be man and wife as long as they should live, but without using a minister or the form prescribed in the Book of Common Prayer, had contracted a legal marriage. Corbett examined both civil and common law and concluded that it was, indeed, a good marriage. He did admit that the Catholics, and by implication, the Anglican Church, had made marriage a sacrament by differentiating between a marriage and the sacrament of marriage. A marriage was made, "say they," by mutual consent "without the presence of a priest," but the sacrament of marriage, "they say," could not be effected "without the presence and assistance of a minister or priest." It was the church's "making of marriage a sacrament," Corbett concluded sardonically, that "without doubt" was the basis for the "*vulgar opinion that marriage cannot be without a priest.*" But the civil law alone, he insisted, favored mutual consent, and the common law concurred, believing in the maxim that *"consensus facit matrimonium."* Nor did any statute law exist that made such a marriage void. Although the Act of Uniformity enjoined the minister to use the forms of prayer, administration of the sacraments, and the celebration of marriages prescribed in the Book of Common Prayer, it did not say "that marriages solemnized in any other manner shall be void." In fact, the statute 3 Jas. I, c. 5, while imposing some constraints on the rights of convicted popish recusants who married in a manner other than by common prayer and openly in an Anglican church before an Anglican minister, did not void such marriages nor did it bastardize the issue or "disinherit the heir." Corbett thus concluded that he had "not met with or heard of any judgment in our common law ever given against the validity of such a marriage as is mentioned in the case first above stated." In fact, he had heard of "some cases wherein the opinions of the judges, bishops, and doctors of the civil law have been given *in private* for the validity thereof." [129]

Another case that indirectly confirmed that opinion was decided at Carlisle assizes in August 1681. Thomas Langhorne, a Friend, explained to Meeting for Sufferings what had occurred. The dispute was between John Lamplough and Margaret Dickinson, a widowed Friend. Lamplough, as lord of the manor, had refused to allow Dickinson's daughter to be admitted as a tenant, and was trying to obtain a forfeiture of her land on the grounds that Dickinson's marriage had been unlawful. The case was heard before Baron William Gregory. "A forfeiture of the land," remarked Gregory, "what a strange thing was that, . . . that should ever be offered!" After all, he continued, there was an heir who, if admitted tenant, was ready to pay the landlord the normal fine. What, Gregory queried, would Lamplough have? He should admit the child, take the fine, and let the "next of kin" sue the child over the marriage "if he will," but the lord of the manor "hath nothing to do in that case." In effect, reported Langhorne, while the marriage was a peripheral issue, Gregory "seemed rather to be for us as to the matter of the marriage," commenting at one point that he knew the "way and manner" of Quaker marriages, which Friends interpreted as a favorable note. [130] By March 1686 Meeting for Sufferings could state with confidence, when speaking of another successful suit, that Quaker couples simply needed to prove "cohabitation at common law," and that if such cases were lost at common law it was "for want of due management." The Meeting did add, however, that cohabitation alone was an insufficient defense "in the ecclesiastical court."[131]

What about the "ecclesiastical court?" Although Friends were liable to prosecution in the church courts for their marriages, such suits do not appear to have been frequent, nor did they cause serious concern.[132] "As for a precedent of trial in the ecclesiastical court," the Meeting responded to a query from Friends in Nottinghamshire, "we have not any, though oftentimes in several parts of the nation Friends have been summoned before their courts, *yet there never came (as ever we knew of) any determinate sentence in the case*, and Friends when they have been thither summoned have sometimes appeared, and sometimes not, as they had freedom." Moreover, the Meeting continued, it was likely that the church courts would not accept Quaker marriages, "they being performed without either priest or their courts' license by which both court and priest lose their unjust gain." In any event, "their ecclesiastical censures cannot determine whether the children shall inherit or not, that being determinable only by common law which allows our marriages legal."[133]

VII

Another serious issue, closely associated with marriages, was that of wills, also in jeopardy because the decedent, witnesses, executors, and beneficiaries were likely to be excommunicates and/or unable to take an oath. Technically speaking, a will dealt with real estate and a testament with personal property, but in practice the two were generally combined in one legal instrument. During the Commonwealth all testamentary jurisdiction had been transferred to a court of civil commission, but with the Restoration the church courts again assumed control. Much of the population apparently did not leave wills, although the church attempted to encourage the practice, while also stressing that "it was a matter of conscience to carry out as fully as possible the wishes of the deceased."[134] To that end, two Restoration statutes had further clarified procedure.[135] The major concerns for Friends were the potential for the church to interfere with the executorship or administration, or for non-Quaker members of the family to challenge the will. An example of both concerns was the case of Richard Lancaster, a deceased excommunicate, who had nominated two executors for his will, one of whom proved it, while the other, his widow, refused to swear and was renounced. That prompted Joseph and Thomas Lancaster, two of Richard's sons by a previous marriage, to enter a libel in the church court at Chester against the will, claiming that the law did not permit any person "dying excommunicated and having continued so for twelve months before his death . . . to make a testament." This situation was the case, they averred, with Lancaster who, in addition, had not been married in accordance with canon law, "but only after the Quakers' form." They desired the administration. The Quakers, alarmed, approached Thomas Corbett who advised them that the excommunication was irrelevant to making a will, for an excommunicate could legally "give or grant his lands or goods or cattle as another man, and so may another man to him." Corbett mustered an impressive array of authorities to support him, including Edward Coke, William Dyer, William Sheppard,[136] Dr. John Godolphin, and Henry Swinburne. But even if the will was voided, he continued, the wife should receive administration, for the marriage could not be questioned after the death of the spouse, and in any case, common law permitted Quaker marriages. Yet if the church proceeded to void the will and refuse administration, the wife should upon motion to the court of King's Bench receive a *mandamus* to the church court commanding the judge to grant her the administration. "I have known the like *mandamus* granted," Corbett added.[137] Unfortunately, he did not discuss the fact that the wife had refused to take the oath.

The following year saw the case of Mark Wapp, a Durham Friend who had died intestate, leaving a substantial estate in lands and goods. He also left two young daughters. His wife's father, probably a non-Quaker, applied to the court of the bishop of Durham and then to that of the archbishop of York for letters of administration to oversee the estate during the minority of the daughters for their use, but both courts refused to grant it, on the grounds that the daughters had not been baptized. Once again, Friends went to Corbett to find out if the administration could be rejected on that basis. He replied in the negative, because the ecclesiastical courts were specifically directed by the statute 31 Eliz. I, c. 3 and by two Henrician statutes "to grant the administration of the surviving parent to the children without any such qualification as that they must be first baptized." In fact, Corbett stressed, "in all my practice or reading I never yet met with or read of such an exception taken against granting of administration nor was such an exception ever yet pleaded in our law to stay any suit as an excom-

munication or outlawry hath been." But if the court persisted in deny-
ing administration on that basis, then once again he advised that
King's Bench would "grant a *mandamus* to command them to grant it
as aforesaid."[138]

Increasingly, it appeared that Friends need not worry about their
rights in relation to wills, despite various and sundry efforts to deny
those rights. But the most definitive legal statement on the matter
came in 1683. In that year, Robert Cole's will made several bequests,
the largest of which was to his widow, Margaret, who was also named
as one of the executors. In addition, prior to his death he had held a
right to several houses for a term of years: these he settled on trustees,
rather than leave them in his will. But his eldest brother, George Cole,
a non-Quaker, contested the will and the settlement, and the Quakers
asked Joseph Fisher of Gray's Inn to examine the case. In his opinion
the settlement was good, as having been accomplished prior to marriage and "grounded upon good consideration," and in such a way
"that none of the brothers or other kindred of the said Robert can in-
termeddle contrary to the same." As for the will, it was also good, and
bound all his kindred. Therefore, although nothing was given to Cole's
brother George, the latter was "as much excluded from claiming any
thing of the testator's estate . . . as if he had been a stranger." In all
cases, Fisher emphasized, "*the law favours men's last wills & supports them
by the most benign constructions that they may take effect*." As for the legality
of the marriage, Fisher concluded that it was a good marriage at common law; in fact, if an action had been brought against Margaret Cole
during her husband's life, "she might have avoided it by pleading
coverture, which would have been tried by a jury," and for evidence
she could cite "consent & cohabitation . . . in a marriage way as man &
wife." Francis Swaine, another lawyer consulted, put it most succinctly:
he was "clearly of opinion that George Cole . . . hath no right, title,
nor interest in any part of his brother Robert Cole's estate, real or personal."[139] Other attempts to invalidate wills or executors were equally
unsuccessful.[140]

While Quaker wills appeared safe, at least where they were challenged on the basis of excommunications or illegal marriages, Friends
were still liable to the oaths necessary to witness or probate a will or to
take out an administration. Moreover, popish recusants were incapable of acting as executors, administrators, or guardians. Yet it seems
clear that there were "no large-scale prosecutions for refusal to com-

ply with the accepted Anglican procedure."[141] The explanation lies, in part, in the nature of seventeenth-century will procedure. For example, it appears that probate of a will of land was unnecessary, since the signed will itself was sufficient to transfer land after death. That was not the case, however, with copyhold land, which could not be devised by will, although the copyhold tenant could convey his lands to trustees for the uses specified in his will. Furthermore, an executor who failed to probate a will could only be excommunicated; if he or she appeared and refused to act, the court normally committed the administration to the person with the largest beneficial interest in the estate, since it was assumed that the intestate's intent was to prefer the kin, unless he named a residuary legatee. In addition, after debts, funeral expenses, and appropriate costs had been met, the goods of an intestate were to be distributed according to a statutory formula that essentially protected the family of the deceased. Since an executor's rights were the same before and after probate, failure to prove a will "might only impede his actions." Also, considering the fees demanded by the church court for probate, many wills were never proved when estates were small and disputes lacking, thereby avoiding court fees and delays. Nor were letters of administration always applied for, except possibly to avoid any potential family dispute or when some pretense of authority was necessary to collect debts or prove title to property.[142]

There is also evidence that both the Quakers and the church courts used other methods to legitimize potentially questionable wills. Quakers apparently used non-Friends, albeit close kin, as witnesses and executors, thereby permitting the necessary oaths to be taken. After all, kinship ties "were particularly strong over the matter of the disposition of property." In other cases, Friends may have used a substitute to swear; that arrangement was particularly likely when the executor was too old or infirm to appear in person. At such times, the church permitted a deputy to attend the court.[143]

There is reason to believe that the church courts were also conniving with Friends. For example, Gervase Benson, a Westmorland Quaker, and a former mayor of Kendal, justice of the peace, proctor at civil law, and commissary of the archdeaconry of Richmond, was able to use his influence "to obtain that favour for Friends that they had the privilege of proving wills & taking letters of administration without oaths."[144] Another hint is contained in an enigmatic minute of Six Weeks Meeting in March 1677:

Upon the Friends' account of the service done by them relating to the recording and registering of wills, administrations, and trusts, their proceeding therein was approved by this meeting, and it's agreed and ordered that the register extend to all monthly meetings in London, Middlesex, and Southwark, and Friends further declare that it is not their intention or purpose to prohibit any person or Friends their freedom *to record or take out the probate of wills or administrations in such manner as heretofore*, and that Friends appointed heretofore for the said service proceed in that work and meet from time to time about the same as they shall see meet and convenient.[145]

In a related development, Six Weeks Meeting kept a register of legacies and trusts, while Meeting for Sufferings mentioned several instances where money was left to the Meeting, sometimes by non-Quakers, often for the use of suffering Friends.[146] These legacies, however, resembled that of Robert Mayott, an Anglican, to the Presbyterian, Richard Baxter, for the use of sixty ejected ministers. The executors proved Mayott's will, but the attorney general exhibited a bill against them and had them subpoenaed, along with Baxter. Lord Keeper North overturned the will as a contravention of the Statute for Superstitious Uses, and decided that the money should be at the king's disposal. Another foreboding precedent occurred in January 1682, in an Exchequer trial where an estate was settled upon the Jesuits. The attorney general gave his opinion that wills should be scrutinized for gifts to nonconformists.[147] But despite these omens, it does not appear, with one exception,[148] that any Quaker legacies were treated in that fashion, another indication of possible collusion by the church courts. In fact, the Quakers expressed concern in November 1686 about a change in attitude of the Prerogative Court of Canterbury, which issued an order "to bar any from proving a will or be executor or administrator thereof without an oath." Meeting for Sufferings asked Roland Vaughan to bring in a "short instruction how to make wills safely among Friends for the probate & execution thereof & also in letters of administration." Interestingly, Vaughan introduced a clause to be inserted into wills, which apparently permitted non-Quakers to act as executors or administrators. It was objected against by those present "as being not so safe for the testator, the estate being put in the power of a stranger."[149] It seems ironical that the Meeting would be concerned about a stranger as executor, since Friends at the local level often used this approach.

It is likely that oaths were also circumscribed with certification of burial in woollen. For example, the absence of any noteworthy prosecution of Friends in Derbyshire for that offense indicates cooperation from neighbors and clergy.[150] But collusion was more clearly evident in Chancery where oaths were needed to formalize an appearance. Roger Haydock, a Lancashire Friend, wrote to Meeting for Sufferings in August 1683 that Friends in that area had been continually subpoenaed into Chancery by "evil-minded men," who were taking advantage of that court's requirement that answers be made on oath, to make spurious claims to Quaker lands and moneys. But much to those plaintiffs' surprise, the Quaker answers in Chancery, although not sworn, "were recorded as accepted upon oath." Unfortunately, Haydock continued, "a late chancellor made a rule of court that no answer should be taken, but in the presence of the plaintiff's attorney," who was to be given six days' notice "of the place, as well as time where and when the commissioners sit to receive our Friends' answer." Consequently, it was proving more difficult for such answers "to be accepted" without oath. Therefore, the attorney for Friends had devised a strategy of learning whom the plaintiff had named to be in the commission, and then finding out when that commissioner was "either abroad or hath such earnest occasion elsewhere, that although 6 days' notice be given him, he cannot meet the other commissioners, which," Haydock added, "if it take effect as several times it hath done, then the Friend's answer is readily taken without oath, but still by the commissioners recorded as accepted upon oath." Was this, Haydock queried, in accordance with Friends' testimony? The Meeting replied disingenuously that Friends could give their testimony "in justice & truth as in the sight & presence of God, and solemnly . . . aver the truth of their answer in His fear." If any court or magistrate, it continued, was "satisfied therewith," and considered it as "equivalent with an oath," recording it accordingly, "it may be in kindness to prevent & frustrate the designs of unreasonable people against them." That did not, the Meeting insisted, "make the Friend or Friends guilty in the sight of God nor men, nor be a spot or blemish to their Christian profession." This situation was also the case with "probates of wills, executorship, freedom in corporations, entries at customhouse[s] & many other things." As long as a "faithful testimony" was given "at the time & places above, & nothing but the truth spoken, whatever others do write or record cannot be charged as evil upon such." More to the point, the Meeting added that since "in diverse weighty cases Friends' testimonies, depositions, & answers," although not on oath, had been accepted and recorded by "officers in trust . . . under the term '*jurat*,' in design only of doing them a kindness," it would appear, the Meeting emphasized, "disingenuous, very imprudent, and unfair in those Friends . . . to make a discovery of this . . . in court against the officers." Such action, it concluded, could cause an officer "to be called in question & perhaps . . . lose his place, and not only so, but by such open discovery of such a nice scruple, *cause the courts to be more inquisitive, strict, & severe upon Friends to their great detriment & damage in many weighty cases & concerns*." [151]

Even the lord chancellor had assisted a Friend. On the advice of the Meeting for Sufferings, Samuel Boulton, prosecuted in Chancery for refusing to give evidence on oath, applied to Lord Chancellor Jeffreys, who ordered a hearing of the case in his chambers. Understanding that Boulton had been taken advantage of simply because he could not swear, Jeffreys decided the case himself in Boulton's favor without forcing him either to come into court or to swear.[152]

What is most significant about these cases of marriages, wills, and oaths was the apparent protection the law afforded to Quakers and other Dissenters, and the concomitant willingness of some officials to act with moderation. Nor were these isolated examples. Having looked previously at royal and parliamentary ambivalence towards religious dissent, at the "tyranny" of the law, and at Quaker reactive lobbying and legal tactics, we need now to focus closer attention on the reasons for the failure of the late Stuart legal system to eradicate the Quakers, and by implication, religious dissent in general.

Notes

1. See *An Account of the Convincement, Exercises, Services, and Travels of . . . Richard Davies*, 6th ed. (Philadelphia, 1832), 73–77, 105–8, 110–11; Horle, "Changing Quaker Attitudes," 34, 36. For Rudyard, see Braithwaite, *Thomas Rudyard*; R. Dunn and M. Dunn, eds., *Papers of William Penn*, 1:240n, 386n, 387; 2:138–40, 184–95, 197–211, 339–41. Some of Vaughan's opinions are discussed in this chapter.
2. Meeting for Sufferings, 4:222; see also 2:163; 3:16, 126–27.
3. Some Friends in certain locales continued to hold meetings in their homes, but fines appear to have been spread among those who attended; see GBS, 1:10–14; 3:421–23.
4. Probably 15 Ric. II, c. 5, and 31 Eliz. I, c. 7.
5. London Yearly Meeting, 1:157–58. In the Warwick case, although Yearly Meeting recorded that Heritage was indicted, *Warwick Records* indicates

that he, with John Wyatt and John Cockbill, were presented at the 1684 Epiphany Sessions for erecting the Quakers' meetinghouse at Brailes (8:73). The meetinghouse was again presented in the same year by the constable of Brailes at both Trinity and Michaelmas Sessions, but there is no mention of an indictment or of any further action (*Warwick Records*, 8:98, 106).

6. Mortimer, ed., *Men's Meeting in Bristol 1667–1686*, 166.

7. London Yearly Meeting, 1:113–14.

8. Meeting for Sufferings, 3:266; 4:127, 144–45, 149, 166 [italics added]. The meetinghouse was prosecuted under the statute 23 Hen. VIII, c. 10 as a superstitious use.

9. Meeting for Sufferings, 4:228, 249 [italics added].

10. Meeting for Sufferings, 2:163–64.

11. Book of Cases, 1:15.

12. Meeting for Sufferings, 2:181.

13. See, for example, the case of Mary Galloway, tenant in the Lewes meetinghouse (East Sussex Record Office: Sussex QM Sufferings [SOF 1/123–24]); or that of Richard Chare in London (ORS, fol. 422).

14. Book of Cases, 1:184–85.

15. Book of Cases, 1:14–18, 47–51 [italics added throughout].

16. More properly, *Qui aliquid statuerit parte inaudita altera, aequum licet statuerit, haud aequus fuerit*: He who decides anything, one party being unheard, though he decide rightly, does wrong.

17. Meeting for Sufferings, 5:195–96 [italics added].

18. See Book of Cases, 1:115–17 [italics added].

19. Book of Cases, 1:113–14, 117–18. There is no record of Friends actually prosecuting John Hellier or the other abusive Bristol magistrates.

20. Ellwood, *A Caution to Constables*, 1–6, 8, 10, 16; Meeting for Sufferings, 3:220.

21. Book of Cases, 1:150.

22. See Meeting for Sufferings, 2:218, 226; 3:9–10, 14, 150, 184, 192, 298, 332–33; 4:105, 283; 5:11. Quarter sessions were obligated to accept appeals where goods were prematurely sold. Although goods should have been appraised, there were instances where they were not, nor any inventory left behind. In at least one case, goods were distrained, appraised, and left in the house because a neighbor had agreed with the undersheriff to redeem them. See Meeting for Sufferings, 2:218, 3:9–10, 14, 307; 4:1, 15, 34, 115, 192; Besse, *Sufferings*, 1:457, 478–79; ORS, fol. 360.

23. Meeting for Sufferings, 2:204. As a result of this advice, Richard Needham later appealed on the goods valued at double their sale price (Meeting for Sufferings, 3:184).

24. *Second Part of Continued Cry*, 65; HSP: Pemberton MSS, 1:69; Meeting for Sufferings, 3:73; 4:76, 82. In May 1683 Yearly Meeting asked Friends in all counties to collect "precedents of appeals that have been beneficial to Friends, and the verdict thereupon," and to have them "attested by the clerk of the peace." They were then to be brought to Yearly Meeting and recorded in a book for that purpose, in order that Friends would "have recourse to them upon occasion for information, in like cases" (London Yearly Meeting, 1:144–45). That book has not been found; see also ORS, fols. 16, 31, 51, 103, 377–78, 390, 395, 397, 452–53, 474, 508–9, 524, 530, 533–34, 556–58, 573, 582, 589–90, 593, 598, 607–8, 737, 822–33; GBS, 5:378, 383, 390–91, 452–53, 478, 480, 483; Jeaffreson, ed., *Middlesex County Records*, 4:200, 205,

234, 244, 259 (examples of successful Quaker appeals). Nor were the Quakers alone in appealing, for Roger Morrice, a Presbyterian, indicated many such trials as well as those in which informers were accused of perjury. In October 1686 he reported 80 appeals at one session (Morrice Entr'ing Book, 1:639; see also 1:346, 377, 416, 569, 623, 633–35, 638, 651–52, 654, 656; 2:9, 20, 34, 44, 48, 52–53, 69).

25. See, for example, ORS, fols. 103, 336, 340, 377, 509, 524, 530, 534, 557–58, 573, 582, 590, 592; GBS, 5:480; 6:527; Besse, *Sufferings*, 1:186; Meeting for Sufferings, 2:167; 3:9–10, 14, 50, 84–85, 87, 110, 239–40, 252, 256, 302, 321, 350; 4:105, 218, 223. In the case of the marriage supper, the owner of a house where the marriage had earlier been solemnized lost his appeal, the justices concluding it was a conventicle because the groom took the bride "to the glory of God" (GBS, 6:527).

26. Meeting for Sufferings, 3:9–10, 78, 206, 210–11, 329, 352; Besse, *Sufferings*, 1:472; Eddington, *First Fifty Years of Quakerism*, 72–74; see also Ellwood, who believed that the burden of proof lay on the informers (*Caution to Constables*, 8).

27. Meeting for Sufferings, 3:142, 186.

28. Meeting for Sufferings, 2:203–4; Book of Cases, 1:158–59.

29. Meeting for Sufferings, 2:223; 3:360. In 1684 an angry Margaret Fox suffered a heavy distraint on a warrant naming her as Margaret Fell, widow. But her legal counsel, Robert Dormer, advised that an appeal against the warrant for the wrong name and addition "will not be so positive against them, she being still the same person & went once under that name." Apparently, the convicting justice had taken one of the distrained oxen and killed it for himself, which led to his being severely censored by Lord Chief Justice Jeffreys when on circuit; see Sarah Meade to [Bridget Fell], 10.v [July].1684, Gooseyes (Dix MSS, z 3); George Fox to Margaret Fox, 26.viii [October].1684, London (A. Midgeley Cash Collection, unpaginated); see also Spence MSS, 3:1.

30. GBS, 3:424; see also the case of Thomas Life, of London, distrained upon for two meetings he had not attended. He did not appeal, "being a man not able to spend time and money to try them" (ORS, fols. 525, 595).

31. Meeting for Sufferings, 3:14.

32. London Yearly Meeting, 1:60; Book of Cases, 1:36–37, 122–23; see also GBS, 4:24.

33. Meeting for Sufferings, 4:170.

34. Meeting for Sufferings, 2:207; 4:113; see also 2:138–39, 179, 187; 4:1–8; Book of Cases, 1:114–15, 131, 166.

35. ORS, fols. 742–43.

36. Richard Pinder to George Fox and George Whitehead, 14.iii [May]. 1684, North Shields (ARB MSS, fol. 106). The "lees" were the basest part, or dregs, of the soap. No record has been found of young Airey's fate; see also ORS, fol. 755, where a constable involved in breaking up a meeting accused Joseph Rogers, a Quaker, of violently laying hands on him. Rogers denied this, but privately admitted that "there was a woman Friend did lay hold on his arms with both hands pulling him" while he was proclaiming that they should depart but, Rogers added, "there was nothing said of that."

37. Meeting for Sufferings, 2:59–60 [italics added].

38. S. Graveson, ed., *The History of the Life of Thomas Ellwood*, (London, 1906), 239, 241–46; *Minute Book of the Monthly Meeting . . . for Upperside . . .*

1669–1690 (High Wycombe, 1937), 5–8. Ellwood was a Latin tutor and friend of Milton (R. Dunn and M. Dunn, eds., *Papers of William Penn*, 1:132n). Ralph Lacey, the perjured informer, had a colorful career: in 1691 he was fined £5 at Buckingham sessions for "speaking scandalous words against their Majesties," and 3*s.* 4*d.* "for keeping a disorderly alehouse" (Hardy and Reckitt, eds., *Buckingham Sessions Records*, 1:368).

39. Meeting for Sufferings, 1:13–14; 3:252 [italics added]. Informations, naturally, were the preferred method used by informers against Quaker meetings.

40. Meeting for Sufferings, 3:50; GBS, 6:110.

41. The following is found in Book of Cases, 1:134–39 [italics added].

42. Meeting for Sufferings, 3:151; GBS, 3:454; see also Meeting for Sufferings, 3:153–54.

43. The following account is based on Whitehead, *Christian Progress*, 591–609 [italics added]. See also Lacey, *Dissent and Parliamentary Politics*, 74; Meeting for Sufferings, 5:211. An attempt by Robert Barclay and George Whitehead in May 1685 to encourage James II to react against the informers had been unsuccessful; see Whitehead, *Christian Progress*, 575–79.

44. See, for example, Meeting for Sufferings, 5:122, 213, 221–22, 227, 230, 247–48, 254, 257–59, 264–65, 275, 277–78, 287–89, 294, 297–99, 306–7, 309, 319–20, 330; HMC, "Fleming MSS," 201, 251; Book of Cases, 1:168–69; *CSPD, 1686–1687*, 315, 329, 389.

45. London Yearly Meeting, 1:148–49.

46. GBS, 1:429.

47. Meeting for Sufferings, 3:259 [italics added].

48. Meeting for Sufferings, 4:14; see also 4:31, 216–17; Besse, *Sufferings*, 1:536–37.

49. Meeting for Sufferings, 3:199, 201; see also Besse, *Sufferings*, 1:154.

50. Meeting for Sufferings, 3:88–89.

51. Meeting for Sufferings, 3:12, 78; GBS, 3:31; see also GBS, 3:53.

52. See, for example, Meeting for Sufferings, 2:225; 3:266; Whitehead, *Christian Progress*, 560; Besse, *Sufferings*, 1:207.

53. Meeting for Sufferings, 3:125, 206, 227, 251.

54. GBS, 1:50; 3:49.

55. Meeting for Sufferings, 4:82.

56. GBS, vol. 2, Somerset, 94–95, 129–30; see also Besse, *Sufferings*, 1:609.

57. Alfred Braithwaite, "'Errors in the Indictment' and Pardons: the Case of Theophilus Green," *Journal of the Friends Historical Society* 49 (1959–61): 24–26; see also GBS, 4:64–71; Jeaffreson, ed., *Middlesex County Records*, 4:24.

58. Book of Cases, 1:108–10 [italics added]. See also Mortimer, ed., *Men's Meeting in Bristol, 1667–1686*, 199.

59. Book of Cases, 1:119–20 [italics added]. For Edward Dolby's comment, above, see GBS, 1:49.

60. Book of Cases, 1:121–22.

61. Thomas Smith supported this contention in his 1680 opinion on behalf of Norwich Friends (Book of Cases, 1:77).

62. Book of Cases, 1:126–29 [italics added]. For the nature of rents-charge, rents-seck, and warrens, see Henry C. Black, *Black's Law Dictionary*, 5th ed. (St. Paul, 1979), 1166, 1425. The opinion was given in March 1683. As

late as January 1685 Meeting for Sufferings was questioned by a praemunired Friend "about securing his goods for the payment of his debts out of the same" (Meeting for Sufferings, 3:332).

63. Book of Cases, 1:105–6; Meeting for Sufferings, 2:93; R. Dunn and M. Dunn, eds., *Papers of William Penn*, 2:196n.

64. Thomas Salthouse to Alexander Parker and George Whitehead, 15.vii [September].1683, Launceston (ORS, fol. 290); Meeting for Sufferings, 2:219 [italics added].

65. Book of Cases, 1:69.

66. Book of Cases, 1:35. But see *Warwick Records*, 7:5, 56.

67. Meeting for Sufferings, 6:58, 128, 150 [italics added]. Ironically, the Quakers again ran afoul of their old nemesis, Sir Daniel Fleming, for in June 1688 Meeting for Sufferings heard that James Fell in Lancashire had been urged "to swear to execute the office of a constable, that he showed the king's order for Friends to take the office . . . without oaths to one Justice Fleming who slighted it, saying he did not matter it without he had it under the king's broad seal" (Meeting for Sufferings, 6:184).

68. Meeting for Sufferings, 2:14; 5:231, 307; see also 2:19–20; 5:353, 273. The case of "smuggling" mentioned here involved John Herron, of Durham, fined £100 on the statute 1 Eliz. I, c. 11, and distrained upon by process from the Exchequer. A witness had sworn that he was smuggling lead and had refused to swear, but Herron denied the smuggling charge and also claimed that he had been willing to answer without oath, which the statute permitted (GBS, 1:390).

69. Meeting for Sufferings, 1:11, 71; MS Minutes of Six Weeks Meeting, 1:83. For the writ of prohibition, see Marchant, *Church Under Law*, 9–10.

70. Book of Cases, 2:351–53; Meeting for Sufferings, 5:355; 6:131–32 [italics added].

71. PRO: P.C. 2/64/379; *CTB, 1672–1675*, 694–98; Book of Cases, 1:10. The king's remembrancer was primarily responsible for collecting the casual revenue of the Crown, and was to enter and prosecute informations on penal statutes, debt, and seizures. He was also to issue and prosecute commissions to find debts due to the Crown. All of the equity proceedings of the court of Exchequer were filed or entered in his office (*Guide to Public Record Office*, 1:49). In response to the king's letter of 5 February 1675, the Lancashire justices ordered constables and churchwardens to present at quarter sessions "*as well all nonconformists* as all popish recusants" (Quintrell, ed., *Proceedings of the Lancashire Justices*, 133–34 [italics added]).

72. Book of Cases, 1:69–70 [italics added]. The clerk of the pipe had custody of the recusancy rolls detailing prosecutions involving seizure of two-thirds of estates (*Guide to Public Record Office*, 1:79). Informers when prosecuting *qui tam* actions were to receive one-third of the fines and could not be prevented by the king from carrying on such prosecutions. This resembled their right vis-à-vis conventicles.

73. Book of Cases, 1:12; Meeting for Sufferings, 1:168–69; see also Meeting for Sufferings, 1:8.

74. In effect, the equivalent of a plea of "not guilty."

75. Book of Cases, 1:16, 18, 53–57.

76. Book of Cases, 1:139–40.

77. Book of Cases, 1:77–78; see also 1:33.

78. Thomas Rudyard, *The Case of Protestant Dissenters* (London, 1680;

R2178), 5–6; Meeting for Sufferings, 1:45; Algernon Sidney to Benjamin Furley, 13 April 1678 (*Journal of the Friends Historical Society* 11 [1914]:68; see also 69); William Penn, *Reasons why the Oaths Should not be made a part of the Test* (London, 1683; P2178), 7; Book of Cases, 1:71. For the Quaker parliamentary campaign, see Meeting for Sufferings, 1:45–46, 49, 51–52, 56–57, 61, 71, 73, 84, 88, 92, 95, 99, 124; 2:12, 15–22, 24–26, 32, 34–36; Book of Cases, 1:41, 63; Besse, *Sufferings*, 2:144; Whitehead, *Christian Progress*, 493–96.

79. GBS, 3:794–97; Book of Cases, 1:69; see also ORS, fols. 442–43; *CTB, 1676–1679*, 1256–57; Meeting for Sufferings, 1:83; GBS, 1:502; Pemberton MSS, 1:97. Perhaps as a concomitant to these events, the Lancashire justices on 25 August 1679 ordered enforcement against Dissenters for *weekly* absence (at 12*d.* per week) as opposed to *monthly* absence (at £20 per month) (Quintrell, ed., *Proceedings of the Lancashire Justices*, 139–40).

80. PRO: P.C. 2/67/67; P.C. 2/68, 20; see also Meeting for Sufferings, 1:127, 172; 2:2; ORS, fol. 463.

81. See PRO: P.C. 2/67/131; P.C. 2/68, 20; P.C. 2/69, 215; Book of Cases, 1:87–88, 95–98; Meeting for Sufferings, 2:44.

82. ORS, fol. 460; Meeting for Sufferings, 2:35, 38–39, 51, 58–60; Book of Cases, 1:93–95; see also Meeting for Sufferings, 2:61, 72–73, 75.

83. "Fleming MSS," 183; PRO: P.C. 2/69, 382; Book of Cases, 1:101.

84. Meeting for Sufferings, 2:85 [italics added].

85. Fleming to Jenkins, 18 January 1681/2 ("Fleming MSS," 184). Late in December 1681, when told by Westmorland Quakers that Charles Howard, fourth earl of Carlisle, had signed a certificate for Friends, Fleming, along with Christopher Phillipson, agreed to sign the same certificate if it was brought to them, but "would not make another over his head" (ARB MSS, fol. 149).

86. See Meeting for Sufferings, 2:84–85, 94–95, 109, 117, 119, 123, 125, 127, 140, 159–61, 165; 3:1, 14; 4:21; ORS, fols. 421, 478, 484–89; Book of Cases, 1:139–40, 163–64; Miller, *Popery and Politics*, 204.

87. Morrice Entr'ing Book, 1:330, 355–56, 368; Luttrell, *Brief Relation*, 1:248; see also Turner MSS, 15:208a, where the justices at Bristol Quarter Sessions overruled similar "popish recusant" arguments. But not all justices of the peace reacted unfavorably towards this argument; see, for example, the charge given by Henry Booth at Knutsford (*CSPD, 1682*, 456–58), and the action of the North Riding justices in July 1684 (Atkinson, ed., *North Riding Quarter Sessions*, 7:69–70).

88. This statement is not entirely correct, for indictments were also based on presentments by hundred juries, constables, and churchwardens.

89. Book of Cases, 1:78–80.

90. London Yearly Meeting, 1:110–11, 157.

91. See Meeting for Sufferings, 4:123, 139, 143, 153–54, 167, 171, 200; Besse, *Sufferings*, 1:548–51.

92. London Yearly Meeting, 1:104; see also Meeting for Sufferings, 3:295; 4:202; ORS, fol. 398; Besse, *Sufferings*, 1:574.

93. See Meeting for Sufferings, 1:157, 166, 168–69; 2:54, 57, 121, 149, 153–55, 157, 161, 164, 183, 190, 206, 211, 213, 215–16, 219; 3:33, 41, 50, 57, 62, 71, 192, 222, 310; 4:153, 215.

94. Meeting for Sufferings, 4:212, 221.

95. Meeting for Sufferings, 3:308; 4:212, 221; London Yearly Meeting, 1:114–15; see also Meeting for Sufferings, 1:157; 2:57–58; 3:71, 89, 91, 135, 146, 180, 309; 4:96, 141. Delay was more difficult in cases of proclama-

tion after presentment, for suspects were obliged to surrender to the sheriff before appearance at the next assizes or sessions; see John Kelyng, *A Report of Divers Cases in Pleas of the Crown . . . in the Reign of . . . King Charles II* (London, 1708), 35.

96. Meeting for Sufferings, 3:35–36; see also 3:30, 51, 251; 4:141; and Besse, *Sufferings*, 1:505

97. See Craig W. Horle, "Death as a Felon: Richard Vickris and the Elizabethan Conventicle Act," *Quaker History* 76, no. 2 (Fall 1987):95–107.

98. London Yearly Meeting, 1:77.

99. Besse, *Sufferings*, 2:18–19; GBS, 3:430–31. Fortunately for the appellants, the minister died during the proceedings and the case fell; see also Besse, *Sufferings*, 2:22.

100. GBS, vol. 2, Oxfordshire, 8.

101. Book of Cases, 1:18–20; Pemberton MSS, 1:20.

102. See, for example, GBS, 3:790; Besse, *Sufferings*, 2:18; Meeting for Sufferings, 5:313, the latter in a wapentake court of Thomas Preston, deputy-lieutenant and justice of the peace in Cartmel, Lancashire, and farmer of the tithes under the bishop of Chester. On occasion, Friends had successfully demurred to local court jurisdiction against Preston, who retaliated by putting the Conventicle Act into execution (GBS, 3:790–91, 793).

103. Meeting for Sufferings, 1:111.

104. Meeting for Sufferings, 1:73; 5:339; 6:104, 149, 152; see also 1:84, 111, 129; 2:62, 70, 86, 114; 4:209; 5:370, 6:138, 142 [italics added]. For the instructions from Roland Vaughan, see text preceding n. 120.

105. R. Tregennow to J. Brain, 6.v [July].1682, Bodmin prison (ORS, fol. 412).

106. Meeting for Sufferings, 1:107–8.

107. See, for example, GBS, 1:60–61, 77, 199–200; vol. 2, Sussex, 10; 3:594–95, 780–81, 823, 840, 996; 4:206, 322–23; 5:1, 3–4, 500; 6:45, 198; ORS, fols. 8, 436; Meeting for Sufferings, 2:194; Harvey MSS, fol. 15; Penney, ed., *Sufferings of Quakers in Cornwall*, 38–39, 105; Besse, *Sufferings*, 1:7, 82–83, 160, 202, 240, 263, 322, 326, 712, 719. Robert West, when called upon for legal advice on avoiding actions on this statute, told Friends they would be well advised to set out the tithes (Book of Cases, 1:78).

108. London Yearly Meeting, 1:90, 111.

109. Book of Cases, 1:172; Meeting for Sufferings, 5:362; 6:17; see also 6:5. Richard Burn, when speaking of church rates, emphatically stated that "if any refuse to pay the rates, being demanded by the churchwardens, they are to be sued for in the ecclesiastical courts *and not elsewhere*" (*Justices of the Peace*, 1:331 [italics added]).

110. Marchant estimates that another ten percent did not take their religious obligations seriously (*Church Under Law*, 227).

111. Helen Forde, "Derbyshire Quakers 1650–1761" (Ph.D. thesis, University of Leicester, 1978), 63.

112. See, for example, GBS, 1:136, 141, 353, 373, 577; vol. 2, Westmorland, 17; vol. 2, Yorkshire, 44; 3:824–25, 878; 4:256, 627, 665–66, 668–69, 671–75; 6:401; Meeting for Sufferings, 1:129; 2:70; 6:73, 77, 81, 127–28, 138, 158, 186; Besse, *Sufferings*, 1:104, 326; 2:28, 138, 140, 167, 169. Barry Reay believes that the number of Quaker imprisonments for excommunication has been underestimated ("Authorities and Quakerism," 78). For example, he sees eighty such cases from 1662 to 1664 alone; see also Appendix 1. Nor was imprisonment the only liability from excommunication; in theory,

excommunicates were unable to plead at law in cases between parties, except those involving their own real property, were unable to act as executors, and could face discrimination by landlords and employees. A minister could warn the people of the parish not to have any dealings with them, nor let them have any kind of provision, either for money or credit, on pain of excommunication themselves.

113. See, for example, Meeting for Sufferings, 1:127; 2:1, 3, 35–36, 68–69, 74, 118, 150, 183–84, 186; 4:183.

114. Book of Cases, 1:16–17, 50–51, 117 [italics added].

115. Meeting for Sufferings, 2:25.

116. Book of Cases, 1:8. The Meeting advised the Friend, John Furley, to move for a *habeas corpus* to remove him to King's Bench for his release. A cursitor was a Chancery clerk.

117. Book of Cases, 1:33. The Meeting believed that "in case the court will proceed to sentence a person contumacious, they ought to signify it and proceed by writ of *excommunicato capiendo* as has been the judges' opinion." Thus Friends were to procure a writ of *habeas corpus* to come before the judges at Westminster "who must discharge them, and the cost will be *at least £30 every man*" [italics added].

118. Meeting for Sufferings, 3:202. The Meeting advised him to write to the gaoler for a true copy of the writ, and to return to prison if he received it. If the gaoler did not have a copy nor any warrant to remand or detain him, however, then he was free and was "not bound to return to gaol."

119. London Yearly Meeting, 1:112–13.

120. Book of Cases, 1:175–76.

121. See Chapter 4, The Lamb's War, nn. 13–14.

122. Meeting for Sufferings, 1:76–77, 81–82; 2:102; Book of Cases, 1:44–46; see also Meeting for Sufferings, 1:78.

123. London Yearly Meeting, 1:78 [italics added]; see also Meeting for Sufferings, 2:117–18, 123.

124. Richard Grey, *A System of English Ecclesiastical Law*, 4th ed. (London, 1743), 142–43. "Matrimony is not accounted consummate by our law, until it be celebrated and solemnized in *facie ecclesia*" (Sheppard, *Epitome of the Laws*, 720 [italics added]).

125. Normally involved where disputes arose over legacies dependent on the propriety of a marriage.

126. Swarthmore MSS, 4:127.

127. The following account is based upon Book of Cases, 1:28–29, 93; George Whitehead to Norwich Friends, 1688 (Eddington, *First Fifty Years of Quakerism*, 257); Martin Mason MSS, 16–20; Fox, *Journal*, ed. Nickalls, 421–22; Lincolnshire QM Digests of Births, Marriages, and Deaths. The opinion by Coke can be found in his discussion of *Articuli Cleri*, in his *Second Institutes*, 6th ed. (London, 1681), 614.

128. Book of Cases, 1:112; Whitehead to Norwich Friends (Eddington, *First Fifty Years of Quakerism*, 257); see also Meeting for Sufferings, 1:50.

129. Book of Cases, 1:64–65 [italics added].

130. T. Langhorne et al. to George Whitehead, 4.vi [August].1681, Carlisle (Book of Cases, 1:91–92); see also Whitehead to Norwich Friends (Eddington, *First Fifty Years of Quakerism*, 258); Book of Cases, counsel's opinions on marriage, unpaginated; Meeting for Sufferings, 4:48–49, 51, 282; 5:31; 6:156.

131. Meeting for Sufferings, 5:9. This was confirmed by former Chief

Justice Pemberton in a 1695 opinion to Friends; see Craig W. Horle, "Judicial Encounters with Quakers 1660–1689," *Journal of the Friends Historical Society* 54 (1976–80):99–100.

132. See, for example, GBS, 1:89, 164, 513; 3:104, 493; Meeting for Sufferings, 1:62, 77, 79, 81; 4:15; Mortimer, ed., *Men's Meeting in Bristol, 1667–1686,* xxv, 134; ORS, fol. 513; Besse, *Sufferings,* 1:318–19; see also GBS, 4:259, where William Scarce of Wortham, Suffolk, was imprisoned in August 1675 on a writ *de excommunicato capiendo,* having been presented in the bishop's court as not legally married, "notwithstanding it hath been made appear since to the chancellor of the same court under the hands of the priest who married him, and other witnesses (and that before he was called a Quaker) that he was married according to the manner of the Church of England."

133. Book of Cases, 1:30 [italics added].

134. Anthony J. Camp, *Wills and their Whereabouts* (London, 1974), ix, xxvi; Sheppard, *Epitome of the Laws,* 931. Helen Forde found only twelve Quaker wills in Derbyshire prior to 1696 ("Friends and Authority: A Consideration of Attitudes and Expedients with Particular Reference to Derbyshire," *Journal of the Friends Historical Society* 54 [1976–80]:117).

135. 22 & 23 Chas. II, c. 10; 29 Chas. II, c. 3.

136. Sheppard, however, believed that while an excommunicate could devise his lands by will in common law, he could not in civil law (*Epitome of the Laws,* 934).

137. Book of Cases, 1:26–27.

138. Book of Cases, 1:40; see also 1:101; Meeting for Sufferings, 1:78–79; 2:76, 78.

139. Book of Cases, 1:149 [italics added].

140. See, for example, GBS, 4:332–34; Meeting for Sufferings, 2:222; 4:205.

141. Forde, "Friends and Authority," 117.

142. Camp, *Wills,* xi, xvii, xx, xxxvii; Grey, *Ecclesiastical Law,* 163–64.

143. Forde, "Friends and Authority," 117, 119. In fact, a curate or vicar was actually used in several Derbyshire Quaker wills.

144. Penney, ed., *First Publishers of Truth,* 251. My thanks to Nicholas Morgan for this reference.

145. MS Minutes of Six Weeks Meeting, 1:52 [italics added].

146. See MS Minutes of Six Weeks Meeting, 1:50, 85, 99, 107; Meeting for Sufferings, 2:218, 220; 3:125, 167; 4:189–90, 211, 214, 225; 5:15.

147. Morrice Entr'ing Book, 1:324, 435; Anthony Wood, *Life and Times,* 5 vols. (Oxford, 1891–1900), 3:36; PRO: S.P. 44/71/317.

148. In 1671 the legacy of £200 left by George Watkinson of Scotton, Yorkshire, to the use of Scotton Friends, was confiscated by the Crown and given to Lord Frescheville, "as of our free gift without account" (Penney, ed., *Extracts from State Papers,* 330–32).

149. Meeting for Sufferings, 5:283, 295; see also 5:292. The Meeting, examining all possibilities, also asked Vaughan to look into "settling estates without a will" (5:321). Similarly, the Meeting shortly thereafter minuted a letter from Berkshire, "desiring that a form of a will may be drawn up of settling estates personal . . . and to make settlements instead of wills to prevent the coming into court" (5:327; see also 5:302, 314, 329, 336, 340, 345). Vaughan may have been encountering difficulties, for the Meeting in February 1687 was still asking him about the matter (5:349).

150. Forde, "Friends and Authority," 124.

151. R. Haydock to Meeting for Sufferings, 11.vi [August].1683 (GBS, 3:830); Portfolio 16/32 [italics added]. My gratitude is extended to Nicholas Morgan for these references; see also his "Lancashire Quakers and the Oath, 1660–1722," *Journal of the Friends Historical Society* 54 (1976–80):235–54.

152. Meeting for Sufferings, 5:332. This episode reveals Boulton's dedication to Quaker principles to be slightly suspect, as also the ethical posture of his adversary's attorney, who was now forced either to return the £20 he had received from Boulton "for respiting the proceedings for some short time or to lay him by the heels" (5:332).

Chapter Six

THE LEGAL SYSTEM RECONSIDERED

He answered he was sorry that it lay not in his power to release me. He hath carried pretty fair towards Friends in these parts hitherto, and as far as I perceive by him hath no desire at all to meddle with us if he can any way avoid it.

Richard Smith to George Fox, 7.3 [May].1665, Chester Castle gaol, speaking of Sir Job Charleton, Chief Justice of Chester: Swarthmore MSS, 1:99

In 1972 and 1976, respectively, London Yearly Meeting and Meeting for Sufferings celebrated their three-hundredth anniversary, a testimonial to Quaker adaptability, their religious message, and the English reliance on the rule of law. As we have seen, Quaker resistance to "persecution" had incorporated a broad range of tactics whose cumulative effect may have been to frustrate and embarrass law-enforcement officers, while also protecting Friends from serious and prolonged prosecution. Quaker records indicate that such enforcement, for whatever reason, was sporadic, varying from place to place and according to circumstances. Legal officials often acted with moderation, as did the Crown. The Catholic sympathies of Charles II and the conversion to that faith of his brother James II were significant factors. While both kings at times enthusiastically supported the laws against dissent, they lacked any consistent approach. Their apparent willingness to assist prosecuted Quakers, including their leader, George Fox,[1] was often resented by those justices anxious to execute the law, and signified the Crown's lack of will to suppress religious dissent thoroughly. This hesitancy was further exemplified by the religious characteristics of the "Cabal," which acted as a proto-cabinet under Charles II prior to the 1672 Declaration of Indulgence, and by the meaningful role played by William Penn at the court of James II. While granting Penn a colony could have been construed by contemporaries as a way to siphon off those prominent English Quakers who were leading the legal resistance, it could also have been viewed as an unwarranted gift to the heretical son of a disreputable creditor of the Crown.[2] The Quakers did appear to have remarkably easy access to the court throughout the period, although Charles II demonstated the constraints of his position in January 1670 when confronted by Richard Carver, a Quaker seeking assistance for his coreligionists. Carver handed him a paper listing praemunired Quakers, prompting Charles to remark that there were "many of them," that they would only be imprisoned again "*in a month's time*," and that the country gentry were complaining to him that they were "so troubled with the Quakers." Nonetheless, he agreed to release some of those on the list.[3]

The Quakers also tried to influence members of Parliament. Unlike the Crown, however, M.P.s appeared determined to limit the religious and political rights of Dissenters, and thereby displayed a firmer loyalty to the Established Church than the two men who were its titular head. Even comprehension of the Presbyterians was anathema to many of them, let alone toleration for the Quakers. But as we have seen, Parliament wavered in its resolve as its membership changed, and from 1679 to 1681 it supported efforts to end the prosecution of Protestant Dissenters as popish recusants. At that time the Quakers had their greatest success, despite what Algernon Sidney had viewed as lingering bitterness by some members towards them. Yet Friends had also received support from Sir Christopher Musgrave, son of their formidable antagonist Sir Philip Musgrave. When the bill for ease to Protestant Dissenters was committed after its second reading, Musgrave, a member of Parliament for forty-three years, came before the committee, some of whose members opposed any concessions to the Quakers. Sir Christopher, however, warned that the prisons were filled with Quakers, often for small matters, which he viewed as a shame and scandal for the church. The resulting bill was favorable towards Friends, but it fell when Charles dissolved Parliament to prevent an exclusion bill.[4]

Despite the general hostility of Parliament towards Friends, some members, in their capacity as justices of the peace, were potentially more accessible; more vulnerable to effective lobbying; and therefore more likely to act with moderation. Some justices, in fact, despite opposition from their colleagues, acted reasonably towards Friends—securing their release, preventing their imprisonment, or providing sufficient opposition to delay proceedings. Joseph Hull, a Suffolk justice, found this out the hard way in 1684, when he encountered protracted resistance from his colleagues at quarter sessions to his efforts to praemunire numerous Quakers for refusing the Oath of Allegiance. Although the first refusal had occurred as early as the April sessions, the Friends were remanded each succeeding sessions, despite Hull's obvious frustration at the delay, before they were finally praemunired in October.[5] In an incident replete with modern overtones, Theophila Townsend and another Quaker appeared in March 1682 before the assembled justices at a petty sessions in Cirencester. One of the justices was James George. Having acted harshly towards the two Friends, George was caught off guard when Townsend gave him a copy of the paper he had distributed to Quakers when he campaigned for Parliament, and in which he "pretended his great kindness to honest people," and his intention "so to continue as long as he lived." Mistaking the paper for a petition, George was about to read it aloud, when Townsend warned him to look at it first to see "whose name was at it" before beginning. "I would have no man," she chided, "let fall a good resolution." George, embarrassed, called the Quakers "a pack of rogues," who had voted against him. "I will be even with them," he exclaimed, "and be revenged on them before I have done." After fending off a question from his colleague, Lord Herbert, as to what was in the paper, George attempted to persuade Herbert and Philip Shepard, another justice, to tender the Oath of Allegiance to the two Quakers. They refused to permit it, however, and simply bound them over to answer at quarter sessions.[6]

John Gratton, although a prisoner at Derby, wrote to Yearly Meeting that the justices there "for some years" had been "very kind and moderate to us," and therefore he did not think it "meet" to make his imprisonment public knowledge, while at Bolton, Lancashire, in 1679 a new constable named Townley, having often threatened the Quakers, attempted to break up their meeting and have them imprisoned, but Justice Lever "bade him hold his tongue, he would not meddle in it himself." Nor did matters improve for Townley, for after a particularly unpleasant distraint upon Phineas Pemberton, he was reprimanded by the justices, one of whom, having heard that a cow had been returned to the Quaker, snickered that "the cow had more wit then Townley." James Harrison, in fact, was happy to report that "our enemies are very still & quiet at present, & seems to be much down, Townley being repulsed at the quarter sessions for his carriage against Phineas & I perceive in most companies much blamed." Thus Townley had found the work "heavier then he thought it was when others was in the office, or than he thought when he took the office upon him."[7]

Nor were justices always willing to be pestered by informers, as Hester Collingwood discovered in London. Three Quakers had been taken from Devonshire House meeting on a blank warrant to break up meetings. She took one of them to Sir William Pritchard, a justice, who refused to get involved, forcing her to seek out the more compliant Sir Thomas Jenner. Sir Geoffrey Shakerley, at a meeting of justices in Chester, reacted against an informer who was presenting meetings twice a week. Informers were not, he ordered, to present "for every meeting; once a quarter might serve."[8] Also, justices often accepted Friends' promise or "engagement" to appear, without the requirement of bail or sureties.[9]

Yet justices of the peace were often substantially influenced by assize judges, a point strongly emphasized by the Quakers. According to Thomas Rudyard, enforcement of the laws against dissent, whether on statutes or otherwise, was "generally prosecuted as the judges give in charge, countenance, or discourage." The grand juries, he stressed, observed the judges; the justices of the peace took their direction from them; and the counties where they traveled were influenced by their "moderation" or "stirred up" by their "contrary countenance."[10] At times that stirring up was evident, as at Taunton in April 1684 when Chief Justice George Jeffreys, sitting on the Crown side, was "very severe," calling for the laws against Dissenters to be put in execution, and "telling the justices that if they would not do it, he would put in them that should," since which time, Friends complained, "some of the justices seem very severe." At Norwich in April 1664 Friends reported that since the assizes meetings had been "broken up in some places of these parts, for the *judge was very high and severe against the phanaticks so called in his charge and proceedings.*"[11] At the quarter sessions in Hertford in October 1664, after Orlando Bridgeman had dealt sharply with Quakers at the summer assizes, the presiding justice, Henry Chauncey, interrupted a Quaker defendant who claimed that the court had proved only that more than five Quakers had met together. "The wise, judicious, and worthy Judge Bridgeman," Chauncey told the jury, "was of this opinion: That if any person shall meet with others, above five in number, at such houses which are their common houses of meeting, and can give no good account what they did there, that is a presumption in law, and not only a presumption,"

Chauncey continued, "but a violent presumption." The defendants, he concluded, "say they meet in the fear of the Lord to worship him in spirit; this they confess." [12]

Yet judges and justices were often at odds. Although Friends in York complained that Judge Holloway at the assizes in August 1684 "made the justices severe against Friends," leading to several fines at the following quarter sessions, the justices overall were "moderate, discharging the officers from prosecuting any & that they had nothing to say to them." Twelve Quaker prisoners remained who had been convicted three times on the Quaker Act, and were at the king's mercy, but by September it was learned that they "had liberty home." [13] In April 1664 Friends imprisoned for refusing the Oath of Allegiance were not called at Yarmouth gaol delivery. When asked the reason, the clerk explained that the court was doing them a favor, for had they been called, they would have been indicted, retendered the oath and praemunired. He added that if they would put in sureties for good behavior, they could go about their business. One of the prisoners, a prominent ministering Friend named William Caton, then wrote to the judge and bailiffs and gave the letter to one of the justices, who willingly took it to the judge "& did plead our cause pretty much and the judge was a moderate wise man, and willing that we should have our liberty and though he was in much haste to be gone out of the town, yet he prescribed them a way how they might clear us." He suggested that Friends take any one man from the quay, "though but a porter," and he could stand bond "for a hundred of us." When next returning, he "would take it off the file, so that we should not be called." Nor were the prisoners, he added, expected to appear further and, "he knowing our tenderness of conscience, ordered that the clerk should take nothing of us; neither would he have had us further troubled or longer detained." Nonetheless, as soon as the judge was gone, "some of our grand adversaries consulted together & resolved to perpetuate our bonds, except we would yield and give our consent unto the recognizance . . . and because we cannot satisfy them, therefore are our bonds continued." [14] Similarly, at the Lent assizes 1684 in Northampton, Judge Thomas Street received a petition from imprisoned Quakers "very moderately," and noted that London Friends "had been with him and that he would do what he could." He left an order that Sir Roger Norris was to take bail for the women and for those men not imprisoned for refusing the oath, to appear the following sessions. But after Street was gone the justices demanded that the Friends post bond for good behavior, which they refused to do.[15]

Even after the coronation pardon of March 1686, when the judges of assize generally acted with moderation and restraint, going beyond the extent of the pardon in several cases,[16] justices at sessions and officers in corporate towns did not always follow suit. That was particularly the situation in Bristol, but also in Cambridgeshire, Sussex, Cumberland, the West Riding of Yorkshire, and Southampton.[17] Indicative of the frustration the judiciary often experienced with justices of the peace was a 1660 episode, mentioned by Friends some years later. It seems that Judge Hugh Wyndham at the Thetford Lent assizes publicly reproved "some of the justices upon the bench, because they committed men to prison and had bound over none to prosecute them, nor had any evidence against them in the court, when the prisoners were at the bar."[18]

The above cases indicate that assize judges were not always hostile towards the Quakers. In fact, the Quakers had particularly kind words for Sir Matthew Hale, who at the trial of John Crook in March 1661 expressed sadness at being unable to accept Crook's subscription of the Oath of Allegiance without the word "swear," and who had advised him to seek the assistance of the king and Council. Likewise, in 1664, shortly after passage of the first Conventicle Act, Friends reported that at Bath assizes Hale "appeared a moderate man . . . not willing to afflict the innocent," while it was reported from Exeter that "the Quakers were through his means found not guilty because no sedition appeared under the exercise of religion," Hale insisting that the act was "not made against religious meetings, but seditious conventicles." Even Judge Bridgeman, whose severe behavior towards Friends at Hertford has been chronicled, showed restraint on that same circuit at Kingston upon Thames where four Quakers were charged with refusing the Oath of Allegiance. As at Hertford, Bridgeman contended that he desired their reformation, not their punishment; but when they refused the oath, he asked if they would subscribe to its substance, for he was willing to "omit the form that made it an oath." Having told them to consider it, they proceeded to draw up and sign a paper, which one of the prisoners, Samuel Fisher, gave to Bridgeman, who agreed to show it to the king. He told Fisher "to come to him after his return from going circuit," but warned him that a newly worded indictment had been brought against the prisoners, although he did not think it dangerous. The Friends were returned to prison, but were likely to have "pretty much liberty as prisoners, so that although we may not so well go to meetings as otherwise, yet we may visit friends *as we have done*."[19]

On several occasions Quakers claimed that judges had accepted their word, rather than force them to swear.[20] There are also many examples of judicial moderation in regard to the recusancy statutes. When, for instance, numerous Friends were indicted for the penalty of £20 per month at Surrey assizes, Judges Francis Pemberton and Edward Atkyns simply thanked the officers for their care and did nothing further.[21] In some cases judges appeared willing to prosecute Friends on the Quaker Act, asking them to incriminate themselves by admitting they would not swear in any case. Friends would cooperate in this to avoid having to take the Oath of Allegiance, the refusal of which carried much harsher penalties. In addition, judges often refused to intervene where Quakers awaited trial for rejecting the Oath of Allegiance; such inaction was beneficial to Friends, as it delayed a praemunire. This influenced Judge Turner at York assizes in 1662. When asked by Quaker prisoners (who had refused the oath at sessions) why he was insisting on sureties for good behavior, he "started up and said he did it to favour them."[22]

Judges on circuit might, of course, be swayed by local justices. Sir Henry Every, foreman of the grand jury at Derby Lent assizes in 1683, and also a justice of the peace, persuaded his fellow jurors to refuse to find the bills against numerous Quakers indicted for recusancy, much to the annoyance of Judge William Gregory. He took Every aside, but the justice successfully argued that it was not the king's pleasure to ruin his subjects. As a result, Quakers were indicted only for 1*s.* per Sunday, while none was called or served with any assize processes. Moreover, Every and Sir Simon Degge, another justice, having received a letter from John Gratton, an imprisoned Derby Friend, importuned Gregory to speak with the king to release Gratton. Gregory, no doubt feeling slightly bewildered, agreed not only to speak with Charles II, but to send down the release, if it could be procured. Ironically, Gregory's "moderation" earned him the sobriquet of "Whig" from his enemies. At the following sessions, on the initiative of the two justices, neither the many Quakers presented by constables, nor those indicted at assizes for three weeks' absence from church, were called.[23]

On the other hand, justices could attempt to influence judges to act with severity. George Whitehead, writing many years after the fact, complained that in the early years of the Restoration, "it was no strange thing" for what he called "ill natur'd persecuting justices" to act as both "accusers and judges upon the bench against our Friends and also (like invidious informers) to endeavour to incense the judges against us by unjust insinuations and undue accusations with intent to stir up prejudice and hard usage against us."[24] In March 1664 Francis Howgill, a leading Quaker, was brought to trial at Appleby in Westmorland for having refused the Oath of Allegiance,[25] a case which typified the atmosphere assize judges often encountered in hostile localities, where they were forced to mix diplomacy with law, often against their personal feelings. Judges Christopher Turner and Thomas Twisden presided at the trial, with Twisden giving the charge to the grand jury. Denouncing those people "who under pretence of conscience and religion," and under "colour" of the Declaration of Breda "hatched rebellions, treasons, and the like," he ordered the grand jury to "make enquiry of them for the preservation of the peace of the nation." But Twisden and Turner both acted moderately towards Howgill, only to have that inveterate anti-Quaker justice, Daniel Fleming, depict the prisoner as an influential preacher whose loss would be a great blow to the Quakers. Twisden replied that Howgill could be what he wished if he would but enter a bond. That led Sir Philip Musgrave and Sir John Lowther to complain that Quaker meetings were dangerous and the Quakers insolent. Howgill now joined the debate, defending both the principles and peacefulness of the Quakers, and then asking for liberty without posting bond until the next assizes. He next disputed a contention by Musgrave that the Quakers had been active in the Northern Plot. The trial lasted at least an hour. Ultimately Howgill refused to post bond and was remanded. "By accident," Howgill commented, he saw an account of the assizes

> drawn up by Philip Musgrave, which was sent by the post to the king, and so I believe will come in the newsbook to do us harm. The thing was this: Declaring about the plot, 2 young men, he saith, came from Leeds that were Quakers and gave intelligence to Captain Atkinson. The evidence in court was this: That two young men that were strangers came to Captain Atkinson. They asked what they were, and the evidence said he knew not, they wear 'sober' men, and Philip hath put it in 'Quakers.'[26]

Another judge caught in a similar predicament was Chief Justice Francis North, presiding at Wells assizes in 1675. When John Anderdon, having been accused of speaking against the king, refused to take the Oath of Allegiance, "many did account the proceedings very hard." But with Bishop Peter Mew, of Bath and Wells, along with several other church officials present "desiring the restraint of the said John Anderdon," whom they characterized as a "ringleader of the Quakers," Judge North "to do them a kindness, as it's believed, put him off to the next assizes and left him in bonds."[27]

Yet efforts by justices and churchmen to influence assize judges were not always successful. "The judge was very moderate," wrote Bridget Fell to her sister from Lancaster assizes in March 1661, "though he was incensed by some of the justices against Friends." Fortunately, she added, he "would not take notice of it except they could prove what they had said." In March 1662, William Watcher, imprisoned for failing to find sureties after writing a paper attacking Presbyterian occasional conformists, was brought to Maidstone assizes. One of the justices warned the judge that Watcher was a Quaker who needed to be dealt with, but the judge discharged him by proclamation.[28]

Nor were churchmen uniformly opposed to the Quakers. As seen previously, there is evidence of collusion between Anglican churchmen and the Quakers in relation to wills. Bishops may also have been culpable. William Penn was a close friend of Francis Turner, the bishop of Ely,[29] while Gilbert Latey was on good terms with Thomas Lamplugh, bishop of Exeter, who had done Latey "several favours in respect to friends under sufferings in his diocese." Latey, in fact, mentioned having visited him in 1679 "according to his wonted custom." Far more revealing was a letter from the bishop to Latey in March 1684:

I had acknowledged the receipt of your civil letter before now, but that I stayed till our assizes were over, that I might see what proceedings were made against any of your persuasion: and I can hear of none. I find no process of late against any of them in any of my courts, for I have examined my officers about it. What the justices of peace have done in their monthly meetings I know not; but sure I am, that such as live quiet and peaceable in the land, by any order from me, are no way disturbed; and I believe the justices are gentle enough to such as do not affront them. I never was, nor will be for persecution, but shall endeavour that by any amicable way, such as have erred may be brought into the way of Truth, and that we may all enjoy one another in heaven. I am now somewhat indisposed; writing is irksome to me. God Almighty bless you.[30]

Nathaniel Crew, bishop of Durham, complained that the Quaker meeting there was so close to his house that he was "disturbed" as he walked "in his room." Yet Meeting for Sufferings learned in January 1682 that several Friends had been discharged at the past sessions in Durham, apparently "by the moderation of the bishop," while at quarter sessions in July, he "seemed rather to discourage the informers than otherwise." In Wales, the Meeting heard in November 1685 that none of the many writs *de excommunicato capiendo* had been executed by favor of John Lloyd, the bishop of Bangor.[31] Even Henry Compton, bishop of London, in September 1685 had stopped a writ *de excommunicato capiendo* against one Friend, while others imprisoned in Wood Street Compter by that writ were given some liberty by his "connivance." But when petitioned to assist imprisoned Chelmsford Friends, Compton grumbled that "the men at court blame him for giving away their fees"; therefore, he advised the petitioners to see "whether they could persuade them to forego their fees." In fact, in November, having received certificates of peaceable behavior for those prisoners and under pressure from Meeting for Sufferings, the bishop absolved them. The gaoler at first insisted on his fees, but soon set them free.[32] As we have seen, justices and clergy had signed a number of such certificates for Quakers, either mentioning their peaceable behavior or their not being popish recusants.

Nor were lesser officers of the law adverse to assisting the Quakers. Constables or other officers often refused to execute warrants for distraint, to sell distrained goods, or to prosecute meetings.[33] In one instance, a sharp-tongued London constable when ordered by Alderman Peter Daniel in April 1683 to disperse a meeting and pull down a speaker, retorted that "he was no porter . . . [and] could not carry them on his back, for he had desired them to depart." He added that "he had no warrant to disperse the meeting, he being there only to keep the peace." A Leicestershire constable, after an informer had prosecuted a meeting where only four Quakers were present, took neighbors as witnesses before the justices to swear that only four had been present, "the constable doing this for his own security because the informer threatened him." Nonenforcement must have been rife in Essex, for in 1670 two informers complained to the justices and caused a churchwarden, two constables, and four overseers of the poor to be fined for neglect of duty in regard to distraints on Quakers.[34]

Occasionally, moderation proved to be more trouble to the officer than it was worth. In April 1680 Meeting for Sufferings learned that Richard Stephens, imprisoned for tithes, had been given liberty by the gaoler of the Marshalsea at the request of Thomas Moore, the minister who had originally sued him. The release was predicated on Stephens' returning to gaol upon notice. Shortly afterwards Moore died, but Stephens did not return. Moore's executor then sued both the sheriff and the gaoler for permitting Stephens to remain at liberty, and won damages which the gaoler paid. He, in turn, demanded satisfaction from Stephens. Friends were very concerned, for the gaoler was "greatly enraged" and threatened "other Friends that are or shall be brought into his custody." Assisted by the Meeting, Stephens paid. In a bizarre case, Thomas Marsh of Newbury, Berkshire, imprisoned by a writ *de excommunicato capiendo*, was "never discharged from it, nor detained very little in prison, but the gaoler in favor to him let him go home so soon that very few of his neighbors were sensible that he was a prisoner." In fact, he "followed his employment publicly as before all along, and kept to meetings as constant as any." Ironically, when "other Friends were taken, he was taken and put in prison with them and so remained as the rest do."[35]

Although assistance from the Crown, law-enforcement officers, and churchmen was important for the Quakers, the pivotal factor in seventeenth-century enforcement was the reaction of neighbors and relatives of those prosecuted. The Quakers reported numerous instances where neighbors either refused to purchase distrained goods or bought them at very low prices, returning them again to the victims.[36] A different approach was adopted in March 1685, when William Gill of Bethnal Green, Middlesex, suffered a distraint. A neighbor came and bought the goods before they were taken away, apparently leaving them with Gill. As if that neighbor's action was not enough to thwart law-enforcement officials, matters worsened. The constable had already sent for a cart "to carry away the goods," but the carter, "understanding for what the goods was seized . . . refused to come," while a joiner, who had been sent for "to take down the goods" when he heard "for what the goods was seized, went back again & would not do it."[37] The fact that distrained Quaker goods were often not sold or were purchased cheaply and returned to the offenders, sent a clear signal to informers and officers that distraints were largely meaningless in such locales.

Similarly, fines were often paid or bail put up, usually by relatives or neighbors, but occasionally by officers or others. Perhaps the wildest example occurred on 17 April 1684 in London, when more than one hundred Quakers had been taken from White Hart Court meeting and were brought before the mayor, who fined each of them 5s., "but people threw many of their fines in over their heads, saying here is such a one's, and a woman neighbor to the mayor paid down 30, or 40s." Consequently most were released, but "about 20 poor men, for whom there were none to pay their fines, were sent to prison." Similarly, at Uxbridge meeting in October 1683, twelve Quakers were taken and fined; but the lesser officers and neighbors, "rather than let their peaceable neighbors go to prison, paid the money for them."[38]

Far more challenging to Friends' testimony, however, were those cases where good behavior was demanded. Despite Quaker opposition to any such promise, it could not always be avoided. Two Norwich Friends discovered this in September 1671 when they were released after Edwin Bensley, a non-Quaker, entered bond for their good behavior, while in Suffolk in March 1685 "some friendly people having paid the fines for some former prisoners . . . say they have promised for them the good behavior."[39]

Not all Quakers were amenable to neighborly benevolence. Four London Friends in June 1683, taken from Bull and Mouth Meeting and brought before the mayor, refused to accept the 20s. in fines paid in by a stranger. Unfortunately the court, wisely preferring money to Quaker prisoners, accepted the generous offer and discharged the Friends. Early in 1682 Meeting for Sufferings learned that "neighborly tenderness" had resulted in the bailing of several Bristol Quakers "without their desire or approbation." Fearful for their testimony, the Friends asked the Meeting for advice, for they had heard that the bond was not only for their appearance, "but behavior also." Predictably, the Meeting advised that "as far as may be, they do tenderly discourage all their acquaintance[s] from engaging so for them." Friends that "go out," the Meeting continued, should "be free, not obliged or . . . constrained to their houses, not . . . bound to the good behavior."[40] Neighbors also helped in other, less expensive ways, such as those who sent a certificate to the bishop of London testifying to the poor and sickly condition of Susanna Fallow, an aged, bedridden widow in Essex, prosecuted for her refusal to pay church rates; or those neighbors in Lincolnshire who sent a certificate of protest to Sir John Newton, whose impropriator had caused the imprisonment of two Quakers for nonpayment of tithes.[41] One neighbor, however, assisted Friends in his own unique style, after the town clerk of Launceston in January 1665 had caused several Quakers to be imprisoned in extremely bad conditions. As one of the imprisoned Friends later explained, a captain asked the clerk why "he could not let his neighbors live quietly," and not receiving the answer he desired, then "hewed and wounded him and beat him till they say he is almost killed." Although the Quaker commentator presumably opposed violence, he casually added that the clerk had garnered "a part of his reward which I said he should receive."[42]

Perhaps the most welcome assistance given to Friends was that rendered in the mid-1660s by ship captains and crews who resisted orders transporting banished Quakers to the colonies. That the authorities were serious in their efforts to transport Quakers can be seen with the several orders for their departure issued by the Privy Council. For example, sixty Quakers were to sail in the *Black Eagle* to Jamaica, fifty more in the *John and Sarah* to Barbados, with others in the *Daniel* for the same island, thirty in the *Nicholas* to any colony except Virginia and New England, while the authorities in Bristol in September 1665 issued warrants for fifteen Quakers to be transported to Barbados. Other ships used included the *Jamaica Merchant*, the *Mary Fortune*, and the *Anne*. At one point, the government considered sending the London Quakers sentenced to transportation in a prize ship. At least one shipmaster, however, was imprisoned for refusing to take Quakers, while there is ample evidence of resistance by crews. During the height of the plague, in August 1665, thirty-seven men and eighteen women were put aboard the *Black Eagle* below Greenwich, despite the sailors' refusal to assist in their boarding. The ship lay seven weeks in the river before making the Downs, the master having been imprisoned for debt and the crew threatening to desert. During that time, half the Quakers died. The ship, still in the Downs in January 1666, was ultimately captured by the Dutch; and the surviving Quakers were able to return to England. Some Friends, however, were successfully transported to Jamaica, Nevis, and Barbados, while one was sent to Virginia as a slave. But of more than two hundred fifty Quakers sentenced to transportation, only about twenty were actually transported.[43]

The Quakers, of course, also helped themselves through their lobbying, their legal strategy, and their flexibility. They were able to muster resources far superior to informers or ministers; to prosecute a Quaker became an expensive proposition. Their use of delaying tactics, appeals, demurrers, and conveyances of goods was all calculated to defeat their adversaries. Although the legal advice they received was often self-serving and questionable, they still had far greater likelihood of success on legal grounds than most of their opponents. Some Friends, however, preferred a different form of self-reliance. Flexibility for them implied avoidance of prosecution or imprisonment. A movement as large as the Quakers and as firmly based as it was on the leadings of an Inner Light was bound to have some difficulty in strictly enforcing its testimonies on all those who regarded themselves as Friends. It is possible, therefore, that some Quakers were paying fines themselves, or arranging for them to be paid, ostensibly without their knowledge. This would help to account for those instances in their records in which a smaller number of Friends were tried than were arrested, or where fines were imposed on many Quakers for riots, where distraint was not permitted, and yet few were imprisoned.[44] There is stronger evidence, particularly in connection with the Wilkinson-Story separatist movement in Westmorland in the 1670s, that some Friends met surreptitiously to avoid informers, and that the testimony against tithes was not always followed. Yet there is no indication that such behavior, before 1689, included more than a disillusioned minority unhappy over the increasing bureaucratization of Quakerism under the aegis of George Fox and London Friends.[45]

In quantitative terms, although it must be kept in mind that criminal statistics are often misleading, Quaker records clearly signify that the prosecution of Friends was sporadic and capricious.[46] In London and Middlesex, for example, most of their recorded sufferings were for meetings (or suspicion of plotting in meetings), tithes, and failure to provide men for the militia. Tithe convictions, beginning with the rebuilding of London after the Great Fire, were generally consistent, as were militia distraints. Prosecutions for meetings were substantial, however, only in the periods 1660–65, 1670–71, and 1683–86. At most other times, they were virtually nonexistent. London sessions records specify, in fact, that there were no prosecutions of Quaker meetings from 1666 through 1669. The severe periods of prosecution are identifiable with the plot scares in 1661 and 1662, the first Conventicle Act in 1664, the second Conventicle Act in 1670, and the reaction by Charles in the 1680s against those who had supported Exclusion.[47] With the exception of a brief period in the 1680s, cases where recusancy penalties were levied are completely lacking. In Cumberland, perhaps reflecting that county's agricultural bias, tithe prosecutions were extremely heavy and, with the exception of the middle 1660s and early 1670s, very consistent. Prosecutions for meeting, however, were haphazard and very light. Nor is there much evidence of violence or petty harassment against Friends there. On the other hand, recusancy enforcement, although generally 12*d*. for each Sunday, was somewhat more prevalent there than in London and Middlesex. Like those two counties, Bristol saw heavy prosecution of meetings in 1661, 1664, and again in 1682, but none at all for long periods; there were none for tithes, either, and few for the militia. Alternatively, recusancy enforcement in the early 1680s was extremely high. Finally, Durham and Northumberland saw the most consistent pattern of prosecutions for meetings. Yet tithe prosecutions, while steady, were light; and recusancy fines and forfeitures, despite Durham's status as a bishopric, were relatively rare. These statistics show geographical and chronological variation, but there is one constant—prosecutions were often nonexistent or relatively rare for many years. One surprising statistic is the apparent infrequency, except for the 1680s, of recusancy prosecutions. It is likely that Friends regarded recusancy presentments and convictions in the same way they viewed excommunications, that is, as not worthy to record unless they resulted in distraint, sequestration, or imprisonment. Support for this interpretation comes from John Miller, who lists 776 Norfolk Quaker recusancy convictions (comprising 369 individuals) from 1664 to 1685, a figure exceeding by 120 the combined recorded total for the six counties listed in Appendix 1. Joseph Besse, whose figures generally approximate those of the "Great Book of Sufferings," lists only 81 Norfolk recusancy cases for the same period. Of Miller's 776 convictions, 215 occurred before 1681. Since C. D. Chandaman discloses that until Easter term of 1681 recusancy receipts in the Exchequer for the entire country totaled only about £3500, there is little doubt that before 1681 recusancy convictions rarely resulted in a levying of the penalties.[48] The reasons for this are unclear, although the tremendous numbers of presentments and convictions, combined with the slow, cumbersome procedure of distraint, sequestration, and accounting surely played a critical part. Moreover, it is highly probable that sheriffs and their assistants were often reluctant to enforce such severe penalties on their neighbors, even where the offenders were Quakers. On the other hand, Quaker records confirm Chandaman's statistics, which indicate that the levying of recusancy fines dramatically increased in the 1680s. He calculates that the Exchequer received over £25,500 between the Easter terms of 1681 and 1687.[49]

All of these figures, of course, fail to convey the quality of the often harsh sufferings that Friends underwent, or such petty harassment as meetings forced to be held in the rain and cold, or vandalism and minor violence. Nor do they reflect the fact that the breadth of Quaker principles caused many legal actions to continue for years, although they were recorded only once in their records. Nor can anyone quantify the severe emotional impact upon Friends of a habitual threat of violence, imprisonment, distraint, and disruption of family life. Nevertheless, the considerable gaps in Quaker records suggest, at most, inconsistent enforcement of the law. That conclusion is further supported by Friends' correspondence, which implies that at any given date prosecutions varied markedly from area to area. Even within London, while some meetings on a particular day were being harassed or prosecuted, others were not.[50] Many Friends were able to amass sufficient wealth to purchase substantial estates in West New Jersey and Pennsylvania.[51] Hard work, honesty, and a more restrained pattern of personal religious behavior all contributed to the growth in wealth and status of leading Friends and influenced the survival of the Quakers as a religious entity.

Yet while the behavior of Friends was significant to their survival, the English legal system and the restraint of neighbors must not be overlooked. For any system of law to work effectively, there must be a high degree of cooperation between those who legislate, those who enforce, and those who are law-abiding members of the community. From 1660 to 1689, in the contentious area of religion, that prerequisite was entirely lacking. Despite the apparent power of the Crown, the restored Stuarts were circumscribed by their own religious inclinations, their desperate need for money from Parliament, and their deep reliance on the English gentry, often jealous of their own rights and privileges and suspicious of the motives of their rulers. The system also depended on a plethora of amateur lesser officers, often unwilling and incompetent, backed by a horde of unreliable, disreputable informers. There was little professionalism or direction in law enforcement—no police force, no county prosecuting solicitors, no director of public prosecutions, nor in most cases any prosecuting counsel. To a large extent, the system was held together by fear and self-interest, with officers laboring under the threat of punishment for failure to carry out their duty, and enticed always by the possibility of corruption. Although such considerations are not altogether absent in a professional police force, they were present to a disproportionate extent in the seventeenth century, and were exacerbated by often primitive procedure, jurisdictional complexity, legal fictions, time-consuming writs, and imprecise legislation. Uncertainty and ignorance only exaggerated the potential for abuse. Far too much was expected from those men who served as constables, bailiffs, and other officers in the lower echelons of the legal system. The difficulty of filling the lesser posts, the ineffectiveness of threats of dismissal from burdensome, unpaid offices, and the slight qualifications required were further complications. There was far too much scope for inaction, illegal behavior, or outright corruption. That potential was particularly evident in the entire process of distraint.

The system might have been mobilized by strong leadership at the top, but with the Crown and Parliament so often at odds over religion, and with Quakers often gaining their freedom through royal interference, effective law enforcement was unlikely. It is difficult to assess with precision the rationale behind the occasionally severe and widespread prosecutions. The Crown and Parliament appear to have initially feared a resurgence of insurrection, and may also have desired a measure of revenge against those who had supported the overthrow of the monarchy and the church and who for two decades had "turned the world upside down." Often "ringleaders" were the object of particular attention.[52] In the 1680s, on the other hand, an embittered Charles II reacted against the Dissenters for supporting parliamentary efforts to exclude his brother from the throne. Although any effort to suppress religious dissent was generally supported by the hierarchy of the Anglican Church, it appears that the impetus behind royal and/or parliamentary action against Protestant dissent was political and economic, rather than religious. Often the bitterest theological disagreements were among the Dissenters themselves. Yet the absence of a concerted and consistent effort to suppress them enabled the Dissenters to survive, and the secular basis for their prosecution became increasingly apparent. Consequently, religious "persecution" became less tenable and toleration more acceptable, although political and economic restraints would remain.

But even had Parliament and the Crown acted in concert, the Quakers and other Dissenters might still have survived, for any legal effort to destroy them depended upon the willingness of the superior common-law judges to carry out often unpopular policies, and the degree to which they were supported by the justices of the peace. In fact, the judges were rarely as obsequious to the Crown as contemporaries liked to believe. They were subject to numerous pressures apart from the Crown—from Parliament, from local officials anxious for their prejudices and policies to be confirmed, from the influence of tradition, and from the law itself. Nor were the judges in this period young, ambitious careerists. Most were middle-aged men with extensive legal experience, now at the pinnacle of the legal profession, and often from solid, respectable, gentry families with a long tradition of service in the law and politics.[53] For such men to have been mere pawns of the Crown would have destroyed their integrity, that of the law, and of the institutions they represented. At the same time, however, lords lieutenant and justices of the peace, sensing a threat to their supremacy in the counties, and often considering themselves socially superior, resented interference from the judiciary. For their part, the judges were venturing twice each year into potentially volatile circumstances, knowing little of local rivalries and prejudices. "Wrong" decisions could lead to serious trouble for Stuart judges, who were often haughty, aggressive, and arrogant in the courtroom, resorting in many cases to sarcasm or ridicule as weapons against willful or impertinent magistrates. That tendency did not improve the potential for sound law enforcement; nor did the fact, already noted, that the judges were heavily reliant on local participants—justices, sheriffs, constables, and other law-enforcement officers—for the production of suspects, witnesses, evidence, and the return and trial of indictments.[54] It is not surprising, therefore, that Quaker records often reflect disparities between royal instructions and judicial conduct on circuit, or that justices varied greatly in their application of the law. Unfortunately for the Quakers, the lack of direction and inherent conflicts, combined with the general unwillingness of many justices to attend quarter sessions, enabled zealous justices, churchmen, and corporation officials to pursue their own agenda of consistent enforcement. Quakers often reserved their venom for officers they regarded as the sole cause of much of their "persecution"—men like Daniel Fleming, Philip Musgrave, Richard Browne, William Armorer, John Hellier, Archbishop Gilbert Sheldon, and above all, Sir Thomas Jenner. The system also depended to an inordinate degree on informers. Far more than mere informants, they were an integral feature of law enforcement, acting as witnesses, prosecutors, and motivators of reluctant officers. Their ability to continue prosecuting Quakers despite the opposition of the Crown and many high-ranking officials was inexcusable.

Ultimately, however, the system depended on the popularity or unpopularity of Quakers in the localities, for a system of law enforcement based on amateurs who lived in the neighborhood and who resented the duties thrust upon them, could lead to the neglect of unpopular legislation. Local officers were understandably reluctant to undertake a burdensome and thankless task that might pit them against their neighbors or relatives. Alternatively, rumor and gossip could be powerful incentives for prosecuting Quakers. But it often took unusual fervor by law officers or tremendous dislike of the victims, for effective enforcement of penal statutes against religious dissenters. In effect, law-enforcement officers, pressured from above and below, influenced by local loyalties, family connections, political, religious, and personal prejudices, were continually exercising preferences and choices in determining whom to prosecute.[55] Consistent law enforcement in these circumstances was unlikely at best.

In the final analysis, however, what may have aided the Quakers more than anything else, and essentially defeated the legal system, was the tremendous breadth of religious criminality. The rule of law depends primarily on the willingness of most of the population to act within a legal framework. In seventeenth-century England, the depth of religious opposition to the Anglican Church and the legislation its supporters had enacted, combined with the potentially devastating economic consequences of repression, and with the belief that Protestants, including Quakers, must unite against the Catholic "threat," was sufficient to undermine respect for the law and those who enforced it. Of itself this might not have saved the Quakers, but in conjunction with inconsistent royal leadership, centrifugal forces within the law-enforcement system, alienation of many Englishmen from the Catholicism of the court, the developing "respectability" of Friends, and their increasingly sophisticated use of legal and pressure group tactics, their survival and toleration were ultimately assured. Nor were they alone. Protestant dissent would never again be proscribed in England to the extent it was during the period 1660–88. Ironically, eighteenth-century Quakerism, reputable and unemotional, was a pale reflection of that exciting, millenarian movement that had spread southward in the 1650s, challenging the law and the state to a degree unparalleled in seventeenth-century England.

Notes

1. Fox was released in 1660 and again in 1666, each time at the behest of Charles II, while Margaret Fell was released in 1668 (Fox, *Journal*, ed. Nickalls, 385–91, 501–2). Daniel Fleming was particularly upset with Fell's release, believing that her discharge "doth not a little encourage that rabble of fanatics, & discourage all magistrates from acting against them" (Fleming to Joseph Williamson, 21 August 1668, Rydal, PRO: S.P. 29/245/20).

2. Sir William Penn had been impeached and suspended from the House of Commons in 1668 for selling, as admiral of the fleet, between £1,000 and £2,000 worth of captured Dutch merchandise, the proceeds of which he kept (R. Dunn and M. Dunn, eds., *Papers of William Penn*, 1:174n). Those enemies who believed that Quakers would flock to Pennsylvania to avoid prosecution failed to perceive Friends' strong testimony against fleeing persecution; see J. William Frost, "William Penn's Experiment: Promise and Legend," *Pennsylvania Magazine of History and Biography* 107 (October 1983):588 and n.

3. Swarthmore MSS, 1:50 [italics in the original].

4. Whitehead, *Christian Progress*, 493–96.

5. See Meeting for Sufferings, 3:101; Besse, *Sufferings*, 1:684–86; GBS, 6:221–24; see also Meeting for Sufferings, 3:154, 214–15.

6. ORS, fol. 111.

7. J. Gratton to London Y.M. [1686], in Besse, *Sufferings*, 1:144; James Harrison to Roger Longworth, 20.ix [November].1679, Bolton (HSP: Gratz Collection, case 2, box 12); Phineas Pemberton to Roger Longworth, 20.xii [February].1679/80 (Pemberton MSS, 1:129); James Harrison to Roger Longworth, 24.xii [February].1679/80 (Pemberton MSS, 1:130).

8. Meeting for Sufferings, 4:219; Pemberton MSS, 1:35; see also *Second Part of Continued Cry*, 15.

9. See, for example, Meeting for Sufferings, 2:225; 4:6; GBS, 3:162–63; Besse, *Sufferings*, 1:630–31, 634.

10. Book of Cases, 1:57.

11. GBS, 6:125; Swarthmore MSS, 4:278 [italics added].

12. GBS, 1:474; see also 6:205.

13. Meeting for Sufferings, 3:224, 227, 251.

14. William Caton to James Moore, 18.ii [April].1664, Yarmouth, in Swarthmore MSS, 4:278. The assize judges were Sir Robert Hyde and Sir John Kelyng.

15. GBS, 5:543, 549, 551, 553.

16. See, for example, Meeting for Sufferings, 5:18, 32, 47–50, 60, 65, 67, 73, 75, 79, 81, 86, 93; GBS, 3:888; 6:281–82; Besse, *Sufferings*, 1:330, 646–47, 732–33; Penney, ed., *Sufferings of Quakers in Cornwall*, 135–36.

17. See Meeting for Sufferings, 5:45, 59, 61, 67, 77–79, 87–89, 92, 99, 111. The actions of the town clerk in Bristol especially angered Friends, as he refused to cooperate in releasing Quaker prisoners, even those whose fines were now discharged by the former sheriffs, Sir John Knight and Richard Lane. Exasperated, the prisoners told Meeting for Sufferings that they were "willing that our case be presented to the king" (Meeting for Sufferings, 5:112).

18. *Second Part of Cry of Oppressed*, 41–42.

19. GBS, 1:508–10; vol. 2, Somerset, 125; PRO: S.P. 29/102/137; Samuel Fisher and Joseph Fuce to George Fox, 31.v [July].1664, near London, in Swarthmore MSS, 3:106 [italics added]. See also GBS, vol. 2, Somerset, 109, 124.

20. See, for example, GBS, vol. 2, Shropshire, 3, 7–8; vol. 2, Warwickshire, 5–6.

21. Meeting for Sufferings, 3:1, 14; see also GBS, 5:545–46; 6:466–67; ORS, fol. 240; Meeting for Sufferings, 2:70–71, 74, 83–84, 91, 98, 105, 118–19, 122–23.

22. GBS, vol. 2, Yorkshire, 41; see also GBS, 1:582; vol. 2, Sussex, 12; Meeting for Sufferings, 3:223; PRO: S.P. 29/100/36.

23. ORS, fol. 240.

24. Whitehead, *Christian Progress*, 250.

25. The following account is derived from Francis Howgill to Ellis Hookes, 24.1 [March, 1664] (GBS, 4:422–26); Francis Howgill to George Fox, 23.1 [March].1663/4, Appleby (ARB MSS, fol. 92); see also Besse, *Sufferings*, 2:11–17. Howgill was praemunired at the August 1664 assizes (GBS, vol. 2, Westmorland, 4–6). Howgill complained that "all the justices in the county incensed the judge against me," causing the praemunire, although he believed the judges "would have washed their hands [of it]" (F. Howgill to George Fox, 3.vii [September].1664, Appleby, in ARB MSS, fol. 93). In 1666 Howgill had an opportunity to gain his liberty, but was unwilling to pay the necessary charges for an attorney to effect it (F. Howgill to Margaret Fell, 1666, Appleby, in Swarthmore MSS, 3:159). He died in prison in January 1669 (Braithwaite, *Second Period*, 37).

26. GBS, 4:426.

27. GBS, vol. 2, Somerset, 144–45. Anderdon was subsequently praemunired at Taunton assizes in March 1676 by Judge Richard Rainsford (GBS, 4:214, 226; 6:57). See also ORS, fol. 398.

28. B. Fell to Margaret Fell, Jr., 23.i [March].1660/1 (Spence MSS, 3:2C); GBS, 1:548; PRO: Assizes 35/103/4, m. 2. Unfortunately for William Watcher, soon after his release, when he and his wife were at the burial of a relative, and the minister was reading the prayer, Watcher's wife remarked aloud that the blind would continue to lead the blind until they both fell into the ditch. The minister caused a justice to demand sureties from the Watchers; they refused and were imprisoned at Maidstone, where Watcher died soon thereafter. His wife was released at the summer assizes (GBS, 1:548); see also Meeting for Sufferings, 4:137; Besse, *Sufferings*, 1:533; GBS, vol. 2, Somerset, 23–24.

29. Unfortunately, Penn and Turner were both suspected of treason by

the govenment of William III; see HSP: Penn-Forbes collection, 2:45–47; PRO: S.P. 45/13/61.

30. T. Lamplugh to G. Latey, 24 March 1683/4, Exeter, in *A Brief Narrative of the Life and Death of . . . Gilbert Latey*, comp. R. Hawkins [London, 1707], 109–10.

31. Meeting for Sufferings, 2:8–9, 90; 4:212; Book of Cases, 1:115; see also GBS, 3:420. Ironically, the marquis of Worcester had also refused to assist Friends on the pretext that their meeting was "so near unto his house" (Meeting for Sufferings, 2:133). As for the bishop's complaint, Friends denied that the meetinghouse was nearby. In fact, they insisted it was "almost at the other end of the town," while his house was "so far within the walls (being a castle) that if a meeting were at the wallside, . . . he could not hear a voice, though a loud one, into his chamber" (Meeting for Sufferings, 2:13–14). In 1689 Thomas Robertson, along with two other Friends, visited Bishop Crew in Durham, who did not know Robertson. "I told him," Robertson later wrote, "that I was at London when we made application to him for our Friends in this county, and received help and kindness from him, and now I being in the country was willing to give the acknowledgment of it to him." Flattered, Crew welcomed him. "I indeed received order from King Charles II," responded the bishop, "to break up your meetings, and I sent to my neighbor Tonsdale and wished him not to meet so near me, but he would not, but they kept . . . in their usual place, and so their goods was distrained." The Lord knew, however, "the tribulation that I [was] in." Robertson added that when he and his companions were ready to leave, Crew "would not let us, but sent for a bottle of wine, and we drank and came our way" (Thomas Robertson to George Fox, [1689?], in ARB MSS, fol. 150).

32. Meeting for Sufferings, 4:126, 133, 140, 200, 209.

33. See, for example, Fox, *Journal*, Nickalls, ed., 148–49; GBS, 1:118; vol. 2, London and Middlesex, 9, 11; 3:397, 936; 5:389; Besse, *Sufferings*, 1:221; Meeting for Sufferings, 2:205; 3:247; ORS, fols. 506, 767; *Declaration of Present Sufferings*, 14; Jeaffreson, ed., *Middlesex Sessions Records*, 4:183, 213 (the cases of constables Richard Mason and William Field, each accused of refusing to execute a warrant of distraint against Samuel Hodge and Patience Ashfield, respectively, identified by Besse as Quakers [*Sufferings*, 1:440, 482]); W. J. Hardy and W. L. Hardy, eds., *Hertfordshire County Records*, 1:349 (the case of a constable named Marston, accused of failing to disturb a Quaker meeting held every Sunday at Wood Green).

34. GBS, 5:324; Meeting for Sufferings, 5:312; Besse, *Sufferings*, 1:204; see also 1:463; Meeting for Sufferings, 2:173; 5:248, 259; GBS, 3:968; 6:381–82. On at least two occasions, Sir Peter Leicester, when charging the grand jury, complained of the serious negligence of constables in refusing to disturb conventicles, including those of Quakers (see Leicester, *Charges to Grand Jury*, ed. Halcrow, 80, 93).

35. Book of Cases, 1:73; Meeting for Sufferings, 1:148, 154–55; 2:46; ORS, fol. 516; see also the case of Sussex Friends in jeopardy with the marshal of King's Bench prison (Meeting for Sufferings, 2:30–31), and the case of an Aylesbury gaoler named Birch, who was fined £5 "for suffering the Quakers committed by this court to go at large" (Hardy and Reckitt, eds., *Buckingham Sessions Records*, 1:149).

36. See GBS, 1:11–12; vol. 2, Westmorland, 12–13; 3:128, 308–9, 423, 425; 4:182; 6:418–19; Besse, *Sufferings*, 1:111, 132, 142, 253, 345, 611;

Meeting for Sufferings, 3:300, 316; 4:25; W. J. Hardy and W. L. Hardy, eds., *Hertfordshire County Records*, 1:343.

37. GBS, 5:488–89; see also GBS, 3:344; Meeting for Sufferings, 3:316; 4:25.

38. GBS, 5:375–76; ORS, fol. 767; see also GBS, 1:382, 392, 394; 3:1023; 5:333–34, 363, 369, 407–26, 441, 453, 459, 464–66, 468–69; ORS, fols. 312, 545; Meeting for Sufferings, 3:266; 4:59; 5:5; Besse, *Sufferings*, 1:110, 207, 468, 470, 632, 687; *Life of Ellwood*, 284–86; Dix MSS, a25s; Whitehead, *Christian Progress*, 560. It is difficult to evaluate what impact the paying of fines for some Friends had on those less fortunate Quakers who remained in prison.

39. Eddington, *First Fifty Years of Quakerism*, 76; Meeting for Sufferings, 4:7.

40. Meeting for Sufferings, 2:89, 216–17.

41. Meeting for Sufferings, 6:211–12, 220, 228, 244–45; see also Meeting for Sufferings, 6:109, 160–61; GBS, 3:794–97; ORS, fols. 421, 486, 489.

42. Josiah Coale to George Fox, 12.xi [January].1664/5, the Darkhouse, Launceston (ARB MSS, fol. 64).

43. PRO: P.C. 2/58/39; 2/58/55; 2/58/100; Braithwaite, *Second Period*, 44–54, 655; William C. Braithwaite, London Friends Sentenced to Transportation, 1664–65 (typescript in FLL); Penney, ed., *Extracts from State Papers*, 230–31, 240; GBS, 1:89; vol. 2, London and Middlesex, 99–100; Besse, *Sufferings*, 1:247; Thirnbeck MSS, fol. 3; see also ORS, fol. 89; P.C. 2/58/37; S.P.44/22/48. The imprisoned shipmaster was Captain Thomas May of the *Anne*, of London. It appears that captains and crews were not alone in resisting the transportation of Quakers. When eight transported Friends arrived at Nevis, "the governor . . . would not receive them unless they were willing to come ashore." It is possible that the governor had learned the fate of the ship's captain, who had been "struck . . . dumb, and about a fortnight after, . . . died and was thrown overboard about 4 days before they came to land" (Esther Biddle to John Smith, 29.ix [November].1665, London, in ARB MSS, fol. 94).

44. See, for example, Besse, *Sufferings*, 1:109–10, 621, 628–29.

45. See Braithwaite, *Second Period*, 77–78, 296n, 297–99, 374–75.

46. The following can be found in Appendix 1, the introduction to which should be read with care.

47. Even these figures can be misleading. London authorities from 1683 to 1686 tended to keep Friends out of their meetinghouses, taking away preachers to be fined or imprisoned briefly, while simply dispersing listeners or arresting them for short periods and light fines. In addition, since Friends increasingly had their fines or bail paid, they were assisted by the decision of the London magistrates to try them for riots, which effectively eliminated the rewards for informers provided by the second Conventicle Act. There are also indications that justices were not staying at home on Sundays, making it difficult for informers or lesser officers to locate them in order to convict Quakers and, presumably, other Dissenters; see GBS, 5:318–26, 342–54, 356, 365–80, 383–84, 386–89, 400, 403–4, 427–29, 436–40, 447–51, 455, 459–61, 464–65, 468–70, 483, 503.

48. Miller, *Popery & Politics*, 267; Besse, *Sufferings*, 1:491–518; Chandaman, *The English Public Revenue 1660–1688* (Oxford, 1975), 348–49, 356–57, 360–61.

49. Chandaman, 359–61.

50. See, for example, Thomas Salthouse to Leonard Fell, 26.xi [January].1662/3, Bristol (Abraham MSS, fol. 6); John Stubbs to Margaret Fell, 25.viii [October].1670, Enfield (Abraham MSS, fol. 13); John Higgins to George Fox and Margaret Fell, 26.v [July].1664, London (ARB MSS, fol. 82); Josiah Coale to George Fox, ll.ix [November].1663, Chalfont St. Giles (ARB MSS, fol. 88); William Storrs to Samuel Hooton, 30.xi [January].1666/7, Chesterfield (ARB MSS, fol. 95); John Lawrence to Joseph Miles, 29.xi [January].1681/2, Wramplingham (ORS, fol. 488); James Harrison to Roger Longworth, 6.v [July].1670, Bolton (Pemberton MSS, 1:35); John Crook to George Fox, 25.vi [August].1664, Ipswich Gaol (Swarthmore MSS, 3:123); Alexander Parker to George Fox, 12.ii [April].1664, London (Swarthmore MSS, 3:149); George Whitehead to George Fox, 4.3 [May].1664, London (Swarthmore MSS, 4:96); James Parkes to John Lacon, 7.xi [January].1664/5, Blubery, Berkshire (Swarthmore MSS, 4:128); Guli Penn to Margaret Fox, 24.vi [August].1684, Warminghurst (Caton MSS, 3:496–97); Ellis Hookes to Margaret Fell, 2.vi [August].1666, London (Thirnbeck MSS, fol. 5); Esther Biddle to Francis Howgill, 17.viii [October].1664, Bridewell Gaol, London (PRO: S.P. 29/103/75).

51. See John E. Pomfret, *The Province of West New Jersey, 1609–1702* (Princeton, 1956); R. Dunn and M. Dunn, eds., *Papers of William Penn*, 2:636–64.

52. See, for example, John Whitehead, *The Written Gospel-Labours of that Ancient and Faithfull Servant of Jesus Christ, John Whitehead* (London, 1704), 203; GBS, 1:34; vol. 2, London and Middlesex, 57; vol. 2, Shropshire, 7–8; Reay, "Authorities and Quakerism," 71–73; Besse, *Sufferings*, 1:262.

53. For more information on the superior common-law judges in this period, see Horle, "Judicial Encounters with Quakers," 91–92n. As for accusations of judicial obsequiousness, see Horle, "Judicial Encounters," 85, nn. 4–5.

54. Cockburn, *Assizes*, 101–2, 132, 164–65.

55. *Essex Sessions*, xxxii; *Warwick Records*, 7:lxxvii; T. C. Curtis, "Quarter Sessions Appearances and their Background: a Seventeenth-Century Regional Study," in *Crime in England*, ed. Cockburn, 144, 148; M. J. Ingram, "Communities and Courts: Law and Disorder in Early Seventeenth-Century Wiltshire," in *Crime in England*, 128; Sharpe, "Crime and Delinquency," 107–8; see also Marchant, *Church Under Law*, 183; Dowdell, *Hundred Years*, 21; *Kesteven*, cxxvii–cxxviii. In Cheshire, the justices of the peace indicted seventy-three constables in 1682, generally for neglect of duty (Curtis, "Quarter Sessions," 144–45).

SUFFERINGS, 1660–1688

The following lists are drawn from the first six volumes of the MS Great Book of Sufferings which was compiled from accounts sent by Friends to London. Although some accounts were scribbled on scraps of parchment, many were included in lengthy letters to London Friends or to the London-based county correspondents for Meeting for Sufferings. There were also annual tabulations of sufferings for each county. All of these were gathered together, edited, and recorded by Ellis Hookes, or by others after his death. A large number of these original accounts, particularly for London and Middlesex, can be found in the MS Original Records of Sufferings. There also exist local records of sufferings for a number of counties, which often provide additional information. Future Quaker local historians would be well advised to consult these as a supplement to the Great Book of Sufferings.

Crime statistics involving Quakers in this period are difficult to categorize and tend to be misleading, failing as they do to reflect the fear and anxiety, violence and petty harassment (including destruction of meetinghouses) that often plagued Friends. As noted in the text, violence against Quakers was sufficiently common to warrant their concern.

Nonetheless, such statistics are useful as indicators of the general level of law enforcement. I have chosen to include only those instances where some legal action took place, for example, detainment, imprisonment, fines, distraints, and sureties. Private suits are included only where a penalty was assessed. For example, if two hundred Quakers were dispersed from a meeting, but only fifty detained by the authorities, only those detained would be included. In a substantial number of cases, the Oath of Allegiance was tendered to suspects originally arrested for other causes. I have listed *only the original pretext*, rather than refusal of the Oath, or refusal to post sureties or bail, or to pay fines; excommunications are treated similarly. I have listed under the general heading of "meetings" those instances, particularly in 1661, in which Friends were rounded up on suspicion of involvement in plots such as that of the Fifth Monarchists. Quaker records are often unclear as to whether the suspects were taken after a meeting or at work, at home, or elsewhere. Miscellaneous crimes include hat-honor, opening shops on the Lord's Day or holy days (particularly Christmas), contempt shown to a magistrate, intruding into churches, or crimes left unspecified. To indicate the potential seriousness of tithe prosecutions, I have included below three of the tables the number of imprisonments for that crime. The figures presented below represent the number of prosecutions, not the number of different individuals involved. Some Friends were prosecuted in the same year more than once for the same crime (or different crimes), particularly under the first Conventicle Act, which required three convictions before the offender could be transported. The Great Book is also slightly vague at times on the exact year in which a crime occurred. For example, the 662 cases in Bristol in 1682 may actually include cases in 1681 and 1683. I have attempted, however, to be as precise as possible, with the result that most figures are included within the appropriate year. For a discussion of the figures given below, see Chapter 6, The Legal System Reconsidered.

TABLE 1.   *Cumberland*

Year	Meeting	Oaths	Tithes/ Rates	Recu- sancy	Militia	Misc.	Total
1660	——	37	8	——	——	3	48
1661	5	9	57	35	——	——	106
1662	15	4	11	1	——	——	31
1663	——	1	263	59	——	——	323
1664	——	3	89	——	——	——	92
1665	1	——	——	——	——	——	1
1666	——	——	——	——	——	——	——
1667	——	——	1	——	——	——	1
1668	——	——	——	——	——	——	——
1669	——	——	——	——	——	——	——
1670	55	——	——	——	——	——	55
1671	——	——	——	——	——	——	——
1672	——	——	3	——	——	——	3
1673	85	——	20	——	——	——	105
1674	——	1	138	——	——	——	139
1675	6	1	109	——	——	——	116
1676	10	——	189	9	——	——	208
1677	——	——	7	——	——	——	7
1678	——	——	256	5	——	——	261
1679	16	——	268	——	——	——	284
1680	12	——	262	2	——	——	276
1681	——	——	243	——	——	——	243
1682	——	3	231	4	——	1	239
1683	8	2	336	3	——	——	349
1684	12	4	223	——	——	1	240
1685	17	1	205	——	——	——	223
1686	——	——	235	——	——	——	235
1687	——	——	266	——	——	——	266
1688	——	——	232	——	——	——	232
TOTAL	242	66	3,652	118	——	5	4,083

Deaths in prison numbered four.
Recusancy convictions were generally one shilling each Sunday with distraint.
Indications of violence are very rare for this county.
Imprisonments for tithes totaled eighty-six.

TABLE 2.   *Durham and Northumberland*

Year	Meeting	Oaths	Tithes/Rates	Recusancy	Militia	Misc.	Total
1660	6	—	—	—	—	—	6
1661	87	14	5	—	—	2	108
1662	2	1	3	—	—	—	6
1663	1	1	9	4	—	—	15
1664	31	—	6	1	—	—	38
1665	39	—	12	—	—	—	51
1666	29	—	1	—	—	13	30
1667	—	—	—	—	—	—	—
1668	—	—	3	—	—	—	3
1669	—	—	—	—	—	—	—
1670	38	—	—	1	—	—	39
1671	11	—	3	—	—	—	14
1672	—	—	8	—	—	—	8
1673	—	—	9	—	—	—	9
1674	—	—	2	—	—	—	2
1675	63	—	5	—	—	3	71
1676	18	—	2	2	—	—	22
1677	—	—	—	—	—	—	—
1678	22	—	1	—	—	—	23
1679	12	—	2	—	—	1	15
1680	62	1	—	32	1	—	96
1681	14	—	2	—	—	—	16
1682	85	—	2	94	—	1	182
1683	74	—	—	9	—	5	88
1684	49	—	—	9	—	7	65
1685	18	—	1	5	—	—	24
1686	—	—	4	—	—	—	4
1687	—	—	15	—	—	—	15
1688	—	—	—	—	—	—	—
TOTAL	661	17	95	157	1	32	950

Deaths in prison numbered six.

Most recusancy violations were one shilling each Sunday, although three hundred convictions and prosecutions for £20 occurred in 1686, but were apparently not levied, due to a moderating of royal policy.

Imprisonments for tithes totaled forty-two.

TABLE 3.   *Bristol*

Year	Meeting	Oaths	Tithes/ Rates	Recu- sancy	Militia	Misc.	Total
1660	——	——	——	——	——	——	——
1661	178	1	——	——	1	6	186
1662	2	——	——	——	——	——	2
1663	29	——	——	——	——	——	29
1664	610	——	——	——	1	5	616
1665	12	——	——	1	——	——	13
1666	——	——	——	——	——	——	——
1667	——	——	——	——	——	——	——
1668	——	——	——	——	——	——	——
1669	——	——	——	——	——	——	——
1670	3	——	——	——	——	——	3
1671	——	——	——	——	——	——	——
1672	——	——	——	——	——	——	——
1673	——	——	——	——	——	——	——
1674	——	——	——	——	——	——	——
1675	——	——	——	——	——	——	——
1676	——	——	——	——	——	——	——
1677	——	——	——	——	——	——	——
1678	——	——	——	——	1	2	3
1679	——	——	——	——	——	1	1
1680	——	——	——	——	——	4	4
1681	4	——	——	41	——	——	45
1682	662	4	——	50	——	——	715
1683	32	——	——	191	——	1	224
1684	——	——	——	——	——	——	——
1685	——	——	——	——	——	——	——
1686	——	——	——	——	——	——	——
1687	——	——	——	——	——	——	——
1688	——	——	——	——	——	——	——
TOTAL	1,532	5	——	283	3	19	1,841

Deaths in prison numbered five.

A great deal of violence is indicated in the records, particularly against Friends attending meetings.

It was reported in 1682–83 that over five hundred Friends were under prosecution in the Exchequer for recusancy.

Imprisonments for tithes totaled four.

TABLE 4.   *London and Middlesex*

Year	Meeting	Oaths	Tithes/Rates	Recusancy	Militia	Misc.	Total
1660	14	—	—	—	—	5	19
1661	324	—	—	—	—	14	338
1662	305	6	—	—	—	3	314
1663	6	10	—	—	—	—	16
1664	1,729	—	—	—	—	—	1,729
1665	319	—	—	—	—	—	319
1666	—	—	—	—	—	—	—
1667	—	—	—	—	1	—	1
1668	—	—	3	—	1	—	4
1669	—	—	1	—	—	—	1
1670	515	—	1	—	3	—	519
1671	17	—	12	—	2	4	35
1672	1	—	15	—	2	—	18
1673	—	—	6	—	2	4	12
1674	—	—	15	—	2	1	18
1675	—	2	14	—	2	—	18
1676	—	—	22	—	—	—	22
1677	—	1	17	—	—	—	18
1678	5	—	23	—	1	—	29
1679	—	—	22	—	17	—	39
1680	—	—	5	—	4	6	15
1681	—	—	16	—	13	2	31
1682	5	—	12	—	3	—	20
1683	401	—	15	7	18	—	441
1684	440	2	14	10	9	—	475
1685	209	—	6	23	4	—	242
1686	83	—	7	46	7	—	143
1687	—	2	6	—	11	—	19
1688	—	5	—	4	11	—	—
TOTAL	4,373	23	237	86	106	39	4,855

Deaths in prison numbered 114.

These accounts are rather confusing, because of the complexity of prosecutions and the time they were entered in the Great Book of Sufferings. There may be some overlap.

Militia prosecutions often included numerous years.

Collection of tithes or their equivalent was simplified after the rebuilding of London. Many arrested in 1661–62 were tendered the Oath of Allegiance, then soon released, with the exception of those perceived as ringleaders.

LAWYERS CONSULTED OR UTILIZED BY FRIENDS, 1660–1690

The source in which the name of the particular lawyer is mentioned has been provided in brackets. Information has not been found for all those mentioned. It is possible that they were Dissenters who could not take the required oaths to pursue a legal career, or that perhaps they had attended the Inns of Chancery, whose records have not survived. In addition, the Inner Temple has not published admittance records past 1660, with the result that several of the lawyers, who were called to the bar while members of that Inn, have been provided with speculative admission dates. Some of the references by Friends mention only a surname; in those instances, I have attempted to provide identifications by matching lawyers with the same surname to the county in which the case took place. I have supplied the first name in brackets. It should be stressed that these identifications are speculative. Information has been gathered from the following sources: Cockburn, *Assizes*; Edward Foss, *A Biographical Dictionary of the Judges of England 1066–1870* (London, 1870); Joseph Foster, *The Register of Admissions to Gray's Inn, 1521–1889* (London, 1889); Reginald J. Fletcher, ed., *The Pension Book of Gray's Inn 1569–1669* (London, 1901), and *The Pension Book of Gray's Inn 1669–1800* (London, 1910); *Students Admitted to the Inner Temple 1547–1660* (London, 1877); F. A. Inderwick, ed., *A Calendar of the Inner Temple Records 1603–1660* (London, 1898), and *A Calendar of the Inner Temple Records, 1660–1714* (London, 1901); *The Records of . . . Lincoln's Inn: Admissions 1420–1799* ([London], 1896); *The Records of . . . Lincoln's Inn: The Black Books 1586–1660* ([London], 1898); *Register of Admissions to . . . the Middle Temple*, vol. 1 (London, 1949); Charles Henry Hopwood, ed., *A Calendar of the Middle Temple*

Records (London, 1903); J. Bruce Williamson, *Middle Temple Bench Book*, 2d ed. (London, 1937); *Dictionary of National Biography*; PRO: Docket Book (series c); R. Dunn and M. Dunn, eds., *Papers of William Penn*, vol. 2.

John Ashley [Fox, *Journal*, ed. Nickalls, 698]
    Unidentified
—— Athrop [Penn, *Second Part of Continued Cry*, 67–68]
    Unidentified
James Bird or Byrd, gentleman, of Brougham, Westminster [ORS, fol. 461]
    Admitted to Gray's Inn, 27 February 1673/4
    Called to the bar, 7 July 1685
    Called to Ancients, 6 February 1701/2
Samuel Blackerby, son of ——, clerk, of Stowmarket, Suffolk [Book of Cases, 1:184–85]
    Admitted to Gray's Inn, 10 February 1670/1
    Called to the bar, 16 November 1677
    Called to Ancients, 6 February 1701/2
    Called to the bench, 11 February 1705/6
Robert Blaney [Meeting for Sufferings, 1:78]
    [Admitted to Inner Temple, c. 1670]
    Called to the bar, 25 November 1678
John Coates [Book of Cases, 1:112; Eddington, *First Fifty Years of Quakerism*, 257]
    Associate clerk, Midland assize circuit, 1657–1673
Thomas Corbett, second son of Edward Corbett, Esq., of Leighton, Montgomeryshire [Book of Cases, 1:14–18, 26–27, 35, 37–39, 40, 47–51, 53–57, 64–65; Meeting for Sufferings, 1:14]
    Admitted to Gray's Inn, 24 May 1642
    Called to the bar, 26 November 1649
    Called to the Grand Company, 18 May 1667
    Reader of Barnard's Inn, 19 November 1669
[Charles] Cox, of Gloucester [ORS, fol. 411]
    Admitted to Lincoln's Inn, 6 August 1677
    Called to the bar, 3 June 1684
    Called to the bench, 7 May 1707
    Treasurer, 1711
Sir Charles Dallison, son of Thomas Dallison, Knight, of Greetwell, Lincolnshire [Book of Cases, 1:28–29]
    Admitted to Gray's Inn, 7 February 1619/20
    Was called to the bar and later created a serjeant [dates not found]
    Reader of Barnard's Inn, 20 November 1641
John Darnell, son and heir of Ralph Darnell, Esq., of Lawton's Hope, Herefordshire [ORS, fol. 520; Book of Cases, 1:134, 157–59; Meeting for Sufferings, 3:9–10, 41]
    Admitted to Gray's Inn, 2 December 1662
    Admitted to Middle Temple, 7 June 1670
    Called to the bar, 22 November 1672

Robert Dodsworth [Book of Cases, 1 : 112–13, 120–22]
  Admitted to Inner Temple [c. 1672]
  Called to the bar, 28 November 1680
Robert Dormer, second son of John Dormer, barrister, of Ley Grange and
  Purston, Buckinghamshire [Book of Cases, 1 : 130; Dix MSS, Z3]
  Admitted to Lincoln's Inn, 20 May 1669
  Called to the bar, 27 January 1675/6
  Associate of the bench, 6 November 1695, at that time chancellor of the
    county palatine of Durham and an ancient barrister of the Society
  Called to the bench, 20 May 1696
  M.P. for Aylesbury, 1698; M.P. for Buckinghamshire, 1701; M.P. for North-
    allerton, 1702
  Treasurer, 1702
  Master of library, 1705
  Dean of chapel, 1706
  Serjeant and justice of Common Pleas, 1707–26
Sir William Ellis, second son of Sir Thomas Ellis, of Grantham, Lincolnshire
  [Book of Cases, 1 : 112; Eddington, *First Fifty Years of Quakerism*, 257]
  Admitted to Gray's Inn, 6 November 1627
  Called to the bar, 6 February 1634/5
  M.P. for Boston, Lincolnshire, 1640, 1654
  Bencher, 1654
  Appointed solicitor general, 24 May 1654
  M.P. for Grantham, Lincolnshire, 1656, 1659
  Reader, Autumn 1663
  Serjeant-at-law, 26 August 1669
  King's serjeant and knighted, April 1671
  Appointed justice of Common Pleas, 18 December 1672, but dismissed in
    October 1676
  M.P. for Boston, Lincolnshire, March 1679
  Justice of Common Pleas, May–December 1680
Joseph Fisher [Book of Cases, 1 : 149, given as of Gray's Inn]
  Unidentified
[Stewart] Forster, fifth son of Sir Humphrey Forster, baronet, of Aldermaston,
  Berkshire [*Life of Thomas Ellwood*, ed. Graveson, 245]
  Admitted to Middle Temple, 13 May 1655
  Called to the bar, 22 November 1661
John Haggatt, of New Inn, son and heir of Francis Haggatt, gentleman, of
  Mark, Somersetshire [Book of Cases, 1 : 18–19, 154]
  Admitted to Middle Temple, 11 December 1645
  Called to the bar, 28 May 1647
  Chief Justice of Carmarthen, Cardigan, and Pembroke, 1653–60
  Recorder of Abergavenny, 1657
  Associate bencher, 5 November 1658
Thomas Hunt, son of Richard Hunt, Esq., of London [Book of Cases,
  1 : 19–20, 155]
  Admitted to Gray's Inn, 12 November 1650
  Admitted to perform and to bar moot, 14 May 1658
  Published barrister, 4 February 1658/9

Ancient, 17 April 1676
Called to the bench and reading, 14 November 1679
[Sir] W[illiam] Jones, son of Richard Jones, of Stowey, Somersetshire [Book of Cases, 1:69]
Admitted to Gray's Inn, 6 May 1647
Called to the bar [date not found]
Solicitor general, 11 November 1673
Attorney general, 25 June 1675; resigned, November 1679
M.P. for Plymouth, Devonshire, 3 November 1680, and March 1681
Edward King, son and heir of Henry King, gentleman, of Bromley, Kent [Book of Cases, 1:33; Meeting for Sufferings, 1:38]
Admitted to Middle Temple, 7 July 1660
Called to the bar, 25 November 1664
Thomas Langly [Meeting for Sufferings, 1:23]
[Admitted to Inner Temple, c. 1663]
Called to the bar, 27 November 1670
[Sir William] Leeke, or Leake, son and heir of William Leeke, of Wimeswould, Leicestershire [Penn, *Second Part of Continued Cry*, 67–68]
Admitted to Gray's Inn, 23 June 1653
Called to the bar, to be published and confirmed a barrister, having been former bailiff of the moots, 8 November 1661
Ancient, 17 April 1676
Serjeant, 12 February 1678/9
Baron of Exchequer, 8 May 1679; resigned before 28 May 1679
John Merefield, or Merifield [Book of Cases, 1:18–19, 154]
[Admitted to Inner Temple, c. 1614]
Called to the bar, 15 October 1620
Called to the bench, 4 November 1638
Charles Molloy, or Mulloy, son and heir of John Molloy, armiger, of Ireland [ORS, fol. 520]
Admitted to Lincoln's Inn, 7 August 1667
Admitted to Gray's Inn, 28 June 1669
[Sir Edward] Nevil, or Neville, Second son of Henry Nevil, of Bathwick, Somersetshire [GBS, vol. 2, Somersetshire, p. 141]
Admitted to Gray's Inn, 21 October 1650
Called to perform bar moot, 14 May 1658
Published barrister, 19 November 1658
Ancient, 17 April 1676
Called to the bench, and read, 19 November 1679
Knighted as recorder of Bath, June 1681
Serjeant, January 1684
Baron of Exchequer, 11 October 1685; dismissed 21 April 1686
Baron of Exchequer, 11 March 1689
Justice of Common Pleas, 1 October 1691–8 August 1705
[Henry] North, of Suffolk [Book of Cases, 1:96]
Admitted to Middle Temple, 11 June 1680
Called to the bar, 29 May 1685
Sir Francis Pemberton, son of Ralph Pemberton, of St. Albans, Essex [Book of Cases, opinion on marriage, unpaginated; Meeting for Sufferings, 3:360]
Admitted to Inner Temple, 14 October 1645

Called to the bar, 27 November 1654
Bencher, 5 February 1670/1
Lent Reader, 21 January 1673/4
Serjeant, 21 April 1675
King's serjeant, 16 August 1675
Justice of King's Bench, 5 May 1679; dismissed, 16 February 1679/80
Chief Justice of King's Bench, 11 April 1681
Chief Justice of Common Pleas, 22 January 1682/3; dismissed, 7 September
    1683
[Thomas] Pettitt, of Oxted, Surrey [Book of Cases, 1:153]
    Admitted to Inner Temple, November 1657
    Called to the bar, 12 February 1664/5
    Called to the bench, 9 June 1689
    Reader, 17 May 1692
Sir Henry Pollexfen, son and heir of Andrew Pollexfen, of Shorfolde, Devon
    [Book of Cases 1:101, 119–20, 165; Meeting for Sufferings, 2:178]
    [Admitted to Inner Temple, c. 1651]
    Called to the bar, 1658
    Bencher, 1674
    Attorney-general and knighthood, February 1689
    Chief Justice of Common Pleas, 4 May 1689– 15 June 1691
G[eorge] Prickett, son of Marmaduke Prickett, gentleman, of Allerthorpe,
    Yorkshire [Book of Cases, 1:160]
    Admitted to Gray's Inn, 15 June 1656
    Called to the bar, 29 May 1663
    Grand Company of Ancients, 26 November 1680
    Called to the bench, and read, 29 January 1685/6
    Admitted to the bench, 3 May 1686
    Serjeant, 1692
Sir Thomas Rokeby, second son of Thomas Rokeby, of Barnby, Yorkshire
    [Book of Cases, 1:160]
    Admitted to Gray's Inn, 17 May 1650
    Called to the bar, June 1657
    Ancient, 1676
    Justice of Common Pleas, 8 May 1689
    Justice of King's Bench, 29 October 1695–26 November 1699
Sir John Rotherham, son of Thomas Atwood Rotherham, vicar, of Farleigh,
    near Luton, Bedfordshire [Book of Cases, opinion on marriage, unpagi-
    nated]
    Admitted to Gray's Inn, 2 August 1647
    Called to the bar, 18 May 1655
    Ancient, 16 November 1671
    Called to the bench, 10 February 1676/7
    Reader, 7 May 1677
    Treasurer, 26 January 1684/5, 25 January 1685/6
    High Steward of Maldon, Essex, January 1687/8
    Serjeant, 18 June 1688
    Baron of Exchequer, 7 July 1688–December 1688
    Knighted, 13 July 1688
Thomas Rudyard, of Staffordshire and London [ORS, fol. 412]

No record found of any legal training
Secretary and register of East New Jersey, 16 September 1682
Deputy-governor of East New Jersey, c. December 1682–January 1684
Emigrated to Barbados, 1685
Sir Edmund Saunders, of Barnwood, near Gloucester, later of New Inn [Book of Cases, 1:113–14, 117–18]
 Admitted to Middle Temple, 4 July 1660
 Called to the bar, 25 November 1664
 Bencher, November 1682
 Knighted and appointed Chief Justice of King's Bench, 13 January 1682/3 to 19 June 1683
Thomas Smyth, or Smith, son and heir of Thomas Smyth, gentlemen, of London [Book of Cases, 73–74, 76–78; ORS, fol. 467]
 Admitted to Middle Temple, 16 November 1648
 Called to the bar, 21 November 1656
 Bencher, 24 October 1673
 Reader, Autumn 1679; Lent 1680
John [Lord] Somers, son of John Somers, Esquire, of Clifton, Severn Stoke, Worcestershire [Book of Cases, 1:185]
 Admitted to Middle Temple, 24 May 1669
 Called to the bar, 5 May 1676
 Bencher, 10 May 1689
 Solicitor general, 4 May 1689
 Knighted, 31 October 1689
 Attorney-general, 2 May 1692
 Lord Keeper, 23 March 1692/3
 Speaker of House of Lords, 2 May 1693
 Lord chancellor, 22 April 1697
 Peerage, 2 December 1697
 President of the Council, 1708
[George] Starkey, son and heir of George Starkey, gentleman, of New Windsor, Berkshire [*Life of Thomas Ellwood*, ed. Graveson, 245].
 Admitted to Gray's Inn, 6 July 1633
 Called to the bar, 1 June 1641
 Called to be of Grand Company of Ancients, 21 May 1658
 Refused to read and was fined, having accepted call to the bench and to read, 20 November 1668
 Refused to read and was fined, 26 January 1671/2
George Strode, son of Sir John Strode, of Dorsetshire [Fox, *Journal*, ed. Penney, 2:266–67]
 Admitted Lincoln's Inn, 16 June 1646
 Called to the bar, 20 June 1653
Francis Swaine, or Swane, son and heir of Francis Swaine, gentleman, of York [Book of Cases, 1:149]
 Admitted to Gray's Inn, 1650
 Admitted to bar moot, 13 November 1657
 Called to the bar, 25 November 1657
William Thomson, or Thompson, son and heir of Henry Thomson, gentleman, of Hobbinghose, parish of Ripon, Yorkshire [Book of Cases, 1:108, 124–26]

> Admitted to Middle Temple, 24 November 1664
> Called to the bar, 13 May 1670

Joseph Tily, or Tilly, son of Joseph Tily, merchant, of Bristol [Book of Cases, 1:126–29]

> Admitted to Lincoln's Inn, 9 August 1671
> Called to the bar, 1 December 1681

Roland Vaughan [ORS, fols. 215, 398, 487, 520; Book of Cases, 1:78–80, 134–40, 175–76; Meeting for Sufferings, 2:218; 3:259]

> Nothing found relating to his legal training

John Viney, or Vining, son and heir of John Viney, gentleman, of Maidstone, Kent [Meeting for Sufferings, 1:76–77, 81–82, 2:102]

> Admitted to Middle Temple, 15 February 1669/70
> Called to the bar, 25 May 1677
> Bencher, 24 January 1700
> Reader, Lent 1702
> Treasurer, 1713

[Sir] Edward Ward, second son of William Ward, of Preston, Rutlandshire [ORS, fol. 290; Book of Cases, 1:69–70, 108–10, 124–26, 172]

> Admitted to Inner Temple, June 1664, having been previously admitted to Clifford's Inn
> Called to the bar, 1670
> Bencher, 1687
> Justice of Common Pleas, 12 April 1689, but excused after four days
> Lent reader, 1690
> Treasurer, 1693
> Attorney-general, 30 March 1693
> Chief Baron of the Exchequer, 8 June 1695–16 July 1714

Edward Webb, of Newington Bagpath, Gloucestershire, gentleman [Meeting for Sufferings, 2:58]

> Admitted to Lincoln's Inn, 15 November 1666
> Called to the bar, 18 June 1673, but not published until the following term

Robert West, son and heir of James West, Esq., of Banbury, Oxon [Book of Cases, 1:78]

> Admitted to Gray's Inn, 29 January 1668/9
> Called to the bar, 3 July 1674
> Admitted to the Middle Temple, 15 June 1681, which lists his former admission to Gray's Inn as 27 October 1668. Given as of Banbury, Oxon, and therefore presumably the same person listed in Gray's Inn records as admitted and called to the bar

Bibliography

Primary Sources: Unpublished

1. Library of the Religious Society of Friends, London [FLL].
   A. Midgeley Cash Collection, "Original Letters written by George Fox, (Admiral) W. Penn, Benjn. Holme."
   A. R. Barclay MSS [ARB MSS].
   Abraham MSS.
   Book of Cases. 2 vols., to 1700.
   Caton MSS, vol. 3.
   Derby and Notts. QM Digest of Burials.
   Dix MSS.
   Gibson MSS. 6 vols.
   Gloucester and Wilts QM Digest of Burials.
   Great Book of Sufferings. 6 vols., to 1690 [GBS].
   Harvey MSS.
   Leek MSS.
   Lincolnshire QM Digests of Births, Marriages, and Deaths.
   London and Middlesex QM Digest of Burials.
   London and Middlesex QM Sufferings Book, 1654–1753.
   Martin Mason MSS.
   Minutes of the Meeting for Sufferings. 5 vols., to 1690 [Meeting for Sufferings].
   Minutes of London Yearly Meeting, vol. 1.
   Minutes of Six Weeks Meeting, vol. 1.
   Original Records of Sufferings [ORS].
   Penn MSS.
   Portfolio 16.
   Portfolio 36.
   Spence MSS. 3 vols., the first two being the manuscript version of George Fox's "Journal."
   Swarthmore MSS. 6 vols.
   Swarthmore MSS: The Letters of John Audland.
   Thirnbeck MSS.

2. Friends Library, Swarthmore.
  Penn MSS, Small Collections.
3. Dr. Williams' Library, London [DWL].
  G. Lyon Turner MSS.
  "Roger Morrice MS Ent'ring Book." 3 vols.
4. American Philosophical Society.
  Penn Letters and Ancient Documents.
5. British Library, London [BL].
  Additional MSS [Add. MSS].
  Stowe MSS.
6. East Sussex Record Office, Lewes.
  Sussex QM Sufferings. 2 vols.
7. Historical Society of Pennsylvania [HSP].
  Penn-Forbes Papers.
  Pemberton MSS, vol. 1.
  Gratz Collection, Case 2, Box 12.
8. Public Record Office, London [PRO].
  State Papers Domestic. Charles II [S.P.].
  State Papers Domestic. James II [S.P.].
  Privy Council Registers. Charles II [P.C.].
  Privy Council Registers. James II [P.C.].
9. Wiltshire Record Office, Trowbridge [WRO].
  Collection of the Sufferings of . . . Quakers in Wilt-Shire, 1653–1702.
  Collection of the Sufferings of . . . Quakers in Wilt-Shire, 1653–1773.
  Booke of Regester . . . of Sufferings of . . . Quakers in . . . Wilts.

Primary Sources: Published

[Allen, Robert]. *The Cry of Innocent Blood* . . . . [London], 1670. A1045B.
An Easie Way to Get Money. London, 1671. E109B.
Another Cry of the Innocent. London, 1664. A3256.
Audland, Anne. *A True Declaration of the Suffering of the Innocent.* London, 1655. A4195.
Baker, Daniel. *A Single and General Voice.* London, 1659. B485.
———. *The Guiltless Cries and Warnings of the Innocent.* London, 1660. B482B.
Baxter, Richard. *The Quakers Catechism.* . . . London, 1655. B1362.
Benson, Gervase. *A True Tryal of the Ministers.* London, 1655. B1903.
Besse, Joseph. *A Collection of the Sufferings of the People called Quakers for the Testimony of a Good Conscience.* 2 vols. London, 1753.
Blome, Richard. *The Fanatick History.* London, 1660. B3212.
Brief Relation of the Persecutions and Cruelties . . . Quakers, A. London, 1662. B4629.
Brownsword, William. *The Quaker-Jesuite.* Kendal, 1660. B5215.
Burrough, Edward. *Something in Answer to a Book.* B6025. In Francis Howgill, *The Fiery Darts of the Divel Quenched.* London, 1654. H3159.
———. Prefatory epistle. In George Fox, *The Great Mistery of the Great Whore Unfolded*, B2. London, 1659. F1832.
———. *To the Camp of the Lord.* 1655. B6037. In Edward Burrough, *The Memo-*

rable Works of a Son of Thunder and Consolation, edited by Ellis Hookes, 64–67. London, 1672 [not in Wing].

———. *A Message for Instruction . . . how far the Magistrates Power Reacheth*. London, 1658. B6013.

———. *To Charles Fleetwood Steward*. London, 1659. B6035.

Byllynge, Edward. *A Word of Reproof, and advice*. London, 1659. B2903.

———. *A Mite of Affection*. London, 1659. B2902. [The author's name is misspelled in Wing as Billing.]

Camm, John. *Some Particulars Concerning the Law, Sent to Oliver Cromwell*. London, 1654. C391.

The Case of . . . Quakers . . . Especially upon old Statutes made Against Popish Recusants. In John Whiting, *Persecution Expos'd*, 33–34. London, 1715.

Chandler, John. *A True Relation of the Unjust Proceedings . . . Against . . . Quakers*. London, 1662. C1929.

Clark, Henry. *Here is True Magistracy Described*. London, 1660. C4455.

———. *A Rod Discover'd*. London, 1657. C4457.

Coke, Sir Edward. *The First Part of the Institutes of the Laws of England or a Commentary upon Littleton*. London, 1628.

———. *The Fourth Part of the Institutes of the Laws of England*. London, 1644.

———. *The Second Part of the Institutes of the Laws of England*. 6th ed. London, 1681.

———. *The Third Part of the Institutes of the Laws of England*. London, 1660.

Collier, Thomas. *A Looking-glasse for the Quakers*. London, 1657. C5290.

Coveney, Thomas, et al. *For the King and both Houses of Parliament. Being a Short Relation*. London, 1661. F1435.

Crook, John. *An Epistle of Love*. London, 1660. C7204.

———. *Sixteen Reasons Drawn from the Law of God*. London, 1661. C7213.

———. *Tythes no Property*. London, 1659. C7225.

Cry of the Innocent & Oppressed for Justice, The. London, 1664. C7450.

Cry of Oppression and Cruelty. London, 1677. C7449A.

Curtis, Samuel, et al. *The Lamentable Sufferings of the Church of God in Dorsetshire*. London, 1659. C7691.

Dalton, Michael. *The Countrey Justice*. 5th ed., rev. and enl. London, 1635.

Davies, Richard. *An Account of the Convincements, Exercises, Services and Travels of . . . Richard Davies*. 6th ed. London, 1825.

Declaration of the Present Sufferings, A. London, 1659. B5993. [This work is wrongly attributed by Wing to Edward Burrough.]

Ellwood, Thomas. *A Caution to Constables*. London, 1683. E616.

———. *A Discourse Concerning Riots*. London, 1683. E618.

Farnworth, Richard. *The Liberty of the Subject by Magna Charta*. London, 1664. F489.

Fell, Margaret. *A Declaration and an Information from us*. London, 1660. F628.

Fisher, Samuel, et al. *This is to thee, O King, and thy Council*. London, 1660/1 [not in Wing].

For the King and both Houses of Parliament. For You (who have Known . . .). London, 1660. F1436.

Fox, George. *A Collection of Many Select and Christian Epistles. Second Volume*. London, 1698. F1764.

———. *The Copies of Several Letters*. London, 1660. F1778.

———. *For the King, and both Houses*. London, 1661. F1821.

———. *A Journal*. Edited by Thomas Ellwood. London, 1694. F1854.

———. *Journal*. Edited by John L. Nickalls. Rev. ed. London, 1975.

———. *Journal*. Edited by Norman Penney. 2 vols. Cambridge, 1911.

———. *The Law of God the Rule of Law-makers*. London, 1658. F1856.

———. *Newes Coming Up Out of the North*. London, 1654. F1867.

———. *Our Covenant with God*. London, 1660. F1871B.

———. *To the Parliament of the Comon-wealth of England. Fifty-nine particulars*. London, 1659. F1958.

———. *Several Papers Given Forth*. London, 1660. F1901.

———. *A Small Treatise Concerning Swearing*. 1675. F1906. In *Gospel Truth Demonstrated in a Collection of Doctrinal Books Given Forth by . . . George Fox*, 469–82. London, 1706.

Fox, George, et al. *A Declaration from the Harmless and Innocent People of God Called Quakers*. London, 1660[1]. F1786.

Fox, George, John Stubbs, and Henry Fell. *For the King and his Council, these*. London, 1660/1. F1822.

Fox, George, the Younger. *A Noble Salutation and a Faithful Greeting*. London, 1660. F2007.

———. *A True Relation of the Unlawful and Unreasonable Proceedings*. London, 1661. F2014.

Gibson, Thomas. *Something Offered to the Consideration*. London, 1665. G678.

Grassingham, Robert, et al. *For the King and Both Houses of Parliament. The True State and Condition of the . . . Quakers*. London, 1661 [not in Wing].

Grey, Richard. *A System of English Ecclesiastical Law*. 4th ed. London, 1743.

Gutch, John, ed. *Collectanea Curiosa: or Miscellaneous Tracts Relating to the History and Antiquities of England and Ireland*. 2 vols. Oxford, 1781.

Higginson, Francis. *A Brief Relation of the Irreligion of the Northern Quakers*. London, 1653. H1953.

Hookes, Ellis. *For the King, and both Houses of Parliament*. London, 1675. H2661.

Horn (or Horne), Andrew. *The Booke called, The Mirrour of Justices*. London, 1646. H2789.

Hubberthorne, Richard. *Truth Cleared, and the Deceit*. London, 1654. H3241.

Ives, Jeremiah. *The Quakers Quaking, or the Translation of their deceit shaken. . . .* London, 1656. I1103.

Jacob, Giles. *A New-Law Dictionary*. London, 1729.

Jura Ecclesiastica: or A Treatise on the Ecclesiastical Laws and Courts . . . By a Barrister of the Middle Temple. 2 vols. London, 1742.

Kelyng, John. *A Report of Divers Cases in Pleas of the Crown . . . in the Reign of . . . King Charles II*. London, 1708.

To the King and both houses of Parliament. Here are some of our sufferings. London, 1680. T1489A.

To the King, and both houses of Parliament, now sitting in Westminster. Being, I. a Representation. London, 1666. T1490.

To the King and both Houses . . . the suffering condition of the . . . Quakers. London [1685?] T1491.

Lambarde, William. *The Duties of Constables, Borsholders, Tythingmen and Such Other Lowe and Lay Ministers of the Peace*. Enl. ed. London, 1614.

———. *Eirenarcha, or of the Justices of Peace*. Rev. and enl. ed. London, 1614.

Latey, Gilbert. *A Brief Narrative of the Life and Death of . . . Gilbert Latey*. Compiled by R. Hawkins. London, 1707.

Legal Examination of Abuses of Law, A. London, 1682. L943.

Moon, Paul. *Some Passages and Proceedings in Courts*. In George Fox, *An Instruction to Judges and Lawyers*, 31–40. London, 1658. F1848.

Morris, William. *All You Perticuler Baptists in Ireland, These Things are to You* [not in Wing]. In George Fox, *Severall Warnings to the Baptized People*. N.p., 1659 [not in Wing].

Nayler, James. *A Discovery of the First Wisdom*. London, 1656. N273.

———. *A Salutation to the Seede of God*. 4th ed. London, 1656. N311A.

———. *Weaknes above Wickednes*. London, 1656. N327.

News from the Country: or the Plough Man's Lamentation. London, 1706.

Pagitt, Ephraim. *Heresiography*. 5th ed. London, 1654. P180.

Pearse, Edward. *The Conformists Fourth Plea*. London, 1683. P975.

Pearson, Anthony. *To the Parliament of the Commonwealth of England, Christian Friends*. London, 1653. P992.

———. *The Great Case of TYTHES, Stated*. London, 1657. P989.

———. *A Few Words to all Judges*. London, 1654. Wing P988.

Penn, William [Philanglus, pseud.], *One Project for the Good of England: That is, Our Civil Union is our Civil Safety*. London, 1680. P1334. In *A Collection of the Works of William Penn*, edited by Joseph Besse. 2 vols., 2:682–91. London, 1726.

———. *The Peoples Ancient and Just Liberties Asserted in the Tryal of William Penn*. London, 1670. P1335.

———. *The Peoples Antient and Just Liberties Asserted in the Tryal of William Penn*. London, 1670. P1336A.

———. *Reasons why the Oaths Should not be made a part of the Test*. London, 1683. P2178.

———. *Truth Rescued from Imposture*. London, 1670. P1362A.

The Proceedings of the Barons of the Exchequer, at Westminister, in their Court of Equity, for Tythes and Oblations. London, 1705.

Prynne, William. *The Quakers Unmasked*. London, 1655. P4045.

Pyott, Edward, et al. *The West Answering to the North*. London, 1657. F1988. [Wing wrongly attributes this work to George Fox.]

Reports and Arguments of . . . Sir John Vaughan Kt, late Lord Chief Justice . . . of Common Pleas. 2d ed. London, 1706.

Rudyard, Thomas. *The Second Part of the People's Antient and Just Liberties Asserted*. London, 1670 [not in Wing].

———. *The Case of Protestant Dissenters*. London, 1680. R2178.

Sheppard, William. *England's Balme*. London, 1656. S3183.

———. *An Epitome of All the Common & Statute Laws of This Nation now in force*. London, 1656. S3184.

———. *The parsons guide: or the law of tithes*. London, 1654. S3204.

Smith, William. *The Innocency and Conscientiousness of the Quakers*. London, 1664. S4308.

——— *A true, short, impartial Relation*. [London], 1664. S4341.

Something in Answer to a Petition to Oliver Cromwell. London, 1654. S4659.

S[tarling], S[amuel]. *An Answer to the Seditious and Scandalous Pamphlet*. London, 1670. S5295.

Starling, Samuel. *An Answer to the Seditious and Scandalous Pamphlet*. London, 1671. S5296.

Tomlinson, William. *Seven Particulars, Containing*. London, 1657[8]. T1851.

Underhill, Thomas. *Hell Broke Loose*. London, 1660. u43.

Wastfield, Robert. *An Equal Ballance*. London, 1659. w1033.

Wastfield, Robert, et al. *For the King, and his Councill at White hall. Being a breif relation*. London, [1661]. f1436a.

Watkins, Morgan. *The Perfect Life*. London, 1659. w1068.

Watson, William. *The Clergyman's Law, Or: the Complete Incumbent*. 4th ed. London, 1747.

Whitehead, George. *The Christian Progress*. London, 1725.

Whitehead, John, et al. *This to the King*. London, 1660. w1983.

————. *The Written Gospel-Labours of that Ancient and Faithfull Servant of Jesus Christ, John Whitehead*. London, 1704.

Whiting, John. *Persecution Expos'd . . . .* London, 1715.

Wingate, Edmund. *The Body of the Common Law*. London, 1655. w3006.

Secondary Sources

Allen, D. H., ed. *Essex Quarter Sessions Order Book 1652–1661*. Chelmsford, 1974.

Atkinson, J. C., ed. *Quarter Sessions Records*. The North Riding Record Society, vols. 6, 7. London, 1888–89.

Baker, J. H. "Criminal Courts and Procedure at Common Law 1550–1800." In *Crime in England 1550–1800*, edited by J. S. Cockburn, 15–48. London, 1977.

————. *An Introduction to English Legal History*. 2d ed. London, 1979.

Barbour, Hugh. *The Quakers in Puritan England*. New Haven, 1964.

Barbour, Hugh, and Arthur Roberts, eds. *Early Quaker Writings*. Grand Rapids, 1973.

Barclay, A. R., ed. *Letters &c of Early Friends*. London, 1841.

Barnard, T. C. *Cromwellian Ireland*. Oxford, 1975.

Bate, Frank. *The Declaration of Indulgence, 1672: A Study in the Rise of Organized Dissent*. London, 1908.

Beresford, M. W. "The Common Informer, the Penal Statutes and Economic Regulation." *English Historical Review*, 2d ser., 10 (1957):221–37.

Bittle, William. "James Nayler: A Study in Seventeenth-Century Quakerism." Ph.D. diss., Kent State University, 1975.

Blackwood, Bruce Gordon. "Agrarian Unrest and the Early Lancashire Quakers." *Journal of the Friends Historical Society* 51 (1965):72–76.

Bossy, John. *The English Catholic Community 1570–1850*. London, 1975.

Bowler, Hugh, ed. *London Sessions Records 1605–1685*. Catholic Record Society, vol. 34. London, 1934.

Braithwaite, Alfred. "Early Friends' Experience with Juries." *Journal of the Friends Historical Society* 50 (1962–64):217–27.

————. "Early Friends and Informers." *Journal of the Friends Historical Society* 51 (1965):107–14.

————. "Early Friends Testimony against Carnal Weapons." *Journal of the Friends Historical Society* 52 (1968–71):101–5.

————. "Early Tithe Prosecutions: Friends as Outlaws." *Journal of the Friends Historical Society* 49 (1959–61):148–56.

————. "'Errors in the Indictment' and Pardons: the Case of Theophilus

Green." *Journal of the Friends Historical Society* 49 (1959–61):24–30.

———. "George Fox's Last Imprisonment." *Journal of the Friends Historical Society* 51 (1965):159–66.

———. "Imprisonment Upon a Praemunire: George Fox's Last Trial." *Journal of the Friends Historical Society* 50 (1962–64):37–43.

———. *Thomas Rudyard.* Friends Historical Society, supplement no. 27. London, 1956.

———. "Were Penn's Jury 'Starved?'" *Journal of the Friends Historical Society* 53 (1972–75):58–61.

Braithwaite, William C. *The Beginnings of Quakerism.* 2d ed. Cambridge, 1955.

———. *The Second Period of Quakerism.* 2d ed. Cambridge, 1961.

———. "London Friends Sentenced to Transportation, 1664–65." Typescript in FLL.

Brinton, H. H. "The Two Sources of Quaker Mysticism." *Friends Quarterly* 8 (1954):10–13.

Bryson, W. H. *The Equity Side of the Exchequer.* Cambridge, 1975.

Burn, Richard. *The Justice of the Peace and Parish Officer.* 11th ed. 4 vols. London, 1770.

Cadbury, Henry J. "An Obscure Chapter of Quaker History." *Journal of Religion* 24 (1944):201–13.

———. *George Fox's "Book of Miracles."* Cambridge, 1948.

Calamy, Edmund. *The Nonconformists' Memorial.* Abridged and enlarged by Samuel Palmer. 2d ed. 3 vols. London, 1802–03.

Calendar of State Papers, Domestic Series, 1603–1704. Edited by Mary Anne Everett Green et al. 85 vols. London, 1857–1972 [CSPD].

Calendar of Treasury Books, 1660–1718. Edited by William A. Shaw et al. 32 vols. London, 1904–1962 [CTB].

Camp, Anthony J. *Wills and their Whereabouts.* London, 1974.

Carroll, Kenneth L. "Early Quakers and 'Going Naked as a Sign.'" *Quaker History* 67 (1978):69–87.

———. *John Perrot.* Friends Historical Society, supplement no. 33. London, 1970.

———. "Quaker Attitudes Towards Signs and Wonders." *Journal of the Friends Historical Society* 54 (1976–80):70–84.

Chandaman, C. D. *The English Public Revenue 1660–1688.* Oxford, 1975.

Cockburn, J. S. "Seventeenth-Century Clerks of Assize—Some Anonymous Members of the Legal Profession." *American Journal of Legal History* 13 (1969):315–32.

———. *A History of the English Assizes 1559–1714.* Cambridge, 1972.

Cole, W. Alan. "The Quakers and Politics 1652–1660." Ph.D. thesis, Cambridge University, 1955.

———. "The Quakers and the English Revolution." *Past & Present,* no. 10 (November 1956), 39–54.

Cragg, Gerald. *Puritanism in the Age of the Great Persecution 1660–1688.* Cambridge, 1957.

Creasey, Maurice. "Early Quaker Christology." D. Phil. thesis, University of Leeds, 1956.

Curtis, T. C. "Quarter Sessions Appearances and their Background: a Seventeenth-Century Regional Study." In *Crime in England 1550–1800,* edited by J. S. Cockburn, 135–54. London, 1977.

Davies, C. S. L., "Popular Religion and the Pilgrimage of Grace." In *Order and Disorder in Early Modern England*, edited by Anthony Fletcher and John Stevenson, 58–91. Cambridge and New York, 1985.

Davies, Godfrey. *The Restoration of Charles II 1658–1660*. London, 1955.

Doncaster, L. Hugh. "Diversity and Unity in the Society of Friends." *Friends Quarterly* 19 (1975):107–14.

―――. "That State in Which Adam Was." *Journal of the Friends Historical Society* 41 (1949):13–24.

Dowdell, E. G. *A Hundred Years of Quarter Sessions: The Government of Middlesex from 1660 to 1760*. Cambridge, 1932.

Duncan, G. I. O. *The High Court of Delegates*. Cambridge, 1971.

Dunn, Richard, and Mary Maples Dunn, eds. *The Papers of William Penn*. 5 vols. Philadelphia, 1981–87.

Eddington, Arthur. *The First Fifty Years of Quakerism in Norwich*. Privately printed, 1932.

Edwards, George W. "The London Six Weeks Meeting." *Journal of the Friends Historical Society* 50 (1962–64):228–45.

Elton, G. R. *Star Chamber Stories*. London, 1958.

Eusden, J. D. *Puritans, Lawyers and Politics in Early Seventeenth Century England*. New Haven, 1958; reprint [Hamden, Conn.], 1968.

Evans, Eric J. "A History of the Tithe System in England, 1690–1850, with special reference to Staffordshire." Ph.D. thesis, University of Warwick, 1971.

Firth, C. H., and R. S. Rait, eds. *Acts and Ordinances of the Interregnum 1642–1660*. 3 vols. London, 1911.

Fletcher, Anthony. *A County Community in Peace and War: Sussex 1600–1660*. London and New York, 1975.

―――. *Reform in the Provinces: The Government of Stuart England*. New Haven and London, 1986.

Forde, Helen. "Derbyshire Quakers 1650–1761." Ph.D. thesis, University of Leicester, 1978.

―――. "Friends and Authority: A Consideration of Attitudes and Expedients with Particular Reference to Derbyshire." *Journal of the Friends Historical Society* 54 (1976–80):115–25.

Foss, Edward. *The Judges of England*. 9 vols. London, 1848–64.

Frost, J. William. "William Penn's Experiment: Promise and Legend." *Pennsylvania Magazine of History and Biography* 107 (1983):577–605.

Glassey, L. K. J. *Politics and the Appointment of the Justices of the Peace 1675–1720*. Oxford, 1979.

Graveson, S., ed., *The History of the Life of Thomas Ellwood*. London, 1906.

Greaves, Richard L. *Deliver Us from Evil: The Radical Underground in Britain, 1660–1663*. New York and Oxford, 1986.

Green, I. M. *The Re-Establishment of the Church of England 1660–1663*. Oxford, 1978.

Green, Thomas A. *Verdict According to Conscience: Perspectives on the English Criminal Trial Jury, 1200–1800*. Chicago, 1985.

Gretton, Mary Sturge. *Oxfordshire Justices of the Peace in the Seventeenth Century*. Oxford, 1934.

Guide to the Contents of the Public Record Office. 3 vols. London, 1963–68.

Hale, Sir Matthew. *The History of the Common Law of England*. Edited by Charles M. Gray. Chicago and London, 1971.

Hardy, William J. and William Le Hardy, eds. *Hertfordshire County Records*. 9 vols. Hertford, 1905–39.

Hardy, William Le and George Reckitt, eds. *County of Buckingham: Calendar to the Sessions Records*. 4 vols. Aylesbury, 1934–51.

Hartley, T. E. "Undersheriffs and Bailiffs in some English Shrievalties, c. 1580 to c. 1625." *Bulletin of the Institute of Historical Research* 47 (1974):164–74.

Havighurst, Alfred F. "The Judiciary and Politics in the Reign of Charles II." *Law Quarterly Review* 66 (1950):62–78, 229–52.

———. "James II and the Twelve Men in Scarlet." *Law Quarterly Review* 69 (1953):522–46.

Henry, Philip. *Diary and Letters*. Edited by M. H. Lee. London, 1882.

Heward, Edmund. *Matthew Hale*. London, 1972.

Hill, Christopher. *Economic Problems of the Church from Archbishop Whitgift to the Long Parliament*. Oxford, 1956.

———. *The Experience of Defeat*. London, 1984.

———. *The World Turned Upside Down*. Paperback reprint. Harmondsworth, 1975.

Hirst, Margaret. *The Quakers in Peace and War*. London, 1923.

Historical Manuscripts Commission [HMC]: *Report on Manuscripts in Various Collections*, vol. 1. London, 1901.

Historical Manuscripts Commission [HMC]: *Twelfth Report*, Appendix, pt. vii, "The MSS of S.H. Le Fleming of Rydal Hall." London, 1890.

Holdsworth, Sir William. *A History of English Law*. 16 vols. London, 1903–52.

———. "The Constitutional Position of the Judges." *Law Quarterly Review* 48 (1932):25–34.

Horle, Craig W. "Changing Quaker Attitudes Toward Legal Defence: The George Fox Case, 1673–75, and the Establishment of Meeting for Sufferings." In *Seeking the Light: Essays in Quaker History*, edited by J. William Frost and John M. Moore, 17–39. Wallingford, Pa., 1986.

———. "Death as a Felon: Richard Vickris and the Elizabethan Conventicle Act," in *Quaker History* 76, no. 2 (Fall 1987):95–107.

———. "Judicial Encounters with Quakers 1660–1688." *Journal of the Friends Historical Society* 54 (1976–80):85–100.

———. "Partridges Upon the Mountains: The Quakers and the English Legal System, 1660–1688." Ph.D. diss., University of Maryland, 1985.

———. "Quakers and Baptists 1650–1660." *Baptist Quarterly* 26 (1976):218–38.

Hudson, W. S. "A Suppressed Chapter in Quaker History." *Journal of Religion* 24 (1944):108–18.

Ingram, M. J. "Communities and Courts: Law and Order in Early-Seventeenth-Century Wiltshire." In *Crime in England 1550–1800*, edited by J. S. Cockburn, 110–34. London, 1977.

Jeaffreson, John Cordy, ed. *Middlesex County Records*, 4 vols. London, 1886–92.

Jenkinson, Hilary, and Dorothy Powell, eds. *Surrey Quarter Sessions Records*. Surrey Record Society, vols. 35, 36, 39. London, 1934–38.

Jessop, Augustus, ed. *The Lives of the Norths*. 3 vols. London, 1890.
Jewell, H. M. *English Local Administration in the Middle Ages*. Newton Abbot, 1972.
Jones, W. J. *The Elizabethan Court of Chancery*. Oxford, 1967.
Journals of the House of Commons. Charles II.
Journals of the House of Lords. Charles II.
Kenyon, J. P. *Stuart England*. London, 1978.
Lacey, Douglas. *Dissent and Parliamentary Politics in England 1661–1689*. New Brunswick, 1969.
Landau, Norma. *The Justices of the Peace, 1679–1760*. Berkeley, 1984.
Leicester, Sir Peter. *Charges to the Grand Jury at Quarter Sessions, 1660–1677*. Edited by Elizabeth M. Halcrow. Chetham Society, 3d ser., vol. 5. Manchester, 1953.
Levack, Brian P. *The Civil Lawyers in England 1605–1641*. Oxford, 1973.
Lloyd, Arnold. *Quaker Social History*. London, 1950.
Luttrell, Narcissus. *A Brief Historical Relation of State Affairs from September 1678 to April 1714*. 6 vols. Oxford, 1857.
MacGregor, J. F. "Ranterism and the Development of Early Quakerism." *Journal of Religious History* 9 (1977):349–63.
Maclear, J. F. "Quakerism and the End of the Interregnum: A Chapter in the Domestication of Radical Puritanism." *Church History* 19 (1950):240–71.
Marchant, Ronald A. *The Church Under the Law*. Cambridge, 1969.
Mather, Jean. "The Parliamentary Committees and the Justices of the Peace 1642–1661." *American Journal of Legal History* 23 (1979):120–43.
Matthews, Arnold G. *Calamy Revised*. Oxford, 1934.
Matthews, Nancy L. *William Sheppard, Cromwell's Law Reformer*. Cambridge, 1984.
Miller, John. *James II: A Study in Kingship*. Hove, Sussex, 1978.
———. *Popery and Politics 1660–1688*. Cambridge, 1973.
Milward, John. *The Diary . . . September 1666 to May 1668*. Edited by Caroline Robbins. Cambridge, 1938.
Minute Book of the Monthly Meeting . . . for Upperside . . . 1669–1690. High Wycombe, 1937.
Morgan, Nicholas. "Lancashire Quakers and the Oath, 1660–1722." *Journal of the Friends Historical Society* 54 (1976–80):235–54.
Morrill, J. S. *Cheshire 1630–1660*. London, 1974.
Mortimer, Russell J., ed. *Minute Book of the Men's Meeting of the Society of Friends in Bristol, 1686–1704*. Bristol Record Society Publications, vol. 30. Bristol, 1977.
———, ed. *Minute Book of the Men's Meeting of the Society of Friends in Bristol, 1667–1686*. Bristol Record Society Publications, vol. 24. Bristol, 1971.
———. "Quakerism in Seventeenth Century Bristol." M.A. thesis, University of Bristol, 1946.
Morton, A. L. *The World of the Ranters*. London, 1970.
Muddiman, J. G. *The King's Journalist 1659–1689*. London, 1923.
Nuttall, Geoffrey F. *The Holy Spirit in Puritan Faith and Reason*. Oxford, 1946.
———. *Studies in Christian Enthusiasm*. Pendle Hill, Pa., 1948.
———. *The Welsh Saints 1640–1660*. Cardiff, 1957.
Oliver, Pamela. "The Problems of Authority, Discipline and Tradition in the

First Century of English Quakerism." *Friends Quarterly* 19 (1975):115–25.

———. "Quaker Testimony and the Lamb's War." Ph.D. thesis, University of Melbourne, 1977.

———. "The Quakers and Quietism." Master's thesis, University of Melbourne, 1972.

Penney, Norman, ed. *The First Publishers of Truth*. London, 1907.

———, ed. *Extracts from State Papers Relating to Friends 1654–1672*. London, 1913.

———, ed. *Record of the Sufferings of Friends in Cornwall, 1655–1686*. London, 1928.

Pepys, Samuel. *The Diary*. Edited by Robert Latham and William Matthews. 11 vols. Berkeley and Los Angeles, 1970–83.

Peyton, S. A., ed. *Minutes of Proceedings in Quarter Sessions for the Parts of Kesteven in the County of Lincoln, 1674–1695*. 2 vols. Lincoln, 1931.

Ploughman, James. *The Law of Tithes: Adapted as a Practical Guide to the Country Gentleman, Parson, and Farmer*. London, 1829.

Plowden, Francis. *The Principles and Law of Tithing*. London, 1806.

Plucknett, Theodore F. T. *Concise History of the Common Law*. 5th ed. London, 1956.

Prest, Wilfrid R. *The Inns of Court Under Elizabeth I and the Early Stuarts 1590–1640*. London, 1972.

Quintrell, B. W., ed. *Proceedings of the Lancashire Justices of the Peace at the Sheriff's Table During Assize Week, 1578–1694*. The Record Society of Lancashire and Cheshire, vol. 121. N.p., 1981.

Ralph, Elizabeth. *Guide to the Bristol Archives Office*. Bristol, 1971.

Ratcliff, S. C., and H. C. Johnson, eds. *Warwick County Records 1629–1690*. 8 vols. Warwick, 1935–53.

Reay, Barry. "The Authorities and Early Restoration Quakerism." *Journal of Ecclesiastical History*, 34 (1983):69–84.

———. "Popular Hostility Towards Quakers in mid-Seventeenth Century England." *Social History* 5 (1981):387–407.

———. "Quaker Opposition to Tithes, 1652–1660." *Past & Present*, no. 86 (February 1980):98–118.

———. *The Quakers and the English Revolution*. London, 1985.

———. "The Quakers, 1659, and the Restoration of the Monarchy." *History* 63 (1978):193–213.

———. "The Social Origins of Early Quakerism." *Journal of Interdisciplinary History* 11 (1980–81):55–72.

Request to the Justices not to make Convictions, A. London, 1684. ʀ1120.

Roots, Ivan. "Cromwell's Ordinances: The Early Legislation of the Protectorate." In *The Interregnum: The Quest for Settlement 1646–1660*, edited by G. E. Aylmer, 143–64. London and Hamden, Conn., 1972.

Ross, Isabel. *Margaret Fell: Mother of Quakerism*. London, 1949.

Rutt, John Towill, ed. *Diary of Thomas Burton*. 4 vols. London, 1828.

Schofield, Russell G. "Some Ranter Leaders and their Opinions." *Bulletin of the Friends Historical Association* 39 (Autumn, 1950):63–73.

Sharpe, J. A. "Crime and Delinquency in an Essex Parish 1600–1640." In *Crime in England 1550–1800*, edited by J. S. Cockburn, 90–109. London, 1977.

————. *Crime in Seventeenth-Century England: A County Study.* Cambridge, 1983.

Smith, Edward. *The Life of William Dewsbury.* London, 1836.

Smith, Joseph. *A Descriptive Catalogue of Friends Books.* 2 vols. London, 1867.

Spurrier, Wayne W. "The Persecution of Quakers in England, 1650–1714." Ph.D. diss., University of North Carolina, 1976.

Squibb, G. D. *Doctors' Commons: A History of the College of Advocates and Doctors of Law.* Oxford and New York, 1977.

The Statutes at Large from Magna Carta to 1806. 46 vols. Cambridge, 1762–1807.

Steele, Robert, ed. *A Bibliography of Royal Proclamations of the Tudor and Stuart Sovereigns and Others Published Under Authority 1485–1714.* Oxford, 1910.

Stenton, Dorothy M. *English Society in the Early Middle Ages.* 4th ed. Harmondsworth, 1971.

Sylvester, Matthew, ed. *Reliquiae Baxterianae.* London, 1696.

Taylor, Ernest E. "The First Publishers of Truth: A Study." *Journal of the Friends Historical Society* 19 (1922):66–81.

Thomas, Roger. "Comprehension and Indulgence." In *From Uniformity to Unity 1662–1962,* edited by Owen Chadwick and Geoffrey Nuttall, 189–253. London, 1962.

Turner, Edward Raymond. *The Privy Council of England in the Seventeenth and Eighteenth Centuries 1603–1784.* 2 vols. Baltimore, 1927–28.

Underdown, David. "Settlement in the Counties 1653–1658." In *The Interregnum: The Quest for Settlement 1646–1660,* edited by G. E. Aylmer, 165–82. London and Hamden, Conn., 1972.

Underwood, T. L. "The Controversy Between the Baptists and the Quakers in England 1650–1689: A Theological Elucidation." Ph.D. thesis, University of London, 1965.

————. "Early Quaker Eschatology." In *Puritans, the Millennium and the Future of Israel,* edited by Peter Toon, 91–103. London, 1970.

Vann, Richard. *The Social Development of Early Quakerism.* Cambridge, 1969.

Veall, Donald. *The Popular Movement for Law Reform 1640–60.* Oxford, 1970.

Western, J. R. *Monarchy and Revolution.* London, 1972.

Whiting, C. E. *Studies in English Puritanism from the Restoration to the Revolution, 1660–1688.* London, 1931.

Wood, Anthony à. *Life and Times.* Collected by Andrew Clark. 5 vols. Oxford, 1891–1900.

Index